MIXED COMMUNITIES

Gentrification by stealth?

Edited by Gary Bridge, Tim Butler and Loretta Lees

First published in Great Britain in 2012 by

The Policy Press
University of Bristol
Fourth Floor
Beacon House
Queen's Road
Bristol BS8 1QU
UK
Tel +44 (0)117 331 4054
Fax +44 (0)117 331 4093
e-mail tpp-info@bristol.ac.uk
www.policypress.co.uk

North American office:

The Policy Press
c/o The University of Chicago Press
1427 East 60th Street
Chicago, IL 60637, USA
t: +1 773 702 7700
f: +1 773-702-9756
e:sales@press.uchicago.edu
www.press.uchicago.edu

British Library Cataloguing in Publication Data
A catalogue record for this book is available from the British Library.

Library of Congress Cataloging-in-Publication Data
A catalog record for this book has been requested.

ISBN 978 1 84742 492 1 paperback

Cover design by The Policy Press.
Front cover: image kindly supplied by www.alamy.com
Printed and bound in Great Britain by TJ International,
Padstow
The Policy Press uses environmentally responsible print
partners.

Contents

List of tables, figures and photographs

Tables

Figures

Photographs

Acknowledgements

The chapters in this volume originated with presentations and discussions at a series of seminars on 'Gentrification and social mix' held in London, Bristol and Edinburgh in 2008/09 (as well as other invited contributions). The Economic and Social Research Council (ESRC) funded the seminars (grant RES-451-26-0340), and we are very grateful to them. Our thanks also go to Tom Slater (University of Edinburgh) who, along with the editors, was a co-organiser of that seminar series. We are also grateful to the anonymous referee whose comments on the typescript were very helpful. Finally our thanks go to Alison Shaw, Leila Ebrahimi and Laura Vickers at The Policy Press for all their efficient and supportive work on the book.

Notes on contributors

Martine August, Trudeau Foundation Scholar, PhD Candidate, Department of Geography and Program in Planning, University of Toronto, Canada. Martine's doctoral research focuses on socially-mixed public housing redevelopment in Toronto, Canada.

Marie-Hélène Bacqué, Professor, Université Paris Ouest-Nanterre La Défense, Paris, France; sociologist and town planner and director of the Mosaics Laboratory.

Joshua Bazuin, PhD candidate in Community Research and Action, Department of Human and Organizational Development, Peabody College of Education and Human Development, Vanderbilt University, Nashville, Tennessee, USA.

Jürgen Bruns-Berentelg, Chief Executive Officer, HafenCity, Hamburg GMbH (public company owned by the City of Hamburg and charged with the development of HafenCity), Germany. Jürgen studied Geography and Biology, and is also a real estate economist; he publishes regularly on questions of urban development.

Talja Blokland, Professor for Urban and Regional Sociology, Institute of Social Sciences, Humboldt University of Berlin, Germany. Talja's research interests include social theory, relational theory, urban sociology and social policy.

Gary Bridge, Professor of Urban Studies, School for Policy Studies, University of Bristol, UK. Gary's research interests include work in social/urban theory and class, gentrification and urban social change.

Tim Butler, Professor, King's College London, UK. Tim's current research focuses on issues of education, ethnicity and gentrification in East London, an area that has not, until recently, been favoured by the middle classes.

Paul Cheshire, Professor Emeritus of Economic Geography, Department of Geography and Environment, London School of Economics and Political Science, London, UK. Paul's current research interests include the spatial applications of economics, urban policy, growth and territorial competition, urban land and housing markets and the economic consequences of land use regulation.

Mark Davidson, Assistant Professor of Geography, Graduate School of Geography, Clark University, Worcester, MA, USA. Mark's current research interests include urban revisioning and the gentrified city; post-industrial urban spaces and governance; politics, policy making and sustainability in Sydney and Vancouver; and social class in the post-political city.

Joe Doherty, Professor Emeritus, School of Geography and Geosciences, University of St Andrews, UK.

James DeFilippis, Assistant Professor, Edward J. Bloustein School of Planning and Public Policy, Rutgers University, New Brunswick, NJ, USA.

Gwen Van Eijk, Assistant Professor, Department of Sociology and Anthropology, University of Amsterdam, The Netherlands. Gwen's research interests include urban sociology, criminology, socio-spatial segregation and mixed urban settings, cross-category relationships, boundary work, the construction of disorder, public space and mixed methods.

Yankel Fijalkow, Professor in Urban Planning, Université d'Evry Val d'Essonne, Evry, France.

James Fraser, Associate Professor of Human and Organizational Development, College of Education and Human Development, Vanderbilt Peabody College, Nashville, TN, USA. James' work focuses on urban environment, revitalisation and public policy, governance and expressions of community; social inequality and poverty; human-environment studies; organisational culture and behaviour; and research methods.

Sarah Glynn is an architect and academic. She is an Honorary Research Fellow at the University of Strathclyde in Glasgow and an Associate Member of St Andrews Centre for Housing Research. Her recent publications include work on multiculturalism, Islamism, and immigrant political mobilisation, and on social housing, housing policy under neoliberalism, and tenant activism.

Maarten Van Ham, Professor of Urban Renewal, OTB Research Institute for the Built Environment, Delft University of Technology, The Netherlands. Maarten's research interests can be broadly defined as the causes and consequences of family migration: why do people move residence and what are the consequences of moving for the housing, household and labour career?

Patrick Le Galès, Director of Research, Centre d'Etudes Européennes, Sciences Po, Paris, France. Patrick works and teaches in comparative public policy in Europe, urban sociology and economic sociology and the political economy.

Loretta Lees, Professor of Human Geography, Social Science and Public Policy, King's College London, UK. Loretta's research interests include gentrification, urban regeneration, urban policy, urban public space, and the geography of architecture.

David Ley, Professor and Department Head, Department of Geography, University of British Columbia, Canada. David has always been concerned with processes of social and spatial change in older inner-city neighbourhoods. A principal focus has been gentrification, processes of urban reinvestment leading to housing renovation or redevelopment and the replacement and displacement of poorer households by the middle class.

Pauline Lipman, Professor, Educational Policy Studies, College of Education, University of Illinois at Chicago, USA. Pauline's research focuses on 'race' and class inequality in schools, globalisation and the political economy and cultural politics of 'race' in urban education. Her recent publications focus on the interrelation of education policy and neoliberal urban development.

David Manley, Research Fellow, Centre for Housing Research, School of Geography and Geosciences, University of St Andrews, UK. David has recently been involved in a project to create innovative statistical measures of deprivation with regard to health status (www.hpi.org. uk). His current research focuses on longitudinal data and investigates the relationship between deprivation and neighbourhoods in the UK.

Kirsteen Paton, Research Fellow, Sociology, University of Glasgow, UK. Kirsteen's research interests include stratification; working-class lives; urban restructuring; and problematic forms of consumption and risk by marginalised social groups.

Kate Shaw, ARC Research Fellow in Architecture, Building and Planning, The University of Melbourne, Australia. Kate's research interests include cultural diversity, social equity, housing markets, gentrification, urban policy and planning regulatory systems.

Wendy Shaw, School of Biological, Earth and Environmental Sciences, University of New South Wales, Sydney, Australia. Wendy focuses in particular on the contemporary field of whiteness in postcolonial Australia. Her ongoing research explores the theoretical debates about identity, specifically concerning urbanism and urbanity, cosmopolitanism and the complex realities of (post)colonial urban life in Australia, and beyond.

Rebecca Tunstall, Lecturer in Housing, Department of Social Policy, London School of Economics and Political Science, UK.

Mathieu Van Criekingen, Assistant Professor, Department of Human Geography, Free University Brussels (ULB), Belgium. Mathieu's research interests include neoliberal urbanism; politics of city building; gentrification as process and policy strategy.

Alan Walks, Associate Professor, Department of Geography, University of Toronto, Canada. Alan's research is concerned with analysing urban socio-spatial polarisation from a number of different angles, including the relationship between state policies and neighbourhood change, political ideology and urban form, gated communities and gentrification, and the politics of automobility.

ONE

Introduction: gentrification, social mix/ing and mixed communities

Loretta Lees, Tim Butler and Gary Bridge

> Does neighbourhood economic development mean driving out the poor and encouraging the presence of a new population or does it mean improving the life circumstances of the residents? (Taub et al, 1984, p 497)

Introduction: the scope of the book

In recent years there has been a resurgence of interest among urban policy makers, planners and urban scholars in the concept of 'mixed communities' or 'social mix' in cities, particularly at the neighbourhood scale (Forrest and Kearns, 1999; Atkinson and Kintrea, 2000; Goodchild and Cole, 2001; Tunstall, 2003). In this book we focus on the relationship between these social mix policies and plans and gentrification. We define gentrification as the movement of middle-income people into low-income neighbourhoods causing the displacement of all, or many, of the pre-existing low-income residents. Rhetorically and discursively disguised as social mixing, these policies and plans are promoting and spurring gentrification in a number of different countries (Lees, 2008). The morally persuasive and neutered terms policy makers use such as 'mixed communities', 'social mix' and 'diversity' politely avoid the class constitution of the processes involved (Lees, 2003). Rose (2004) has called this 'a particularly slippery area of social mix discourse'. It is hard to be for 'gentrification' as it is a dirty word (see Smith, 1996; also Lees et al, 2008, pp 154-9), but who would oppose 'social mixing' or 'mixed communities'?

It would be difficult to deny that there is something inherently and unquestionably positive about cities, neighbourhoods, streets, buildings and civic spaces in which we might see the broadest possible range of identities, backgrounds, wealth of experiences and personal biographies. Boosters of cities, property developers and estate agents often promote a place based on its diversity or cosmopolitan make-up, tapping into human desires for variety, difference and eclecticism. Social mix appears even more positive when scholars, politicians and journalists talk negatively about segregation – a mixed, socially diverse community is invariably pitched as the desegregating solution to lives that are lived in parallel or in isolation along income, class, ethnic and tenure fault lines. This is particularly glaring in the US, where the demolition of public housing projects to eradicate 'concentrated poverty' in favour of mixed-income development (under the US Department of Housing and Urban Development's HOPE VI programme [Home ownership and Opportunity for People Everywhere]) is producing a markedly different urban landscape (Wyly and Hammel, 2001; Crump, 2002; Lees et al, 2008; Hyra, 2008). It has been happening in the UK and elsewhere in Europe too, as the examples of Newcastle City Council's thwarted 'Going for Growth' strategy (Cameron, 2003), the regeneration of Elephant and Castle in London (DeFilippis and North, 2004), and the Dutch policy of 'housing redifferentiation' (Uitermark et al, 2007) demonstrate. To the journalist, planner, politician and marketing agency, a city with socially mixed neighbourhoods is usually seen as a healthy, liveable city (Rose, 2004).

As such, encouraging socially mixed neighbourhoods and communities by bringing middle-income people into low-income neighbourhoods has become, and for the moment[1] is continuing, as a major planning and policy goal in North America and in a number of West European countries. The largest and most heavily funded programmes have been in the US, the UK and the Netherlands (see Lees, 2008), but programmes have also been present, *inter alia*, Canada, Ireland, France and Australia. Although social mix policies and plans enacted through gentrification have all emerged within the specific political and policy contexts of different countries and are various in their historical referents, such as the garden city movement in the UK or notions of balanced communities which developed in the US in the 1950s, they share as many similarities as they do differences. In large part this is due to the increasing professionalisation, internationalisation and mobilisation of policy makers and policy transfer (see McCann, 2010). For example, it is well known that the British Social Exclusion Unit under the then New Labour government was influenced by US workfare programmes and the US Department of Housing and Urban Development's HOPE VI programme of poverty deconcentration, and that New Labour's Urban Task Force visited cities around the world in developing its ideas for the urban renaissance of English cities.

Those nations who have promoted policies or programmes of social mixing in inner-city neighbourhoods share something very particular in common, something that the gentrification literature is only beginning to think through now – they are all functioning liberal democracies and have welfare programmes of one variety or another. This is important because despite claims about the revanchist nature of gentrification in the Global North from a number of authors (for example, Smith, 1996), the fact is that welfare programmes, no matter how limited and problematic they may be, will still act as mediators against the worst atrocities of gentrification. This is rarely the case in the Global South, because in cities such as Mumbai, Karachi and Shanghai, gentrification is much more visceral – the displacements quantitatively and qualitatively larger – and in these countries the state makes no effort to conceal it (see Lees, in press). So even though this book acts as a critique of social mix policies that have enacted gentrification in a number of Western cities, we are very conscious that many countries outside of those included in this book are unlikely to even consider social mixing as a policy, or welfare, objective.

Social mix in a comparative perspective

Moving beyond 19th-century utopianism and associated normative principles on what constitutes a 'liveable' urban area (Sarkissian, 1976; Dansereau et al, 1997; Rose, 2004), the concept of 'mixed communities' or 'social mix' re-emerged in the 1990s in reaction to the large concentrations of socially homogeneous populations of poor people residing in the inner cities and inner suburbs of cities in Western Europe and North America. Social mix policies and programmes in the UK, the US, the Netherlands, Canada, Ireland and France have one dominant objective, that is, to deconcentrate or dilute large concentrations of low-income/poor households. The welfare programmes that built large-scale modernist estates, the project-based public housing policies enacted in the UK, the US, the Netherlands, Canada, France and Ireland, in the 1950s and 1960s, have been blamed for creating monolithic, socially segregated areas of poverty and social deprivation in the inner city.

In his *The truly disadvantaged* William Julius Wilson (1987) argued that the flight of the middle classes (especially the black middle classes) from central cities in the US had caused the downward spiral of many inner-city neighbourhoods: 'the exodus of the kind of the middle- and working-class families from many ghetto neighbourhoods removes an important "social buffer" that could deflect the full impact of prolonged and increasing joblessness' (p 129). For Wilson, the economy was central in alleviating poverty, but he argued that the outmigration of the black middle class had weakened community organisations and the social infrastructure. He believed that the return of the middle classes to the central city would improve conditions for low-income residents. Wilson, like others (see Kotlowitz, 1992; Lemann, 1992), was critical of the federal urban renewal programmes from the 1950s and 1960s that had ghettoised (segregated) low-income African-Americans into big public housing projects with excessively high violent crime rates. Wilson's voice was heard, and US policy makers began to seek ways to 'excise the cancer' of concentrated poverty in projects, to 'save US cities' (Katz, 2009, p 21). In 1992 Congress passed the US Department of Housing and Urban Development's HOPEVI programme of poverty deconcentration, the result of the National Commission on Severely Distressed Public Housing. This programme has begun to demolish large public housing projects at the centre of US cities and to disperse (displace) the projects' residents through Section 8 rental vouchers, that supposedly enable the recipients to relocate to areas of less concentrated poverty elsewhere in the city (see Varady and Walker, 2003). In their place they are building new mixed-income communities following new urbanist design principles – low rise, high density, traditional layout. The contemporary notion of mixed-income communities in the US offers similar arguments to those made in the 1950s around 'balanced communities', the idea being that social diversity would enrich the lives of residents (both adults and children), promote tolerance of social and cultural differences and offer educational and work role models. The goal has been to combine public housing units with market-rate homeownership units so as to provide an opportunity for people from different socioeconomic groups to live together as a community (US HUD, 2000). HOPE VI, however, is under increasing criticism for not delivering a truly mixed community nor the benefits supposed to come with this new mixed community. Joseph (2006) argues that low-income residents in mixed developments might benefit from increased informal social control and access to higher quality goods and services, but they are unlikely to benefit from social interaction. Fraser and Nelson (2008) claim that these new mixed-income developments have been more successful in satisfying middle-income residents than in helping low-income residents. Others argue that the same or better results could be achieved without income mixing – with good housing design, good management and careful tenant selection (see Vale, 2006). As Wilson (1987) made clear, reintegration with the middle class alone is not enough to generate social mobility; there needs to be a change in the structural economic conditions that inhibit access to employment, and so on.

Photograph 1.1: Cabrini Green, Chicago, being demolished to make way for new mixed-income development

In the UK, as former Prime Minister Tony Blair's New Labour government sought to lift the most disadvantaged out of poverty, they drew on HOPEVI and developed a 'New Deal for Communities' (see Imrie and Raco, 2003; Lees, 2008; Lupton and Fuller, 2009). As the then Deputy Prime Minister testified to Parliament: 'The division between areas exclusively of owner occupation and exclusively of renting, which was very much a creation of the 20th Century, has not been a happy one in our view and it has led to social polarisation and social exclusion' (Select Committee on Environment, Transport and Regional Affairs, 2001, p 2). Like the US, the UK began to demolish its larger public housing estates, indeed the largest public housing estate in Europe – the Aylesbury Estate, near Elephant and Castle in central London – is in the process of being demolished.[2] There are disturbing similarities between the demolition and rebuilding of Cabrini Green in Chicago (see Smith, 2001) and the proposals for the Aylesbury Estate in London (see Photographs 1.1 and 1.2). Other countries have also promoted 'mixed communities' for similar reasons. Anti-segregation policy in the Netherlands, first adopted by Rotterdam (see Uitermark, 2003; Uitermark et al, 2007; Musterd and Ostendorf, 2008) and later by the Dutch national government in its 'Big Cities Policy' (see Bolt and van Kempen, 2010), allows local authorities to refuse unemployed or under-employed households to locate in rental housing in neighbourhoods deemed to have too high a concentration of low-income, unemployed people. This is a policy of income regulation in certain neighbourhoods that was designed to prevent 'unliveability', but the real intention can be found in the detail of the policy documents – it is about diluting ethnic concentrations (see van Eijk, 2010b). Canada has pursued social mixing through both infill development (Rose, 2004), the use of planning tools to 'rebalance the population' (Slater, 2004) and demolition (August, 2008), and Ireland, through new-build developments, tenant purchase (like the English Right to Buy) and demolition; indeed in Ireland many former social housing areas are now completely, or almost completely, privately owned (see Norris, 2005; Redmond and Russell, 2008). In France social mixing has been enacted through legislation requiring local authorities to ensure that at least 20% of housing is social housing or face a fine, but often communes take a decision to pay the fine rather than enforce the quota (Blanc, 2010). There have been related discussions about social housing in Belgium, but to date social mix has only been selectively implemented (Loopmans et al, 2010). In Germany, particularly in the former East Germany, large concentrations of public housing have also come under attack, where whole estates have been bought up by private capital, although many of the companies have subsequently gone into liquidation leaving tenants in a very vulnerable situation (Bernt et al, 2010). Social mix has also been operationalised in Australia, where balancing social mix is also attached to addressing social and behavioural issues on postwar public housing estates (see Arthurson, 2010).

The concept of social mix in these various programmes is vague and slippery, it is not easily defined (see Lees, 2008) and as such, planners and policy makers can, and do, use it in different ways. They are seldom explicit about the exact parameters, in terms of composition (type of

Photograph 1.2: Aylesbury Estate, London, in the process of being redeveloped as a mixed-income community

heterogeneity), concentration (relative percentages of different social groups) and geographical scale (block, neighbourhood), and so the rhetoric and the reality of social mix rarely match up (Davidson and Lees, 2005).

Mixed communities policy is seen to be a positive, productive process; the idea is very politically attractive. Yet despite all the positive policy rhetoric floating around mixed communities (see, for example, Cisneros and Engdahl, 2009), criticisms and critiques are numerous and on the increase (see, for example, Goetz, 2005, 2010; Hyra, 2008). Scholars researching gentrification have been at the forefront of subjecting social mix and all its supposed remedial qualities to trenchant academic criticism, and three main lines of argument have emerged.

First, in the recent literature on contemporary gentrification, numerous researchers have argued that social mix is a one-sided (government) strategy, as it is seldom advocated in wealthier neighbourhoods that may be just as socially homogeneous as the deprived neighbourhoods where social mix is pitched as a heterogeneous remedy. To scholars critical of gentrification, 'social mix' is nothing more than rhetoric that obfuscates a gentrification strategy whereby the middle classes are invited into socially and economically challenged neighbourhoods to 'save' them from permanent decline through consumption practices that boost the local tax base (N. Smith, 2002; Lees, 2003, 2008; Blomley, 2004; Slater, 2004, 2006; Davidson and Lees, 2005). Social mix is but a transitory phenomenon on the way to complete gentrification (social homogeneity). Indeed, gentrification theorists have long dismissed social class mix within gentrifying neighbourhoods as a transitory phenomenon, a stage on the way to the complete bourgeois conquest of working-class neighbourhoods (Rose, 2004), and recent detailed statistical research has proven this (see Walks and Maaranen, 2008). Here mixed-income developments are seen as a 'neoliberal approach to the problems of the urban poor that seeks to recapture prime urban real estate despite the resultant displacement of many of those households that the strategy is purported to help' (Joseph and Chaskin, 2010, p 2349).

Second, gentrification scholars have questioned the extent to which it is realistic to assume that people from a highly diverse range of backgrounds, cultures and customs will *actually mix*. In fact policy makers have given little consideration to how these groups will interact as neighbours (Galster, 2007b). As Butler with Robson (2003) reported from research in Brixton, London, the arriving middle classes celebrate local diversity yet do not actually engage with that diversity in their everyday lives, leading to the construction of a 'Brixton in the mind', with 'tectonic' social relations (little or no social interaction) forming as a consequence. In short, the promotion of the residential propinquity of different social groups is based on the dubious assumption that close *physical* ties will lead to close *social* ties (Blokland, 2003; Butler, 2003; Bridge, 2005). Davidson (2008, 2010) and Davidson and Lees (2010) look at levels of social mixing between gentrifying and incumbent communities in neighbourhoods undergoing new-build gentrification along the Thames in London. They find little evidence of substantial interactions between populations and few shared perceptions of community. Davidson (2010) argues that the particular character of new-build gentrification has played an important role in generating this socially tectonic situation.

Third, there is the related assumption that a more mixed community lays the foundations for producing a more harmonious, cohesive, *socially balanced* community, even though it could be equally plausible to assume that more mixed neighbourhoods, where different classes, cultures and values may clash, will in fact engender even more conflicts and tensions, and thus an unstable, unbalanced community (Goodchild and Cole, 2001). Cheshire (2006, 2007b) has recently taken this further, arguing that 'forcing neighbourhoods to be mixed in social and economic terms is treating the symptoms of inequality, not the cause ... on a par with applying leeches to lower a fever', and wonders whether gentrification-induced social mix threatens the welfare benefits and supportive networks that emerge from living in neighbourhoods with complementary and similar households. These arguments echo those made much earlier by Herbert Gans (1961, p 181), who wrote that heterogeneity at the block level 'is unlikely to produce relationships of sufficient intensity to achieve either a positive social life or the cultural, political, and educational values sought through the balanced community'. The evidence emerging seems to support this; for example, Joseph and Chaskin (2010, p 2359) found that few respondents in the newly planned mixed communities in Chicago they researched described positive social interactions with neighbours. They quote one of their interviewees: 'There has been no interaction at all, and like I said, we see people all the time and people just kind of walk by and they don't make an effort to get to know you or speak or anything. So I kind of feel like there's a divisiveness ... we have the people who live in the apartments and ... those people who own' (Joseph and Chaskin, 2010, p 2360).

Furthermore, with the exception of recent studies by Freeman (2006) and Davidson (2008, 2010), there has been little to no discussion concerning the question of the degree to which social mixing *actually takes place* where gentrification is occurring. We feel that the wider policy debates on mixed communities are taking place without the important insights to be gained from a growing knowledge base on gentrification and social mixing. This book seeks to address that omission, and in so doing we have drawn together academic experts from different countries/cities with research interests and empirical findings specifically in this area. We hope that this book will significantly advance the critique of mixed communities policy by showing how social mix *policies* are accepted and sometimes deployed uncritically by various levels of urban governance in the face of evidence that suggests they will not be successful in terms of social inclusion and poverty uplift, and that they are leading to significant gentrification and ironically, social segregation, albeit an inversion of the previous social segregation (see Hyra, 2008, on this 'new urban renewal').

The chapters in this collection question the evidence base for social mix policies and rhetorics that advance processes of gentrification. We are not ideologically averse to 'social mix*ing*' as a policy objective, indeed as a 'moral landscape' it is hard to argue against 'social mix*ing*'. But we do question recent policies and plans around social *mix*. We highlight both the lack of an evidence base and contradictory evidence with respect to policies of social mix, and importantly we offer new evidence about social mix policy in a number of different national, city, neighbourhood and indeed temporal contexts.

The book has three main objectives. First, the different chapters demonstrate the proliferation, differences and similarities between social mix policies enacted through urban renaissance/gentrification policies in countries around the world. Second, we evaluate the claim that gentrification (introducing middle-income people into low-income neighbourhoods, usually of public housing) can break down socially segregated or socially homogeneous, deprived areas in positive ways. And third, we hope to advance debate on social mix policies that promote gentrification between gentrification researchers, policy makers, planners and housing groups.

Within each of these main objectives the book considers whether social diversity at the neighbourhood scale, as evidenced by census and other data, conceals a lack of social mixing between different class/income groups within neighbourhoods. We look at what kind of social mixing actually takes place in gentrifying neighbourhoods. And importantly, we question whether the aspirations of social mix policy sit well with the lived realities of daily conduct by different social groups. In so doing we hope to advance international debate by publishing research here from around the world that has begun to address these issues.

As William Julius Wilson (1987, p 18) has said:

> ... if the liberal perspective on the ghetto underclass is to regain the influence it has lost since the 1960s, it will be necessary to do more than simply react to what conservative scholars and policymakers are saying. Liberals will also have to propose thoughtful explanations of the rise in inner city social dislocations.

In contemporary vein, we want to do more than simply react to neoliberal policies, and we see this book as the first step towards research into more thoughtful explanations and socially just policies for the urban poor.

Overview of the book

The book begins with this introduction and ends with an afterword written by ourselves, and the middle of the book is divided into five thematic parts, including 18 chapters in total. The contributors to this collection are a mix of geographers, sociologists, urban researchers, policy analysts and the chief executive officer of the largest redevelopment project in Europe. This mix of academic disciplines as well as practitioners has enabled us to draw together different insights into the issues of social mix and social mixing, perhaps in ways not previously achieved where – for example – urban geographers and urban sociologists have ploughed somewhat separate furrows, and where academics and activists have criticised social mix as gentrification while paying little attention to the academically grounded complexity of some plans for social mix (see Lees, 2010, on HafenCity). The contributors all have specific expertise in gentrification research and/or social mix interventions in different national contexts. Some were selected from a group of invited researchers who took part in an international seminar series we co-organised on 'Gentrification and Social Mixing' funded by the Economic and Social Research Council (ESRC). We approached other contributors separately in the knowledge that they were undertaking in-depth research or had considerable research expertise on this topic.

Part 1 includes a series of *reflections on social mix policy* from around the world. The authors of these chapters all have good strategic knowledge of mixed communities (or the lack thereof) in relation to forms of governance and policy making in particular national contexts. In **Chapter Two** Paul Cheshire reviews the evidence, particularly that from the US, as it relates to the impact of social and economic mix on the welfare of those living in segregated neighbourhoods. He argues strongly that attempting to cure or reduce deprivation by engineering neighbourhood social mix, mistakes symptoms for causes. In **Chapter Three**, reflecting on social mix policy in Europe, Patrick Le Galès discusses the difficulty in defining social mix/ing, the question of scale, and the fact that different countries are differentially invested in the term. In **Chapter Four** Rebecca Tunstall argues that the policy of achieving 'mixed communities' became the overarching goal of New Labour's urban and housing policy in the UK, although its success in achieving this was much less certain. And in **Chapter Five**, Wendy Shaw reminds us that social mixing is not on the policy agenda of most countries in the rapidly urbanising world of Australasia.

Part 2 focuses on two *case studies of exemplary social mixing in urban renaissance projects*, one from Canada in the 1960s and 1970s and one from Germany that is contemporary. These two case studies demonstrate how ideas of social mix have progressed in planning for socially mixed communities over time, and they illustrate the contextual mediating factors such as politics, governance, economy and society. In **Chapter Six** David Ley traces the historical geography of gentrification and its relation to ideas of social mix. He discusses the neighbourhood of False Creek South in downtown Vancouver that was redeveloped in the 1960s and 1970s by planners enacting policies of social mixity. He reflects on the 'moral landscape' of False Creek South as a socially and tenurially mixed neighbourhood, comparing it with the contemporary development pressures on Downtown Eastside, an impoverished neighbourhood that is resisting social mix (in the form of gentrification) to preserve the supportive functions of the neighbourhood for low-income and marginalised groups. Ley contrasts social mix in an era of progressive liberal urban policies with today's neoliberal policy context. In **Chapter Seven** Jürgen Bruns-Berentelg, the chief executive of HafenCity Hamburg, discusses the novel planning measures that have been used to encourage social encounter and social mix in the new build district of HafenCity in Hamburg – currently the largest redevelopment project in Europe. He shows how he has developed a complex agenda for social mix in HafenCity, which includes tenurial mixing, functional mixing (for example, commercial and residential), mixing of social groups (by age, ethnicity, identity, cycle in life course) and research to investigate the successes and failures of its social mix agenda. Whether HafenCity is, or will be, another example of a gentrified downtown is being debated in Hamburg and elsewhere – at the moment the verdict is open.

Part 3 considers *social mix policies and gentrification* in a number of different national contexts. In **Chapter Eight** Pauline Lipman draws on her work on education policy to show how mixed-income housing policies and school policies are joined, discursively and practically, in attempts to socially mix inner-city public schools in Chicago. She locates these policies in relation to neoliberal urban development and the politics of 'race' (the schools being mixed are mainly black schools). She argues that the contention that lower-income and black students will benefit from proximity to middle-class students ignores research on the constellation of structural, cultural and pedagogical factors that perpetuate 'race' and class inequalities in educational experiences and outcomes. In **Chapter Nine** Marie-Hélène Bacqué and Yankel Fijalkow examine the link between gentrification and so-called social mix policies in Paris, and show how, despite an often inclusive rhetoric, gentrifiers in one of inner Paris's remaining black settlements pursue an agenda that is antagonistic to the needs of those living in social housing, particularly when they come from poor and black backgrounds. In **Chapter Ten** Kate Shaw shows how social mix strategies (there are no policies) in Australia are almost invariably associated with the large-scale regeneration of public housing estates. In her detailed study of several housing estates in Melbourne, Shaw points out that, even allowing for the changing party political context, estate redevelopment represents gentrification given the increased financial risks for government.

Part 4 considers the *rhetoric and reality of gentrification and social mix*. Mixing communities by bringing middle-income people into low-income communities (gentrification) is sold to us as social inclusion (the mark of a decent society) and plain good sense (a society which allows some to be excluded loses the benefit of their contribution). The function and value of 'social mixing' is simply taken for granted, it is seen to be the medicine for the exclusionary forces of housing segregation, both social and spatial, but here we see that the policy rhetoric does not measure up in reality. In **Chapter Eleven** David Manley, Maarten van Ham and Joe Doherty critique the rhetoric of neighbourhood social mix through quantitative research that investigates the effect of different levels of neighbourhood housing tenure mix on transitions from unemployment to employment and the probability of staying in employment for those with a job using data from the Scottish Longitudinal Study. They find long-lasting negative effects of living in deprived neighbourhoods, but only a small, if significant, benefit of living in mixed tenure (40%–80% social housing) streets and blocks for the unemployed. In **Chapter Twelve** Mathieu van Criekingen shows how notions of 'social' and 'functional mix' have acted as core values in urban policies and planning frameworks in Brussels since the early 1990s; critiquing this, he explores the migratory dynamics associated with the 'revitalisation' of Brussels' historic core. The results suggest trends towards rising socio-spatial inequalities fuelled by diverse gentrification-induced displacement processes. In **Chapter Thirteen** Sarah Glynn draws on her experience as an activist and architect to question the motives behind plans for the demolition of two multi-storey blocks in Hilltown, central Dundee, Scotland, and for the subsequent redevelopment of the site. Glynn shows how politicians and councillors in Dundee have convinced themselves, and others, that the active promotion of policies that encourage gentrification is for the common good. In **Chapter Fourteen** James Fraser, James DeFilippis, and Joshua Bazuin examine the real life experiences of residents in four HOPE VI developments in Nashville, Tennessee; their findings urge them to call for modesty in the claims made by proponents of HOPE VI.

Part 5 looks at the experience of *social mix policies and gentrification on the ground*, how social mix policies have been enacted by moving/attracting middle-income groups into poor neighbourhoods, displacing some of the poor and moving the others back into a very different community than what was there before. In **Chapter Fifteen** Mark Davidson draws on in-depth research in a number of Thames riverside areas of new-build gentrification in London to show that the neighbourhood-based social relations emerging in affected areas show a lack of mixing and therefore signal an important social policy failure, but also that mounting urban changes are simultaneously generating worrying displacement pressures. In **Chapter Sixteen** Kirsteen Paton presents a detailed study of social mix and gentrification in the redeveloped (gentrified and socially mixed) neighbourhood of Partick in Glasgow, Scotland. She questions the advocacy role of middle-class residents in helping to improve the fortunes of neighbourhoods, and argues that encouraging middle-class residents into poorer neighbourhoods might not result in welfare gains for poorer residents but argues, importantly, that the working-class residents who are able to remain have been able to benefit from the area's gentrification. In **Chapter Seventeen** Martine August and Alan Walks explore what socially mixed public housing redevelopment in Toronto might mean for tenant participation, organisational structure and political capital. They show how the imposition of social mix is already affecting public housing tenants negatively, and that this negative affect is likely to increase down the line. In **Chapter Eighteen** Talja Blokland and Gwen van Eijk focus on the actual experience of social mix in their comparison of the social networks of people living in two different but gentrifying urban neighbourhoods in Rotterdam. The authors contend that the social interaction and social mixing found are not those envisaged in Dutch policy prescriptions.

We conclude the book with an **Afterword**, asking whether policy makers and governments should be aiming to produce socially mixed neighbourhoods through the introduction of middle-class residents into low-income/working-class areas. In addition, we ask if there is scope for methodological development with respect to researching social mix, and consider how quantitative and qualitative techniques might be combined to shed light on the ways in which different social groups do, or do not, interact in places where social mix is a policy priority.

Notes

[1] Although the worldwide recession/financial crisis is impacting this. In the UK, the Localism Bill is due to displace the mixed communities initiative with a system of 'community rights' that may empower communities to resist affordable housing and cause greater social segregation.

[2] Although this particular programme is currently in jeopardy due to a significant cut in government funding.

Part I
Reflections on social mix policy

Why do birds of a feather flock together? Social mix and social welfare: a quantitative appraisal

Paul Cheshire

Introduction

One of the peculiarities of utopian visions of the 'good' urban society is how little attention the visionaries pay to how people choose to live. As an urban economist, my starting point is that the choices people make for themselves are the best way of discovering what their preferences are, what makes them happy. Of course to an economist it is self-evident that such choices are constrained by people's incomes. Poor households cannot choose to play polo, nor buy private healthcare. That is because they are poor and polo and private healthcare are expensive. Strangely this rather obvious insight does not seem to translate into our discussions about neighbourhood segregation or how cities generate (and distribute) welfare.

Since this chapter is about 'social' rather than ethnic mix, it is inevitably about gradations of income. The attributes of people that determine their incomes are very closely correlated with their social status since the key factors determining social status are education, skills and training, which in combination largely determine incomes. Planners and social engineers have long hankered after 'balanced' (or mixed) communities, and significant policy effort over the years has been put into trying to force people to live in such communities – for example, by the requirement to include affordable housing in new residential developments. The trouble is that cussed people still seem to choose to live in neighbourhoods with their peers – subject, of course, to their choices being constrained by their incomes.

This political or social aspiration for mixed neighbourhoods seems to survive regardless of the evidence which continues to appear that welfare gains for poor people from living close to richer neighbours are nil to negligible. Sometimes, as an urban economist, I nearly despair:

it seems that when we can find no evidence to support the improving effects of policies we want to impose on people we just invent some new and untested aspiration mixed communities should serve. Living together with richer neighbours may not make poor people any better off but there must be some other social reason for trying to enforce it (and so diverting resources from actually doing something effective to address poverty). Not only is there almost no good evidence that poor people benefit in welfare terms from having richer neighbours, there is some evidence that people – both poorer and richer – gain welfare from living in neighbourhoods – again subject to their choices being constrained by income – with compatible peers rather similar in lifestyle and needs to themselves.

The problem may be that two quite separate questions have got confused: do we like to see poverty – more obvious when spatially concentrated? The answer for most civilised people is: no. Indeed most progressive people would favour an explicit redistribution of income and opportunities and effective policies to address concentrated poverty.

The second question is whether poor people are made poorer or lose welfare – all else being equal – if they live in poor neighbourhoods? They are, of course, more visible if concentrated, but the evidence, discussed below, is pretty strong that they are not made poorer by being concentrated. It is hard to find convincing evidence that poor people gain significant net benefits from having richer neighbours, while at the same time they may lose an important advantage from living in a poor community. This is not all that surprising since the proposition that poorer people gain from having richer neighbours must depend on there being some benign externality that seeps from richer households to poorer ones close by, whereas what mainly happens is that richer households bid up local prices and drive out shops and other facilities that serve poor households. There is a certain patronising aspect to the view that a *Sun* reader must benefit from having a *Guardian*-reading neighbour.

The underlying problem is that those characteristics of neighbourhoods which attract richer households – make them 'nicer' – are all capitalised into house prices or reflected in rents (see, for example, Cheshire and Sheppard, 2004; Cheshire, 2010; Hilber, 2010). These include access to higher paying jobs: the fundamental driver of systematic difference in the costs of residential space within an urban area is the costs of accessing better paid jobs. It also includes access to upmarket local facilities such as gastropubs or good delis, better schools or high quality parks or National Trust sites. It is not that poor people would not like to consume any of these features of nicer (and more expensive) neighbourhoods, but rather that some of them would be of no value (access to highly skilled jobs or upmarket gastropubs) and others, while nice, are not high enough in the priority list of poor households' budgets to be worth paying a premium for. Access to Hampstead Heath is a wonderful amenity but it is not as important as being able to feed your children.

Evidence on neighbourhood effects

The idea that poor households gain from living in proximity to richer households is usually known as 'neighbourhood effects'. The problem is that while there is not surprisingly ample evidence that people who live in poor neighbourhoods have lower incomes, worse health and are less skilled, there is virtually no evidence that these adverse effects are the results of living in poor neighbourhoods. Correlation does not demonstrate causation, and the sorting mechanism exercised by income provides a clear casual explanation. Poor households who exhibit these adverse characteristics in terms of skills, jobs, health or exposure to crime can only afford to live where housing is cheap.

There have been a series of rigorous studies over the past 20 years or so that seem to demonstrate this lack of causal effect, that is, no significant adverse neighbourhood effects. Methodologically it is difficult because of self-selection to identify the causal relationship, but two main methodologies have emerged. The first comes from studying outcomes for people who are more or less randomly moved from poor to rich neighbourhoods or vice versa. The second is cohort studies that look at outcomes for people who originated in different types of neighbourhoods.

The most widely quoted, and in some ways most thorough, of the first type of study were those based on the US Moving to Opportunity programme. This deliberately set out to offer re-housing into more affluent neighbourhoods for a more or less randomly selected sample of poor people from neighbourhoods of concentrated poverty. Participants were divided into three groups. Group 1 got housing vouchers conditional on moving to more affluent neighbourhoods and significant professional help to assist them to find new housing; Group 2 got the housing vouchers but no help and could move where they chose; Group 3 – the control group – got no assistance in moving and nor did they get housing vouchers. The most rigorous analysis of the results of this programme appeared in papers by Kling et al (2005, 2007). They found that there were very few statistically significant differences in long-term outcomes between these three groups. A consistent finding was that there was no improvement at all in the economic or labour market position of the adults in Groups 1 or 2 compared to those in Group 3, the control. For younger people there were some, mainly not statistically significant, differences. Adolescent girls seemed to do rather better in the educational system and in various behavioural ways, but differences between the groups were not statistically significant. Adolescent boys who moved to more affluent neighbourhoods tended to do worse in the educational system 10 years after the programme started, and did worse in terms of criminality, especially property crime. This was one of the few statistically significant differences between those who moved and those who did not.

Other studies have exploited exogenous enforced moves connected with the housing system to try to identify causal links between aspects of neighbourhoods and outcomes for individuals. Edin et al (2003) is an interesting study but not strictly relevant to the present chapter since it was concerned with any impacts of ethnically homogeneous neighbourhoods on labour market outcomes. They exploited the Swedish policy of housing political asylum seekers in non-ethnically concentrated neighbourhoods. They found this was harmful and statistically significantly harmful to the later earnings of refugees. Refugees in more ethnically concentrated neighbourhoods gained 13% in earnings for a one standard deviation increase in the ethnic concentration of their neighbourhood.

A more relevant study with comparable findings is that by Weinhardt (2010). This exploits the fact that transfers into social housing in Britain are essentially exogenous. When a family's name gets to the top of the list they have to take what is offered or wait for an unknown time. This produces a transfer of children between schools and yields a large sample of random moves from better neighbourhoods and schools (in terms of public examination or testing results) to very bad ones. Weinhardt compares the change in the achievements of adolescents before and after the move. Failing to control for family and personal characteristics yields the usual result that moving to a 'bad' school worsens a child's performance. However, once personal and family characteristics are controlled for, this finding disappears. Moving to a really badly performing school in a neighbourhood of severe deprivation has no statistically significant effects on educational outcomes – at least over the span of children's lives covered by this analysis.

The other rigorous approach to establishing the significance of neighbourhood effects is to track individuals over time – cohort studies. One of the earlier convincing studies was Oreopoulos (2003), using Canadian data. He tracked individuals originating in social housing in Toronto over a 30-year period. Their neighbourhoods of origin exhibited great variation with respect to deprivation indicators. But over a 30-year period, and once personal characteristics had been fully taken into account, there was no statistically significant effect of the characteristics of the neighbourhood of origin on any measure of labour market successor earnings. In Britain, Bolster et al (2007) published the results of a 10-year tracking of individuals. They used a random sample of individuals and experimented with different 'concepts' of neighbourhood from the very small to the quite extensive. Again they could find no statistically significant impact of neighbourhood of origin on any measure of labour market success or earnings once personal characteristics had been standardised for. Indeed, although not statistically significant, the result suggested a perverse effect: other things being equal, people from poorer neighbourhoods had higher earnings 10 years later.

The most recent British cohort study is by van Ham and Manley (2010). They used the Scottish Longitudinal Study, a 5.3% sample of the Scottish population linked over successive population censuses. The authors were interested in the impact on labour market outcomes of tenure mix in the neighbourhood of origin because this linked closely to the policy of mixed communities and the enforced provision of social or affordable housing in new, market, residential estates. Their conclusion was that most existing non–experimental studies of neighbourhood effects suffered from the problem of 'reverse causality', that is, finding apparent neighbourhood effects because of self-selection of individuals with adverse characteristics into poor and deprived neighbourhoods. They found no evidence that a concentration of social renting or, for those in socially rented housing, coming from more deprived neighbourhoods, had adverse effects on labour market outcomes 10 years later. They did find some evidence suggesting that for owner-occupiers originating in the most deprived neighbourhoods there was a statistically significant adverse effect on labour market outcomes 10 years later but, as they added, the adverse neighbourhood effects found for homeowners seem likely to provide evidence of '(self) selection not causation'. They suggest the self-selection was driven by house price difference which, given the findings of Cheshire and Sheppard (2004), seems highly plausible.

Benefits of living with peers

Given the observation that there is substantial self-selection in neighbourhood choice, it would be surprising if living close to other like-minded and socially similar people did not provide a significant welfare benefit. Here the detailed empirical evidence is far sparser, although Edin et al (2003) provide indirect evidence supportive of the proposition. Furthermore, the mounting evidence that the assumption of spatial equilibrium in urban housing markets is a quite close approximation of what is observed (see Cheshire, 2010) suggests that self-selection – house hunting – in housing markets is an effective and sophisticated process. There really are very few households in a typical city that, subject to their incomes, could move house and improve their welfare.

One of the great but largely under-investigated agglomeration economies of cities is not their contribution to productivity but their contribution to welfare. They provide a far more diverse range of goods and services as well as more competition between sellers. One of the most important services in welfare terms is the amenities people derive from the particular locations in which they live, including the congeniality/complementarity of their neighbours. This is obvious in ethnic neighbourhoods. If you want access to a mosque or a synagogue then there are important advantages of living in an ethnically appropriate neighbourhood, or a conservative as opposed to a liberal synagogue. The same logic applies if you want access to Korean food or a Spanish language school. But this argument applies more widely still. There are advantages for households with young children if they live near other households with young children; if your hobbies are music or theatre, or golf or tennis, so, too, you will gain welfare from living with similar neighbours.

There is clear evidence, for example, in Musterd (2006), that in Amsterdam particular social groups – of similar income – choose to live in different parts of the city. There is significant evidence, mainly from the US, supporting the important part played by neighbourhood contacts in job finding, and more particularly finding long-term suitable jobs for lower skilled workers. Bayer et al (2005) showed that for a very large sample of employed people in Boston, there was a very strong tendency for people who lived in the same neighbourhood – a census block – to work in the same census block. Having eliminated the effects of transport networks and other factors that might explain this finding independently of social interactions with neighbours, they found convincing evidence that it was interactions between neighbours that strongly influenced the job locations of neighbours. They further found that such interactions were more influential if neighbours were of a similar level of education, both parties had children and were of a similar age. Their conclusion was that social interactions within neighbourhoods, between people similar to each other, are a significant mechanism matching jobs and workers.

Both sets of findings are consistent with earlier US research (see Blau and Robins, 1992) on the importance in job search of informal networks with friends and relatives. They found that while this was a frequent – but not the most frequent – method of job search, and particularly important for the less skilled, it was the most successful form of job search from the point of view of both workers and employers. It produced the highest rate of job offers per contact and the highest rate of job offer acceptances. In their review, Ioannides and Loury (2004) report that, in addition, such jobs found through personal contacts lasted longer, so that around half of all jobs were held by people who had found them via friends and neighbours. Friends and neighbours were also more important in job searches for the currently unemployed than for the employed, so not just more important for the less skilled but also the less fortunate. Ioannides and Loury also report a persistent increase in the use of informal contacts as a means of job searching over time – despite the rise in the internet – and that it is more prevalent the larger a city is: in cities of more than 500,000, more than half of unemployed job searchers relied on friends and acquaintances; in cities smaller than 100,000, less than 10% did. Since the larger a city is the more (apparent) intensely socially segregated neighbourhoods it has (see Krupka, 2007), it follows that homogeneous, socially segregated neighbourhoods are one of the advantages large cities confer on their citizens in the job matching process.

Conclusion

This has necessarily been a selective review of the evidence as it relates to the impact of social and economic mix on the welfare of those living in segregated neighbourhoods. While it has not been possible to include all significant work, all the work surveyed has been of the highest standards of analytical and methodological rigour. It is a very difficult business to determine the direction of causation. However, my reading of the best research we have is that the causal chain runs from attributes – low skills, poor education, bad health – which make people poor, to low incomes which constrain them to live in cheap neighbourhoods. Neighbourhoods we think of as nice – places with the attributes sought by upper middle-income, liberal professionals, including good transport connections to well-paid jobs or accessible high quality parks – cost too much for poor people to afford to live in them. Moreover, many of the attributes that help make nice neighbourhoods expensive would have little or no value to households living on benefits. Households on the poverty line cannot afford to pay extra to have good access to highly skilled jobs, and nor would such access be likely to benefit them since they tend to lack the skills to qualify for such jobs. And while poor neighbourhoods may not be 'attractive', they are cheap; they have attributes such as access to cheap takeouts and neighbours with similar problems and needs who may have relevant and useful contacts. The most deprived neighbourhoods of all may confer very limited benefits, but still the question remains: is moving their inhabitants to more affluent neighbourhoods any kind of solution to their problems? The evidence suggests it is not.

Attempting to cure or reduce deprivation by engineering neighbourhood social mix mistakes symptoms for causes. As I have said elsewhere, it is like trying to cure fevers by attaching leeches. Moreover, policies to try to engineer neighbourhood mix cost substantial resources (even if those resources are not visible to the public finances because they are paid by developers who are forced to provide 'affordable' or social housing within their developments), and may destroy significant sources of welfare. We devote disproportionate resources towards trying to mix neighbourhoods with little evidence of real benefit in poverty reduction; even our research efforts are distorted to trying to find evidence for, or disprove, neighbourhood effects when we would get more useful results from researching the underlying causes of poverty and how best to equip people to escape from it.

THREE

Social mix and urban policy

Patrick Le Galès

Introduction

A first difficulty that is encountered in producing a book such as this is the question of definition: what does 'social mix' really mean beyond the spatial coexistence of different social and ethnic groups in a given neighbourhood? The least that can be argued is that social mix is not very stabilised as a concept. All societies are mixed one way or another. Social mix could be defined by what it is not: the extreme concentration of some social or ethnic groups, that is, super-bourgeois neighbourhoods, ghettos or ethnic enclaves. As the editors of this book rightly emphasise, the question of social mix is, of course, first and foremost, seen as concerning poor neighbourhoods where the concentration of the upper middle class is more an issue for social mix. In other words, in most neighbourhoods, there are some elements of social mix. In parallel to the notion of social integration or social cohesion, there is a major discrepancy between the way those words are used and put into practice in everyday and/or policy discourse and a more rigorous academic analysis. This, of course, is very often the case, and there is room for extensive analysis of the use of social mix and other such terms by different actors in different contexts.[1] We may have no clue about what social mix is really supposed to mean but at the same time understand that policy makers have to show they are doing something in the face of staggering spatial inequalities – given that politics is supposed to create common good, to give a sense of unity to a society, and to prevent the most obvious threats to social order such as riots (Driant and Lelévrier, 2006).

The second problem for the analysis and for policy makers is, of course, the question of scale. The debate, for example, in the French context between two leading scholars, E. Maurin and E. Préteceille, was very telling. By analysing social mix at the level of very small areas, Maurin (2004) draws conclusions in the case of France about the rise of extreme segregation and the decline of social mix. By contrast, using data at the level of 2,000 inhabitant units (IRIS for the national statistical institute INSEE), Préteceille (2006, 2009) shows, for the Paris region, an indisputable overall decline in social segregation leading to more social mix in residential terms albeit with a concentration at the extremes – notably the rise of a number of rich enclaves in the west of Paris and the centre of Paris as contrasted to a massive concentration of poverty in the Seine St Denis neighbourhoods to the east. Therefore, by using data at the level of communes or urban areas as a whole, contradictory results are not perhaps unexpected. More generally, interactions between individuals of different social groups may take place within neighbourhoods, in public spaces, in shopping malls, at schools, through networks, through engagement in different activities or at work. We can measure networks and levels of interaction that contribute to the making of society and social mix beyond residential mixity. It is possible to measure these forms of interactions and network activities and how they contribute to the overall level of social engagement in ways that are not possible for residential social mix, largely because the latter lacks the dynamic interaction inherent in social networks.

Third, as with so much else in social science, the social mix question has to be contextualised. The question of social mix has different stakes in different societies. The comparative macro analysis of society tradition is sometimes lost by urban scholars. Social inequalities, gender inequalities and ethnic inequalities obviously vary massively from one country to the next. What is at stake in cities often accentuates structural characteristics of a given society, as argued in the classic urban sociology literature, from Simmel to the Chicago School. Public policies designed to encourage socially mixed neighbourhoods are more likely to have an impact when the level of inequality (both social and spatial) is lower. The work being undertaken by Atkinson and Piketty (2010) has been crucial in helping to underline the role played by structural inequalities over time in different societies. To put things more precisely, when a generous welfare state prevents child poverty and limits inequality, the issue of social mix is not a major one, even if it is argued otherwise in public debates. By contrast, when inequalities are more massive, or growing, the question becomes more sensitive.

Fourth, the development of social mix policies sometimes relies on a strange representation of the population. In the massive French urban renovation policy currently under way, the priority accorded to 'social mix' assumes that the population will be stable in renovated neighbourhoods. Assessment and measures of future mixity are based on a representation of neighbourhoods as places where people stay over time. This is often plain wrong. Lelévrier's (2007) forensically precise analysis of the ongoing process of urban renovation shows that, with or without urban regeneration policy, about half of the population moves over two years – which is only just a little less than the third of the population that moved in highly distressed parts of London at the end of the 19th century. There is therefore massive mobility in neighbourhoods with a high degree of poverty. Urban regeneration policy only increases mobility and changes the parameters of the filtering process. This dynamic over time is seldom taken into account in evaluating social mix policy. Without exaggerating the fluidity, those flux are certainly influenced by housing policy, but many other factors also play a role: the upgrading of a good school (with good connections to elitist higher education organisations) or transport may play a bigger role than the residential element. Social mix, therefore, can also be the result of mobility, rather than a set of fixed social characteristics.

Fifth, the question of social mix lacks a solid theoretical underpinning. From the pioneering research undertaken in the 1960s by Chamboredon and Lemaire (1970) in what has become a cult paper in French sociology, most urban scholars are familiar with the idea that when very different social or ethnic groups live in the same building or the same neighbourhood, this rarely leads to social mixing but rather to strategies of avoidance and distinction. Most social groups play a complex game of distance and proximity with other social and ethnic groups. The question therefore becomes not whether the residential dimension of a socially mixed neighbourhood matters, but to what extent it matters. Beyond the residential dimension, one has to take into account the practice of using various services, schools, hospitals, leisure, consumption, but also interactions in public space. What might appear as lovely social mix in the park with children from different origins (that is, in public space) may disguise severe residential segregation and segregated schools. Making sense of different dimensions is not easy. Social mixing, as social avoidance between different social or ethnic groups (or genders or generations) takes place in numerous ways within cities and some are more important than others; the analysis, however, has to be contextualised. Beyond the discourses and the amazing rhetoric on middle-class models for other groups (see Raco, 2009), social scientists appear somewhat lost in understanding what is going in the urban fabric. We know, for instance, that in most cases, whatever the level of mixed social composition, people hardly talk to their neighbours.

Middle classes in contemporary Europe

In my own research in European cities (see Andreotti et al, 2011: forthcoming) we show that the upper middle classes tend to develop a plural and complex game of distance and proximity in relation to other social groups in order to select, control and choose the dynamics of these interactions. Socially mixed neighbourhoods are one dimension of the more general question of the making of society, in which inter-group social dynamics in urban space are generally more complex than extreme mutual avoidance (constrained only by real estate prices, urban policies or the physical layout of the city) on the one hand, or the colonisation of neighbourhoods on the other. In our research, we show that most upper middle-class households do not aim to live in isolation, complete segregation or absolute secession, and for them it is, most of the time, a matter of skilfully combining proximity and distance in relation to other social groups. Just as the middle classes studied by Chamboredon and Lemaire (1970) in socially mixed neighbourhoods compensated for their geographical proximity to neighbouring communities of working-class people through complex strategies of distancing, we argue that today's urban upper middle-class managers develop their own combinations of practices which allow them to select the dimensions they are willing to share with other social groups, and those in which they search for a more segregated social environment for themselves and their families. In other words, we try to show that the upper middle classes want some form of socially mixed environment, as long as they control it and they can develop compensating strategies or avoidance strategies when needed. Our hypothesis, complementary to the processes of secession and gentrification, suggests that the upper middle classes are distancing themselves from lower social strata, but that this does not necessarily need to take the form of a complete physical segregation from those groups. They search to distance themselves in certain domains (but less so in others) by developing 'partial exit' strategies that allow them to select the dimensions of the public sphere they decide to share with the lower classes. These strategies of distance and proximity in relation to other social groups imply that the upper middle classes (at least those in France, Italy and Spain) remain strongly embedded in the territory of their neighbourhoods and cities through their interaction with dense social networks, their selective use of public services or the frequentation of certain public spaces. In this context, their residential trajectories, in combination with the density and structure of their social networks, and their 'partial exit' strategies, allow them to inhabit socially mixed urban areas without having to renounce their specific values and practices.

These remarks therefore signal that social engineering through housing policies that promote social mix/ing are unlikely to achieve some of the normative goals mentioned by policy makers. Similarly, most of the evidence in the French context, as seen in this book, does not support the view that gentrification creates social mix as such. Apparent instances of this tend not to last.

Does this argument suffice to undermine all public policies in that domain?

Within the field of urban studies, public policy has a bad name. Urban scholars have developed their critical thinking and analysis against the normative and technocratic bias of urban planners or urban officials supporting growth coalitions (Cochrane, 2007). In the urban field in particular, the policy studies tradition has led to the search for best practices, or endless descriptive comments on new policy initiatives. The lack of explanations and theoretical perspectives has also been a classic feature. Quite tellingly, the more governments develop 'new' programmes, policies or initiatives, the bigger the literature becomes which describes, and sometimes analyses, those programmes. Policies to develop socially mixed neighbourhoods are no exception. The making of this volume bears witness to the rise of new policy labelled in those terms, and is a welcome departure in foregrounding a critical analysis rather than either simple and uncritical adulation of the policies, on the one hand, or a blanket rejection of them, on the other.

Among many, two lines of criticism are usually launched against urban policies. First, in the Marxist or post/neo-Marxist tradition, urban policy is something used by state elites to stabilise capitalism. In classic approaches, the state-driven transformation of society is typically analysed, and in these accounts, the state plays an essential role, namely in connection with the primitive accumulation of capital and ideology, the latter a reflection of the dominant material force in society. The state first intervenes through public policy as guarantor of social order, namely through ideology and by regulating the various social interests. As social order is an essential condition for real estate investment, it later intervenes in the accumulation phase, making below-market price land or subsidies available to real estate developers. New markets are subsidised by the state, the state puts in place the conditions required for investment, and, in some cases, speculation. According to these accounts, such are the dynamics of public policy.

There is indeed often close cooperation – growth coalitions – between financial interests and the main state economic actors for the purpose of ensuring economic development. The state in this case does not disappear; indeed it organises the accumulation phase. The role of urban policy is analysed as being the maintenance of social order, to ensure the reproduction of the labour force, and to establish the conditions for market-based accumulation. This argument is well known in the gentrification literature. Political themes, modes and slogans are indeed often used to justify urban policy in the interest of dominant classes.

A second classic line of criticism stresses the limits of the rationalisation process associated with state and urban policy in particular, the illusion of modernity, public policy failures and the resistance it encounters (Scott, 1999). Criticism of the modernist project in cities underlines the violence of the planning process, of urban policy, the displacement and exclusion of populations in the name of the common good, or of policies making possible processes of gentrification in the name of social mix. In an urban world described as chaotic and/or as a fluid process, urban policy is thus bound to fail and to create more intended or unintended effects. This argument makes sense. The urban is as unsettled as ever, urban regions organised in networks, metropolitan areas, global cities, ever-increasing suburbs, towns, neighbourhoods, all of which may become the target of urban policy. Such policies face a whole range of problems: new forms or renewed forms of inequalities, poverty, competition pressure, illegal immigration, extreme right voting, urban renewal issues, pollution, crime, suburbanisation, health alerts, creation of gated communities, globalisation, lack of social housing, and so on. In such an environment, policies to encourage socially mixed communities are bound to fail or to have little impact. They reflect the illusory social engineering tradition of planning that has been so often criticised for its numerous failures.

It is this context that brings us to the argument about governance. Governing the residential strategies of households is far from an easy task. Much of the governance literature fails to question what is really governed in cities, for instance. The less positivist research rightly builds on policy failures. Governing activities, more often than not, fail to achieve the goals set for them.

These two sets of arguments are generously mobilised in the critical literature about gentrification, for instance, and often for good reasons. However, one may want to come back more precisely on those concerned with 'social mix policy'.

Is it the vagueness of 'social mix' that is such a problem for public policies? At the risk of being provocative, one is tempted to answer 'not so much'. Instead of analysing urban policies as they are labelled by governmental agencies – for instance, with respect to social mix policy – it is first useful to remember how, over time, different sets of policies are labelled. Most of the time, a 'new policy' results from the re-organisation of existing pieces of public policy that are re-assembled, brought together and re-branded as 'new urban policy'. Re-assembling and re-framing elements of public policies is a major activity within government for two reasons: (1) policies die hard, and (2) there is a constant pressure for ministers to be visible in the public debate, to start new initiatives, to launch new policies, to start innovative programmes. In other words, at least in the French case, there are cases where the new policy imperative in favour of 'social mix' leads to absolutely no change whatsoever when such programmes are implemented. The only change is that when some social housing programmes are implemented locally, they change the label to brand the 'social' dimensions more obviously. A contrasting case is also taking place, when the 'social mix' priority is used to justify urban regeneration programmes or gentrification dynamics, that is, the exclusion of some disadvantaged groups from neighbourhoods that have become desirable. In most cases, the priority given to 'social mix' urban policies makes this question much more visible, but has some marginal, incremental influence on the policies which are being implemented. It simply adds another layer of policies to a very rich and institutionalised domain. It follows that critical social scientists should, at the same time, analyse the new discourse and the instrumentation of the new discourse and check out the effect of what is being implemented. The sociology of public policy argues that policies do not change easily and that there is little relation between change of discourses and change of implemented policies. It may or may not take place. Policy makers have to make things visible. As was argued, the focus on 'social mix' may be just a way to reassess the unity of society and to demonstrate a commitment to prevent some forms of extreme inequality at the macro level.

Conclusion: what matters is what works?

There is a further related lesson to be learned from the public policy literature: in a number of public policies, goals and discourses do not matter very much if one is interested in the output. The logic is well known (Lascoumes and Le Galès, 2008); in many domains, public policies fail, or do not achieve their goals, or may only get results in the much longer term. Societies are difficult to govern, people protest and entrenched interests are very strong. On the other hand, because of the increasing influence of new media in the dissemination of information, there is increasing pressure for policy makers to legitimate their actions by their results and therefore to show their effectiveness in solving problems. One way to react is for politicians to adopt blame avoidance strategies by appearing hyper activist, by developing new policies every day and to change the policy all the time before any clear evaluation of it can be made. This was a strategy that was adopted by President Sarkozy in France, Prime Minister Berlusconi in Italy and the former Prime Minister Tony Blair in the UK. An alternative strategy is to be as vague as possible in setting out the goals of the policy, or to try and achieve a large number of goals so that at the end, it will be difficult to assess whether the policy has failed or not. In the midst of such a plethora of policy initiatives, goals, reviews and outcomes, politicians are usually able to claim that something has worked – and, as Blair is once reported as saying, 'what matters is what works'. In France, most new flagship policies have always set out, at the very least, to contribute to sustainable development, social cohesion and economic development. In one major law concerning the environment, we managed to identify 23 different goals, including major contradictions between them. In other words, because it has become difficult to achieve goals, one way out for policy makers has been to rely on consensually vague overarching goals. Social mix policy is a very good example of this.

Finally, and against some *a priori* criticisms on urban policies, it is worth thinking in terms of what happens when social mix policies do not take place. When very large estates comprising large groups of impoverished populations are abandoned by public policies (whatever the type of intervention), what happens? If we accept that governments are supposed to deal with the most fragile population, who governs when nobody governs? If there is no public policy, including social mix policies with all their limitations, market mechanisms operate without constraints and that rarely plays in favour of disadvantaged groups. The policy of mixed communities, in London in particular, was certainly not the best policy and did not compensate for the lack of social housing construction under New Labour. However, if this area of provision is curtailed by the current Coalition government as planned, it is unlikely to produce better housing conditions for the lower classes and will, as the Conservative Mayor of London Boris Johnson puts it, lead to a degree of 'social cleansing' of the centre of London. And when the market does not take over, other regulation mechanisms may develop in the absence of state intervention such as mafias or gangs.

In conclusion, there are no grounds for arguing that the increase in social mix policies (both rhetorically and implemented on the ground) will massively change societies and interactions between various social groups or produce significant social change. It is only one piece in understanding the jigsaw puzzle that constitutes the fabric of urban societies. Many criticisms of social mix policies are therefore well taken because of the instrumental use of the notion to justify and rationalise all sorts of urban policies. Equally, however, their limitations notwithstanding, the complete absence in urban policy of vague goals such as 'social mix' may also be damaging. Long-term concentrated poverty in some neighbourhoods is never good news. That should be addressed and whether that takes place under the rubric of 'social mix' or not may not be as central as some critical commentators have led us to believe.

Note
[1] For the French debate on social mix and urban policy, see Epstein (2011).

FOUR

Mixed communities and urban policy: reflections from the UK

Rebecca Tunstall

Introduction

The 'genealogy' of British mixed communities discourse and policy can be traced back as far as the mid-19th century (Cole and Goodchild, 2001). In the past three decades alone, both Conservative and Labour governments have introduced a wide variety of housing and urban policies which have aimed, at least in part, to increase or maintain tenure or social mix within residential neighbourhoods. Under the 1997–2010 New Labour government, 'mixed communities' looked set to become the overarching goal of all urban and housing policy. Mixed communities policies have been intertwined with the shrinking of social housing from its peak in 1980, increases in home ownership, and growing reliance on the private sector not only as a partner in urban policy but as a principal source of funding for regeneration and new affordable housing (Lupton and Tunstall, 2008), and have run in parallel with high income inequality (Hills et al, 2010).

Over the past three decades, the most overt mixed communities policies have been neighbourhood regeneration policies and planning policies for new developments. First, a series of neighbourhood redevelopment projects have aimed to increase tenure mix in social housing areas and social mix in deprived areas, including Estate Action, which aimed to improve 500 council estates in England (1985–94) (Pinto, 1993), and the Single Regeneration Budget which supported a wide range of schemes in deprived areas (1994–98). More recently, the National Strategy for Neighbourhood Renewal (1998–2009) (Amion Consulting Ltd, 2010) aimed to reduce the gaps between all more deprived neighbourhoods in England and the national average across a wide range of indicators though multifaceted regeneration projects, the New Deal for Communities which did the same in 39 particularly deprived neighbourhoods (1998–2009) (Batty et al, 2010), and Housing

Market Renewal pathfinders, which aimed to restructure local housing markets and increase demand and social mix in nine areas exhibiting housing market weaknesses, such as high vacancy rates, low sales values and neighbourhood abandonment (Cole and Flint, 2007; Allen, 2008). Individual local authorities, social landlords and other partners have developed their own projects, a handful of which came together under the banner of the Mixed Communities Initiative: Demonstration Project (2006 and ongoing) (Lupton et al, 2009). There have also been distinctive programmes in Scotland and Wales.

Policy outcomes

A few government and other programmes have explicitly aimed to create new mixed tenure and mixed income communities, for example through so-called urban villages and millennium villages (Silverman et al, 2005). However, in terms of numbers of homes and new mixed communities produced, mainstream planning policy and development control applied to the market has been more significant. Land costs and not in my backyard (NIMBY) political pressures may tend to steer new social housing development away from areas with more advantaged populations. However, countervailing processes mean that social housing can be, and increasingly has been, built 'in the back yard'. Social and affordable housing has increasingly been funded through conditions placed on planning permissions (termed 'Section 106' agreements in England, and 'Section 75' agreements in Scotland) (Burgess et al, 2008; Fenton, 2010). Planners increasingly require those developing private housing on all but the smallest sites either to provide some homes for low-cost home ownership or social renting, or to make a contribution to off-site development. This form of affordable housing subsidy has had the effect of creating mixed tenure schemes, and also acts to direct affordable housing into regions and local authorities where there is the most private housing development taking place, which tend to have above-average incomes, employment rates and home ownership. Countercyclical policy measures in the two most recent downturns also contributed to the acquisition of social housing 'in the back yard', with the government providing funds for social landlords in England to buy up unsold new homes intended for the private market. The net effect of these policies is the opposite of gentrification: to increase the number of new residential areas with some tenure and income mix within them, and also to increase the proportion of new social homes and tenants in less deprived areas with less deprived neighbours.

For both these overt mixed communities policies, implementation has varied widely between sites and local authorities. However, it has tended to result in less change to tenure or population mix than might have been expected. For example, one of the aims of the Estate Action programme was to diversify tenure by encouraging sales, demolition and building of homes for sale, but many schemes involved few of these processes (Pinto, 1993). The amount of social housing produced from Section 106 policies, the amount produced on site and the degree of mix resulting also varied (Burgess et al, 2008). For example, schemes described as 'mixed tenure' include those with 95% private housing and 5% low-cost home ownership, in a new development at Clarence Dock, Leeds, or 45% private housing and 55% social renting, through neighbourhood regeneration, at Hulme, Manchester (Silverman et al, 2005). Resulting income mixes range from cases where half of households earned under £15,000 (in 2005), as at Hulme, and cases where a fifth earned under £15,000 and a fifth earned over £50,000, as at Greenwich Millennium Village (Silverman et al, 2005). Variation between sites may reflect local political choice, officer effectiveness, resident opinion or the nature of sites and buildings. In practice the greatest influence over actual mixes achieved has been the state of the local housing market, and the need in some cases to maintain provision of social housing for existing residents.

Does the 'Right to Buy', Britain's best known housing policy of the past three decades, count in any way as a mixed communities policy – or perhaps as an anti-mix policy? Introduced in 1980, the Right to Buy allowed existing council tenants to purchase their home at a discount, and has resulted in the transfer of over two million homes to home ownership. Three adjustments to the Right to Buy policy have had the effects of steering purchases into less popular areas: greater discounts for flats from the 1980s, limits on sales in the most popular small rural communities from the 1990s, and in the 2000s, caps on discounts which made purchase less attractive in high-priced areas. However, a substantial body of research has recorded how the rate and pattern of take-up of the Right to Buy has been closely linked to the temporal and spatial patterns of the national housing market (Jones and Murie, 2006). At neighbourhood level, take-up of the Right to Buy has reflected rather than transformed the relative popularity of different areas and relative advantage of their residents. It has created new mixed tenure areas within council-built estates, but has not necessarily increased the number of areas mixed in terms of income. Over time, ex-tenant purchasers have moved on and homes have been allocated through the market, gradually enabling demographic or income change. However, the combination of reduced remaining social housing stock and the disadvantage of those entering it has resulted in a long process of socio-tenurial polarisation, which has, in effect, decreased the social mix in those estates with low Right to Buy sales (Tunstall and Coulter, 2006).

Another set of 'gentry-luring' policies has encouraged wealthier people, people in employment, or potential or actual homeowners to move into and to stay in deprived or social housing areas. The UK has a substantial history of low-cost home ownership programmes. There has been considerable variation in the degree and rationales for spatial targeting of these policies. Some low-cost home ownership has been in lower value areas by default, and some has been linked via Section 106 agreements to market developments in high value areas. However, as with the Right to Buy, buyers of low-cost homes built for sale in or next to deprived council estates may be very similar in income and other characteristics to existing residents (Nevin, 2010).

Some other less well-known aspects of housing policy may have affected local population and income mix without necessarily changing tenure mix. Some social landlords have allocated homes to promote neighbourhood mix over individual need, termed 'balanced housing allocations'. These policies have been superseded by the emphasis on providing some choice for households searching for social rented c homes, through 'choice-based lettings' (Brown et al, 2005). Allowances to renters on low incomes have been another stealth mixed communities policy. Since 1982, Housing Benefit has enabled households on low incomes to live in the private rented sector, in the area of their choice, covering up to 100% of their rent (as well as subsidising social renting tenants on low incomes). From 2008, however, it was capped at the median rent for the relevant local area, so keeping these poorer households out of the higher-priced homes and neighbourhoods. The Coalition government elected in 2010 intends further restrictions that are likely to reduce further neighbourhood choice and the social mixing effect.

In addition, ongoing cross-party support for increased home ownership and reluctance to address neighbourhoods of concentrated home ownership or advantage have contributed important anti-mix policy. The rise of the private rented sector from the 1990s, linked to rising values and the role of housing as an investment, has constituted an area of non-policy, with private renting contributing to tenure mix but with very varied and fluid effects on neighbourhood social mix. Meanwhile, despite substantial policy effort from 1997 onwards, income inequality remains high (Hills et al, 2010).

Have British communities become more or less mixed over this period of energetic policy interest and activity? While there is an increasing group of studies describing long-term trends in neighbourhood mix across Britain, there is no agreed measure of 'mixedness'. In 2005 there was a clash between the incoming chief executive of the Equality and Human Rights Commission, who argued that Britain was 'sleepwalking to segregation', and researchers who argued that ethnic segregation decreased in the 1990s (Finney and Simpson, 2009). This provided a high-profile illustration of the how sensitive assessments are to the measures used.

Dorling and colleagues (2007) calculated an index of dissimilarity for very large neighbourhoods (with an average 45,000 residents) for measures of household poverty and wealth during 1970–2000. They found that in terms of the distribution of 'core poor' households (who made up between 10% and 15% of the British population), communities became less mixed during 1970–80, and then very slightly more mixed during 1980–2000. In terms of tenure mix, the proportion of all people and of social housing residents living in electoral wards dominated by social housing fell sharply during 1971–2001. This was mainly due to the decline in the total amount of social housing, and was accompanied by increases in the number of areas dominated by home ownership. However, owner-occupation rose faster during 1991–2001 in the 3% poorest small neighbourhoods (with an average of 5,500 residents), and faster still in those dominated by social housing (Berube, 2005) and in unpopular council-built estates (Tunstall and Coulter, 2006). Communities with high proportions of these 'core poor' households were those most likely to be the target of neighbourhood redevelopment-type mixed communities policies, so these data are consistent with some policy impact during 1980–2000.

However, in his review of national, regional and urban policy in the 1980s, Robson (1994) found that gaps between neighbourhoods in individual cities on indicators including unemployment rates and people in the key 25-34 age group increased. In a review of studies, Kintrea (2007) found that the number of 'poor' council-built neighbourhoods, one type of unmixed community, did not change over the 1990s. Using a consistent measure over time, Robson and colleagues found that while overall deprivation decreased during 1971–2001, the distribution of deprivation between small neighbourhoods became more unequal (Amion Consulting Ltd, 2010). In addition, returning to Dorling et al's (2007) study, in terms of the distribution of those in the less extreme 'breadline' measure of poverty, their large neighbourhoods became steadily less mixed in each of the decades 1970–2000, and in terms of the distribution of wealthy households, these large neighbourhoods also became less mixed during 1980-2000.

After 1997, neighbourhood renewal policy concentrated on reducing the 'gaps' Robson had described. Looking at trends during 2001–07, he and colleagues found reductions in the absolute and proportionate gaps in employment rates and other indicators, including education levels and health status, between deprived neighbourhoods targeted by the National Strategy for Neighbourhood Renewal and other neighbourhoods (Amion Consulting Ltd, 2010). However, closing 'gaps' does not necessarily mean more even distribution of people in different situations between neighbourhoods. For example, if mixedness is measured in terms of the evenness of the distribution of unemployed people between neighbourhoods (via Gini coefficients for postcode sectors), communities were actually less mixed in 2001 than in 1991, even though both absolute and relative 'gaps' in unemployment were lower (Tunstall with Fenton, 2009). There is thus no *clear* evidence for a general 'gentrification' of poor neighbourhoods.

Conclusion: gentrification by stealth?

What role did mixed communities policy play in these trends and in individual sites, and are there grounds for labelling any as 'gentrification by stealth'? As discussed, many neighbourhood renewal projects did not result in significant change in tenure, income or other measures of mix. This was reflected to some extent in the greater willingness to use demolition in the late 1990s Housing Market Renewal programme (Cole and Flint, 2007), and the government's ambition for its Mixed Communities Initiative: Demonstration Projects to go *'further, faster'* than previous schemes (Lupton et al, 2009). Some staff working in these neighbourhoods were concerned about the potential for *'gentrification'*, or *'social engineering'* (Lupton et al, 2009), and a sizeable minority of residents thought that having more high-income neighbours would not improve the area, and were opposed to building homes for sale (Lupton et al, 2010). However, it has been argued that 'gentrification' is a misnomer for the generally marginal population mix changes seen in the most deprived areas (Nevin, 2010; although see Allen, 2008), and mixed communities policy may have had a limited role in the changes that did occur. Of the small minority of high unemployment communities which at least began to move in the general direction of gentrified population over the 1980s and 1990s (retaining high unemployment rates), only a handful appeared to have experienced mixed communities policies, mostly social housing estate redevelopment, while others had seen an increase in employed residents through market processes or 'studentification' (Tunstall with Fenton, 2009). The evaluation of the National Strategy for Neighbourhood Renewal found the levels of renewal expenditure to be associated with the extent of change, but that many other factors such as neighbourhood tenure mix and the nature of the regional economy were at least as important (Amion Consulting Ltd, 2010). But what would have occurred in the absence of mixed communities policies? Kintrea (200) argued that national, local and neighbourhood housing and environment policies for council-built neighbourhoods during 1975-2000 were likely at least to have prevented problems in these areas getting worse, and to have slowed spatial polarisation. Cheshire (2007) argued that market mechanisms make some degree of unmixedness inevitable, but we do not know what degree of mix or number of mixed communities that might exist with untrammelled markets reaching equilibrium. Market trends may influence the effectiveness of mixed communities policies. Robson (1994) commented that it was harder to close gaps between neighbourhoods during recessions, while evaluations of urban policy in the 2000s commented on the favourable economic context in that period (Amion Consulting Ltd, 2010; Batty et al, 2010). However, just as income inequality can fall – somewhat counter-intuitively – in recessions, if community mix is measured in terms of the evenness of the distribution of unemployed people between neighbourhoods, between 1985 and 2009 communities were most mixed in times of recession and high unemployment in the late 1980s and 2000s, and least mixed in times of growth and low unemployment (Tunstall with Fenton, 2009). In their assessment of the Housing Market Renewal programme, Cole and Flint (2007, p 7) concluded, 'the underlying message is that it is very difficult to direct, channel or contain market processes'. Finally, the government elected in 2010 appears less inclined than its predecessors to try.

FIVE

Gentrification without social mixing in the rapidly urbanising world of Australasia

Wendy Shaw

Introduction

For the first time in recorded history the world has a higher urban than rural population, and much of this shift has occurred in Australasia. According to the United Nations (UN) Department of Economic and Social Affairs, Population Division, Population Estimates and Projections Section (2010), Asia has the largest number of megacities in the world (in 2010) and will have another five by 2025. In this context, urban change has included a rapid rise of urban skylines, with the march of residential towers in places where older, poorer housing once stood. The notion of 'social mixing' as a policy construct is therefore far removed from urban (re)building which is largely driven by global economic forces – of private investment – and external to government structures. The exceptions, which include Australia and Singapore, have engaged with aspects of social mixing policy, but these have largely applied only to government-provided, social or public housing contexts. This chapter considers urban change in the Australasian region, and some of the gentrification contexts that, rather than driven by government or policy initiatives, have proceeded viscerally. In this context, notions of 'social mixing' are largely absent, and where policies have been attempted, they have targeted social/public housing.

A region in flux

As Japan 'opened up' to the world after the Second World War, Tokyo emerged as a global city. Large-scale urban renewal has also accompanied the rise of Singapore, Hong Kong and Sydney (Australia) as international financial hubs. The newly industrialised economies of Malaysia, Taiwan and the Republic of Korea (South Korea) have also experienced dramatic redevelopment since decolonisation. Most recently, China's engagement with globalisation has resulted in another experience of rebuilding, and significant changes to the urban fabric of many larger Chinese cities. The region's entrée into the global economy meant that the processes of urban residential redevelopment have largely moved beyond the realms of conventional notions of gentrification, of the rejuvenation of older inner cities by middle classes.

The few examples of restoration-based gentrification are based on preservation initiatives. In Kyoto, Japan, for instance, urban areas have gained recognition because of their 'heritage' appeal, and therefore escaped demolition. Tokyo too has experienced the 'movement of young professionals to traditional housing in the *shitmachi*, or inner city and relatively poor areas' (Fujitsuka, 2005, p 137). Another example of heritage restoration exists in Thailand, on the island of Phuket. Phuket is a popular tourist destination, particularly for foreigners. Private investors are now restoring parts of Old Phuket to its former Chinatown identity. An 'upmarket' Thai restaurant chain has cemented the process through acquisition and the proposed redevelopment of a derelict late 19th-century Sino-colonial mansion at the centre of town (Janssen, 2009). However, as Fujitsuka (2005) has observed for Kyoto, preservation movements are important for maintaining heritage buildings – which can be good for business – but they do not prevent gentrification and the associated displacement of poorer residents. This has certainly been the case in the 'Austral' cities of Australasia, in Australia (Shaw, 2005), and New Zealand (Latham, 2003; Murphy, 2008). However, the overall regional experience of gentrification is one of demolished 'old towns' and the rise of residential and commercial towers, or the conversion of industrial landscapes into apartments/condominiums.

If we accept the premise that 'gentrification' in the Australasian region must include wholesale redevelopment, which includes the construction or conversion of buildings to apartments/condominiums (Shaw, 2000; Fujitsuka, 2005), then an analysis of the policy context for the concept of 'social mixing' is predicated on the historical geographies of the region. If the legacies of European colonisation have paved the way for flexible forms of advanced capitalism, one manifestation is the (re)building of cities to accommodate shifting financial geographies. Investment in 'real estate' can be precarious, as demonstrated in Jakarta, Indonesia, where the remnants of the economic crisis of the late 1990s left uncompleted high-rise buildings, which sat useless and decaying atop former poorer but functional communities. This reflected some of the worst impacts of a sudden shift in economic fortunes (Goldblum and Wong, 2000). Of course, the global financial crisis of 2008/09 has had repercussions (Grenville, 2010), with approximately 10% of permanent industrial sector jobs being lost during 2009, and around 40% of contractual jobs (IDS UK, 2009). Until recently, the urban poor in Jakarta lived in now demolished or threatened single-storey *kampung* houses. According to Goldblum and Wong (2000), the welfare-oriented *kampung* restructuring policy of the 1960s and 1970s, which assisted displaced residents to move nearby when their homes were demolished, and thereby maintain their social networks and proximity to employment, has failed. Goldblum and Wong (2000, p 30) maintain that the *kampung* restructuring policy 'virtually stopped to function under the impact of ... globalisation and international capital' during the 1980s. With *kampung* eradication at the urban core, food-growing agricultural lands, on the fringes of Jakarta, face increasing numbers of settlers and the ongoing threat of urban sprawl. Home to increasing legions of dispossessed rural workers, Jakarta's newly unemployed industrial workers now occupy a swelling pool of workers all competing for the dwindling city jobs while living at the margins of a bustling metropolis.

A close neighbour, and intricately immersed in Jakarta's redevelopment through investment,[1] Singapore has had a very different style of residential redevelopment experience, with much stricter planning controls. Its powerful positioning on the global economic stage has led to the wholesale demolition of inner-city 'slums', and the redevelopment of the globally connected 'downtown'. However, unique to Singapore, a massive public housing initiative accompanied slum removal. The inner-urban landscape of skyscrapers, with some low-rise restoration in the entertainment district along the foreshore, sits in stark contrast to the public housing 'heartland', a landscape of largely uniform low-rise apartment buildings, which house approximately 80% of Singapore's population (Wong, 2006). According to Wong (2006, p 181), gentrification of Singapore's inner city has followed the 'West' through redevelopment of the waterfront. However, during the 1960s, a 'highly concentrated commercial sector' displaced low-income residents, rather than a group of gentrifiers. Moreover,

> Central Area residents were ... relocated to the self-sustained new towns in the outlying areas. The Urban Renewal Unit of the Housing and Development Board built public housing estates within an eight-kilometre radius from the city centre. Some 54,450 units of public housing were constructed during the period 1960-65. (Wong, 2006, pp 186-7)

Within this highly structured redevelopment context, the Singaporean government has engaged in a form of social mixing through its Ethnic Integration Policy (EIP). The EIP aims to 'promote racial integration and harmony ... [and] prevent the formation of racial enclaves by ensuring a balanced ethnic mix among the various ethnic communities living in public housing estates' (Singapore Government Housing and Development Board, 2010). It appears that while one form of social mixing is encouraged in the public housing estates, the elite that have moved to the now luxurious inner city engage in a different kind of social mixing – a version that accompanies the globalised lifestyles of the cosmopolite.

In quite a different redevelopment scenario, South Korea engaged more directly with private investment to rebuild Seoul. The Joint Redevelopment Programme (JRP), which 'depended on real estate developers' participation in partnership with dwelling-owners', began transforming the city in 1984, with the construction of 'high-rise commercial housing estates' (Shin, 2009, p 906).

> JRP was effectively a market-oriented property development in line with a national housing strategy that favoured increased housing production and home-ownership ... relying on the initiatives of developers and dwelling-owners with less direct intervention by the public sector, the state resorted to market-oriented measures to resolve the problems of dilapidated neighbourhoods. (Shin, 2009, p 916)

The result of this kind of private investment was massive displacement, estimated at nearly 80% of original residents (Shin, 2009). The notion of 'social mixing' in this context was obviously far from the agenda.

Gentrification in the People's Republic of China is a very recent phenomenon, and linked to its sudden emergence as an economic powerhouse, and the subsequent neoliberalisation of urban development (He and Wu, 2009; Wu, 2009). China's *dragon head* city is Shanghai, which 'never pauses in its struggle to rebuild itself as a global city' (He, 2007, p 174). This too has meant the wholesale demolition of old parts of the city for reconstruction. In keeping with the region, this inner-city redevelopment has catered to higher-income earners. A new middle class began to move into previously low-income areas in the early 1990s. Real estate in Shanghai is (again) big business. It has the backing of a powerful state, which aims to 'realize place promotion and local boosterism' (He, 2007, p 177). With the demolition of old housing areas, such as through the 365 scheme, 'to redevelop 365 hectares of low-income neighbourhoods', poorer residents have experienced what is now a familiar trend in the region: displacement to the urban fringes (He, 2007, p 177). Recent interest in 'heritage' – a useful currency for tourism purposes – has also paved the way for more conventional forms of gentrification. In the case of the restoration of Xintiandi,

> The old-fashioned Shanghai-style houses are no longer homes for low-income residents but places exclusively for local elites, expatriates, and tourists ... indigenous low-income residents were ... relocated to suburban areas in the Pudong New Area ... with the help of the local state ... residents have been offered resettlement housing. (He, 2007, p 181)

Although the Chinese government has imposed measures to ensure the inclusion of smaller dwellings, for lower-income affordability within its urban redevelopment planning (He and Wu, 2009; Wu, 2010), escalation in property prices confound this attempt at social mixing. So it seems that the impacts of gentrification (through restoration or redevelopment) includes displacement of poorer people. Be they re-housed at the margins of a city, or not at all, displacement seems to be a common result of the commodification of housing – its conversion to 'real estate'.

Turning to the 'outposts', or the former European colonies now described as 'settler societies', a much more familiar picture of gentrification emerges. Duke (2009, p 103) observed that social mixing policies have targeted public/social housing compositions in the US, Europe, Australia and New Zealand. Such policies sometimes include the relocation of tenants to more affluent neighbourhoods. In some cases, new housing developments must include a proportion of affordable housing for the purpose of public/social housing leases. The other form of social mixing includes attracting different groups to live in close proximity, which, as Davidson (2008, p 2385) suggests, 'smells like gentrification'. In Australia, both forms of social mixing have been attempted. However, as one resident of a newly gentrifying suburb in Sydney noted:

> People have no issue with gentrification or rejuvenation.... The problem is when ... they [the existing residents] can't be part of that community any more. (quoted in Tovey, 2010)

Previously the domain of restoration, of old inner-city areas dominated by Victorian terrace or row houses, Sydney, and to various degrees most Australian cities, are now transforming through apartment development. Displacement of poorer communities, including migrant and indigenous groups, occurred through the more traditional gentrification cycles. With these changes came shifts in the composition of urban areas, with some mixing of public/social housing within gentrified neighbourhoods. However, local and state governments have subsequently sold off much of this housing including social housing stock that existed before gentrification. As elsewhere (in the UK and Canada), tenants' 'right to buy' schemes have existed (Authurson, 2010), but this kind of social mixing has proved to be unpalatable to the new gentrifiers fearing for their amenity, capital gains and safety. The result is that, as a journalist, Lisa Pryor (2007), noticed on a trip to the outer suburbs of Sydney, community diversity exists outside the inner city, where:

> ... the preponderance of cafes ... sign[s] in English.... A white ghetto. The census figures for 2006 ... reveal that some of the trendiest urban villages are ... whitebread.

This mostly middle-class 'whitening' of inner urban neighbourhoods is a far cry from social mixing. In New Zealand, gentrification has similarly moved from the restoration of 'heritage' housing stock to the redevelopment of formerly industrial areas, such as shorelines (Murphy, 2008). Similar to the Australian experience, references to 'social mixing' exist but are usually based on 'a suffused notion of new urbanism' (L. Murphy, personal communication, 27 May 2010). The notion of social mixing therefore tends to mean the development of a range of housing types, rather than groups of people. This is a familiar experience in many parts of the world.

Conclusion

While gentrification may be an 'elastic yet targeted' process of what is 'now global' (Clark, 2005), social mixing policies are not. Described as 'policies ... that are a central part of urban renaissance agendas in much of the developed world' (Lees, 2008, p 2451), social mixing is far from a desired objective in a part of the world that can be variously described as 'developed' and 'developing'. Indeed, it could be argued that the concept, although often well intended, disregards the diversity of ways of living in a variety of contexts. That is, as many have already identified, the desire for 'diversity' often resides within privileged realms of consumption, not necessarily habitation. For instance, in communities that have fought hard for their place in the city, an imposition of social mixing and gentrification policies may be threatening to those communities, such as the Aboriginal community in Redfern, Australia (Shaw, 2007). Moreover, social mixing – of class/income and ethnicity – often *starts* with gentrification, again, to the detriment of those displaced in the process. The kinds of social mixing that occur in the context of rapidly 'developing' economies of eastern Asia are more likely to occur among the elite, and in cosmopolitan, internationalised ways (with the possible exception of state-provided housing in Singapore[2]). Many of these cities have high influxes of expatriates, often 'employed by transnational corporations to open up the markets of the newly emerging economies' (Atkinson and Bridge, 2005, p 3). More social justice-oriented understandings of social mixing and associated policy formations that aim to provide a milieu of mixed classes, ethnicities and so on, are simply not part of redevelopment policies that often work hard to meet the ever-increasing demands of free market forces in an unsettled economic world. With little room to accommodate social diversity, the eradication of 'slum' housing, for instance, is more likely to accompany the repositioning of a society in an increasingly competitive economic world and, where possible, the re-housing of dispossessed residents elsewhere. Where social mixing has been attempted as policy, it has had little impact on the experience of social polarisation that accompanies urban redevelopment – that is, gentrification *en masse*, at the scale of large sections of the city. Overall, for many of the rapidly changing cities of Australasia, and I have considered only a few very briefly here, social mixing is simply not central to the redevelopment agendas where housing has become investment in cities that struggle to support swelling populations. As with gentrification elsewhere – state-driven, sanctioned or otherwise – social mixing policies benefit some but not all in the struggle to gain or maintain a presence on a globalised economic stage.

Acknowledgements

With thanks to Tai-Chee Wong, National Institute of Education, Singapore; Fulong Wu, Cardiff University, Cardiff, UK; and Lawrence Murphy, University of Auckland, New Zealand.

Notes

[1] Goldblum and Wong (2000, p 35) note that 'growth polygons' offer free trade and export-processing zones and that the impacts of these on the development of urban space in many of East Asia's large metropolises needs closer scrutiny.

[2] This chapter is not an exhaustive account of attempts at social mixing, which may have occurred in other cities in the region.

Part 2
Social mix in liberal and neoliberal times

SIX

Social mixing and the historical geography of gentrification

David Ley

Introduction: legacies

Accepting that Ruth Glass coined the term 'gentrification' in an unpublished paper in 1959 (Lees et al, 2007, p 4), the field has just passed its 50th anniversary. Inevitably the contexts of gentrification have shifted over the decades. The process has successively encountered the critical social movements of the 1960s, the high water mark of the welfare state in the 1970s, the ascendancy of neoliberalism in the 1980s, and finally, globalisation, the dominant and multifaceted keyword of the past 20 years. The demographic bulge of the baby boomers, vanguard of gentrification as students and young professionals in the 1960s, is now filled by retirees and near retirees with different housing needs and aspirations. The relatively specific submarket of the young urban professional, the essential gentrifier of the 1970s, has since broadened to also include middle-class families, empty nesters and international jet-setters. On the supply side, inner-city locations redlined by financial institutions and large development corporations in the early days of gentrification – leaving renovation to be achieved through sweat equity – are now eagerly sought for redevelopment by the largest players in an international property market. Trends that were noted primarily in major Western world cities have now diffused to some smaller towns, rural villages and the mega-cities of emerging nations. The most extravagant gentrification of the past decade has been the state-driven redevelopment of the large cities of China – in Shanghai municipal statistics identify the displacement of 750,000 households between 1995 and 2005, around 10% of the entire metropolitan population (Iossifova, 2009). So gentrification has mutated, albeit the same in the perennial narrative of residential displacement and class succession, yet profoundly not the same in the permutations around that basic process shaped by geographical and political contexts across more than a generation. We can now profitably examine the historical geography of gentrification.

In this chapter I examine how the idea of social mixing of diverse groups has intersected with gentrification, and has evolved from a progressive policy in the 1960s and 1970s to a perceived regressive policy today in some scholarly and activist circles. In examining social mixing we must also consider its other, residential segregation, a condition against which mixing was compared favourably a generation ago, but much less favourably in some – but not all – quarters today. While ranging across a number of North American and Western European sites, I will develop in more detail two cases from Vancouver, a city where I have been studying gentrification since the 1970s.

Segregation and civil rights

A transformational logic has taken hold of the idea of social mixing in gentrification when we examine its changing meaning through time. Among student radicals, artists and the young professionals of the 1960s and 1970s, social mixing was politically progressive. By the 1970s it was being institutionalised by left-liberal governments in the last hurrah of the welfare state, when funds for social programmes were relatively plentiful. The fiscal crisis of the state and a new conservative consensus put an end to all that in the neoliberal 1980s, and since. Today social mixing is often vilified as an underhand strategy of a conspiratorial state to displace the poor. What has changed? Social mixing? Or our framing of it? In the remainder of this chapter, I wish to underscore the progressive intent of inner-city social mixing in the 1960s-1970s and then project that argument against the critical present. My sub-theme is that as the field of gentrification turns 50, we can profitably learn from historical comparison. To do so we need to preserve a lively memory of intellectual legacies.

It is important – as always – to place the early decades of gentrification in historical context. The 1960s was a period of social movements resisting unjust social and political orders. In the US the civil rights movement hit its tragic climax with the assassination of Martin Luther King in April 1968, prompting a season of urban rioting. Progressive social policy aimed to break up segregation, the zones of concentrated black urban poverty and low quality public services that would later be associated with the damning epithet of the urban underclass. US housing policy adopted a scattered-site strategy of locating state housing outside the conventional area of the deprived inner city and mixing poor residents within existing middle-class areas (Ley, 1983). While there was substantial resistance to scattering large projects, there was more success in dispersing smaller subsidised rental and ownership programmes in the US Housing Acts of the 1960s – although at the end of the day, white flight often made the goal of residential integration only a temporary success. Another significant effort at social mixing and a central target of the civil rights' movement was school desegregation, including the bussing of poor inner-city children to schools and school districts with higher levels of attainment. Initial court-directed actions involved the desegregation of school districts in the American South, but by the 1970s attention had turned to northern cities, where segregation levels were often higher. Resistance and evasion (through the rise of fee-paying private schools) occurred throughout the US (Lord, 1977). But the key issue is that political activists and progressive administrations saw desegregation, the mixing of 'race' and class, as a desirable outcome.

The viewing of segregation among racial and low-income populations as fundamentally unjust has survived. The controversial underclass thesis, or the analysis of concentrated urban poverty as it was re-framed, emphasised the penalties of geographical marginalisation where vulnerable groups were separated from jobs and private and public services, perpetuating dependent and dysfunctional subcultures, and condemned to live in high crime areas abandoned by employers and institutions (Wilson, 1987). In their own influential work, Massey and Denton (1993) viewed this marginalised landscape and its consequences as evidence of a pernicious 'American apartheid', provocatively linking segregation in the US with the vicious strategy of racial domination by spatial design in South Africa, where the Group Areas Act, enforcing racial separation in urban areas, was a means to ensure control by a privileged minority (Western, 1997). Massey and Denton were thereby maintaining the explicit association between desegregation, social mixing and civil rights. The progressive torch was picked up again in Loic Wacquant's *Urban outcasts* (2007), with his powerful language describing the 'urban purgatory' (2007, p 80) of Chicago's segregated South Side, although he regarded the primary culprit to be not Wilson's economic restructuring, nor Massey and Denton's racial distancing, but rather the wilful abdication by the state of its responsibilities. Such abdication represented a failure of civil rights; trapped in the ghetto, residents do not enjoy their own right to the city.

Social mixing as progressive urban policy

With this hegemonic ideology, progressive politics has regarded residential segregation of the poor as a profound urban malady, a failure of civil rights, and this taken-for-granted belief is an ever-present backdrop to other arguments in favour of social mixing that are more immediately relevant to the sensibilities of gentrifiers. The zoning and design homogeneity of the post-1945 suburbs was the subject of critical satire by the 1960s youth movement and the gentrifiers who followed them. Wendy Sarkissian's important 1976 paper, 'The idea of social mix in town planning', offered a prescient historical and literature review. Arguments were popularised in Lewis Mumford's voluminous writing, and assumed huge currency in the 1960s with Jane Jacobs' (1961) influential thesis on the delights of her socially mixed inner-city block in Greenwich Village, the ballet of Hudson Street as she called it, in many ways the genesis story of the gentrified inner-city street. Sarkissian set out nine rationales presented in favour of social mixing; in an astute account she noted both that 'very little empirical evidence exists to support the claims of those who favour residential mix', but also that 'although the advantages of the mixed area are hard to measure, it is probably safe to say that diverse areas should be encouraged simply because they are not homogeneous' (1976, pp 243, 244).

Jane Jacobs' seminal thinking promoted diversity of building age, land use type and social and cultural groups as requisites of urbane big city environments. Fainstein (2005) has noted how the pursuit of diversity at different spatial scales in the 1960s and 1970s converged with broader postmodern impulses in urban planning and design. The simplicity and master narratives of urban modernity were challenged as too simple, too standardised, too prescriptive for more complex societies and needs. Master plans gave way to local area plans, the universal abstractions of modern architecture to the nuanced local contextualities and complexities of postmodern architecture. Homogeneous land uses, whether allocated to housing, retailing or leisure, were out of favour and mixed-use developments appeared on the blueprints and landscapes of the contemporary metropolis. Among residents, 'cities of difference' were recognised not only descriptively but also prescribed normatively, although a critical eye would also point out the unequal political and economic geographies of difference (Fincher and Jacobs, 1998). It was no accident that these intellectual developments coincided with growing public diversity of lifestyle and identity, particularly in large cities. Ethnicity and sexuality were being inscribed on urban settings in unprecedented ways. Multiculturalism, although enunciated nationally (in Canada in 1971), was articulated locally in large cities in parades, festivals and a growing acceptance, even welcome, of social and cultural difference. Multiculturalism moved the existence of difference and diversity beyond policy into legislated rights, notably in Canada's Multiculturalism Act (1988) and the Charter of Rights and Freedoms (1982), part of the revision to the Canadian Constitution.

Surveys in gentrifying neighbourhoods in Canadian cities in the late 1970s and 1980s revealed that social mixing and cultural diversity were often regarded as particular advantages of inner-city living (Ley, 1996, pp 38-41). But it was primarily in districts in the earlier stages of gentrification where attitudes most favourable to diversity occurred, and co-existed with the perceived advantage of affordability. In contrast, in several neighbourhoods where gentrification was advanced, property investment potential was mentioned and there was more of an economic than a social appreciation of the district. When prices rose high enough in gentrified areas owners were tempted to protect their equity and some became more cautious about price-threatening diversity. In some instances, for example in Toronto's Cabbagetown, opposing middle-class neighbourhood groups lobbied for and against new social housing.

Pro-diversity attitudes were repeated in local and civic politics. The neighbourhood movement of the 1970s saw a widespread articulation of preservationist attitudes for older districts (Brown-Saracino, 2009). Reviewing this movement in gentrifying districts in six Canadian cities, I identified the typical agenda of 1970s neighbourhood activism: 'down-zonings, the pursuit of social mix, protection and rehabilitation of existing housing, the safeguarding of affordable shelter, enhancement of local amenity and public services, in short a panoply of policies directed to the preservation of the physical and social character of neighbourhoods' (Ley, 1996, pp 241-2). Neighbourhood organisations in these districts not only pressed for affordable housing to preserve social mix, but in some gentrifying districts, including Vancouver's Kitsilano and Ottawa's Centretown, they formed non-profit agencies to build the units with government funding. One of the most impressive examples was in Centretown, where gentrification was accelerating in the 1970s. Its 1976 local plan advocated the preservation of inexpensive dwellings and a decade later its neighbourhood association had constructed 450 units of affordable housing. The adjacent gentrifying district of Sandy Hill evoked the same sentiment in favour of social mix through an endorsement of housing cooperatives: 'The residents of Sandy Hill wish to express their support for non-profit cooperatives in the community as a humane and economically viable alternative

which also provides support to single persons, couples and small families'
(City of Ottawa, 1975).

Segregation and social mixing in neoliberal times

Like so much else in the city, neoliberal policy has brought new
standards for assessing old themes, in this case segregation and mixing.
Under neoliberal governance, social policies may continue to be
promoted but for entirely new reasons. Decentralisation of government
services to local areas and non-governmental organisations (NGOs), for
example, was regarded in the 1970s as a means of enhancing substantive
citizenship by taking service delivery closer to its clients, but by the
1990s it was promoted, if the services survived at all, as a cost-saving
mechanism that would also incorporate potentially adversarial groups
under the discipline of state funding and accountability (Hasson and Ley,
1994). So, too, desegregation and social mix continue to be advanced,
but now from different motives.

The persistence of inner-city poverty and related social problems
became a growing irritant to neoliberal politicians. Margaret Thatcher's
exasperation with '*those* inner cities' (emphasis added) following the
1987 British election (Robson, 1988) was accompanied by wholesale
regeneration programmes in which the well-being of existing residents
was rarely the primary emphasis. London's Docklands was a prototype,
with 1970s plans that had envisaged a commitment to significant state
housing subsidies while re-orienting but not eliminating an industrial
past, replaced in the 1980s by a market-driven post-industrial scenario
of largely private sector housing for white-collar workers in the City
and its new satellite of Canary Wharf (Hamnett, 2003). A principal
casualty in this regeneration process was the downgrading of the role
of subsidised, affordable housing in redevelopment, giving rise to a
landscape of new-build gentrification that has been extended up and
down the Thames waterfront (Davidson, 2008). With no sense of irony,
government policy, wary of segregated poverty in East London, has
sired in Docklands a landscape of segregated affluence instead.

Dikeç (2007) detected a transition that also occurred toward spatially
concentrated poverty in French urban policy. In the name of enhancing
social inclusion in the republic, earlier public policy had for years sought
to address the social and economic problems of the suburban *banlieues*
(suburbs), but from 1993 onwards, the *banlieues* themselves were seen as
the problem, as 'badlands' that were 'potential "threats" to the republic
and its values' (2007, p 95). In some quarters concentrated poverty and
periodic social disorder became interpreted as threatening to national

aspirations, with the *banlieues* bound together in an imagined Islamic communitarianism that 'menaces the integrity of "the republic"' (2007, p 172). The policy response now became more disciplinary and penal in areas of concentrated poverty, in France and also the US (Wacquant, 2007). Genial multicultural cities of difference became redefined as communities of hostile difference.

The spectre of threatening concentrated poverty is an old urban idiom, hearkening back to middle-class fears of the lower-class 'masses' in 19th-century industrial cities (Ward, 1976). In the growing multicultural gateway cities of North America and Western Europe, concentrated poverty is increasingly associated not only with native-born poverty but also with the 'superdiversity' of ethnic and immigrant minorities (Vertovec, 2006; Smith and Ley, 2008). Following ethnic riots and terrorist acts, notably in the last decade, the spectre of hostile difference, seemingly thriving in the ideological hot house of segregated neighbourhoods, has led to something of a moral panic among populist media and policy makers in European cities especially (Ley, 2010). In Britain, Trevor Phillips, then Head of the Commission for Racial Equality, warned in 2005 that the nation was 'sleepwalking toward segregation' in a celebrated response to an official report on the 2001 riots in several towns of northern England. The report drew on the language of 'parallel lives' current elsewhere in Western Europe to highlight the dangers of segregation between marginalised immigrants and the entitled native-born. Even in Canada, with its strong multiculturalism, populist columnists have drawn unfavourable attention to the creation of immigrant enclaves in the gateway cities of Toronto and Vancouver. 'How we became a land of ghettos', raged veteran journalist, Robert Fulford (2006), repeating a lament from respected pollster and political commentator, Allan Gregg (2006), that 'ethnic groups are self-segregating', a tendency he linked to violent events in London, Paris and Sydney.

Such visceral and less than rational fears of segregation among working-class and immigrant poor has motivated a renewed urge for socio-spatial mixing. The normally understated Swedish government established a policy 'to break up segregation' in housing estates populated by immigrants and other poor Swedes (Andersson, 2006). In the US, the vast HOPE VI programme, with its objective of massive redevelopment of public housing sites, is aiming for more mixed-income residents. Chicago, with the nation's most deficient public housing, has the most active rebuilding programme, and anticipated that rebuilt sites would comprise only one third public housing units (Hyra, 2010). Other displaced households would receive vouchers to subsidise their movement into the private rental market. But relocation planning has been deficient and received minimal funding, while the low-end rental market has been unable to accommodate the bulge of voucher holders. While there has certainly been a reduction in the scale of concentrated poverty in Chicago (McDonald, 2004), there are indications that new clusters of segregated and disadvantaged neighbourhoods are being established more distant from downtown and its job opportunities. Critics note the erosion of affordable public housing units and are sceptical that there will be any net benefits for displacees. Public housing in Australia (Arthurson, 2002), the UK (Davidson, 2008), the Netherlands and elsewhere has faced similar redeployment to mixing strategies.

Canada has not been immune to these renewed tendencies to social and income mixing. Some of the oldest public housing projects in the country, Regent Park in Toronto and Little Mountain in Vancouver, are in the process of transformation as almost 60-year-old structures are demolished and replaced by an equivalent number of subsidised units larded with middle-income condominium owners in central locations attractive to gentrifiers. Both projects have been controversial (August, 2008; Thomson, 2010). The argument of the federal Canada Mortgage and Housing Corporation is that privatisation of such sites permits the replacement of obsolete housing with new and improved units for former tenants, with the cost and risk absorbed by the profits from private sales. These arguments are persuasive enough that some members of politically progressive groups in both cities are on side, partly because of an upgrading in quality and no loss of numbers in public units. For while HOPE VI has abandoned one for one replacement of public housing units in the US, its Canadian equivalent is committed to full replacement following the redevelopment of public housing sites.

In support of good segregation

Like the strategies of the 1960s, social mixing today is regarded by supporters as creating more healthy urban environments for residents of varied income groups. For poorer groups the argument is one of enrichment, of improved housing, better peer models to motivate school, family and employment aspirations, and a more secure environment for daily life. In the US, desegregation has been a founding myth of progressive politics, just as correcting socio-spatial exclusion has been a prevalent feature of social democracy in Western Europe. These substantial legacies warrant careful examination (Rose, 2004). To what extent does social inclusion indeed require breaking up segregation?

There is considerable evidence that social mixing has achieved less than its desired outcomes in the short term. A prevalent criticism is that social interaction between diverse neighbourhood residents does not occur, limiting the opportunities for the sharing of beneficial attitudinal and practical information (Davidson, 2010; van Kempen, 2010). What is less certain is whether medium or long-term neighbourhood effects could be more positive. Van Kempen (2010) noted that his European multi-city study examining social mix effects from the rebuilding of public housing undertook two to five years after redevelopment, which might be too short an interval for mixing to have led to positive effects, for example in educational outcomes. But Fainstein (2005) has offered a more substantial criticism. The emphasis on social mixing alone offers an incomplete policy agenda. If poverty and social exclusion are related to unemployment – as they invariably are – then job creation or job training programmes are likely to be more important than social mixing. Even the dispersal programme associated with HOPE VI, which places public housing residents in somewhat better districts, does not address core needs if it does not aid employment opportunities. While such dispersal that takes residents further from downtown might lead to improved educational outcomes for children, it could also penalise the journey to work for their parents.

A detailed review of the effects of HOPE VI and other relocation programmes shows that gains from social mixing are typically slight or absent, and heavily contingent on local conditions (Thomson, 2010). Indeed there are cases where *losses* in social capital accompanied the temporary or permanent dispersal of residents following redevelopment of their public housing units. In these instances well-designed and well-managed projects had generated considerable mutual support among residents that was inevitably eroded with relocation. Such conditions fall within the rubric of what Ceri Peach (1996) called 'good segregation', the segregation accompanied by deep social networks associated with the presence of extended family members, intense neighbouring, hometown associations and active religious institutions. Mutual aid generated by local social capital provides significant resources to residents, reaching beyond casual help to the informal provision of services such as childcare and to housing and employment opportunities. The beneficial effects of such 'urban villages' represented a major plank in the 1960s resistance to urban renewal in the influential work of Jane Jacobs (1961) and Herbert Gans (1962). The tight bonding of society and space, place and identity, the private and the public, created a communitarian sense of place that was worth preserving. In the West End in Boston's inner city, the site of Gans' research with Italian–Americans, 'slum clearance' and the dispersal of a cohesive community not only disrupted place-based social capital but also undercut a deep sense of belonging. In a related study, Fried (1963) documented measurable physical and mental health stresses that occurred among residents following forced evacuation and dispersal from the West End. The former residents were, he determined, grieving for a lost home.

Current policy initiatives seem to have forgotten these seminal lessons from the urban renewal era. Urban villages were typically thought of as ethnically defined, and may continue to be so, although as we saw earlier, such segregated ethnic communities are once again being uncritically challenged (Murdie and Ghosh, 2010). But urban villages need not be restricted to ethnic dimensions. Communitarian cases of good segregation may also be class-based, an argument that has been made concerning the urban clearances associated both with state-driven redevelopment in Chinese inner cities (Iossifova, 2009) and also some of the HOPE VI displacements in the US (Greenbaum et al, 2008; Manzo, 2008). Similar claims have been made in the context of public housing redevelopment in urban Canada (Thomson, 2010), and as we shall see shortly, are repeated by advocacy groups in poor neighbourhoods experiencing state-sanctioned gentrification. The assumption that segregation among the poor necessarily needs to be remedied is not defensible. Like the rich, the poor may benefit from the accrual and dispersal of bonding social capital accumulated in segregated districts.

For social mix: False Creek

In the remainder of this chapter I refer to two cases in inner Vancouver where social mix has been an explicit objective of the state. In the 1970s (South) False Creek, a city-owned brownfield site, was the site of an innovative approach to urban policy following the abandonment of urban renewal. The new-build project included a thorough and largely successful commitment to mixing land uses and social groups. In the current period social mix is again a conscious state policy in the desperately poor inner-city district of Downtown Eastside. But in this context activists are vigorously resisting diversity that they see as providing a pretext for gentrification.

The 1970s in Canada represented the pinnacle of the welfare state before growing public deficits and a neo-conservative majority redefined the relations between public and private interests. Left-liberal representatives of an urban reform movement were elected to city councils in Vancouver and Toronto and matched the experimental liberalism of the federal Trudeau government. This was an unprecedented period of innovative and well-funded initiatives for new social housing and grants for housing renovation. Around 25% of new housing units in the City of Vancouver in the 1970s were non-market units, but by the 1990s the share had fallen beneath 10%. Housing cooperatives, one of the new housing programmes of the 1970s, deliberately included a range of family incomes within each development to enhance economic viability and to avoid the social problems of concentrated poverty (Ley, 1993). However, by the mid-1980s, the cost of the co-op programme led government away from mixing and back to targeting families with the deepest housing need, and in 1992 the co-op programme was cancelled (August, 2008).

Deindustrialisation and the appearance of brownfield sites gave reform city administrations in the 1970s opportunity to show their mettle. Large projects, sharing considerable ideological convergence, began on the inner-city brownfield sites of St Lawrence in Toronto and False Creek in Vancouver. Both projects reveal the deep-seated public commitment to social and cultural mixing. The City of Vancouver's innovative (South) False Creek project (on the edge of downtown) was a testimony to a liberal decade with its emphasis on environmentalism, progressive social planning and design aesthetics (Ley, 1987). The commitment to mixing was fastidious, as the 1,750-unit development was planned by the city to be one third low income, one third middle income and one third high income. Its social and lifestyle diversity was intentional: a design document read, 'Communities which offer little social and physical diversity are unhealthy. People living in them have limited access to the wide range of values, habits and beliefs which are the essential ingredients of urban living ... health in any form is invariably connected to diversity' (Rodger, 1976, p 8). The underlying objective seemed to be the promotion of a democratic cosmopolitanism. False Creek was certainly a virtual Noah's Ark in its inclusiveness. Its housing featured market and subsidised rentals, market and subsidised condominiums and cooperatives for all ages and family types; co-op sponsors included service clubs, an ethnic association, a physically handicapped society and a floating homes society.

In the early heady years of official multiculturalism, False Creek planning documents sought design solutions to differentiate and sustain plural identities, 'to support rather than destroy the vast mosaic of subcultures' (False Creek Study Group, 1972). So important was the pursuit of social mix in False Creek that it was the dominant theme in the official public evaluation (Vischer Skaburskis, Planners, 1980). False Creek was built as a series of juxtaposed enclaves, with each enclave more or less homogeneous, but varying socially from those adjacent to it. Although the project was still quite new, there was a considerable level of neighbouring, with 35-40% of respondents stating they knew at least six residents *outside* their own enclave, and therefore across social divisions, while almost everyone (over 95% of respondents) found neighbours to be compatible (Vischer Skaburskis, Planners, 1980, pp 111-13). While there were imperfections and the planners' lofty objective of democratic cosmopolitanism was rarely voiced, for most residents features of the project other than its social mixing were uppermost in their assessment, which the evaluation team took to be a mark of success.

Importantly, the City of Vancouver owned the land on the south side of False Creek and was able to make the calls on social planning. It is worth comparing this older development with the current Olympic Village nearby (part of which housed athletes during the 2010 Winter Games), on the final brownfield site remaining along False Creek. Also on city-owned land, Olympic Village makes the transition to the present debate on social mixing. It underwent lengthy planning and was intended to be an innovative example of sustainable development in its commitment to the highest environmental standards and also to social mixing. Late in the planning process a right-wing city council demoted the social sustainability criterion from the plan, reducing the social housing component to 250 units out of a total of 1,100 Olympic units and some 6,000 overall, and sold the land to a private developer. Cost overruns on this high-priced site, and financing problems with the withdrawal of the New York lending company in 2009, created a policy nightmare for even this modest allocation of social housing in a high-priced development. The city had to re-assume financing, but including the value of the land it donated, the cost for each social housing unit was estimated at $595,000. To cover the mortgage on that loan the city would have to rent out units for $3,200 a month – a preposterous figure for social housing. But the alternative was a severe fiscal shock for city coffers (Cernetig, 2009). The solution has been to reserve the subsidised units for essential city workers, including fire fighters and the police, thereby moderating the depth of subsidies, but also excluding those with core housing need.

Of course in hindsight, one could say that the privatisation of the Olympic Village site was the fundamental error that exposed the social housing units to 'market imperfections'. This is the risk undertaken by the state in a private–public partnership. In the city's defence, one could point to the cash advantage of the sale, benefiting the development of social programmes elsewhere. But more fundamentally for our present concerns, the very high cost of building for poor households on expensive land offers a formidable barrier to the poverty dispersal model of social mixing. The escalation of urban land prices especially in expensive districts imposes a material barrier to the capacity for state intervention.

The 1970s model of social mixing envisaged the insertion of poor households into brownfield sites, or the maintenance of existing poorer households in neighbourhoods that were gentrifying. Today the upward pressure of property prices in wealthier inner-city areas makes that policy virtually impossible in many cities as the extravagant costs of social housing in Olympic Village testifies. Consequently, saving existing affordable housing is a renewed priority, with caution against any call to social mixing that might threaten it.

Against social mix: Downtown Eastside

Downtown Eastside has become a classic example of what Michael Dear once called the 'public city'. Close to downtown and adjacent to the industrial waterfront, with warehouses, factories and the terminus of two trans-Canada railway lines, the district became home to many single men in cheap residential hotels. Over time that population diversified as working men retired, and were joined by Aboriginal migrants to the city, men and women, and later those suffering from addictions and also groups released from centralised mental hospitals. In the early post-1945 period the district was already widely recognised in Vancouver at large as the city's 'skid road' (Hasson and Ley, 1994). Those conditions have become more visible over the decades, as the district has a startling incidence of HIV and AIDS and Hepatitis C, by far the highest crime rate in the region, and a conspicuous sex and drug trade. It has become the setting of media spectacle, not least as a result of 65 missing women, primarily sex trade workers, who disappeared from local streets, leading to the conviction of a suburban pig farmer as a serial killer. Numerous documentaries, television series and global media reporting during the 2010 Winter Olympics have brought the district widespread attention: a front-page story in the *Globe and Mail* (2009), Canada's national liberal daily newspaper, was entitled 'Our nation's slum: time to fix it'.

In fact considerable effort has been made to fix the district, initially through church and charitable organisations, and since the

1970s through vigorous local advocacy to which the welfare state has responded significantly in shaping the public city. The *Globe and Mail* estimated $1.4 billion in public funds were spent in Downtown Eastside during the past decade alone. By 2007, over 40% of dwelling units for the population of some 16,000 were non-market housing, while the district contained over 35% of the city's social service offices (Ley and Dobson, 2008). As conditions deteriorated – at least in the public view – a tri-level 10-year government planning and servicing programme, the Vancouver Agreement, committed to a policy of 'revitalisation without displacement' (City of Vancouver, 2007). Part of an integrated approach to the district's social problems is to encourage social mixing, with condominium development on selected sites, while maintaining affordable housing as new non-market dwellings take up the dwindling stock of low quality single-room occupancy (SRO) units. There seem to be several reasons for this policy. First, there is a continuing ideological position in favour of social mixing wherever there is a policy opening (August, 2008); second, there is a view that exclusively public initiatives have not been successful in the past, and that private investment will bring not only middle-class residents but also private services like grocery stores and even possible employment; and third, middle-class residents will bring additional surveillance and eyes on the street to mitigate street crime. Some critics, however, add that a more subversive rationale is to disperse poverty so that – like most other Canadian cities – it is less concentrated and therefore less open to political articulation.

Downtown Eastside is ripe for gentrification. It is less than a kilometre from the city's financial district, it has a stock of attractive heritage structures, and some ocean and mountain views. Land prices are anomalously low for a district so close to the urban core. To date gentrification has largely been repelled by crime and a street scene unsettling to middle-class sensibilities. But reinvestment and middle-class colonisation is encroaching on all sides. Local advocacy groups see no future for the poor if the process of social mix unfolds.

Part of their strategic response is discursive. For decades organisers have contested the damaging labels of 'slum' and 'skid road', language that invariably encourages radical urban surgery – and displacement. An organiser in the 1980s observed, 'Our fundamental strategy has been to demand that the Downtown Eastside be recognised by all as a residential neighbourhood and not simply Skid Road' (Hasson and Ley, 1994). Indeed Downtown Eastside seems to be a name invented from within the district. Local advocacy documents are filled with references to 'the community', pointing out not only the long-term presence of many residents, but also the existence of a neighbourhood with social assets: 'residents form decades-long friendships and share resources in a way that builds a communal sense of how to be together that doesn't exist in other Vancouver neighbourhoods' (Pedersen and Swanson, 2010, p 4). The lesson is that there is social capital worth preserving and enhancing. Segregation has its social rewards.

Consequently social mix through gentrification and its inevitable displacement are to be avoided. Segregation has undoubtedly aided the politicisation of the poor, enforcing sometimes reluctant governments to keep funding social housing and services in response to effective lobbying. Segregation has also permitted efficiencies in service delivery by the many agencies in the district. But a severe challenge in maintaining a high concentration of poor people in Downtown Eastside is the scale of public intervention that is required to keep gentrification at bay, with development sites for social housing inevitably rising in cost as gentrification laps around the district. The extent to which the state has an appetite for such deep expenditures when so much has already been spent in past projects is uncertain. Local advocates might respond that these are services not just for one neighbourhood, as they serve a regional population of Canadians who are vulnerable and have become casualties through mental illness, unemployment, poverty, addictions, discrimination and marginalisation in other locations. In a neoliberal era new members are constantly recruited to this disadvantaged population, but there are few places that claim to be as tolerant and non-judgemental in accepting these new recruits. A current statement of 'community values' includes, 'Accepting people without judgement; co-operating; appreciating diversity; providing sanctuary for people who aren't welcome in other places' (Pedersen and Swanson, 2010, p 3). Downtown Eastside draws attention to the casualties of a polarising neoliberal era, and makes visible the flip-side of the over-hyped post-industrial 'creative city'.

The claim that Downtown Eastside displays the multicultural virtues of tolerance and acceptance reveals an unexpected side of the local political culture. While the position of advocates might be criticised as promoting segregation and social exclusion, this is true only if the category in question is social class. In terms of age, gender, employment status, ethnicity, sexuality, disability and lifestyle, there is immense diversity in the district. Moreover, the claims of advocates are voiced in a sophisticated language of rights; the opening statements of their most recent report quote David Harvey and a UN document on the right to the city (Pedersen and Swanson, 2010). Despite the heavy burden of history that elevates desegregation as a civil rights issue, Downtown

Eastside suggests persuasively that the social mixing of social classes is not a necessary route to human rights. A case could be made that, more than most districts, Downtown Eastside, 'Canada's poorest postal code', reveals evidence of the democratic cosmopolitanism sought by the middle-class reformers of (South) False Creek.

SEVEN

Social mix and encounter capacity – a pragmatic social model for a new downtown: the example of HafenCity Hamburg

Jürgen Bruns-Berentelg[1]

Introduction

Social mix becomes an issue not only in cases when a city's development has already led to pockets of social exclusion[2] and thus to negative spatial context effects for households, which sometimes result in political attempts at 'urban repair', but also with respect to such neighbourhoods as that of our case study, HafenCity Hamburg, whose definition as a new city district in economic and social terms within the cityscape is not yet complete. In the first case, the social mix concept can be pursued by intervening to change the socioeconomic environment and institutional structure so that negative context effects at least – be they economic, physical or symbolic – are largely removed, and the neighbourhood context no longer leads to involuntary segregation. However, in the case of projects of 'urban reinvention', such as HafenCity Hamburg presented here, substantial problems arise in defining an operational and adequately founded model for determining a new social mix:

- No theoretically founded model of social mix based on social theory exists that would lend itself to an operative process, regardless of which form of capitalist society is assumed.[3] Even ambitious ideas of equitable urban development or the 'right to the city' have not been presented in sufficiently elaborate form to serve as a pre-structured concept or theory for the idea of social mix as a spatial model of an inclusive urban society, without relinquishing the benefits of voluntary segregation or the advantages of a differentiated city.[4]
- The political public – also in Germany – regularly calls for urban development policies to facilitate social mix, but a political framework

of norms based on national political goals or far-reaching planning consensus is non-existent. Germany also lacks implementation-oriented national urban development policy goals, if only due to the municipalities' predominant responsibility for their urban development, which fundamentally allows for clear differentiation in local strategies. Social mixing as a stipulation for planning is basically well received by the German public, yet it is not a focus of national urban policy; in comparison with the UK or the Netherlands, at least, fully fledged strategies for action exist only rarely.[5]

• Compared to the welfare state-driven, Fordist approach of 30 or 40 years ago, urban development today is to a far greater degree a process which follows market principles and is borne by private sector investments and protagonists, Germany being no exception. Even if places of work in cities have always been created primarily by private, entrepreneurial investment – both in Fordist and post-Fordist times – it is only in recent decades that housing construction has become virtually an exclusively private sector, non-public or non-communal project. In Germany, market regulation has largely been relegated to other levels, for example, tenancy law, or targeted support for impoverished households. At the same time, the social mix in core inner cities is indirectly influenced by a multitude of smaller individual measures, such as conservation bylaws, ordinances to protect certain milieus, neighbourhood improvement measures or social reorganisation of land holdings (for example, in Munich) (Jekel and Frölich von Bodelschwingh, 2008). Thus, what 'social mix' can mean in a given market-driven context remains an open question to be addressed.

• At the spatial level, the question arises of what social mix means for certain levels of measurement of urban development, but particularly what it means for specific locations. A pragmatic determination of social mix might be possible for new residential neighbourhoods based on the existing planning context, since there are general rules that can be applied to the concept of social mix in residential areas as a central living environment. By contrast, what social mix entails for a central New Downtown[6] district such as HafenCity Hamburg, with a sizeable proportion of housing but predominantly non-residential uses, remains an unanswered question.

In terms of social theory and urban development policy, social mix in Germany can thus be likened to a 'black box', lacking sufficient theoretical corroboration and international context. Yet in practice, the issue cannot be ignored. While it may still be acceptable for individual, small-scale urban development ventures to proceed without an underlying conception, it is certainly not viable for a 157-hectare regeneration project like HafenCity Hamburg. This extensive urban redevelopment project will increase the size of the 'new downtown' of Hamburg, Germany's second-largest city with about 1.75 million inhabitants, by 40% over a period of 25 years. Apart from some 45,000 service sector jobs, this will create approximately 5,800 housing units, and an urban environment including institutions with an exceedingly high profile. This in itself would already result in social mixing – whatever its nature or appropriateness – based on a multitude of uncoordinated individual decisions. Even without a forward-looking concept, the urban development process will result in social mix – in the extreme case in a 'non-mixed' form, that is, a fairly high degree of social homogeneity. Despite the considerable theoretical and practical deficits afflicting the concept of social mix, an explicit and reflective approach within the context of large-scale urban redevelopment is preferable to a non-reflective, implicit utilisation of the concept and implementation. Even with all the theoretical and practical shortcomings of the concept, it would be scarcely conceivable to employ a strategy that excludes the aspect of social mix. Therefore, we are conducting our own process of strategic social deliberations for the HafenCity project, focusing on how to achieve social mix, independent of national or municipal specifications.

For HafenCity, the basic model for social mix leads back to the potential of the city location and the planned urban spatial structure, and thus follows a bottom-up conception and implementation strategy. At the same time it expands the idea of 'social mix' beyond the notion of mixed household types in a residential environment by adding constituent levels: public urban spaces and institutions with public appeal – although these cannot be described in detail. We are moving on from the predominant view of social mix relating to residential quarters, augmenting it with the idea of capacity for social encounter. In the process the different levels interact intensively and also change; although spatially planned, they cannot be interpreted as a 'spatial fix'.

The following section presents the waterfront project and new city area of HafenCity Hamburg, while the second section goes on to outline the framework concept of 'social mix' and encounter capacity. Subsequent sections describe how these ideas will be applied to attain social mix in HafenCity's housing sector and these are then presented in a wider context, before a number of conclusions are put forward.

HafenCity Hamburg[7]

A summary of the development of Hamburg's HafenCity breaks down into three characteristics. First, HafenCity falls in the category of large-scale waterfront projects. It covers 157 hectares, of which 127 hectares are on land, structured by the harbour basins, situated on the northern bank of the Elbe river, whose southern shore is dominated by an active general cargo port and, a few kilometres westward, by one of the world's top 10 container ports. It is within this maritime context that HafenCity is now being developed, the project having been announced in 1997 and brought under way by a masterplan in 2000. Being a waterfront project, it is flanked not only by the Elbe over a 3.1km stretch, but characterised by a number of port basins which altogether provide the city with 10.5kms of new waterline for development. The aesthetic and emotional assets of the waterfront location can thus be translated into qualities of economic and symbolic allure.

Second, and to enhance the waterfront qualities further, HafenCity has been designed to achieve a dynamic and compelling pairing of authenticity and aesthetic, architectural reinvention. Harbour basins and quay walls have been preserved, old materials incorporated into embankments, old harbour cranes restored and set up beside the promenades. At the same time the maritime tradition is being carried

Figure 7.1: HafenCity (highlighted in black) within Hamburg

Source: Freie und Hansestadt Hamburg, Behörde für Stadtentwicklung und Umwelt, Amt für Landesplanung

on: a traditional ship harbour has been constructed, and the cruise activities are being integrated into HafenCity, with two temporary terminals already operating successfully. A large maritime museum has opened in one of the preserved buildings, while construction is progressing on Hamburg's new landmark, the Elbphilharmonie concert hall, set atop an existing port warehouse which itself measures 35m in height; by 2013 the 110m-high, maritime hybrid with added hotel and residential use will be ready. Indeed, in urbanistic and architectural terms, HafenCity also implies the far-reaching reinvention of the city as such. Since only a few buildings in the former harbour landscape – consisting largely of single-storey warehouses – were considered worth preserving, HafenCity is implicitly a completely new urban architectural creation. Apart from six existing buildings, hundreds of new, mostly five- to seven-storey structures, will be erected – the products of architectural competitions, referencing the historic inner city – with higher buildings marking prominent locations in this part of the city. Thus, despite consisting almost completely of new-built structures, HafenCity blends in with the cubature and building height of Hamburg's existing downtown instead of dominating the cityscape as a modern, vertical city. HafenCity is a hybrid, perpetuating authentic structures while redefining urbanity through the means of modern architecture and urban redevelopment.

Third, in terms of uses, HafenCity's location predestines it to become a new city; at its core it is just 800m from Hamburg's town hall and less than 600m from the central railway station, with only the narrow strip of historic Speicherstadt buildings separating it from the city centre. HafenCity poses a question for Hamburg: what role should this new downtown play in future? It is the big cultural institutions such as the Elbphilharmonie, the International Maritime Museum and Science Centre, a new university for the built environment (HafenCity University and a private university), as well as important urban spaces that are giving this idea a real face. In the core area of HafenCity and beyond, retail stores and eateries are prevalent at ground level; HafenCity is becoming a major tourist attraction. At the same time, HafenCity is a business location; some 50% of the available floor space is used by companies rendering services, ranging from small local enterprises to big multinationals; HafenCity is the place in Hamburg where 'glocalisation', that is, locally embedded global integration, manifests itself in a new form. These links are realised by constructing buildings greatly varying in size, ranging from 4,000 to 40,000m^2 in the different neighbourhoods and specifying ceiling heights of 5m for ground floors, where public amenities predominate. This very fine-grained mix of uses – creating neighbourhoods in which certain core uses dominate, yet providing for residential use even in densely built, predominantly commercial zones, while also integrating office and retail space into residential zones – is the result of concerted urban planning. The considerable extent to which HafenCity suspends the functional division of uses is unprecedented world-wide in large-scale downtown redevelopment. After all, a good third of the useable area is taken up for residential use, and along with around 45,000 jobs, some 5,800 new housing units will be created. Thus, HafenCity is not merely perpetuating the known downtown model, but taking on the challenge of redefining the city between the competing interests of globalisation and local continuity.

The characteristics that distinguish the development of HafenCity are thus: (1) waterfront development; (2) a hybrid of authenticity and modern architectural aesthetics; and (3) the redefinition of the city. Together they form an image of new urbanity for a new downtown. This urbanity, however, is not simply an expression of the commercially successful generation of urban uses. It is, in the first instance, the expression of a strong regulatory position and municipal management. Hamburg plays a significant regulative and formative role, despite the considerable weight of private investment which amounts to over €6.6 billion for the projected 2.3 million m² of newly constructed gross floor area. Public investments in infrastructure, public urban spaces, public cultural and educational facilities, amounting to about €2 billion, once again largely funded through the sale of plots to the developers of individual private ventures, are being undertaken, reinforcing the degree of public influence on the quality and character of urban development. Through the linkage between the City of Hamburg's role as landowner and a sales strategy toward private investors highly geared to competition and innovation, as well as the substantial position of public investment in the area and strong development management by a city-owned urban redevelopment corporation, HafenCity Hamburg GmbH,[8] the city enjoys considerable leverage over and above traditional planning instruments. Hamburg's ambition amounts to more than the creation of high commercial quality by the private sector accompanied by public investment. Rather, the aim is to achieve emancipatory potential for HafenCity through its intrinsic urban character and its high ecological sustainability. This ranges from focusing strongly on issues of sustainable, ecological urban structure and achieving urbanity for HafenCity that is also emancipatory.

The future context of a completed HafenCity will consist of approximately 12,000 residents and some 45,000 people working here, along with an expected number of 80,000–100,000 daily visitors. 'What does this new urbanity mean?' is the central question in HafenCity's development, not merely as a commercially distinguishing characteristic of a place, but also as a public good whose scope and influence is felt well beyond the market. This is the background against which questions regarding social mix and capacity for urban encounter unfold.

Currently three HafenCity neighbourhoods have been completed, another three are under construction and four are in the planning stage or undergoing infrastructural development. The International Maritime Museum has opened, several large public spaces have been completed, and the city's waterfront has grown by 1.7km. The first primary school has opened, as have the first kindergartens. Already 1,500 people live in HafenCity and as many as 270 companies from various industries with a total 6,000 staff have located here; both the completed section and the part currently under construction are major tourist attractions.

Social mix and possibilities of urban encounter[9]: a conceptual outline

A place with considerable surplus meaning, such as the HafenCity of the future, is defined simultaneously as a place of work, as a place of culture and consumption oriented towards visitors, and as a dwelling place. Local employees, the residents and up to 100,000 visitors per day should be able to see their interests and needs represented within the fine-grained mix in HafenCity. However, the spatial coexistence of the uses and actors connected with this place will not *a priori* generate lasting social coexistence between the actors spatially, and certainly not socially, as the social and economic evolution of the place progresses. If there is too large a gulf between the expectations and needs of these groups, they will move out or segregate, probably initially from the home users, who regard their private sphere as at risk.

The first step of any requirement of the physical and acquired physical structure is that of a layout which enables a spatial density with at least a (weak) form of social mix and encounter potential and reproduces the urban everyday practices of a city. With reference to the basic parameters for a diversified city described by Jane Jacobs (1961), this will be abbreviated here as 'Jane Jacobs' urbanity'. Of course the claim for a largely newly built city like HafenCity lacking the advantages of a mix with older buildings as stipulated by Jacobs to draw on is extraordinarily high. Beyond Jane Jacobs' everyday urbanity, qualities and social structures should be able to emerge to create emancipatory potential (see, for example, Lees, 2004). Consequently for HafenCity this means not only the requirement of suitability for urban daily life but also of the emancipatory potential of appropriated physical space, and for the city as a whole. HafenCity's new social milieus must regard themselves as discursive and reflexive; public spaces and institutions must develop socially, to enable discourse and inclusive learning. It therefore follows that the notion of social mix – which means housing in everyday discourse – is an insufficient objective in the context of a new city development with larger emancipatory aspirations. How can this aspiration be achieved?

The social mix that develops out of the market effects of the different commercial real estate projects is not adequate, because it is geared exclusively to the economic performance of households at the time of purchase or when use commences. The mix that emerges reflects the economic efficiency of the households, not their 'urbanistic efficiency', which at best would be created as a coincidental by-product. Under the most favourable circumstances, the big city dweller mentality described by Georg Simmel (1903), with its complacency and blasé attitude, will be engendered in relation to the place and to the other actors. In the less favourable case, a symbolic or spatially factual claim to power will develop out of the success culture of the market society (see Neckel, 1994) in which privileged residents, who finance their homes out of their own means, also restrictively mark out the urban context as private extensions to their own dwellings, for example, to keep to a minimum potential disturbance by others in public spaces. This spatial claim to power, as long as it is not limited to a minority of households, is linked to the emergence of a sense of entitlement to a 'mental gated community', transcending any homogeneity of residential milieus. With respect to a mix whose development is exclusively market-related therefore, no emancipatory programme and no new city as a public good can be realised, even though it consists to a large extent of residences. The private, exclusively market-related demands of housing destroy or undermine the character of the new downtown as a public place.

So let us turn to the distributive concept in the form of mixed dwelling of basic socioeconomic groups as an emancipatory basis. In the first phase of the development of HafenCity the opportunity to benefit from funding of subsidised house building did not exist, there were no relevant schemes, nor was there a relevant planning concept for the City of Hamburg as a whole. This barred the route to a distributive form of social mix for residential households from the start. However, a strongly distributive model of social mix – in addition to the necessity of a direct or indirect subsidy – does have the conceptual disadvantage that, at best, it can only contribute indirectly to an emancipatory model of the new city. For HafenCity as a place, orienting social mix primarily towards a socioeconomic distributive model of the city overlooks the fact that only a limited social effect in terms of an emancipatory city is to be expected. The distributive form of social mix and the socially emancipatory substance of HafenCity do not simply coincide – although this does not mean that the former might not be meaningful for other reasons. Instead emancipatory substance is founded more on a strategy of recognition that gives higher priority to households in the strategic context of social mix for a new city which (help to) support the public (discursive) social character of the emerging place. This means that a key role in social mix is designated to social actors who influence the appropriated physical space as 'social urbanites' rather than as 'individualistic urbanites'. Recognition[10] of these social actors does not result from a pre-existing social and economic identity but, unlike the typical identities of recognition policy such as gender, ethnicity and 'race', although much more weakly configured, can develop and be partially triggered in the social sphere of the new city.

Specifically, it follows that to establish the social presence of the residents of HafenCity as an emerging emancipatory urban place and to activate social mix in such a way that the public place and the 'social urbanites', where appropriate, assert themselves against the possessive behaviour of a homogeneous, exclusionary neighbourhood and a social community turned inward on itself, the social mix of the residents, at least for HafenCity, should not therefore be aimed at the ideals of an inward-looking community or classical neighbourhood. Two consequences of social mix can be formulated, according to the conceptual approach. First, a balance must be found within the framework of market processes that at an early stage places social actors well-disposed towards collective urbanity in a key structuring position vis-à-vis social life, as well as ensuring that they are proportionally numerous in comparison with the overall number of households. Second, this social structuring role is not predefined in terms of reification of characteristics, but must be created within the context of social appropriation, also of the space, by the actors themselves through joint activities and mutual sense-making, as well as in the face of those who show an individually possessive attitude towards the city, and actors who do not occupy the place with the same social intensity (for example, local employees or visitors). It follows that social mix, however it is defined, cannot be the ultimate aim of the strategic development of the new city, but that the objective is the potential for encounter (not solely commercially determined), ascribed to the physical, social and economic place. Possibility of encounter can transform into the encounter capacity of a place, which makes it clear that, dependent on the social actors, spaces and time of day involved, these can be understood as relational potential spaces with at least ambiguous influence, but which can also be developed. They function beyond urban everyday life – not (yet) over years or during very short periods of time (for example, squares during cultural or political events) – as emancipatory places, while other places, for example, educational institutions, can largely attain this quality from the start and continuously in everyday practice.

Capacity for encounter is manifested primarily in two socio-spatial forms:

- public and private but publicly used urban spaces; and
- public or seemingly public private institutions including some commercial spaces.

These are the social places which allow non-commercial encounters, public discourse and public learning, also for residents, outside the private situations of dwellings and workplaces. Social mix among residents and the capacity for encounter in public-social places are mutually dependent: public places of encounter must be socially available for collective urbanistic purposes in order to have emancipatory effects, and the urban role of residents – rooted in the city through the private character of residence – can unfold meaningfully and to a considerable extent in such public social places. This is even possible in the age of the internet. On the other hand, the balance of power in favour of encounter and discourse in public places can only be achieved through a suitable social mix of people living here and their activities. The development of the social mix (in the housing sector) and of the capacity for encounter (in different public places) together also constitute the possibility of the emancipatory urbanity of a core inner city. In the following sections, the first specific development following on from these ideas of social mix is illustrated.

Development of social mix and encounter capability[11]

The central question regarding the development of a socially mixed residential population in HafenCity is not only what type of mix to strive for, and to what end, but how and by which means this mix can be achieved if housing construction is pursued with private funds, while HafenCity Hamburg GmbH, on behalf of the City of Hamburg, exerts a strong market influence as the landowner and has the power to intervene at various other critical levels of urban realisation. HafenCity Hamburg GmbH's activities can be broken down into three levels :

- (indirect) selection processes;
- communication consolidation processes; and
- institution–generating processes.

Each of the three levels is closely linked. They should not be understood as deductive settling and planning processes, but as processes of incentive and interaction between various protagonists, in particular between HafenCity Hamburg GmbH as the urban development corporation and the residents.

Selection processes

Residents of HafenCity are at no point directly chosen; instead they are effectively 'pre-selected' through two concurrent processes:

- the bidding process for plots and thus the determination of price-setting parameters and institutional financiers for housing construction and ownership; and
- HafenCity Hamburg's exhaustive information process regarding the project's development goals, as well as the increasingly concrete opportunities for perceiving HafenCity as a public place.

Having initially sold residential plots divided into small sections (parcel by parcel) but at top prices, as provided for in the masterplan of 2000, HafenCity GmbH began in 2003 to put plots for housing construction out to tender on a fixed-price basis in small sections in order to achieve a sufficient degree of social differentiation; the first site was offered at prices per gross floor area of between 430 and 480 €/m² and were thus priced deliberately 30% to 50% lower than office space in comparable locations. Since each investor was only allowed a single successful bid (one plot containing between 30 and 100 apartments), this resulted in considerable institutional diversity among the builders. Since to a certain extent joint ventures were also formed, 20 different builders completed a total of 640 units in this first phase – for a large project this represented a considerable small-scale breakdown in the tender process (requiring significant management effort). The builders' institutional backers ranged from cooperatives and joint building ventures to property developers in various market segments, as well as private investors. This creates a pattern of different residential use concepts within immediate proximity – from joint building ventures and cooperative-owned flats to luxury apartments with price bands ranging from 9.50 €/m²/month (rent without ancillary costs) for inexpensive cooperative-owned flats to 2,850 €/m² for reasonably priced flats for sale by joint building ventures, and purchase prices of 8,000 to 10,000 €/m² for luxury apartments.[12]

Figure 7.2: Differentiation in a mixed-use residential construction site (approximately 640 homes) by concept and funding type (approximately 75% proportion of overall area for residential)

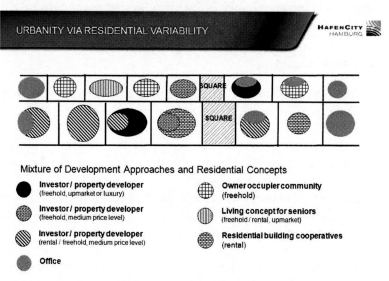

Based on 2009 micro-census data for Hamburg, which shows that Hamburgers spend 30% to a maximum of 40% of household income on housing expenses, 42%–57% of two-person households, 23%–49% of three-person households and 28–41% of four-person households in Hamburg theoretically have the means to live in HafenCity. Taking into account the reduced costs of mobility,[13] if peripheral locations are compared with the new HafenCity downtown and its optimal mass transit connections, almost 150,000 jobs within 20 minutes' walk, and a high density of social, cultural and local amenities, and adding these savings to the available housing budget as disposable income, the number of households increases markedly: 57%–73% of two-person households, 51%–70% of three-person households and 47%–66% of four-person households could afford the HafenCity location.[14]

Despite the fact that the lower price bracket in particular is prone to crowding-out effects due to demand backed by higher purchasing power, this statistical view shows that the greater part of Hamburg's households are potential residents of HafenCity if the reduced costs of mobility are factored in. This is due to the fairly inexpensive offerings from housing cooperatives and their relative resilience to being crowded out by the upmarket range, as well as the presence of joint building ventures. The tender and pricing strategy for the plots thus results in a comparatively wide socioeconomic base of different households despite the market-based approach and high building costs for residential units in waterfront locations.

Furthermore, HafenCity's information strategy plays a significant part in achieving social mix quality in the selection process. The information centre opened in 2000, and the combination of numerous public presentations, cultural and entertainment events, informative literature and a monthly television broadcast, produce a consolidated communication of HafenCity's ambitions to generate an urban context and public place. Accordingly, not only is there an emphasis on the presence of the residents who are part of a dense urban, waterside residential community, but also on the co-presence of various groups of urban protagonists with non-residential interests, of which visitors and employees in particular constitute large groups. This gave rise to yet another, in this instance subjective, selection filter favouring such households that accept a strongly interactive spatial context for residence and regard the residential environment of HafenCity Hamburg as part of the public good.

Social and communicative consolidation

It is important to move from the co-presence of households towards a social network and thus to social and communicative cohesion among residents as part of the social mix process. To a large extent this process is one of self-socialisation on the part of residents, supported by external protagonists, for example, church representatives or HafenCity Hamburg GmbH. This process – which could also be described as a process of spatial creation of social capital – has been followed, and in part structured by HafenCity Hamburg GmbH from the very beginning. Initially it engaged in complementary socio-scientific research (for example, in the form of group interviews) and, from 2006, one year after the first occupants had moved in, enlisted the aid of an urban sociologist. In essence, however, the urban neighbourhood socialisation process must be understood as a process of self-organisation.

Beginning with meetings in an apartment reserved for such uses by the housing cooperative, informal networks gradually evolved, given that the buildings were completed successively and new occupants could thus be quickly integrated. The opening of the first shops and kiosks, eateries and pubs created additional venues serving as informal meeting points. HafenCity Hamburg GmbH underpinned these first steps taken by residents with regular events on HafenCity planning and development issues (occupants' events), and provided each household with an information kit covering topics regarding HafenCity's development as well as network contacts, meeting places, and the like. At the same time, the urban sociologist appointed by HafenCity Hamburg GmbH continues to work as a provider of information, organisation supporter and trouble-shooter. One important aspect from HafenCity Hamburg GmbH's point of view was to network households with small children through group interviews, which led to participatory planning of the first playground and to the development of a children's playhouse funded in part by HafenCity Hamburg GmbH and also by companies that had been approached by the parents. Following the signing of a contract with HafenCity Hamburg GmbH, the playhouse is now run by parents. While face-to-face networking among the occupants progressed, a simultaneous strong consolidation of communication evolved via the internet and later in print media. Residents' internet portals were established very early on, facilitating a continuous exchange on neighbourhood and HafenCity-related issues. One of the internet platforms spawned a monthly gazette (*HafenCity Zeitung*), publishing articles by residents as well as journalists. One individual (a photographer and journalist), whose work often takes him to HafenCity, launched the quarterly journal, *Das Quartier*, which consciously includes HafenCity and adjacent neighbourhoods in its coverage. Both printed publications are distributed free of charge and have an avid readership. They are characterised by bottom-up journalism.

As the number of residents continued to grow, new annual local events were initiated, for example, a flea market on the promenade that also attracts many visitors from outside HafenCity; the annual residents' festival is held in the HafenCity cruise terminal with the participation of many businesses, and more recently, a St Nicholas market. Through network building, the development of internet- and print-based communication channels, as well as local events and activities, strong communication links have grown up between the residents, which are also starting to branch out to companies and people outside HafenCity. Through this communicative consolidation, residents have also generated a strong identification with HafenCity as a social place, over and above its physical and aesthetic attributes.

Institution-building

There is a direct link between the social communication process and the formation of residents' or public institutions. This is how parents came to form the registered association Spielhaus HafenCity e.V. (*eingetragener Verein*, registered association) and took over the running of the children's playhouse as a contractual party. The sports club, established early on, is active both within and outside HafenCity, using facilities in other parts of town (there is no sports ground yet) and also attracting many young members from surrounding city neighbourhoods. Another newly formed association is Kunstkompanie HafenCity e.V., that organises cultural activities in HafenCity and beyond. The most significant launch is probably Netzwerk HafenCity e.V., a network with members from HafenCity as well as from neighbouring districts (Altstadt, Neustadt and Rothenburgsort). The founding of Netzwerk e.V. as a superordinate organisation came about due to the fact that after the first large neighbourhood had been completed, HafenCity Hamburg GmbH partially pulled out of managing this part of HafenCity. It became obvious to the residents that direct, personal contact with the management corporation would no longer suffice to exercise their interests, but that it was now crucial to consult at a higher political level. Netzwerk e.V. focuses on specific issues pertaining to HafenCity Hamburg (for example, future traffic developments and environmental certification); it functioned as a contact platform for residents during the revision of the HafenCity masterplan, and also, for example, as the institution which will determine the composition of the advisory board of the central commercial neighbourhood, Überseequartier. The network also includes members and residents from outside HafenCity; the borders of the redevelopment area are frequently crossed. Nonetheless the essential protagonists in these activities are residents of HafenCity – who often describe themselves as 'pioneers'.

To the empathetic onlooker, the impression is that the main proponents of these activities are occupants of cooperative housing (tenant groups) and joint building ventures (owner groups), although not exclusively so. This may be partly due to the fact that the cooperative-built properties in the core area were the first residential buildings to be completed and could therefore serve as a meeting place. However, the philosophy behind the residential cooperative, even if no longer associated with such obligations today, is expected to provide an important impetus for involvement in the newly forming neighbourhood and its social fabric. The same can be said of the residents of joint building venture homes, who need to combine a strong entrepreneurial spirit with the will to cooperate in the process of redesigning and constructing a large building themselves (20-50 households) with expert support. This 'spirit of cooperation' of both groups is carried through into the formation of a collaborative network and the creation of institutions; attitude and involvement evolve into 'social place-making' ability. Therefore, the significance of housing cooperatives and joint building ventures not only derives from their role within the market segment of low-cost, unsubsidised housing (except in terms of plot prices) with a comparatively stable user structure, but also from their residents' role in social networks and as social entrepreneurs. Thus, in the concept of social mixing they occupy the central role, not based on economic factors but arising from their social role. It is the role of housing cooperative and joint building venture residents which lends particular legitimacy to keeping land prices at a level that allows these groups of protagonists a presence in HafenCity. It is the recognition of their social function, not primarily of their economic status, which, resulting from a selection process, the consolidation of social communication, and the creation of institutions geared to cooperation and exchange, gives rise to their importance for the social mix.

The intrinsic form of social mix among HafenCity residents in turn evolves spatially and socially from the context of a high capacity for encounters in the whole urban milieu, in a form that is neither aimed primarily at residents, nor supported by them. For the process of selection, communicative consolidation and the formation of institutions at resident level is embedded in an all-embracing process of the formation of social encounter capacity at public area level and of public or semi-public institutions. A few pointers should suffice. While public places in the public sphere were in the past overestimated in their capacity to provide opportunities for social interaction, today the opposite is true (see, for example, Amin, 2002). In the case of HafenCity it is clear that its public places, because of their varied physical design, in intensive use for everyday and cultural purposes, generate a dense field of communication pregnant with social encounter capacity for residents and non-residents alike (see Bruns-Berentelg, 2010).

At a second level, the development of encounter capacity emerges through the extension of the roles of institutions and the creation of institutions. Thus the first primary school in HafenCity was planned – and is intensively used – as a community centre (Läpple et al, 2010).

Other institutions which are extending their functional scope are private businesses which regard their (semi-public) spaces as places for social interaction, as well as HafenCity Hamburg GmbH itself, which has evolved far beyond its original role as a real estate development corporation. In addition a large number of new institutions which see communicative concentration as a central role are evolving or already active. Social interaction and encounter, albeit sometimes thematically limited, are central aspects, for example, for the Hamburg America Center, the Ecumenical Forum, Designport in connection with Greenpeace' headquarters, the Stadthaushotel with its disabled workforce, the deportation documentation centre, the HafenCity information centre with its many public events, etc. In addition to classical meeting places such as museums, the concert hall, universities and event spaces in hotels, restaurants and cafes (some still under construction), a milieu for social encounters is taking shape that goes far beyond that generated by residents. Thus, the development of high encounter capacity is taking place throughout a variety of places and institutions.

It is the social embeddedness of HafenCity residents that is emerging in this environment of encounter possibility that first creates the preconditions for the social mix of occupants to be viewed in the context of an evolutionary process in the city and in the debate about urban society. At the same time, the external milieu of encounter possibility stabilises residents' own aspirations, as well as their expectations of other residents to become part of the public milieu of encounter potential in the new downtown and not just be part of the residential community.

Conclusion: gentrification and social mix

To conclude, we now discuss the connection between gentrification and social mix. If gentrification is not merely understood as a process of economically weaker households being displaced, but more comprehensively, as a process of social segregation and social polarisation (see, for example, Lees et al, 2008), the question emerges of whether gentrification can be avoided at all in the context of large-scale urban redevelopment, or whether economic selectivity caused by high-cost new-builds does not in itself force gentrification. This contribution takes the view that this does not have to be the case. That does, however, presuppose an explicit concept for social mix. In the context of a new development area, the frequently assumed strategic argument (see the editors to this volume's critical assessment in Chapter One) that gentrification will achieve a ('better') social mix in existing residential areas looks very different: to avoid wholesale gentrification of newly built areas a specific form of social mix is necessary. Taking the example of the HafenCity Hamburg new-build project, the social mix strategy has been described, including processes of selection, as well as social and communicative consolidation and institution building, which results in the creation of a new inner city which, although its resident population is far outnumbered by visitors and jobholders, essentially defines itself through the high social encounter capacity of its inhabitants. This capacity for encounter, which manifests itself in physical places, as well as in institutions and residents' manifold activities and relationships, is both the yardstick for measuring the acceptability of the social mix of the place and for assessing whether or not gentrification is an issue.

HafenCity Hamburg serves as a case in point that the requirements of a new downtown as a public place with high social encounter capacity and 'supercharged' with surplus economic, social, cultural and physical importance gives rise to specific demands of its social context as a residential environment and the attitude of its residents to want to be part of this special, public context. Life here is imbued with a very public dimension and thereby loses a substantial part of its usual, private character. In order to achieve an adequate social mix of inhabitants the strategy has to focus on the dimension of social interactivity in the mix of households, instead of on social mix, as is frequently the case, when based on a distributive social model geared to an appropriate socioeconomic distribution of household types in the place concerned. The usual distributive component of social mix in HafenCity is secondary to the component born of recognition that the inner city is a public social and cultural place not only for those who live there, but for others as well. This puts the argument into the theoretical context of, for example, Young (1990, 2000) and Fraser (2009), who place much greater emphasis on 'recognition' in their socio-philosophical analyses instead of basing equity exclusively or predominantly on distributive, income-related aspects. In the case of HafenCity, recognition is founded on the willingness of residents to make a contribution to (or at least to tolerate) the locality's public character as a place of social encounters, and not on an (implicit) socioeconomic model of distribution as license to be present in HafenCity. Recognition processes in the context of HafenCity are twofold:

- Recognition by resident households of the other protagonists; because they view themselves as possessing local social interaction potential in the spatial context of HafenCity, they are thereby able to create openness for fellow residents and others using the place, in particular visitors and employees. These households are the crucial protagonists in networks, some of whose reach extends well beyond HafenCity.

• External as well as political recognition which these potential and actual actors of social encounter capacity receive through regulative and incentive-creating activities on the part of the HafenCity Hamburg GmbH urban development corporation and political decision makers.

In pursuing this specific form of social mix, the pragmatic intent of the development strategy for HafenCity is distinguished by a particular theoretical legitimation and poses questions about a concept of equity for a new downtown, which cannot be discussed here. The social pattern of HafenCity's population, therefore, certainly differs from Simmel's view of the big city dweller, whose individualism and blasé attitude can at best be interpreted as a toleration strategy towards the presence of others (Simmel, 1903). The co-presence of big city dwellers as described by Simmel does not create a social structure with the constitutive attitude needed to support the capacity for social encounters. This requires a modern society, as opposed to a traditional one, as described, for instance, by Tönnies (2005), charged with the task of developing basics such as the formation of identity and social capital, and a democratic attitude (Rosa and Strecker, 2010). If exclusion is to be avoided, this also applies to local contexts. The local community of HafenCity Hamburg can therefore also be described as a post-traditional society in which voluntary and temporary involvement in the socio-spatial agglomeration are constitutive elements (cf Hitzler et al, 2008). More specifically, in the case of HafenCity and its residents' high degree of identification with HafenCity, it could even be understood as the spatial and social manifestation of a brand community (Pfadenhauer, 2008).

The voluntary and temporary character (residents as part of a mobile local society or who, if they leave, could mutate into big city dwellers in the sense of Simmel) of the brand community of HafenCity residents makes it clear that the habitus of a post-traditional community can also function in the shape of a local social community and not just as a largely placeless network. It is this quality of a local post-traditional society that should generate social mix in the form of high capacity for social interaction. The brand community of HafenCity residents is characterised both by a strong identity and in the sense of differentiation from other districts in Hamburg – to term it segregation would be wrong – and by an attitude of urban openness and willingness to communicate.

However, the image of the HafenCity population as a brand community does not necessarily mean that the majority of the residents share this self-perception. What is essential, however, is that a substantial number of the inhabitants accept the view that it is a social place with the capacity for social interaction as opposed to being oriented towards privacy. Observation of HafenCity leads to the assumption that it is not a numerical majority of the residents that is required but a critical proportion of households able and ready to articulate this vision, along the lines of Schelling's 'tipping point' model (1978), to maintain the balance in favour of high capacity for social encounters and for it to develop further. In HafenCity, a 20–30% proportion of cooperative housing and joint building venture residents (plus participants from other institutional residential contexts) appears to be a solid foundation for strong social interaction. HafenCity's population structure is by no means homogeneous, as became very clear during the 2009 federal elections. HafenCity showed the highest voter turnout of any polling district in Hamburg (87.4%), thus demonstrating strong democratic and political interest. On the other hand, the liberal Free Democratic Party (FDP), whose programme leans more towards performance and individualism and therefore arguably represents a certain closeness to Simmel's big city dweller, received 27.5% of the votes, double the party's Hamburg average. At the same time, the percentage of votes for the Green Party (GAL) was above-average, at 17.9%, and the share of the conservatives (CDU) slightly above the mean; the Social Democrats (SPD), closest to the distributive model, came out well below average, while small parties from the political left and right were hardly represented at all.[15] However, how closely the post-traditional, spatially and socially based brand community with its high capacity for social interaction is linked to political orientation remains an open question and requires empirical investigation.

Nevertheless, there is ample evidence to show why social differentiation and social segregation in a place like HafenCity should not be categorised as gentrification.[16] Gentrification, in a broad sense, does not exist if the social interaction potential of a place is so pronounced within the post-traditional community of residents that it – as in the case of the new HafenCity – creates a place which not only offers a high degree of urbanity in daily life, but also has a strong communicative density, as well as internal and external networks, and which is recognised as an urban, open place. Therefore, gentrification in a broader sense is not always the outcome in large-scale urban redevelopments. However, as the example has shown, this requires a social mix that is interaction-based and not primarily understood in the distributive sense. A strategy oriented towards distributive social mix does not contribute sufficiently to the creation of internal (targeted at residents) and external (targeted at protagonists and residents outside HafenCity) social interaction capacity because it views social encounter of households as an automatism and also fails to utilise the differentiation resulting from different lifestyles productively. For a public place such as the new HafenCity downtown, the distributive component is therefore secondary in significance to the subject of social mix. Hamburg media reports, sometimes critical of HafenCity's social development (for example, 'rich people's ghetto'), viewing the distributive component as the essential characteristic of social, does, however, in turn, pose a threat to the recognition of an exchange-based approach: it is not those residents who contribute to the public character of the locality through their own activities and attitude who would receive special support, but primarily those with an economic eligibility to be present in HafenCity.

Indeed, given that media stigmatisation[17] of such a large newly built district could be powerful enough to undermine the locality's capacity for social encounter on all levels except everyday urbanity, it was decided in 2009 under the aegis of Hamburg's residential development plan and reinforcement of subsidised house building in Hamburg overall, that even HafenCity would henceforth also include a 20% proportion of households eligible for social support. Although this distributive component certainly does not replace the recognition-based component of social mix, it gives it additional legitimacy. The example of HafenCity Hamburg also shows that, intentionally or not, the relationship between social mix and gentrification is complex. Recognition-based social mixing (now supplemented by a distributive level) is necessary and should be at the core of the development strategy in order to open up social encounter potential in the new centre of a major city, despite considerable socioeconomic differentiation between households. As shown, this goal can be attained through market mechanisms, but the process must be embedded in a comprehensive regulative framework such as that provided by the HafenCity Hamburg GmbH development corporation. Only then will the 'newly built downtown' not automatically spell 'new-build gentrification'.

Notes

[1] The author's contribution is a personal one and does not necessarily represent the view of the Free and Hanseatic City of Hamburg.

[2] In Germany much of the discussion about social mix is conducted implicitly, for example, in connection with the concept of exclusion/inclusion (see, for example, Häussermann and Kronauer, 2009 or Kronauer et al, 2006).

[3] For an overview of research into social mix in residential areas, particularly in Germany, see Friedrichs (2010). Overall, there has been very little research on this issue in Germany.

[4] See, for example, the internationally oriented works of Marcuse et al (2009) or Soja (2010).

[5] If at all, the issue of social mix at national level can be regarded as being 'embedded' within the strategy of 'social urban development' in Germany (see Güntner, 2007, for a summary). However, these programmes and approaches do not focus on the city as a whole.

[6] The term was coined by Professor Ilse Helbrecht, an urban geographer at Humboldt University, Berlin.

[7] General and up-to-date information can be retrieved at www.hafencity.com

[8] Regarding the function and role of HafenCity Hamburg GmbH, see also Clark et al (2010).

[9] The argument can be outlined here, without detailed substantiation.

[10] A simple introduction to the theory of recognition can be found in Becker (2010).

[11] Additional empirical information on population and neighbourhood structure and motives for moving into HafenCity is contained in Menzl (2010) and in Menzl et al (2011). This description places greater emphasis on the process of indirect and direct influence.

[12] An overview of household types in HafenCity can be found in Menzl's description (2010).

[13] The new inner city White Paper of the German Federal Ministry of Transport, Building and Urban Development assumes possible savings of €300 to €400 per household per a month due to reduced mobility costs (cf BMVBS, 2010, p 23).

[14] Information regarding the calculation base may be requested from the author.

[15] A general overview of election milieus and the German party system is provided by Walter (2008).

[16] General empirical arguments, that do not need to be enlarged on here, can be found on HafenCity's website. The assertion that gentrification is taking place in HafenCity is rejected thus:

> Occasionally the term gentrification is used in connection with HafenCity because the housing being built is of high quality and negative repercussions are feared. But this criticism is not valid. The phrase was coined in 1964 by Ruth Glass to describe the crowding out of households from their traditional living quarters by new groups of higher-income residents who can afford to invest in the buildings, thus increasing property values in the neighbourhood. This process, to be observed in the Hamburg districts of St Pauli, St Georg or Schanzenviertel, is not taking place in HafenCity; as the district never boasted any housing, no established residents exist to be squeezed out of their homes. Indirect gentrification in new-build areas is not evident either. HafenCity is separated by the Speicherstadt from other inner-city residential quarters and, because they are subsidized, homes close to HafenCity are better protected against increasing rents than old buildings in other inner-city locations. Direct gentrification is not to be expected because the volume of new-builds outside HafenCity within the surrounding inner city is small. On the other hand, it is important that a large quantity of high-quality house building is developed in HafenCity. It increases the proportion of high-value homes which is below average in the inner city and in this way upgrades the quality of social and recreational infrastructure for city-centre residents surrounding HafenCity. At the same time, the development of expensive homes in HafenCity lessens the pressure for redevelopment in areas close to the inner city. So HafenCity is actually making a contribution towards less gentrification in Hamburg (www.hafencity.com).

[17] Refer to the study by Jansson (2005) examining the Expo cooperation project and new development quarter Bo01 in Malmö, Sweden.

Part 3
Social mix policies and gentrification

Mixed-income schools and housing policy in Chicago: a critical examination of the gentrification/education/'racial' exclusion nexus

Pauline Lipman

Introduction

Mixed-income development is an increasingly popular strategy to deconcentrate poverty in the US (Brophy and Smith, 1997; Popkin et al, 2004; Joseph, 2006). In several US cities, mixed-income housing is linked to newly created mixed-income schools (Raffel et al, 2003; Lipman, 2008). Mixed-income strategies in housing and education share a similar set of assumptions: deconcentrating the 'poor' and dispersing them into mixed-income contexts will give them access to the cultural and social capital and political and economic resources of the middle class, thus improving their economic and academic situation. Proposals to move low-income students to mixed-income schools and low-income families to mixed-income developments invoke the democratic goals of the common school and struggles for racial integration and open housing. They also invoke the New Urbanist programme for liveable and communitarian cities designed to encourage social mixing and integrated housing, work and recreation in a people-centred urban environment. Although framed in terms of class, or poverty, in the US the subtext is 'race' – students and families to be displaced and relocated are generally African American.

Chicago, the third largest public school system in the US, has been at the forefront of neoliberal education initiatives in the US. In 2004, Chicago launched Renaissance 2010 (hereafter Ren2010), the first phase of a radical reform to close 'failing' public schools and open new schools of 'choice', the majority run by private operators (charter schools). Some charter and Ren2010 public schools were to be 'mixed income'.The origins of this plan are in the city's corporate boardrooms. Ren2010 was proposed by the Commercial Club of Chicago, a civic organisation of the city's most powerful corporate and financial leaders, and was announced by the mayor at a Commercial Club event.

In 2000, Chicago also launched a $1.6 billion Plan for Transformation of public housing (PFT), as part of the HOPE VI programme (Home ownership and Opportunity for People Everywhere). The PFT was to demolish or 'rehab' high-rise public housing projects. The residents were dispersed to scattered-site, small public housing projects or the private rental housing market, and 6,000 of the original 25,000 public housing households were to be relocated in 10 new mixed-income developments. This is the most extensive revamp of public housing in the US (Bennett et al, 2006b). The national impact was summed up by the MacArthur Foundation, which awarded $50 million in support, including loan guarantees for investors: 'Chicago ... has the potential to demonstrate, at scale, the impact of mixed-income housing on neighborhood revitalization' (MacArthur Foundation, 2005).

The MacArthur Foundation also underscored the role of schools in the PFT: 'The city has made a commitment to improving the local schools, without which the success of the new mixed-income communities would be at great risk' (2005). The confluence of mixed-income schools and housing is strategic. As Lupton (2006) notes, schools are positioned as agents of neighbourhood transformation by attracting new residents through 'school-centred housing development' (Bruce Katz, quoted in Lupton, 2006). This strategy is particularly salient in Chicago's Mid-South area, an African American community with a concentration of high-rise public housing, where Chicago Public Schools (CPS) promised to 'reinvent the area's 25 schools and make them a magnet for the return of middle-class families' (Olszewski and Sadovi, 2003). "We're aiming for dramatic change; we're not going to recreate the status quo," said Arne Duncan, chief executive officer of CPS. "No other school system in the country has pursued this link between community revitalisation and school development." (Olszewski and Sandovi, 2003).

In this chapter, I examine the notion that mixed-income schools in newly constructed mixed-income communities are generative of educational equity and social justice. I locate these policies in relation to neoliberal urban development and the politics of 'race'. My analysis addresses: (1) the ideological basis and intellectual origins of mixed-income strategies in the US; (2) their relation to neoliberal urban restructuring; (3) evidence for mixed-income schools and housing; and (4) implications for educational equity and social and economic justice. I focus on the case of Chicago where mixed-income housing and school policies are joined, discursively and practically.[1]

My analysis is grounded in six years of participatory qualitative research, including observation of, and participation in, school board meetings, public hearings, community and school meetings, rallies, press conferences, planning sessions, coalition meetings and forums on housing and school policy. It is also based on review of archival documents on education, housing and urban development; ongoing conversations and formal interviews with parents, students, teachers, school staff, school level administrators, community organisation leaders and members, teachers and school employee unions, school reform organisations, community-based research groups, policy makers and local government officials; and data from a collaborative project studying the intersection of education, housing and urban development (Data and Democracy, www.uic.edu/educ/ceje/resources.html).

Neoliberal urbanism

Brenner and Theodore (2002b) argue that, 'cities have become strategically crucial geographic arenas in which a variety of neoliberal initiatives ... have been articulated' (p 351). Cuts in federal funding for cities in the US instigated 'roll-back neoliberalism', paving the way for 'roll out' neoliberal policies and institutions (Peck and Tickell, 2002a). To make up for shortfalls in federal funding, and driven by market ideologies, the entrepreneurial city looks to public–private ventures, privatisation of public services and reliance on real estate taxes and debt financing to address budgetary needs. This increases the power of bond rating agencies and real estate developers to regulate urban policy (Weber, 2002; Hackworth, 2007). Neoliberal development is characterised by downtown residential and corporate development and gentrification.

Facilitated by municipal government, gentrification has become a pivotal sector in neoliberal urban economies (Smith, 2002; Hackworth, 2007) and a critical factor in the production of spatial inequality, displacement, homelessness and racial containment. This dynamic is located in the 'spatial fix' (Harvey, 2001) – 'the built environment is junked, abandoned, destroyed and selectively reconstructed' (Weber, 2002, pp 520-1) for capital accumulation. Today's 'third-wave' gentrification intertwines state, local, national and transnational investment capital and real estate interests in the production of gentrification complexes of housing, consumption and leisure that spread beyond the city's inner ring to neighbourhoods distant from downtown (Smith, 2002). For example, Chicago's plan to transform public housing is backed by $1.5 billion in federal funds that will jump start billions of dollars of additional investment in retail, housing and other consumption outlets.[2] The 'inner city' – an icon of vilified Keynesian welfare state policies (for example, subsidised public housing, public health clinics and public hospitals) – is now a site of mega real estate investment projects and extreme transition and a 'soft spot' for neoliberal experimentation (Hackworth, 2007). Mixed–income developments are located in this dynamic.

'Race' has been pivotal to capital accumulation and structures of domination in the US (Barlow, 2003), and neoliberal restructuring is no different. The cultural politics of 'race' provide the ideological soil for a racially coded neoliberal ideology of individual responsibility and reduction of 'dependency' on the state as grounds to restructure or eliminate government-funded social welfare and public institutions. In turn, neoliberal economic restructuring has intensified the structural inequality of people of colour. For example, between 1980 and 2004, the hourly wage gap in Illinois between white workers and Latino workers widened by 24%, and the gap between whites and blacks widened by 162% (Heartland Alliance, 2006). In Illinois' restructured economy, people of colour are concentrated in low-wage service jobs, including day labour where immigrants are more than five times as likely as non-immigrants to be employed (Applied Research Center, 2007). Meanwhile, many African Americans can find no work at all in the new economy (Barlow, 2003). This disproportionate impoverishment is a product of sedimented racial inequality intensified by neoliberal economic restructuring.

Over the past three decades Chicago has been transformed from an industrial city to a centre of global business services and finance, international tourism, downtown development, luxury real estate and retail expansion in gentrified neighbourhoods alongside socially isolated very low-income communities of colour and immigrant enclaves. Stable manufacturing jobs have been replaced by service jobs paying significantly lower wages. Inequality is magnified by the mayor's aspirations to make it a first-tier global city – a command centre of the global economy. Chicago is also a showcase for neoliberal experimentation. City government's aggressive support for capital accumulation and corporate involvement in city decision making includes a rich menu of incentives to developers, including Tax Increment Financing (TIF),[3] tax abatements and incentives for corporate and banking interests, and high-level public–private partnerships. As I will go on to argue, education and housing policy are also implicated. City government has also withdrawn funding for social welfare, leased public assets to private companies (for example, the Chicago Skyway bridge, the city's parking meters), and turned over public institutions – housing and schools – to private interests. These measures are coupled with intensified policing and surveillance of communities of colour and militarisation of schools in African American and Latino areas (Lipman, 2003). Housing and education policy are key arenas of neoliberal policy implementation.

In this chapter I explore the connections between neoliberal policies of marketisation in education and welfare policy and the implementation of social mix policy. The study suggests how the labelling and pathologising of sections of the population and urban space acts a precursor to open up areas of the city to marketised policies in welfare and education that, alongside social mix initiatives, enhance housing market profits through gentrification and the displacement of poorer African American residents.

Mixed-income strategies, neoliberal development and racial exclusion

Hackworth (2007) contends that '[I]nequitable real estate development in cities is the knife-edge of neoliberal urbanism' (p 192). Closing schools in mixed-income HOPE VI areas, displacing and dispersing public housing and public school populations, and opening new schools of choice associated with mixed-income developments are part of this 'knife-edge'. In Chicago, school policy is strategically linked with housing in the neoliberal structuring of the city. When Ren2010 was unveiled in 2004, the Chicago Metropolitan Planning Council (2004), an organisation of business and elite civic leaders which is closely involved in the PFT, made the connection explicit:

> Looking ahead, a number of issues should be addressed as Renaissance 2010 unfolds, including how to coordinate the development timelines of mixed-income communities with the openings and closings of schools nearby, how to establish ongoing communication mechanisms to report on the status and progress of Renaissance 2010 to all of the stakeholders involved in the process, and how to market these new schools to parents considering moving into the new mixed income communities.

Good schools and options within the public school system are important in the global competition to attract highly skilled knowledge workers, to entice investors to gentrification projects and to subsequently market gentrified and gentrifying areas to new middle-class residents. Closing schools is part of a strategy of softening up areas for development. It creates additional instability in an already unstable housing environment and contributes to pushing people out of the neighbourhood. As one community resident said, "When you destroy a community's school, you destroy a community" (quoted in field notes, 17 February 2005).

Before communities can be gentrified, they have to be devalued, prepared for redevelopment and re-imagined as places of value. To do so it is necessary to construct a reality of 'easily discardable people and social life' (Wilson et al, 2004, p 1181). 'Race' is at the centre of this process in the US. Closing schools in African American communities is facilitated by their construction in the media and public policy as 'dysfunctional' and 'violent'. These portrayals mask the nexus of racialised public policy and investment decisions that produced deindustrialisation, disinvestment, unemployment and degradation of public health, the built environment and education in communities of colour over the past 50 years. Closing schools to re-open them with new identities that mark them as middle class and that appeal to whites even when initial gentrifiers are African American is part of erasing communities' historically constituted 'race' and class meaning and 'rebranding' them for a new clientele. For example, CPS closed neighbourhood public schools serving low-income working-class black and Latino students and opened selective enrolment and specialty schools to appeal to the upper middle class (for example, a prestigious language academy, a school of global studies, a Montessori school).

When people are uprooted and relocated to mixed-income communities/schools not of their own making, at stake are issues of identity, place, solidarity and historical meaning. In particular, black urban communities in the US, in the context of racial segregation and terror, were forged as spaces of cultural and political resistance and survival (Haymes, 1995). Thus, their eradication through gentrification has historical, political and cultural significance that surpasses bricks and mortar. This seems lost on policy makers who presume to know what is best for these communities. As Greenbaum (2002) points out, the contention that relocation to mixed-income developments will address public housing tenants' deficit of social capital, assumes that the social support networks forged in low-income neighbourhoods are not valuable. In fact, the reciprocal services, support networks and institutions that low-income households rely on are ruptured when they are displaced and dispersed, actually diminishing their collective social capital.

Representation of black urban space as pathological is yoked to the supposedly regenerative and disciplining effects of the market and proximity to the middle class. According to this racialised neoliberal logic, while public housing and public schools breed dysfunction and failure, private management, the market and public–private partnerships foster entrepreneurship, individual responsibility, choice and discipline. The chief executive officer of the Chicago Housing Authority claimed that the PFT would not displace those who "want to work hard" and "share in the success" (quoted in field notes, 12 November 2005). HOPE VI and charter school selection criteria and behaviour rules codify the policing of these virtues (Lipman, 2011).

HOPE VI and mixed-income schools

HOPE VI set out to remake public housing in the US through rent subsidies for the private housing market, requirements that public housing residents become self-sufficient and promotion of home ownership. The act called for revitalising or demolishing 'distressed' units and relocating public housing residents in scattered site housing, giving them private housing market vouchers and financing mixed-income developments. A key 1995 revision eliminated one-to-one replacement, thus opening up public housing sites to large-scale private market-rate mixed-income development and gentrification. An assumption of the mixed-income strategy is that middle-class residents will deploy their social capital to connect low-income residents to job markets and resources, intervene to promote safety and social harmony and bring resources to the community.

Mixed-income schools are part of many HOPE VI plans. The assumptions are similar to those underpinning the deconcentration thesis and mixed-income housing – income mixing in schools will improve the educational performance of low-income students just as mixed-income communities will increase their social mobility (Raffel et al, 2003; Varady et al, 2005). HOPE VI policy documents and academic advocates also contend that mixed-income schools play an important role in creating and sustaining mixed-income communities. Under Chicago's Ren2010, CPS proposes to create mixed-income schools in new mixed-income developments. Drawing on egalitarian discourses, mixed-income policies seem democratic, but I want to look more closely at their consequences and implications for social justice.

Mixed-income schools

Richard Kahlenberg (2001), Century Foundation Fellow and leading proponent of mixed-income schools in the US, asserts a good education '... is best guaranteed by the presence of a majority middle-class student body' (p 1), to whom he attributes a range of behavioural and attitudinal merits contrasted with putatively problematic attitudes, behaviours and values of lower class students. His proposal is to create mixed-income schools with a majority of middle-class students and 'ability grouping' for 'faster' students. As evidence for this strategy, Kahlenberg cites the correlation between academic achievement and social class (or in US literature, socioeconomic status – SES). Kahlenberg also extrapolates from research on peer influence to argue for the positive impact of middle-class students on their low-income classmates. Although framed as a class issue, concretely the students affected in urban schools are primarily low-income students of colour.

The correlation of social class with educational experiences and outcomes is well established (Knapp and Woolverton, 2004; Sirin, 2005). Studies show a strong correlation between family SES and the school and classroom environment to which the student has access, school quality (for example, teacher quality, instructional resources, teacher–student ratio), and the relationship between school personnel and parents. The correlation of poverty with low-academic performance, school completion and other education indicators is also well documented (Anyon, 2005), as is the relationship between 'race'/ ethnicity and educational outcomes (Darling-Hammond, 2004). These correlations are, however, moderated by various factors such as school location, 'race' and school level (Sirin, 2005). There is mixed evidence for the benefits of moving low-income students to low-poverty schools and to the suburbs. Results from the national Moving to Opportunity programme appear to show no significant increase in test scores at any age for students who were assigned housing vouchers to move from public housing to lower poverty neighbourhoods (Sandbonmatsu et al, 2006), and virtually no impact on employment, earnings or public assistance (Varady, 2005). Some researchers found positive effects of moving low-income students to suburbs under the Chicago Gutreaux housing desegregation programme (Rubinowitz and Rosenbaum, 2002), although there are questions about the methodology that produced these findings (Goering et al, 2002).

Although there may be social class composition effects on educational outcomes, we do not know why. Kahlenberg and others infer the benefits to low-income students of middle-class schools are due to the positive influence of middle-class students and parents; however, they might just as well be attributed to superior instructional and material resources, better prepared teachers and higher academic expectations in these schools. If the latter is the case, then equitable funding, teacher professional development and educational reform (rather than income mixing) would seem to be an important remedy for educational disparities due to social class, particularly given stark disparities in school funding in the US between affluent school districts and those with a high percentage of low-income students.[4] In fact, studies published in the past 15 years show that higher school funding has a positive effect on student learning, regardless of school composition, particularly when funding is used to obtain better quality instruction and resources for instruction (Darling-Hammond, 2004).

The contention that lower-income students will benefit from proximity to middle-class students ignores research on the constellation of structural, cultural and pedagogical factors that perpetuate 'race' and class inequalities in educational experiences and outcomes (Darling-Hammond, 2004; Knapp and Woolverton, 2004). Evidence of the persistence of these factors (for example, tracking or streaming, teacher attitudes and expectations, Eurocentric curricula) in mixed-race, mixed-income schools indicates that they continue to produce racial disparities in academic achievement, assignment to academic tracks and student discipline, despite strong pro-school attitudes among students of colour (Minority Student Achievement Network, http://msan.wceruw.org/). Yet, academic tracking is built into Kahlenberg's proposal. In fact, 'mixed-income' proposals deflect attention from the centrality of racial subordination and marginalisation in the production of educational inequality, although 'race' and putative deficiencies of low-income children and families of colour are quite clearly the subtext of proposals for 'economic integration' (Orfield, 2001). Mixed-income proposals neither acknowledge the intellectual and cultural strengths of low-income students of colour, nor consider the extensive literature on the importance of culture, language, 'race' and ethnicity in schooling. Proposals to 'reform' low-income students of colour by exposing them to middle-class norms and behaviours run counter to 30 years of scholarship on multicultural, multilingual education and on the role of racial and ethnic subordination in the perpetuation of educational disparities and inequities (Banks and Banks, 2004), and they perpetuate deficit notions about these students.

The assumption that the school involvement of middle-class parents will benefit low-income students is also questionable given evidence that middle-class families deploy their material and cultural resources to secure educational advantages for *their* children (André-Bechely, 2005), particularly in the context of school choice (Ball, 2003; Butler with Robson, 2003). There is also evidence that middle-class parents seek to insulate their children from lower-achieving students and lower-income students of colour (Oakes et al, 1997). This is confirmed by studies of HOPE VI mixed-income developments that found little cross-class or cross-race mixing with low-income students (Raffel et al, 2003; Varady et al, 2005).

Finally, it is questionable that low-income students will actually be enrolled in substantial numbers in new mixed-income schools in Chicago. Both formal school policy and informal social and cultural mechanisms are exclusionary. Despite claims that students from closed schools will not be excluded from Ren2010 schools, CPS policy states students have the right of return 'to the fullest extent possible' (Board of Education, 2007). Unlike regular neighbourhood public schools, which must admit all students, Ren2010 schools have admission stipulations and processes that may exclude them (for example, complicated application processes and parent interviews). Students from the Cabrini Green housing development were initially guaranteed 10% of the slots in a new state of the art selective magnet school in the gentrifying area, but they were excluded after the first year of operation on the grounds that they could not keep up with their academically selected classmates. Interviews and observations indicate some students are unable to enrol or are pushed out of both Ren2010 public and charter schools, and that admissions favour those low-income students with the cultural capital to navigate the system (Fleming et al, 2009; Lipman, 2011). Ren2010 mixed-income schools have significantly fewer low-income students than the original schools. Even for those Ren2010 schools that are initially enrolling students demographically similar to those displaced, in gentrifying areas the goal is to attract middle-class school 'consumers'. CPS's chief executive officer remarked to the press, 'For far too long, middle-class families have gone private or Catholic or fled to the suburbs. We're starting to reverse that trend' (quoted in Duffrin, 2006). Thus the primary result may be displacement.

Concerns about mixed-income schools as a tool of permanent displacement are a central theme in my field notes from community meetings, public hearings, press conferences and rallies opposing Ren2010 across the city (Lipman, 2011). Most displaced public housing students have been relocated to schools academically and demographically similar to those they left, with 84% attending schools with below-average district test scores and 44% attending schools on probation for low test scores (Catalyst Chicago, 2007). In general, displaced elementary students transferred from one low-performing school to another with virtually no effect on student achievement[5] (Gwynne and de la Torre, 2009).

Mixed-income housing

Moreover, research on HOPE VI elsewhere shows original residents' children are not attending new mixed-income schools because of displacement (Raffle et al, 2003; Varady et al, 2005). While HOPE VI has transformed some public housing units into more attractive buildings and communities and improved living conditions for some public housing residents, there is substantial evidence that many have not benefited. Serious problems include inadequate relocation support, continued racial segregation, lack of meaningful resident participation in relocation and in new developments, insufficient affordable housing options and exclusion of public housing families from mixed-income developments (Popkin et al, 2004). HOPE VI developments generally create fewer units than they tear down, and many of the new units are not affordable to displaced families.

Maximising returns on investments is driving this outcome. In the 1990s, private developers interested in investing in public housing redevelopment exerted pressure to change the formula from one-to-one replacement of public housing to no more than one third public housing residents. They claimed a larger percentage would jeopardise the attraction of market rate and affordable buyers (Bennett et al, 2006a). Renée Glover, chief executive officer of Atlanta Housing Authority, said in 2005, 'The long-term success of mixed-income communities must be driven by the same market factors that drive the success of every other real estate development' – attracting market rate renters is the priority and keeping public housing residents below 40% is a principle. Mixed-income developments in Chicago follow the formula one third public housing, one third affordable,[6] and one third market-rate units. Indeed, some scholars question whether mixed income is actually the goal (Bennett, 2006).

Studies of HOPE VI mixed-income developments lead one to question claims that middle-class residents will deploy their social capital to benefit low-income residents. Bennett, Hudspeth and Wright (2006a) could identify only a 'smattering of evidence' that mixed-income communities improve the life chances of low-income people. The assumption of New Urbanists that proximity will lead to social connections is also questionable. Researchers found little social interaction across class, and in some cases conflict between public housing residents and homeowners in HOPE VI mixed-income developments (Raffel et al, 2003; Varady et al, 2005). In the Orchard Park development adjoining the Cabrini Green public housing in Chicago, developers erected a fence to separate market-rate from public housing units. And Boyd's (2005) research shows that although middle and upper middle class black homeowners returning to the gentrifying African American South Side believed they were contributing to the upgrading of everyone in the community, black gentrification as a strategy for racial uplift misses the differential opportunities for low and middle-income African Americans to live in and participate in the new communities. Similarly, Joseph's (2008) study of early resident experiences at a new mixed-income development on Chicago's South Side found limited social relations across class.

In Chicago, evidence suggests that the PFT has generated displacement and racial containment, not mixed-income living, for most public housing residents. Demolition has far out-paced replacement construction. In the first six years of the PFT (up to September 2005), Chicago Housing Authority had constructed or rehabilitated only 766 public housing units in mixed-income communities (Wilen and Nayak, 2006). In 2009, 54% of the original Madden/Wells public housing residents surveyed were using rent vouchers in the private market, 29% were living in public housing and 17% no longer received housing assistance. Just 18% of all respondents lived in PFT mixed-income housing and the developments were located in predominantly low-income and African American neighbourhoods (Buron and Popkin, 2010). This confirms Wilen and Nayak's (2006) estimates that only about 20% of former residents would be able to return to their original locations revamped as mixed-income developments because of a lack of one-to-one replacement housing, the inadequate size of new apartments, settlement elsewhere after years of displacement and inability to meet the new developments' selection criteria. Under the 1998 Quality Housing and Work Reform Act, designed to promote 'self-sufficiency', public housing tenants in HOPE VI mixed-income developments must meet a strict set of eligibility criteria, including being lease-compliant, working at least 30 hours a week, having no unpaid utility bills or recent criminal convictions and passing drug tests (Hackworth, 2007). Moreover, they must submit to regular drug screening and housekeeping checks and specific behaviour rules (Joseph, 2008). Joseph's study of early resident experiences concludes that the public housing tenants who moved into the mixed-income development were substantially different from non-movers. They had better mental and physical health, higher incomes, smaller families, more education, and met all the selection criteria. As Janet Smith (2006) concludes, 'We can expect poverty to go down in some of these new mixed-income communities but not necessarily because poor people have escaped poverty – rather because poor people have been moved out and replaced by higher income families' (p 277).

Democratic deficits

In mixed-income housing and school policy in Chicago, public–private partnerships and appointed advisory groups typify the democratic deficits that characterise neoliberal governance. In a school district that is 85% low income and 91% students of colour, a mayoral-appointed school board comprised of corporate chief executive officers, bankers and real estate developers decides school closings with little genuine public participation. The exclusion of African American and Latino students, parents and the schools' teachers from decisions that deeply affect them is a prominent theme in the rallies, press conferences, town hall meetings and forums related to Ren2010. In my interviews with those affected, a consistent criticism is that the school community was not consulted. Some teachers and families reported that they were not even informed in advance that their school was to be closed:

> We were not informed [even] a month ahead of time. It was like a couple of weeks. And we were not informed by word of mouth. We had a flier. Basically, it was like this. Read this. Take it home and read it. And I mean, it's like, it's closing and there's nothing we can do about it. No voting, no taking a stand or nothing. This is law. (Parent interview in Lipman et al, 2007, p 39)

This parallels the experience of public housing residents systematically locked out of decisions about their housing. As Bennett et al (2006a) write in their study of the transformation of public housing in Chicago: 'From the standpoint of the city and CHA [Chicago Housing Authority], effective dialogue with public housing residents appears to be consultation in which the residents, at the outset and throughout the process, agree to premises advanced by city and public housing agency officials' (p 202). As in other HOPE VI cities, Chicago Housing Authority resident organisations had to pry their way in with demonstrations, noisy public hearings, persistent organising, lawsuits, and even the intervention of the UN Special Rapporteur on Adequate Housing (Wright, 2006).

It is not an exaggeration to claim that people who have faced dislocation, containment and moral rectification through slavery, the black codes, segregation, red lining and urban renewal are again displaced, contained and socially engineered through neoliberal housing and education policy. Public housing residents and parents are 'objectified', 'acted on by progressive policy action', and 'treated' through programmes to promote better housekeeping, work motivation and social behaviours in schools (Bennett et al, 2006b, p 10). The 'dispersal consensus' is a colonial model that denies low-income people of colour the capacity to know and act in their own interests, including the right to stay in their own reinvested schools and homes.

'Root shock'

As HOPE VI reached the end of its first decade, far fewer units had been built than were lost under the policy, and few residents had returned to their communities refashioned as mixed income. The same was true for schools under Ren2010. Residents and students suffered the trauma of dislocation, some, numerous times (Popkin, 2006). Fullilove (2005), writing about urban renewal in the 1950s, describes the psychic pain of displacement and loss of community as 'root shock' – 'the traumatic stress of the loss of [one's] lifeworld' (p 20). Fullilove writes,

> People, too, need roots. Human communities, like the tree, cannot produce their "crown" without the massive network of connections that move nourishment from the earth to the entire organism of the group. The evil of urban renewal is that people were stripped of their roots, and forced, without aid, to struggle through the period of shock to replant themselves as best they might. (p 191)

In my interviews and observations, 'root shock' captures the experience of displaced students, often to schools outside their immediate neighbourhoods and in some cases to as many as four schools in three years. Some parents reported they were given little notice and siblings were sent to different schools. A parent described her experience:

> Children were separated, because my boys were separated.... My younger son [age four] was sent all the way to [school].... But they were getting out at the same time, which was hard on me, you know, because my older son [age seven] couldn't get out on time to come get [younger son]. So [my younger

son] he's over here being let out amongst the crowd ... it was very frustrating that whole year. (quoted in Lipman et al, 2007, p 42)

In interviews with parents and teachers, we heard about the anxiety experienced by dislocated students:

> And then another factor which is a factor in education is most students are comfortable when they leave one grade to go to another grade and they know you ... versus transferring to [a new school] and this has been happening with transfer students ... versus going into a school and you don't even know the teachers, you don't know anybody ... so, you've got to make all these new adjustments ... whereas, when a student has been at [home school] since Kindergarten, it's like going home. (Teacher interview, quoted in Lipman et al, 2007, p 30)

Schools in African American and Latino working-class urban communities are often pathologised, but they are far more complex spaces in which community and caring often prevail, although there are also uncaring teachers and inadequate resources. What may appear to outsiders as 'deprived', 'run-down', even pathological communities and 'bad' schools, have far more nuanced meanings for those who live there. The 'choice' to uproot oneself is reserved for the economically and racially privileged. It is qualitatively different from forced removal from one's school and community and relocation to a mixed-income community where one may be marginalised. The meaning of existing community and the traumatic experiences of displacement are not to be found in the planners' designs to engineer mixed-income development. Urban anthropologist Susan Greenbaum (2002) points out that memories of the personal hardships and losses caused by mass relocations under the urban renewal policy should provoke concern about the effects of HOPE VI. Underlying this social engineering is a discourse of cultural and moral deficiency.

Moralising poverty and educational failure

At the core of this policy agenda is a nexus of academic discourses and ideologies that substitute cultural explanations for structural causes of poverty, naturalise the values and behaviours of the middle class, and promote individual responsibility and market solutions. The central premise of HOPE VI is that concentrations of very low-income public housing residents produce social pathologies (violence, drug abuse, gangs, unemployment, low academic achievement), which are at the root of poverty (Popkin, 2006). HOPE VI promotes mixed-income housing with the aim to transform residents as much as to transform housing (Zhang and Weisman, 2006). This is quite explicit in HOPE VI goals: '[T]he intentional mixing of incomes and working status of residents' will 'promote the economic and social interaction of low-income families within the broader community, thereby providing greater opportunity for the upward mobility of such families' (US Department of Housing and Urban Development, quoted in Bennett et al, 2006b, p 20).

Michael Katz (1989) outlines a long history of delineating the 'deserving' and 'undeserving poor' as an 'enduring attempt to classify poor people by merit' (p 9). The concentration-of-poverty-breeds-pathology thesis invokes this tradition in its racialised form. Although temporarily discredited in US public policy discourse in the 1970s (even though it is very much present in cultural deficit theories in education), the 'culture of poverty' was revived with the deconcentration thesis. Bruce Katz of the Brookings Institution cites public housing as 'the most egregious example of how spatial concentration of poverty leads to welfare dependency, sexual promiscuity, and crime' (quoted in Bennett et al, 2006a, p 194). The solution for these 'marginal citizens' is action by the 'therapeutic state' to normalise their behaviours through spatialised forms of resocialisation (Imbroscio, 2008). This civilising discourse is joined to the architectural determinism of the New Urbanist school of city planners who claim the architecture of high-rise public housing shapes the destiny of poor people. As urban sociologist Janet Abu-Lughod (2005) points out, 'The awful conditions in the projects were redefined as a "new pathology" caused by the high-rise architecture itself' (p 299). Thus, New Urbanist architects are enlisted to design mixed-income 'communities' with fewer units on site, pedestrian streetscapes and the majority of units set aside for more affluent households.

The mixed-income schools argument is also rooted in a cultural deficit model. Kahlenberg (2001) tells us, 'Money does matter to educational achievement, but research – and common sense – tells us that the people who make up a school, the students, parents, and teachers matter more' (p 3). He claims middle-class students have greater motivation, superior language skills, more positive attitudes about school and better behaviour than their low-income peers. He also argues that middle-class parents are more likely to promote effective schools for their children, and these advantages will spill over to lower-income students whose parents are, he claims, less involved and effective advocates for their children. There is a long history of locating school failure in the US in the 'deficient' cultures, languages and family structures of immigrants, the working class and people of colour. In this tradition, deconcentration of poverty is a racially coded morality discourse that simultaneously targets for correction African American 'inner-city' communities and the public institutions (housing and schools) with which they are identified. Haymes (1995) argues that the '... concepts "public" and "private" now act as racialized metaphors, the private is equated with being "good" and "white" and the public with being "bad" and "black"' (p 20). Here the logics of capital and 'race' intertwine to eliminate public housing and close schools in black communities, clearing the way for redevelopment, minus the original residents.

Teachers and administrators we interviewed in schools in the Mid-South also recounted a history of disinvestment – shrinking resources, lack of support for teachers and cuts in support staff as they were held to ever-more stringent standards (Lipman et al, 2007). In both housing and schools the discourse of mixed income and Ren2010 reframes displacement and privatisation as choice. In reality, the majority of low-income families in the areas experiencing mixed-income development have little choice. Most will not be able to live in new developments, and they must negotiate an extremely tight housing market. Children are transferred from one school to the next with few good schools available, and they have no guarantee of a place in new mixed-income or charter schools.

Weber (2002) argues that the neoliberal state has to grapple with two contradictory imperatives: creating conditions for capital accumulation and managing potential political resistance (Weber, 2002). Mixed-income policies can be interpreted as a response to these imperatives. They support capital accumulation while deflecting attention from structural roots of poverty and racism and disinvestment in low-income communities of colour.

Conclusion

I am not suggesting that mixed-income schools and communities are fundamentally wrong. Reducing 'race' and class segregation in housing and education has been a central focus of democratic policy and movements for greater social inequality in the US. However, mixed-income developments spawned by neoliberal policy are a far cry from organic and egalitarian communities. Nor are they a result of greater racial tolerance or reduced poverty or equalisation of resources. The evidence from HOPE VI and plans for mixed-income schools brings into question who is served by projects that are framed as 'race' and class uplift. More people are displaced than have access to new mixed-income opportunities, and, in any case, the evidence does not support the efficacy of social mix as a remedy for entrenched educational and economic inequality. Deconcentration policies actually undermine critical social support networks in low-income communities and dilute the political power of low-income people of colour. They obscure structural inequalities and economic and policy decisions that have produced poverty and disinvestment and neglect and deterioration of public housing and urban public schools, discursively shifting the terrain of public policy from economic redistribution to behaviour modification. This obligates the state to do nothing about the structural roots of poverty, racism, substandard and scarce affordable housing, and inadequate schools.

Current mixed-income policies further neoliberal urban spatial restructuring in the interest of capital accumulation, racial exclusion and displacement, and privatisation of public assets. They essentially deny the urban poor the right to place (Imbroscio, 2008). Despite good intensions by some local housing and education advocates, mixed-income schools and housing under HOPE VI legitimate the displacement of those who formerly lived there on the premise of bettering them. In this sense, they contribute to gentrification as a revanchist process of reclaiming the city for the middle classes (Smith, 1996). This is a deeply colonial project that essentialises culture and pathologises low-income people of colour while undermining their participation in fundamental decisions about their lives – where to live and where to send their children to school – all couched in the language of choice.

Poverty and marginalisation of people in 'inner cities' cannot be resolved by their forced mobility. In addition to critiquing the nearly hegemonic 'dispersal consensus' (Imbroscio, 2008), there is an urgency to address the structural and ideological roots of the problem with fresh solutions that do not simply replicate problematic top-down state welfare policies of the past (Clarke and Newman, 1997). Perhaps the most pressing need is for collaboration of scholars, housing and education planners, and communities affected to begin to develop a programme that addresses the economic, cultural/ideological and political dimensions of poverty and marginalisation in urban areas. In part, the power of the deconcentration thesis, even in the face of evidence to the contrary, rests on the lack of an alternative social programme around which critics and those affected might rally.

Notes

[1] This is reflected in Chicago forums and symposia that bring together housing and school officials with key foundation and local political actors (for example, MacArthur Foundation and Metropolitan Planning Council, 2005).

[2] Legends South, a $593 million development where major housing projects stood on the south side of Chicago, is being developed by Michaels Development Corporation with 77% of all investment coming from federal, state and local public funds (personal communication, Michaels Development, 10 December 2004).

[3] Chicago has 157 TIFs that encompass 26% of the city's land area; 77 were created between 1996 and 2002, many in near downtown areas already undergoing real estate development (Smith, 2006, p 291).

[4] Funding disparities range from annual per pupil expenditures of more than $15,000 to less than $4,000 (Biddle and Berliner, 2002). The wealthiest 10% of school districts spend almost 10 times more than the poorest 10% (Darling-Hammond, 2004, p 608).

[5] Eight of 10 students displaced by school closings transferred to schools that ranked in the bottom half of system on standardised tests (Gwynne and de la Torre, 2009).

[6] A household income of 80%-120% of metropolitan area median annual income, $75,000, qualifies for 'affordable' units.

NINE

Social mix as the aim of a controlled gentrification process: the example of the Goutte d'Or district in Paris[1]

Marie-Hélène Bacqué and Yankel Fijalkow

Introduction

This chapter examines the link between gentrification and so-called social mix policies. Based on an analysis of social and urban transformations in progress in Goutte d'Or, a working-class[2] and immigrant Paris neighbourhood, we contend that public policies focusing on social mix often actually serve the ends of gentrification. In the case in point, such policies tend to result in 'controlled' gentrification. We demonstrate that the gentrification process launched in Goutte d'Or partly stems from such policies that thrive in a tight housing market and converge with the residential and territorial investment strategies of middle and upper middle-class households. Urban projects sponsored by public authorities help to create pressure on housing and drum up expectations of social change among these households.

Gentrification and social mix policies have long been tackled differently in urban research and public debates due to their different origins and histories. Gentrification is an academic term first coined by Ruth Glass, and in France, at least, its use has continued to be largely restricted to academia (Glass, 1963). Social mix, however, goes back further to 19th-century urban policies and city planning. Its current success can be attributed to the negative social, political and academic representations of working-class neighbourhoods that are perceived primarily as 'rough' or 'problem neighbourhoods'.

Recent research publications have already pointed up the links between mix and gentrification based on analyses of other national contexts (Atkinson and Bridge, 2005; Slater, 2006; Lees, 2008). They share our reservations concerning the assumptions underpinning social mix policies, their effects and the supposed benefits of gentrification (Bacqué and Fol, 2003; Bacqué, 2005). We wish to pursue this debate further here by analysing the manner in which the rhetoric concerning mix has come to dominate public debate in France to the extent of becoming both a postulate and an objective, as well as the way in which it serves as a screen for gentrification projects. Urban research integrates a phenomenon of globalisation that highlights comparable urban transformation processes in very different national and cultural contexts and has also been influenced by the internationalisation process driven by the increasing importance of international English-language reviews and the way in which networks and exchanges are structured. Concepts, notions and theories circulate before being re-appropriated and transformed from one context to the next (Lees et al, 2008). Nevertheless, an explanation of ideological contexts and schools of research is necessary before we can proceed with any worthwhile comparative approaches, and this chapter is based on this premise.

Our work draws on empirical research conducted over the past six years in the same neighbourhood. We have analysed the different phases in urban policies and projects in the Goutte d'Or district since the 1960s based on municipal archives, various city planning documents and interviews conducted with local actors and elected representatives. We have studied population patterns and data provided by social landlords to assess the profile of social housing occupants and housing allocation policies, tackled the transformation of the stock of private housing through detailed descriptions of buildings based on interviews held with tenants, owner-occupiers and landlords, and analysed recent ownership trends and property developments. Last, we have monitored local associations and self-help groups as well as participation-based structures set up by the Paris Municipal Council since 2002.

In this chapter we first describe and discuss the scientific and political contexts in which the two concepts of gentrification and social mix have been used in the French context and then, how they have been a factor in focusing urban debates and public policies around the middle classes. We then analyse how the objective of social mix has contributed to how the urban and housing policies of the municipality of Paris have been set up and implemented in a working-class and immigrant neighbourhood, La Goutte d'Or. We go on to describe the effects of such policies and discourses; more specifically, how the expectation of urban change for newly arrived residents has created a climate of confrontation and competition between local social groups.

Gentrification and social groups

Research into gentrification was begun in the 1960s by Ruth Glass and has subsequently produced an abundant international – mostly academic – body of literature. It has received a boost in recent times with increased socio-spatial polarisation in urban areas. This research describes the conquest of former working-class neighbourhoods by the middle and upper middle classes and the resulting transformations, and usually deals with the social and cultural profiles of the new arrivals. It only rarely discusses the question of where those who are forced out actually end up living (Slater, 2006).

'Gentrification' did not enter the French urban sociology lexicon until quite late on, and the notion of *embourgeoisement* (literally, becoming bourgeois) had long been preferred for describing this type of change (Fijalkow and Préteceille, 2007). It should be noted in this respect that unlike their Anglo-Saxon counterparts, French inner-city neighbourhoods retained their bourgeois standing and market valuation and the move back into downtown areas was not therefore a marked phenomenon. Although social transformation processes do indeed exist in working-class or mixed neighbourhoods that tend to result in middle-class predominance, as Edmond Préteceille has demonstrated, such processes are of several different types inasmuch as they concern both suburban and downtown territories with contrasting features and involve very different social groups and trajectories (Préteceille, 2007). Even though gentrification is now a major theme in French urban research as illustrated by the recent publication of two special editions of reviews focusing specifically on this issue (*Sociétés Contemporaines*, 2006 and *Espaces et Sociétés*, 2008), it remains a contentious term because of the way in which it is used so broadly and tends to blur different types of *embourgeoisement* involving different social groups – middle and upper middle classes – by assimilating them under a single generic term.

The use of the French notion of *embourgeoisement* also drew on sociological suppositions influenced by Marxism and the sociology of Pierre Bourdieu that assimilated 'the gentrifiers' with the *petite bourgeoisie* and by inference with the ruling classes, or at the very least considered them to be of one purpose with the latter, both culturally and economically. This semantic discussion also masks a sociological debate that is still ongoing in respect of the definition and boundaries of the middle classes and especially their relation to other social groups. Thence, the term gentrification was taken up in the 1980s and used in French sociological research dealing with the 'new middle classes' or 'alternative classes' to describe those groups that worked in the arts, healthcare and the social services as well as their cultural model and basis of engagement (Bidou, 1984; Chalvon-Demersay, 1984). These social groups were presented as vectors for social change and innovators advocating the values of conviviality and exchange. One of their specific features lay in their relationship to their surrounding territory where the neighbourhood was seen as a village in which the 'right dose' of social mix and a cosmopolitan environment was highly valued. In order to continue to exist in this social space, the new middle classes needed the working classes already living there – even as they helped to push them out – while also fearing the arrival of another middle-class group: executives and professionals.

One of the key issues tackled in French and international research has been the relations between the old and new inhabitants, that is, between the middle classes on the one hand, and the working class and immigrant populations on the other. Radically different situations have been described depending on the context and the stage of gentrification (Butler with Robson, 2003), ranging from avoidance to cohabitation and even including confrontation (Smith, 1996). French research has stressed the social and residential trajectories of households in assessing these social dynamics (Simon, 1997; Authier, 2003). Thence the notion of gentrification focuses directly on the definition of the various different groups comprising the middle classes and their strategies for occupying urban space.

Social mix and the middle classes

The middle classes and their relations with the working class also lie at the heart of social mix policies. In the face of an increase in various forms of social insecurity, the 'ideal mix' is presented as a remedy to social and urban exclusion. It pits a 'balanced' society with a harmonious blend of social classes, ethnic groups and different generations against the fear of a rupture in social cohesion. The middle classes act as guarantors of this 'balance' through their involvement in social activities and the values and norms to which they ascribe.

But the theme of diversity and social mix is not new to urban policies and practices (Sarkassian, 1976), and it emerged along with the earliest public housing policies. In the late 19th and early 20th centuries, the issue of dispersing or concentrating social housing in France was the subject of parliamentary debates when the first social housing laws were being deliberated (Magri, 1995). In many European countries and in the US it has played a central role in the reconfiguration of housing policies and urban renovation and regeneration over the past two decades. In France, from the 1980s on, mix was earmarked as a political objective and dealt with in a number of laws, notably the law of July 1991, *loi d'Orientation pour la Ville*, known as the anti-ghetto law, which proclaimed 'access to the city for all'. Within the spirit of this law, combating segregation precluded building neighbourhoods of uniform character and diversity in housing and was insisted on as one of the underlying prerequisites for social cohesion. The law requires communes with a population of over 200,000 and a housing pool comprising less than 20% of social housing to undertake social housing schemes or face paying a tax. But it was at a local level that social mix policies really began to be developed and implemented. Much research has gone into analysing the effects of these policies that have influenced the social profile of major housing developments in France, and are now based on dispersing the lowest-income families throughout the urban space and attempts at diversifying the populations of working-class neighbourhoods. In the US, this debate had already been initiated in the early 1960s by Herbert Gans who, in response to the work of Jane Jacobs, contested the supposed benefits of social heterogeneousness based on his research into the new town of Levittown (Gans, 1961). Ten years later, in what is probably one of the most frequently quoted articles in French urban sociology, two French researchers, Jean-Claude Chamboredon and Madeleine Lemaire (1970), used their research into a major residential complex in the Greater Paris area to show that spatial proximity does not necessarily create social proximity and may be at the root of social conflicts over such things as education standards, for example. In particular, they stressed that social and residential trajectories are essential to understanding the relationship of individuals to their neighbourhood. These findings were corroborated and brought up to date by subsequent research in the 1980s (Pinçon, 1982), even though the notion of 'diversity' continued to be widely used in housing allocation policies.

Recent research criticising the notion of mix abounds and has focused in particular on urban regeneration policies and their effects (Lelévrier, 2007, 2008). It challenges the meaning of this ill-defined notion. What mix are we talking about – that of income, socio-professional categories, generations or origins? At what level is mix determined: building, neighbourhood, city or even conurbation? These researchers analyse the underlying premises, especially the contention that the middle classes act as guarantors of the social functioning of a neighbourhood, that they are the natural coordinators and help educate by example or enhance the social capital and networks of their working-class neighbours. These are the very arguments advanced to justify the gentrification of working-class neighbourhoods or to spread gentrification on the grounds of necessary social mix. Whereas it would be difficult to launch a project advocating the conquest of working-class districts, there is an almost unanimous consensus around projects lauding the benefits of mix in the name of social cohesion for the good of the working class as a whole.

Ambiguities inherent in Parisian municipal mix policies

Paris is an interesting case study inasmuch as social mix was one of the objectives underpinning the city planning and housing policy of the new city council elected in 2001. It is important to bear in mind that this council, headed by the Socialist Mayor Bertrand Delanoé, was the first left-leaning administration to run Paris after decades of rule by the right.

The theme of mix is not new to Paris. It was already raised in the studies carried out at the end of the 1970s by the council's city planning agency, *Atelier parisien d'urbanisme* (APUR – Paris city planning forum) that focused on the 'ghettoisation' of certain districts in the capital. During this period, the council launched projects to renovate working-class districts that contained subsidised social housing programmes for low-income households. But from 2000 on, social mix was promoted essentially via housing policy and social housing projects. The obligation that all new housing schemes had to include 25% of social housing was written into the *plan local d'urbanisme* (local city planning guidelines), as was the push for a geographical redistribution of the social housing pool in affluent neighbourhoods.

This strategy must also be seen in the context of rising property prices. Housing prices affect private sector rents and hamper household mobility. The social housing pool became a safe haven (with a very low turnover rate in the order of 5%) whereas the (frequently old) private sector housing pool shrank slightly, making it more difficult to find affordable accommodation and putting upward pressure on the households awaiting decent accommodation (there was a waiting list for social housing of over 100,000 people).

There has been an undeniable *embourgeoisement* of the capital (defined as the 20 arrondissements that make up central Paris) since 1980 (Pinçon-Charlot and Pinçon, 2004). The number of workers and employees living there has fallen while numbers of higher level managers, executives and members of the liberal professions have increased. The socio-professional categories[3] comprising entrepreneurs, senior managers and intermediary professionals made up 34.5% of the active population in 1954 and 64.8% in 1999; conversely workers and employees accounted for 65.5% in 1954 and 35.2% in 1999. Post-2000 property prices have risen considerably and there has been a catch-up effect in previously unaffected working-class districts. Nevertheless, while Paris as a whole has been subject to a phenomenon of *embourgeoisement*, it is also home to distressed populations of homeless people, people living on *RMI* (*Revenue minimum d'insertion*, social integration minimum income), clandestine immigrant populations or simply the poorest households at the bottom of the social ladder. The presence of these inhabitants has been brought to the attention of the general public by a series of incidents including fires in lodging houses, the squats organised by the association *Droit au logement*, some of which were evicted by the police using force, and by advertising campaigns such as that run by *Médecins sans frontières* which distributes tents to homeless people, or *Don Quichotte*, which set up a camp for homeless people along the Saint Martin Canal and organised a media campaign to highlight their plight.

So social mix policies are not aimed at the most distressed groups. They have a twofold purpose: (i) eliminating pockets of poverty and continuing the city planning strategy pursued by the previous administration since the 1970s; and (ii) keeping working-class and particularly middle-class households in Paris. In a hot property market, the debate is refocusing on the middle classes and worries that they will be forced out, thus accelerating the depopulation of the capital. Split sales (unit by unit) of buildings[4] jeopardise the position of middle-income private tenants while high property prices discourage potential buyers living in social housing from trying to buy property. Thence during the 2007 local election campaign, the right and centrist opposition parties proposed to boost the aid given to middle-class households to enable them to buy property. There is a consensus that the middle classes – who are assumed to be the lynchpin in the whole process – must be preserved in the name of social mix. But exactly what middle classes are we talking about here?

Parisian social mix policies have taken on two forms: a policy of renovating old working-class districts to attract the middle classes and the construction of social housing in high-income neighbourhoods. The Goutte d'Or has been subject to the first of these and gentrification is presented as an inevitable but controllable process based around the construction of social housing for middle-class and working-class families, developing local facilities and using participatory structures to respond to residents' needs.

Goutte d'Or: a working-class, immigrant neighbourhood

Goutte d'Or is one of Paris's last working-class neighbourhoods close to the centre of the city. It dates from the 19th century when it was built on speculative real estate and has always been a working-class area. Apartments were gradually split into bedsits and the Goutte d'Or housing pool is essentially made up of small, old rented apartments offering little in the way of comfort (in 1962, 50% still had no indoor toilet; in 1990, 14%). The area has welcomed successive waves of immigrants from Europe and later from the Maghreb, sub-Saharan Africa, Asia and, more recently, from Eastern Europe (Toubon and Messamah, 1990). Goutte d'Or has gradually become home to the largest proportion of non-French people in all of Paris (11.74% of heads of households in 1962; 34.8% in 1982; 32.7% in 1990), and a major proportion of its residents are still workers (51% of the active population in 1962; 49% in 1982; 21% in 1990). *Petite Afrique* or *Bamako de l'Europe* as it is alternatively known, is an important commercial centre, notably for exotic produce. The neighbourhood contains a well-established African market that serves the entire Greater Paris region.

The area has a rich social and political history. It was a stopping-off point for Algerian immigrants and their political organisations during the colonial war of independence and in the 1970s it was a hotbed of activity for leftist and immigrant defence groups. But it was only in the late 1970s that a network of local associations emerged to tackle social and urban issues at the initiative of mainly middle-class activists.

From renovation to mix

The project to transform Goutte d'Or is part of a long-term strategy and can be analysed in three stages. In the early 1980s, the council approved an initial project to renovate the southern part of the neighbourhood comprising the demolition of 1,400 dwellings, the construction of 900 units of social housing and incentives to invest in private property in the area. The project was based on the findings of a number of reports prepared by municipal departments that stressed the poor quality and dilapidated state of housing and overcrowding as well as the concentration of immigrant populations.[5] A process of gradual dilapidation is described thus:

> These population movements, coupled with uncontrolled development of private property has resulted in a

wave of urban decay that has swept through the entire neighbourhood. [author translation][6]

Squatting, prostitution, illegal bedsits and delinquency all serve as a basis for legitimising the project to: 'develop the Southern part of the area with a view to triggering a physical and notably a sociological transformation' (19 September 1983 [author translation]).[7] The colourful imagery ('urban decay'/'transformation') and hygienist vocabulary are used to justify the renovation. While the issue of diversifying the local population is never far away, it is not addressed officially, although interviews conducted with people who were key actors at that time show that it did exist.

A significant activist movement rapidly developed around the Paris Goutte d'Or association created specifically for this purpose in 1983, and this comprises the second phase. The project was opposed on heritage, social and procedural grounds. First, the association sought out supplementary expert opinions and scientific research to highlight the heritage value of the sites and to countermand the demolition orders. Second, while recognising the necessity of local authority intervention, it demanded that all inhabitants forced to move should be re-housed in the area, particularly immigrant families. It defended the neighbourhood's reputation and contended that its ethnic diversity was a major plus. Last, it denounced the high-handed attitude of the municipality and central government. A coalition made up of about 15 associations grew out of this umbrella association. Most were previously involved in social work or adult education and many were part of the catholic social movement. In 1984, Goutte d'Or was one of 22 experimental sites included in the *îlots sensible* (distressed urban areas) procedure, the first French social and urban development blueprint that bore similarities to North American 'Model Cities'. This blueprint was instrumental in the development of the network of associations. Faced with pressure on several fronts, Paris City Council was forced to highlight the social dimension of the operation, especially as regards the re-housing of Goutte d'Or residents, although this did not prevent large numbers of lodging house dwellers from being overlooked.[8] As a recent study has shown, the resulting social housing received a high proportion of low-income immigrant households which helped bolster the areas' working-class credentials and identity (Merlot, 2006). The associations were granted service concession arrangements to handle part of the local social services that largely contributed to institutionalising them and blunting their power of criticism (Bacqué, 2005).

In the mid-1990s, the council launched a new initiative to renovate the northern part of the neighbourhood that took on board some of the criticisms levelled at the policy's content and methods by the local associations, and this marks out the third phase in the project. In particular, the old strategy of demolishing entire blocks and changing the ground plan gave way to ad hoc demolition of buildings that were then rebuilt one-by-one in almost identical style from an architectural perspective. The council rolled out 'planning with a human face', thus echoing the 1980s slogan of the Paris Goutte d'Or association which maintained that 'our neighbourhood is our village'.[9] The political changeover following the 2002 local elections did not result in any major policy changes except perhaps a wish to accelerate the social and urban transformation of the area. The aim was no longer merely to re-house existing residents, but to diversify the population. The theme of mix came increasingly to the fore in national housing policy. In particular, it was sponsored by the *Agence Nationale de la Rénovation urbaine* (National Urban Renewal Agency) that funded the operation and insisted on a greater diversification in the types of housing being built. Social mix was also a municipal project. The discourse linking the presence of dilapidated buildings and poverty with the decay sweeping through the neighbourhood was replaced by village-based imagery calling for 'requalification' of an area with an inherent urban and social value. Whereas the former had been accompanied by an authoritarian demolition–reconstruction dynamic, the second underpinned a more measured planning approach whose objective was to build 'social mix'. This amounted to de facto gentrification, although this was not mentioned explicitly.

Beginnings of gentrification

This policy of diversification was based primarily on housing production but it also involved transforming the commercial fabric of the area, as well as the commercial basis for letting out and acquiring property. Different financial arrangements were reflected in the different property statuses. 'Intermediary' housing schemes were developed for middle-class households whereas the first phase of the operation had consisted only in social housing. The first housing programmes came under pressure from the *Agence Nationale de la Rénovation urbaine* that helped with financing and insisted that certain programmes were dedicated for the middle classes. Special attention was also paid to the allocation of social housing and the local council was allowed to depart from normal practice and to set one third of the social housing allocation aside for middle-class households. Thus, French social housing has the particularity of not focusing solely on the poorest households: taking account of the related income ceilings, 70% of French households are eligible to apply. Thus, the basis of allocation has come to be of major importance to both social landlords and the council. However, the social transformation was most in evidence in private housing. In the last five years, and especially since 2000, property prices have almost trebled. Statistics about real estate transactions reflect this evolution: since 2002 to 2005, a third of the buyers are managers and professionals: employees and workers sell their apartments to managers and professionals (Bougras, 2008). Rents have gone up over the same period – although not by as much – with average post-2000 increases of 60% (Florentin, 2007): see Figure 9.1.

Figure 9.1: Average price per m² and volume of transactions (1995–2006)

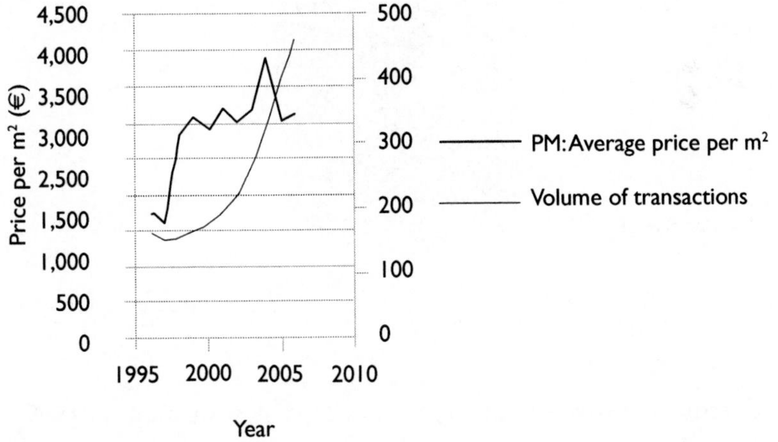

Source: Florentin (2007)

The impact of these policies on the local population profile is statically difficult to assess for the area as a whole. Since 1999, the French census has not been exhaustive. An analysis of changes in socio-professional categories between 1990 and 1999 already shows slight changes in relation to the city-wide trend while highlighting increased social diversity in the population make-up. Although the proportion of people belonging to the higher socio-professional categories in Goutte d'Or is only half what it is in Paris as a whole, in 1999 there were more such households than in 1990, particularly on the periphery and in the west of the area. And while the proportion of workers and employees has fallen, in 1999 it remained higher in the south of the neighbourhood where the social housing put up during the first phase of the project remains predominant. The social housing already built coupled with the number of families rehoused has ultimately consolidated the social and ethnic profile of the population in the southern sector, accentuating the social differentiation with the rest of the neighbourhood (see Figure 9.2).

Figure 9.2: Proprtions of higher socio-profesional category households in Goutte d'Or, 1990 and 19999

Executives, managers and higher intellectual professions in 1990

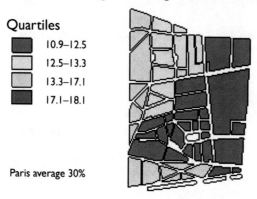

Quartiles

■	10.9–12.5
☐	12.5–13.3
☐	13.3–17.1
■	17.1–18.1

Paris average 30%

Executives, managers and higher intellectual professions in 1999

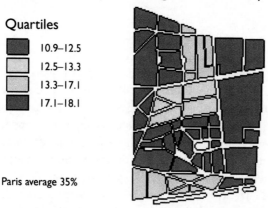

Quartiles

■	10.9–12.5
☐	12.5–13.3
☐	13.3–17.1
■	17.1–18.1

Paris average 35%

Source: Population Census INSEE 1990 and 1999

Two recent studies focusing on new owner-occupiers (Mandel, 2005) and changes in ownership patterns in four old buildings (Florentin, 2007) highlight the recent appearance of the higher intellectual professions (teachers, researchers, journalists, etc) in both rented and owned accommodation. They show that tenants and owners do not behave in the same way or have the same relationship with the surrounding neighbourhood. Tenants – often young with no children – are frequently only passing through, whereas those who have acquired property usually already have children and try to put down roots by exercising influence in property co-owner associations and local groups.

However, these changes are being hampered by the low-end, multi-ethnic business activity based in the neighbourhood. Goutte d'Or is one of the principal African markets serving the entire Greater Paris Region: clothing predominates in the northern sectors, food products in the south of the neighbourhood. The markets bring in a massive influx – particularly on Saturdays – of mostly male, non-French customers who arrive by public transport from all over Paris and its environs. The sheer volume of customers and the traders themselves clog up the public space, and while this activity is evidence of the area's economic vitality, it is viewed as a nuisance by both the council and the new arrivals.

The markets are a major source of grievance and legal complaints for the local residents, particularly the new middle-class arrivals, who complain of the crowds and the attendant illegal activities carried out by street hawkers, the poor quality of the products on sale and most notably the dearth of everyday European products. Closing down or overhauling this activity comprises one aspect of the planning strategy. Several projects are up-and-running such as *une rue de la mode* (a street dedicated to fashion) comprising low-rent commercial premises let out by a public operator to young fashion designers. Other projects to develop *une rue du design* or move the ethnic markets to a *marché des cinq continents* located on the city's periphery have run into opposition due to the economic buoyancy of the activities in question and firmly entrenched social practices. Even so, the commercial fabric of the area is changing bit by bit: witness the range of new stores that include a wine shop run by a former artist, an African art shop, a jazz club, an organic food store, a tea shop and an architect's office.

Thus, different images of the neighbourhood co-exist and are relayed in both the local and national media which alternate features on insecurity ('*l'enfer des crackeurs*' ['the terrifying world of crackheads' – author translation], *Le Monde*, 1 March 2005) with those that stress how the neighbourhood has changed and the resulting property investment opportunities ('*La lente métamorphose de la rue Myhra*' (*Le Parisien*, 30 November 2004).

So the development strategy consists of handling these expectations and helping local associations and decision makers with 'change enablement'. Although the associations previously frowned on the objective of social mix, they have since been made stakeholders in the different working groups tasked with working out the details of the project. They are mostly run by middle-class people – rarely of immigrant extraction – and are struggling to continue to present themselves as a counterweight to established power. Moreover, the council project has taken some of their criticisms on board through resident participation and recognition of local urban heritage. Their approach to social issues is heavily criticised by both the new arrivals who see them as undermining traditional local government practices and call for a return to the 'rule of law', and by the poorest sections of the community who do not feel that anyone is fighting their corner.

Waiting for gentrification: the 'new' residents get organised

Although the neighbourhood newcomers have heterogeneous profiles, different residential trajectories and different relations with their surrounding area, a sub-group of these new residents has tended to prevail in public debates and local participative democracy initiatives. This sub-group is made up of recently arrived residents living in the most upmarket buildings who have got to know each other through friends and cooption. Some of them have banded together in an association called *Droit au calme* (the right to a quiet neighbourhood [author translation]). Another anti-drug initiative has been launched by a group of people who bought apartments in a building sold off by a property developer. It subsequently attracted other like-minded residents who had attended local neighbourhood meetings. These people belong to the upper middle classes (university professors rather than secondary school teachers), and they tend to work more in media and the cultural sphere. They have virtually all acquired property in the area and a core group of about 20 meet in a local bar every week to exchange information, decide on ad hoc initiatives, and prepare meetings and arguments. Everyone is kept informed of current developments by email. This action underpins a wish to 'follow through on their actions' (Ion, 1997, p 23), and to remain in control of their highly individualist initiatives at all times.

These 'new' residents draw on two types of resource: political and cultural. They all consider themselves to be 'on the left' and many already have political experience so they know how to weigh up a potential conflict. They are adept at making themselves heard at a public meeting, using appropriate communication channels and mobilising the public through poster campaigns, petitions or demonstrations. They are able to deal with local representatives on an equal footing and also have direct access to various media as several work as journalists in well-known daily and weekly publications. In addition, they can use their cultural resources to pose as experts or at the very least, as informed citizens. They are perfectly aware of their social standing and public debating skills:

> ... the real problem for the authorities is that they are dealing with people who can speak up for themselves ... we are all property owners because tenants who feel unhappy with the situation prefer to leave while those in a weak position reckon that it's better not to upset their landlord. We are the only ones who aren't afraid of anyone and we're in the area to stay. People living in HLM [council flats] can put up with unbelievable stuff without complaining because most of them are behind with their rent. [author's translation][10]

They believe that their strategy of 'winning back the neighbourhood' is destined to succeed, even if this takes time: "I think we'll win out in the end. There is a coherent approach ... property prices have trebled ... this ultimately has a bearing" [author's translation]. They legitimise their presence in social terms as essential for making the neighbourhood function properly and bringing about the necessary transformation. They have taken up the theme of mix: "the neighbourhood needs people like us to bring the tone up" [author's translation].

Their residential trajectory sheds light on their relationship with their surrounding area and how they mobilise their resources. Most are first-time buyers who have moved from more affluent Parisian neighbourhoods. They bought before the boom when prices in the area – which was the only place in Paris where they could afford to buy – were still quite moderate. So their decision was a rational one guided by the property market. While most claim that they liked the diversity and local colour straight away in spite of slight reservations about the area's reputation, very few were actively looking to live there. Their choice was underpinned by a property investment strategy: many noted the work in progress when they visited the neighbourhood and moved in anticipation of urban and social change. But such change still seems a long way off and many have found the expected 'ethnic rub' and 'lively North African and Black African places' much harder to live in day-to-day. Hope has given way to louder demands and a feeling that the neighbourhood has gone downhill since they moved in. Most of their children go to private schools or public schools outside the area.

In this context, the arrival of these new residents and their active mobilisation provokes reactions and forms of resistance, but this little organised resistance expresses itself very sporadically. During the summer of 2007 several shop windows were broken and a climate of social tension appeared to develop around issues ranging from the approval of building work in jointly owned buildings forcing less well-off owners to sell up, to occupation of public space. Such conflicts are ample evidence that the 'social mix' that has resulted from this first phase in gentrification is a long way from providing the much longed-for harmony and social cohesion.

Conclusion

As we have seen, the principle of social mixing is often presented as a positive component of spatial justice, because this mixing would tend to be the opposite of urban segregation while giving access to all social groups to the totality of the urban space. But, in the case of Paris, characterised by the capital's transformation into a bourgeois city, what we notice is that this principle has been unfairly exploited to justify the changes in the populations of working-class neighbourhoods which are often perceived as degraded, dangerous and concentrations of poverty. The arrival of new populations coming from more middle-class backgrounds gets presented as modernisation and as territorial development, trending 'upwards'. In the name of social mixing, what it is in reality is the gentrification of working-class areas that is being set up by the public authorities. The politics of Paris that have been established by this perception rely on the production of social housing and the control of the way that housing gets populated, on how the public spaces are managed and on the transformation of the commercial apparatus. But they rely as well on the politics of image which presents a neighbourhood in transition and which has as its goal to attract the middle classes. This discourse conveys a negative image of working-class and immigrant neighbourhoods, offering the belief that they can only evolve via outside assistance, and more specifically via the 'middle classes'. There are winners and losers under this policy, and under the current conditions the losers are already the most economically distressed segments of the population. On the other hand, the middle classes, who are waiting for the promised gentrification and who are disappointed at not seeing it come, have begun to develop strategies for the more revanchist conquest of the urban space.

More generally, this reality questions the ideological baggage which comes with the notion of social mixing and which allows the revival of two suppositions. The first affirms that physical proximity would produce social proximity; the second sees within the cohabitation of middle and working classes the possibility of education by example, which is to say structuring of the second by the first or, in a more modern vision, the possibility of acquiring social capital. While this discussion is far from novel in the social sciences (Gans, 1961; Chamboredon and Lemaire, 1970), it doubtless deserves to be pursued by researchers, politicians and practitioners.

Notes
[1] Translated from the French by Neil O'Brien.

[2] Here we encounter the perennial problem of how to translate the French expression *populaire*, as in *classes populaires*, which has no neat equivalent in English. Although generalising here is a hazardous activity – and in any case, the French concept is a more all-embracing one than any equivalent social category in English – it is probably true to say that a lot of working-class people would be better-off than people belonging to the *classes populaires*, but quite a significant portion of the latter would be by no means poor. However, for want of a 'cosier translation', we have fallen back on the unsatisfactory compromise of 'working class'. The author would welcome any useful suggestions in this regard.

[3] Professions and socio-professional categories are classified based on a synthesis of profession (or former profession), grade and status (employee or self-employed). The classification aggregates three levels of overlapping variables: socio-professional groups (8 categories), socio-professional categories (24 and 42 categories) and professions (486 categories). The socio-professional groups are farmers, craftsmen and tradesmen, entrepreneurs, higher managers and executives, the liberal professions, the intermediary professions, employees and workers.

[4] Rental property belonging to institutional landlords is acquired by investors who subsequently sell it off, unit-by-unit, at prices that are unaffordable for the sitting tenants.

[5] APUR (Atelier parisien d'urbanisme) (1983) 'Le plan programme de l'Est parisien', Paris-projet.

[6] APUR (Atelier parisien d'urbanisme) (1983) 'Le plan programme de l'Est parisien', Paris-projet..

[7] The date in parentheses corresponds to a session of Paris Municipal Council.

[8] It is difficult to measure the number of lodging house occupants who left, as such establishments frequently operate illegally.

[9] Association newsletter, 1984.

[10] All author translations are of respondent interviews.

TEN

Beware the Trojan horse: social mix constructions in Melbourne

Kate Shaw

Introduction

From the time of its occupation Australia has been home to people from all over the world. Melbourne is considered the most 'European' of Australia's major cities and is one of the most culturally diverse. About 35% of metropolitan Melbourne's population was born overseas. The postwar inner-city population in particular was a social and cultural melting pot, with immigrants, artists, students, hippies and a solid working class connected mainly by economics and geography as the middle classes gradually abandoned the city for the ever-expanding suburbs.

But just as the white settlers decimated Australia's original peoples in the interests of diversification, so their successors engineer their own form of cultural cleansing in a context of increasing 'social mix'. This chapter tells the story of a city so diverse in cultural, social and economic terms that when a discourse of social mix appears in the public arena to explain a particular policy initiative, those with a genuine interest in diversity have reason to be concerned.

Melbourne's gentrification and its effect on diversity

Melbourne's gentrification is described well by Hackworth and Smith's (2001) three waves. The first wave came to the disinvested, deindustrialising and socially diverse inner city in the late 1960s in a context of ameliorating urban decline. Government strategies such as restoration grants and easing access to home ownership stimulated interest in the large areas of Victorian workers' cottages and terraces (Jager, 1986) that had been a source of cheap rental housing where they were not the subject of slum clearance projects (Logan, 1985; W.S. Shaw, 2005). Gentrification began in the inner city and spread unevenly through the east and south of the inner urban region (Figure 10.1), drawing people apparently attracted to the cultural diversity. The second wave in the 1980s was market-driven and fuelled in the latter part of the decade by a local property boom that followed the global stock market crash. Rapid increases in property values, changes in built form and displacement of the most vulnerable tenants generated significant opposition and a period of left local governance in the city. With support from the Labor government, inner-city councils were able to introduce heritage controls and low-income housing projects that succeeded in tempering the gentrification of some areas, delaying displacement, and maintaining the inner city's social and cultural mix for a while.

Figure 10.1: Inner Melbourne

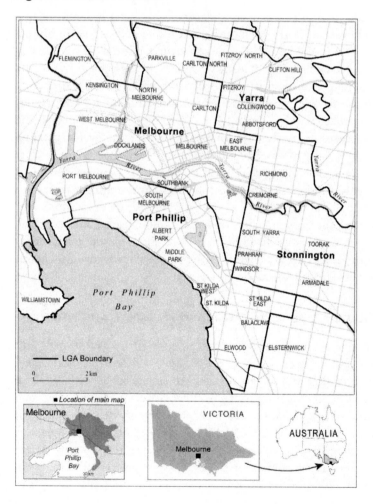

The global recession of the early 1990s ended the second wave of gentrification and the rapidly escalating property boom, and a decade of State Labor government. In 1992 an aggressively neoconservative government came into power on the promise of getting Victoria 'On the Move'. Premier Jeff Kennett instituted a programme of statutory reforms, local government amalgamations and boundary redrawings, privatisation of public services and utilities and disempowering of local communities that was more radical than Margaret Thatcher's in the UK in the 1980s. The third wave of gentrification was much more comprehensive than the first two, extending into areas that involved greater economic risk, requiring and receiving substantial State assistance. Enabled by legislative amendments, special acts of parliament, planning and building deregulations and policies to encourage development and reduce public input, large tracts of land throughout the inner metropolitan region were redeveloped. A joint State government and City of Melbourne initiative called 'Postcode 3000' encouraged residential conversion of warehouses and offices in the central city, led by model developments and financial incentives to building owners. A standard residential code was applied to land within a seven-kilometre radius from the city centre, which produced a large amount of cheaply constructed but highly priced in-fill housing. Inner-city land values increased dramatically through the 1990s, and by the end of the decade the working class and immigrant populations were heavily diminished, having been displaced by rent increases or taken advantage of the extraordinary rises in their once low-value land holdings and relocated to the suburbs. As the economic base of the inner city lifted, inner-Melbourne's socioeconomic diversity narrowed. Then, in the late 1990s, the government turned its attention to the city's public housing estates.

Australia has a very low proportion of public housing, at 5%, provided by the States and funded through a Commonwealth-State Housing Agreement (CSHA). The majority of Melbourne's public stock was built in the late 1950s and early 1960s and concentrated in high-rise towers after the 'slum clearance' programmes in the inner city demolished large areas of the workers' cottages and terraces that became so popular to gentrifiers only a few years later (indeed, early gentrifiers take the credit for the end of the slum clearance programmes and the institution of less concentrated – and more aesthetically pleasing – forms of public housing). Public housing was originally intended for 'working families', but with only small increases in the funding of the CSHA the stock grew slowly, and became increasingly targeted to the most disadvantaged. On the election of the conservative Howard government at the federal level in 1996, funding for public housing was severely cut. In 1997 a 'segmented waiting list' was introduced which gave priority to people who were homeless, at risk of homelessness, refugees, or those with 'special needs' (such as disability, mental health issues, drug and alcohol problems). The massive disjuncture between the number of people on waiting lists and available units meant usually that only those with multiple needs could be housed, producing concentrations not just of poverty but of people with 'high' and 'complex' needs (Commonwealth of Australia, 2004, p 24). The demonisation of Australian public housing estates that began with their construction was compounded by the focus not just on their aesthetics, but on their occupants.

The last frontier: the inner-Melbourne public housing estates

Victorian Premier Kennett had repeatedly expressed his desire to demolish a public housing tower, and in 1998 he announced that a high-rise building on the Kensington estate was the one. Kensington is a small district in the still industrial inner-west. It had been slow to gentrify, partly because of its former use as cattle saleyards and abattoirs, and because the west retained the bulk of Melbourne's residual heavy industry. It had a small but longstanding residential population of about 5,000, of which the public estate made up 30%, with the rest of the housing consisting mainly of remarkably intact workers' cottages. Hulse et al (2004) observe the strong sense of community that existed among the working class and increasingly culturally diverse population, having taken in Italians, Maltese and Greeks in the 1950s, 'people from Vietnam and South America from the late 1970s, from the former Yugoslavia and Turkey in the early 1980s, from China in the late 1980s, and from Horn of Africa countries such as Somalia and Eritrea in the 1990s' (Hulse et al, 2004, p 14). Local residents had formed a number of influential community organisations and facilities over the years, including the Kensington Public Tenants Association, the Kensington Women's Group, a neighbourhood house and a community centre that helped facilitate the development of Melbourne's first community credit cooperative. Most of these involved both public and private residents and made little distinction between them. In the 1980s the saleyards and abattoirs closed, and redevelopment plans were prepared in a participatory process involving the local community groups, with council and State Labor government support. The resulting development included new public housing, private housing, two housing cooperatives and an elderly persons' hostel.

While the tenants were being relocated from the tower prior to its demolition in 1999, the Kennett government canvassed the possibility of selling the entire estate to a private developer. An architectural firm was eventually commissioned to develop options for the site, with no public input. The preferred option proposed that 650 new units be built on the site, and that of these, two thirds be private in order to introduce 'an appropriate range of public and private housing' onto the estate (Government of Victoria, 1999). The Minister for Housing announced the scheme as 'a historic day for public housing in Victoria – the next step in an inner-city estate redevelopment which started with the demolition of the high rise tower', adding that the 'scenario must be attractive to the private sector to facilitate private sector participation in the redevelopment process' (Government of Victoria, 1999). There was no discourse of 'social mix' here: just an open process of assisting the private sector to access a 'high-risk' pocket of the inner city in as pure third-wave gentrification as could be.

Explicit mention of 'social mix' did not appear in government discourses until around the early 2000s, by which time the Kennett government had been replaced by a new Labor government. Victorian Premier Steve Bracks, with his economically conservative Treasurer John Brumby, reviewed the existing Kensington estate redevelopment plan and, notwithstanding their pledge to 'openness and transparency' and repudiation of everything the former government stood for, confirmed that it would proceed. It would be a public–private partnership, and local developer, the Becton Corporation, was awarded the contract in 2001. In addition to the tower already demolished, which had contained 108 units, all the walk-up buildings on the estate would be demolished ('walk-ups' are lower-rise buildings without lifts, usually four storeys).

This meant a loss of a total of 486 public units from the estate. The Office of Housing would upgrade the remaining 252 public units in the two other high-rise towers on the site. The private partner would build 195 new public units (totalling 447 public) and 421 new private units on the extensive public land around the towers, resulting in a total mix on the estate of 51:49. The government saw the redevelopment as 'a test bed for future inner city housing management' (Department of Human Services, 2002, section 4.1; npn). The 'project goals' were outlined as follows:

> To improve the quality of public housing stock and options
> by providing opportunities for reinvigorating the living

environment for all residents through balancing the public and private housing mix and better linking the former estate into the broader Kensington community.... The Kensington redevelopment is an important partnership between the Government, Becton Corporation and the local community to regenerate housing in the area. (Office of Housing, 2008)

In February 2003 a team from the Institute for Social Research at Swinburne University (Melbourne), headed by Kath Hulse, was engaged by the Office of Housing to prepare a social impact study for the redevelopment. By the time the research commenced, the tenants from the walk-ups had been relocated and the blocks demolished (Hulse et al, 2004, p 2). This meant that a longitudinal study of the displaced tenants was not possible (some relocated residents were tracked down but the sample size was not significant). It was also impossible to find out exactly how many bedrooms had been lost (walk-ups usually contain a mix of two-, three- and four-bedroom units). Nevertheless, Hulse et al were able to conclude that 1,800 people had lived in public housing on the site prior to the redevelopment, and that as only 800 people would be living in public housing there at the end of the redevelopment, about 1,000 public tenants were permanently displaced (2004, p xiv). This information is not available through the relevant government departments, which refer only to units and households, not to numbers of beds or people. It was eventually revealed, however, that only 20% of the relocated public tenants 'chose to return after settling in their new area' (Office of Housing, cited in Government of Victoria 2007) – although how much choice they had is contestable.

In an introduction to the report from the Swinburne team in 2004, the Victorian member for Melbourne Province stated that, 'This report is only one part of ongoing evaluation of this project which will continue over the remaining stages of the Kensington redevelopment' (Hulse et al, 2004, p ii). There has been no evaluation since. A substantial proportion of the private housing has been constructed and is already occupied, although the redevelopment will not be complete until late 2011. There has been no assessment so far of the extent of social mixing on the estate beyond the Swinburne team's preliminary findings, and no indication that such an assessment is likely.

It became clear early on that the social mix on the estate was to be structurally limited. Certainly the remaining high-rise towers stand separate and in stark contrast to the lower-rise private housing, which is clustered at the sunny, northern end of the estate. The figures in

Table 10.1 indicate the allocation of public and private units in buildings constructed by 2007.

Table 10.1: Mix of private and public dwellings at the Kensington site

Stage completed	Public dwellings built	Private dwellings built	% of public/ private
Henry St North	20	57	26/74
78 Clifford Terrace	97	0	100/0
65 Kensington Rd	11	0	100/0
Henry St South	0	33	0/100
Gower St South	0	86	0/100

Source: Reproduced from Government of Victoria (2007, p 72)

The 'balance of public and private housing mix' is mainly at a 'block-by-block' level as opposed to a mix of apartments within the buildings. The orientation and location of the new buildings speak volumes: the private housing very clearly connects not to the public housing to the south, but to the older and highly gentrifiable private housing across the road. The advertising for the new private units (with images of beautiful white people enjoying food and wine) is similarly revealing: 'If location is important, if quality is appreciated, if lifestyle matters.... Residents will have ample opportunities to immerse in village life with a mix of uniquely urban cafes, excellent restaurants and interesting shops nearby' (Becton Corporation, 2008). The emphasis is on the privately owned part of Kensington, beyond the housing estate. The property management company set up by Becton to manage residential aspects of the redevelopment makes the following statement on its website, so stark in its assessment of public housing (and by implication, its tenants) that it is worth reproducing at length.

Community sustainability as a key objective

The redevelopment of the Kensington public housing estate is not just a capital works project. The fundamental objective is to build a sustainable community. Consequently both Becton and the Office of Housing (OOH) need to focus on the broader economic, social and environmental aspects of the overall development. Failure to give as much attention to 'building community' as to 'building property' will mean that the problems the redevelopment seeks to overcome, namely the physical, economic and social isolation of public housing tenants, will be repeated.

Internationally, social mix is increasingly being seen as one strategy for enhancing community sustainability. The integration of public and private housing is not just a means to finance the redevelopment of public housing. It is also a strategy to develop a community with greater socio-economic diversity and thereby reduce the concentration of poverty.

Integration however is far more than the intermingling of private and public housing. In this instance it also means connectedness between the new neighbourhood and the broader Kensington community (including residential, commercial and welfare). It also means fostering positive social interaction amongst those who live within the new neighbourhood, regardless of their tenure. Fortunately the suburb of Kensington has a long history of community development and a strong sense of place. Community infrastructure is strong and the existing diverse population share a sense of belonging and commitment to their community. The new neighbourhood will be strengthened if it is effectively linked with this broader community.

In addition to the social objectives there are also commercial objectives for making 'sustainable community' the overarching objective of the redevelopment. Becton's greatest risk is that negative perception about public housing will deter potential purchasers from acquiring a property in the new neighbourhood.

Rightly or wrongly there is a negative perception in the community about public housing; a perception reinforced by the form, condition and social environment of larger public housing estates like the site for redevelopment. Becton's challenge is to convince the public that the new neighbourhood will be fundamentally different to the old. In order to sell the private housing potential purchasers must be convinced that 'estate management' is focused on maintaining a high standard of physical amenity and creating a positive social environment over the long term. Community building is therefore central to Becton's commercial interests.

Source: Kensington Management Company (2008)

'Community sustainability', 'building community' and the development's commercial viability are explicitly linked to the acceptance of the redevelopment and its residents by the broader (privately housed) Kensington community. Hulse et al (2004) suggest that if this is to occur, the composition of that broader community will have to become considerably more gentrified: a process already underway, indeed, and powerfully stimulated by the redevelopment. The researchers were able to interview longstanding private residents in Kensington, most of whom spoke about a loss of facilities and social diversity.

If the desire of the Kensington Management Company for integration of the redeveloped estate into the broader community were realised, it would be at the expense of Kensington's low-income private renters. Hulse et al report that more than two thirds of the local residents they interviewed commented on the changes in Kensington, with most emphasising 'the loss of public housing tenants, families, children and diversity, as well as gentrification and "less friendly" people moving in' (Hulse et al, 2004, p 100).

The immediate effects of the redevelopment on local schools and community facilities were negative. As the walk-ups contained the main stock of multi-bedroom units it is mainly the families on the estate who were permanently displaced, with severe impacts on those families remaining and on the services on which they continue to rely. Both primary schools in the area lost enrolments and funding, and various community facilities had to reduce their services and days of operation:

> We weren't able to have a process for linking the youth into new services. Kids left the programmes virtually overnight. No one asked the tenants whether or not they wanted to continue contact with services or continue to be on mailing lists. We had homework programmes, drop-in programmes and arts programmes, and the estate young people had made up the majority of my workload. The teenage holiday programme is about half now [mid-2003] and the homework programme is about a third now of what it was. (Youth worker, cited in Hulse et al, 2004, p 95)

Of course, this research was conducted after the displacement of most of the public tenants and before enough new construction had occurred to replace demand for those services. Hulse et al note, however, that the new private residents can be expected to have different needs and expectations, and be more likely to send their children to private schools. Those services that continued to have high demand had already noted a change in clientele:

> In the late nineties there was a high multicultural population around here. Now there's not. Culturally the whole area has changed since the flats came down. Now our waiting list is mainly Anglo and those on quite high incomes. (Kensington Community Children's Cooperative, cited in Hulse et al, 2004, p 97)

There is a range of views among the remaining public tenants, which is broadly represented in the following two quotes:

> I think it's the best way to go, to be honest. The mixture will certainly balance it out and there won't be the stigma.

> Land grab going on. Want to see poor, disabled out. See them cringe when you walk past. (Current public tenants, cited in Hulse et al, 2004, p 132)

Kensington has unquestionably become 'hot new real estate'. The coordinated action between the State government and the developer has succeeded in stimulating investment in an area that long resisted gentrification. The project is sealed with a 'place management model' in which one property management company manages the entire estate. Urban Communities describes itself as having evolved from the joint partnership between the Victorian government and the Becton Corporation into a non-government 'not for profit with a business mind' and a real estate licence (Urban Communities, 2010). The company manages the public housing for the Office of Housing and the private rental housing for investors. It acts for public and private tenants, owner-occupiers and the owner's corporation, and handles private sales. Urban Communities states proudly that it offers 'a model for fresh thinking and positive change in the management of mixed tenure communities and urban renewal' (Urban Communities, 2010).

The change in management may well be positive, but as there had been no evaluation of the place management model three years after its introduction, it is hard to know. The Swinburne team's early findings, confirmed by further research and observation, indicate that the objective of 'balancing the public and private housing mix' has resulted in a shrinking of the public housing estate, privatisation of public land, gentrification of the areas around the estate, and little, if any, social mixing of public and private residents. There has been no formal government evaluation of the social and economic impacts of the permanent displacement of 1,000 residents, of the effects of the redevelopment on the remaining public housing tenants and the services they use, nor of the value for money of the public–private partnership. Nevertheless, in 2006, a new public housing estate redevelopment was announced.

The second estate is in Carlton, close to the city centre and the 'university quarter'. Carlton is one of Melbourne's first districts to gentrify and because of a strong Italian community that established there well before the first wave of gentrification, still carries the somewhat romanticised tag as 'the Italian quarter'. The Carlton estate is spread over two separate sites and is larger than the Kensington estate. Unlike in Kensington at the start of the redevelopment, the Carlton sites are surrounded by highly gentrified and valuable properties. The State government again went into partnership with a private developer, but in a slightly different arrangement. The high-rise towers on the estate would remain, and their upgrade would be undertaken by the Office of Housing. The developer, in a consortium of four partners, would demolish the walk-ups containing 192 public units, and build 246 new public and 600 private units. Again, as the walk-up units are mainly family housing and their replacements are for singles and the elderly (seen as the demographic of highest need), an increase in unit numbers does not translate into an increase in the number of people housed. In fact, recent projections indicate that the number of public beds will remain about the same (and may change as the development proceeds).

Unlike in Kensington, then, the public component of the Carlton redevelopment is a case of straight replacement of old public housing with new, with associated public infrastructure and landscaping. For this, the consortium is receiving a money and land package – believed to be AUD$80 million plus the freehold on four hectares in one of Melbourne's more expensive suburbs. It is impossible to get confirmation of these estimates or any financial details as the partnership is protected by commercial-in-confidence provisions. But the general manager of the lead partner in the consortium, Australand, is particularly enamoured with the funding arrangement:

> The multi-staged structure of the redevelopment enables us to re-use capital as stages are completed, making it a very capital efficient project for the consortium partners at a time when many other developers are experiencing difficulty in securing finance.... The inner Melbourne precincts are projected to see strong rental growth for the next four years to 2012-2013 because of the limited new supply coming in during the period, making it a very attractive investment proposition. The redevelopment project is expected to be completed by 2017 and is expected to generate sales revenue of more than $300 million. (Australand, 2009a)

The general manager says he is 'delighted to be taking part in a project set to revitalise key areas in one of Melbourne's most eclectic suburbs' (Australand, 2009a). Again the discourse of connecting the estate to the rest of the neighbourhood is dominant: 'The proposed redevelopment seeks to improve the quality of public housing and be a positive contribution to the streetscapes of Carlton. It will be a combination of public and private housing which aims to reintegrate the estate and its buildings within the neighbouring Carlton community' (Office of Housing, 2008). But in the Carlton case, rather than the redevelopment being a catalyst for the 'revitalisation' of the surrounding area, it is the surrounding area waiting for the estate to 'catch up' in property values.

Interestingly, the discourse of 'social mix' has been almost entirely replaced by 'housing mix'; the Office of Housing talks of integrated public, private and social housing neighbourhoods in Carlton, but no longer of the benefits of 'greater socio-economic diversity ... [reducing] the concentration of poverty' (Kensington Management Company, 2008). Instead, this redevelopment is advertised primarily for the fact that 'the new public, private and social housing will be indistinguishable from the outside' (Office of Housing, 2010). Further, in clear recognition of the values of this gentrified inner-city electorate, the Carlton redevelopment will 'deliver the most environmentally sustainable public housing seen in Melbourne' (Office of Housing, 2010).

Of course public tenants are already in a tiny minority in Carlton, and the redevelopment of their housing is not reducing their concentration. In a panel hearing to consider the rezoning of the area, much discussion occurred around notions of 'salt and pepper' or 'layer cake' mixing, as it did in Kensington. But the Kensington redevelopment sets a precedent for minimal social mixing, and it is clear from the plans that even the 'block-by-block' approach that ultimately defined the Kensington estate is more mixed than will be the case in Carlton. The new private housing in Carlton is as far from the public high-rises as can be, clustered again at the sunny, northern end of the estate, while the new public housing stock occupies the land in between. Australand's lavish marketing brochure for the private units appears to offer an entirely private precinct on the estate:

> Stretch out in Viva's own private garden. Manicured, tranquil and spacious, Viva Retreat is the ideal escape.... Private, quiet and secure, this large space is fully enclosed in the best tradition of a European courtyard garden.... (Australand, 2009b)

'Viva' is the name given to the private housing component which is currently being sold off the plan, and its advertising, with more pictures of beautiful white people, has led to serious concerns of a private gated community within the development. The plans are ambiguous: there is a substantial fence around the private part but the height and extent of enclosure are difficult to verify. Certainly, the brochure's idea of social mix appears more limited than the depictions at Kensington, and a long way from the reality of Carlton in the 1950s and 1960s:

> Carlton offers an invigorating mix of sophisticated chic, heritage elegance and cultural vigour. You'll love the urban elan and festive spirit. Carlton is where Ferraris park nose to tail with Vespa scooters, while their equally fashionable owners sip espresso at al fresco cafes nearby. (Australand, 2009b)

As in Kensington, the Carlton redevelopment involves a substantial shrinking of the public housing estate and quantity of publicly owned land. While the number of public tenants in Carlton is expected to remain the same, the area they occupy will be substantially reduced. The 'concentration of poverty' on the Carlton estate will, in fact, be increased.

'Social mix' and its effect on diversity

The principles behind 'diversity' and 'mix' have existed in Victorian policy at least since the 1970s, when construction of high-rise towers and dedicated public housing estates were abandoned in favour of spot purchases in inner and outer metropolitan areas and, in the 1980s, occasional symbolic developments in gentrifying areas such as St Kilda and Prahran. But this discourse centred on equity and affordability and the principles were enacted by introducing public housing (and increasingly, locally managed community housing) into areas of private housing, or through the construction of diverse new estates on brownfield sites.

The discourse of 'social mix' only appeared in Victorian public policy in the 2000s in association with the clear diminution of public land on both the Kensington and Carlton estates. In Kensington the number of public tenants was clearly reduced; in Carlton the number remains the same (at the time of writing). The residents of the new private housing on both estates are likely to have significantly higher incomes than their public tenant neighbours, more in line with their neighbours in the surrounding areas. According to the preliminary assessments at Kensington, they are more likely to be of Anglo background.

Given the absence of any evidence so far for successful social mixing on the estates, and the strong indications to the contrary, what was driving the Labor government's commitment to the estate redevelopments? Not 'social mix', it would appear: the government's commitment to this was demonstrably thin. It not only wanted no evaluation of its ostensible strategies to increase social mix, but also ignored the growing body of work from Australian researchers that argues that its purported benefits are undemonstrated. Kathy Arthurson (2002, 2004) makes a representative analysis for the academy when she concludes that 'the integrity of claims made for social mix remains inconclusive and it is questionable whether the social benefits the policies purport to generate or the envisaged communities will eventuate' (2002, p 258). Arthurson examined some years ago the social mix strategies in public housing estate regeneration policies in New South Wales, South Australia and Queensland, and found that 'there is no evidence that a balanced social mix is a necessary condition for building inclusive communities' (2002, p 245). Subsequent work from Randolph and Wood (2004) confirms limited benefit from tenure diversification in Australia. This research has little traction.

Neither did 'housing mix' appear to be a significant incentive in itself, given the clear structural limitations on the extent of mixing. If the government's redevelopment programme was a straightforward gentrification strategy, as can reasonably be assumed, with the discourses of social or housing mix only a half-hearted attempt to disguise the fact, then two questions need to be answered. First, why were more towers not demolished, given that they are the most powerful and demonised symbols of 1960s public housing construction and probably the most significant brakes on gentrification in those areas? Second, why weren't all the large inner-city estates, located in districts that are still some way from being fully gentrified in large part because of their presence, also targeted for redevelopment?

Close inspection and the passage of time reveal the answers to these questions. The Kensington tower did not yield the spectacular controlled explosive demolition used to such great effect on American television (in particular, of course, the Pruitt–Igoe estate in St Louis in 1972). The nature of the construction of the Australian towers does not lend them to controlled collapse. Each concrete slab has to be taken down piece-by-piece, taking a long time, costing a great deal, and depriving the responsible politician of the satisfying response to pressure on the detonator. When this factor is taken into account, it becomes clear that not only is the political benefit of demolition low, but so is the amount of land yielded in comparison with the walk-ups. And land was indeed a crucial element of this strategy. It was announced in 2010 that the three remaining large inner-city estates, in Fitzroy, Richmond and Prahran, would also undergo redevelopment. At the time of writing, the announcements indicate only that the public stock will be replaced or upgraded, with 'wider plans for redevelopment' being subject to a future process of 'ongoing consultation with the community' over the next year (Office of Housing, 2010). But the government did reveal that the programme 'will be developed in partnership with private enterprise' (Office of Housing, 2010). If it is a gentrification strategy, we can expect private housing in all these redevelopments.

The redevelopments are undoubtedly a process of third-wave gentrification. But it would not be entirely correct to leave the analysis there, or even to assume that gentrification is the primary objective. This would be a sufficient interpretation of the previous government's intent, given Kennett's open support for market-led development. But the former Victorian Labor Treasurer and subsequent Premier who oversaw these redevelopments and announcements, John Brumby, was driven by slightly different impulses. His objective was to demonstrate conservative economic credentials (average annual surpluses of AUD$500 million) on the basis of the Australian Labor Party's rather unfair reputation for reckless expenditure. He embraced the theory that the private sector is best positioned to deliver public services at least in part because public–private partnerships can absorb, on behalf of government, the political risk of cost blow-outs on major public projects. This ensured that almost every major public infrastructure project under the Labor government between 1999 and 2010 was delivered through some kind of partnership. There had to be incentives for the private sector of course: Melbourne's central station redevelopment came with a massive shopping centre; the new convention centre with a homewares display suite; a new freeway with a private toll. The privatisation of public land was seen as a necessary by-product of replacing or upgrading the ageing public housing stock.

This story is about a discourse of social mix being used less as a pretext for gentrification than as a rationalisation for minimal government outlay on public works (in the short term). The protestation of the Kensington Management Company in 2008 that 'integration of public and private housing is not just a means to finance the redevelopment of public housing' was perhaps unwittingly candid, for this is precisely what it was. This story is about an enduring commitment to public–private 'financing mix'.

The Labor State government not only discouraged any evaluation of social mix strategies, but of its financing partnerships in general.

There was no academic work supported on whether the benefits of the partnerships to date are worth the costs, especially in light of the fact that the private sector borrows at higher rates than governments. There was no publicly released assessment of whether the opportunity costs of giving public land to a developer actually did represent value for money. There was no projection of the relative levels of financial risk carried by the public and private partners in the event that essential public projects really did run aground. This research is difficult to carry out without government support when the commercial and contractual details are not publicly available. It was in part the government's hubris in this regard that led to its surprise defeat in the late 2010 State election. In a pattern that is becoming a little too predictable, the conservative coalition returns with the promise of more 'open and transparent' government.

There has been no funded research on the estate redevelopments since Hulse et al (2004). As in many other parts of the world, funding for research is increasingly tied to partnerships – usually with government – which tend not to seek examination of the principles driving government policies. This is the all-too-common scenario of Labor governments in particular being so intimidated by powerful corporations, with the prospect of financial risk looming larger than ever as a disaster for any government, that they would rather not be responsible for the social and structural forms of the environment. This is not so much gentrification by stealth – indeed, the developers in this story were open enough about the meaning of revitalisation of the estate and integration with the surrounding neighbourhoods – but, on the government's part, gentrification by default.

One thing is certain: gentrification and associated public discourses of increasing social mix in Melbourne result in a reduction of socioeconomic diversity. In this instance it was the result of a forlorn attempt on the part of the proponents of those discourses to secure themselves against risk. Perhaps it was always thus.

Note

After this chapter went to press, I was invited by the Office of Housing to leads an evaluation of the Kensington Place Management Model, including an assessment of the xocial mix, housing mix and finance mix strategies. After careful deliberation I agree, on the basis that the research team be able to publish the findings.

Part 4
The rhetoric and reality of social mix policies

Social mixing as a cure for negative neighbourhood effects: evidence-based policy or urban myth?

David Manley, Maarten van Ham and Joe Doherty

Introduction

There is a widely held belief by government, policy makers and academics that living in deprived neighbourhoods has a negative effect on residents' life chances over and above the effect of their individual characteristics. There is a large body of literature on these so-called neighbourhood effects and neighbourhood effects have been claimed in relation to a variety of outcomes: school dropout rates (Overman, 2002); childhood achievement (Galster et al, 2007); transition rates from welfare to work (van der Klaauw and Ours, 2003); deviant behaviour (Friedrichs and Blasius, 2003); social exclusion (Buck, 2001); and social mobility (Buck, 2001). The current interest in the assumed negative effect of living in deprived neighbourhoods was stimulated by Wilson (1987, 1991), and several theoretical explanations of neighbourhood effects have been developed in the last two decades. These explanations include role model effects and peer group influences, social and physical disconnection from job-finding networks, a culture of poverty leading to dysfunctional values, discrimination by employers and other gatekeepers, access to low-quality public services and high exposure to criminal behaviour (for an overview see van Ham and Manley, 2011: in press).

Policy makers embraced the concept of neighbourhood effects because if concentrations of poverty can make individuals poor(er), then reducing concentrations of poverty would solve the problem. Creating neighbourhoods with a balanced socioeconomic mix of residents is an often used strategy to tackle assumed negative neighbourhood effects. Mixed housing tenure policies are frequently espoused as a vehicle to create more socially mixed neighbourhoods. The idea is that mixing homeowners with social renters will create a more diverse socioeconomic mix in neighbourhoods, removing the potential of negative neighbourhood effects (Musterd and Andersson, 2005). Mixed housing strategies – often involving large-scale demolishment of social housing estates – have been explicitly adopted as part of neighbourhood improvement schemes by many governments including those in the Netherlands, the UK, Germany, France, Finland and Sweden (Atkinson and Kintrea, 2002; Kearns, 2002; Musterd, 2002).

Despite the apparent consensus that neighbourhood effects exist, there is a growing body of literature that questions the status quo (see Oreopoulos, 2003; Bolster et al, 2007; van Ham and Manley, 2010; van Ham et al, 2011: in press). This critical literature demonstrates that there is surprisingly little convincing evidence that living in deprived neighbourhoods really makes people poor(er), and concludes that policies designed to tackle poverty should target individuals rather than the areas within which they live (Cheshire, 2007b). A key problem in the empirical investigation of neighbourhood effects is the (econometric) identification of causal relationships (Durlauf, 2004). Durlauf (2004) also reports that quasi-experimental studies, such as Gautreaux and the Moving to Opportunity programme (Rosenbaum, 1995; Ludwig et al, 2001; Goering et al, 2002) or randomised education studies (see Leventhal and Brooks-Gunn, 2004) find little impact of the neighbourhood on adults' life chances. Within a quasi-experimental setting, selection into neighbourhoods is largely randomised, and the bias that selection mechanisms introduce into the analyses are less prevalent.

It has been suggested that most existing 'evidence' from non-experimental observational (and often cross-sectional) studies suffers from reverse causality. The argument made is that poor neighbourhoods do not make people poor(er), but poor people live in deprived neighbourhoods because they cannot afford to live in more expensive neighbourhoods (Cheshire, 2007b). In other words, poor people self-select themselves into deprived neighbourhoods (through the sorting process of the housing market), and the selection mechanism explains the positive association between deprivation on the neighbourhood level and individual level poverty. Residential location is an outcome largely determined at the level of the individual (or household) and is the result of individual level preferences, resources and restrictions, within a setting of macro level opportunities and constraints (Mulder and Hooimeijer, 1999). In the investigation of neighbourhood effects it is important to fully control for individual characteristics and not, as identified by Buck (2001), merely use neighbourhood difference as evidence of neighbourhood effects. For neighbourhood effects to exist there must be clear causal pathways identifiable. We suggest that the vast majority of the neighbourhood effects literature does not identify causality and therefore over-emphasises the role of the neighbourhood in individual outcomes.

The question whether neighbourhood effects are the result of causation or of selection effects is not only of academic importance, but also has direct policy relevance. Social mixing through creating mixed tenure neighbourhoods obviously only has the desired outcome if neighbourhood effects exist in the first place. The discussion on neighbourhood effects is vital in the development of effective policies to tackle individual deprivation. If neighbourhood effects are not as pervasive as is suggested in the literature, or if selection processes are behind the 'neighbourhood effects' found, tenure mix policies will not help the residents of deprived neighbourhoods. In which case, tenure mix policies will only replace poor residents (social renters) by more affluent residents (homeowners). As a result, the neighbourhood might improve, but not the lives of the original residents.

In this chapter we question the evidence base for social mix policies by examining the current evidence on neighbourhood effects. The structure of the chapter is as follows. The first section provides an overview of the key theoretical explanations of neighbourhood effects. The discussion continues by investigating the methodological challenges for the analysis of neighbourhood effects. The next section discusses the latest empirical evidence on neighbourhood effects. The final section draws together the threads running through the chapter and critically assesses the evidence base of the social mix project and whether current policies are based on an urban myth.

Theoretical considerations

The literature suggests that certain neighbourhood characteristics (mainly deprivation) have a negative effect on a range of individual social, economic and health outcomes. Wilson (1987, 1991) is generally regarded as the starting point of the neighbourhood effects debate, although there have been earlier contributions (see, for instance, Sarkissian, 1976). Wilson developed his notion of negative neighbourhood effects within the context of the labour market and the problem of long-term unemployment. He suggested that concentrations of individuals experiencing long-term unemployment in certain neighbourhoods could lead to outcomes that include 'negative social dispositions, limited aspirations, and casual work habits' (Wilson, 1991, p 642). He posed the idea that certain neighbourhood contexts facilitate the development of an urban underclass whose central problem 'is joblessness reinforced by increasing social isolation in impoverished neighbourhoods' (Wilson, 1991, p 650). Other authors have also identified the potential effect of negative role models as a means through which residents of deprived neighbourhoods suffer disadvantage (Manski, 2000; Blume and Durlauf, 2001). Negative role models are thought to reinforce low expectations of employment, hinder access to job networks and to encourage deviant behaviour. Following Wilson's thesis, in extreme cases the combination of these effects can lead to the development of a 'culture of poverty' (Wilson, 1987), where continued unemployment is not the result of structural (economic or social) problems, but a consequence of the adoption of deviant norms following value systems counter to those adopted by wider society. Potentially, the culture of poverty argument can be seen as a structural neighbourhood effect when, for example, employers refuse to hire residents from certain neighbourhoods because of the reputation of that neighbourhood (see Wilson, 1991; Wacquant, 1993, 2008). Wilson's concentration argument forms the basis of much of the neighbourhood effects debate.

Beyond the work of Wilson, the literature offers a wide range of theoretical explanations of how the neighbourhood context might influence individual outcomes. As there are several excellent overviews, we only discuss these explanations very briefly (see Friedrichs, 1998; Ioannides and Loury, 2004; Galster, 2008; van Ham and Manley, 2011: in press). Manski (1993) identified three categories into which the theoretical explanations can be grouped: correlated effects, endogenous effects and exogenous effects. Correlated effects occur when individuals in the same neighbourhood 'behave similarly because they have similar individual characteristics or face similar institutional environments' (Manski, 1993, p 533). Examples of these include spatial mismatch, external stigma and sparse local institutional resources (Galster, 2008). Endogenous effects relate to the propensity of an individual to vary their behaviour in line with that of the neighbourhood group. Examples include epidemic/social norms, selective socialisation and social network theory. Exogenous effects (also known as contextual effects) relate to the propensity of an individual to behave in some way that varies with the exogenous characteristics of the neighbourhood group. Examples of this include the propensity for minority ethnic groups to favour neighbourhoods with high proportions of co-ethnic residents if they are seeking ethnic solidarity. More recently, Galster (2011b:

forthcoming) offered a more comprehensive list of 15 potential causal pathways for neighbourhood effects, which can be grouped into four categories: social interactive mechanisms (social contagion, collective socialisation, social networks, social cohesion and control, competition, relative deprivation and parental mediation), environmental mechanisms (exposure to violence, physical surroundings and toxic exposure), geographical mechanisms (spatial mismatch of jobs and workers and a lack of quality public services) and institutional mechanisms (stigmatisation, local institutional resources and local market actors).

If empirical studies find evidence for neighbourhood effects, then it follows that at least some, or a combination of, the above mechanisms must be at work. Untangling which of the mechanisms is at work is empirically challenging and may even be impossible. At least theoretically, mixing social groups will introduce positive role models in a neighbourhood that other residents then start to copy. Whether this actually works is contested in the literature; for example, research commissioned by the Joseph Rowntree Foundation to investigate the effectiveness of established mixed communities found little evidence that creating mixed communities helped the interaction between social groups within even very small neighbourhoods (Allen et al, 2005). While an employed neighbour may theoretically set an example and even facilitate access to the labour market for an unemployed resident, the literature also identifies that relative disadvantage within the neighbourhood context can be deleterious and discouraging for residents; socially mixing neighbourhoods and increasing the average affluence in a neighbourhood could serve to highlight relative inequalities. Neighbourhood level interactions between different social groups, including households across different tenures, households with different levels of affluence and households belonging to different ethnic groups, are a crucial element of neighbourhood effects explanations. However, without clear evidence that there are basic interactions between groups of residents, it is difficult to conceptualise how any positive transmission processes would work.

To complicate matters, the literature has identified that the working of neighbourhood effects, if and where they exist, may not be linear. Galster (2008) identified that threshold levels are important, an idea that links directly back to Wilson's original thesis on *concentrations* of poverty. The idea is that below a certain threshold level, the socioeconomic composition of the neighbourhood may not be of significance for individual outcomes. Only when the concentration of, for instance, unemployment, reaches a certain threshold will the negative effects begin to accrue to individuals in the locale resulting in, as Wilson suggested, deviant behaviours moving away from societal norms. Building on this idea, Galster suggested that neighbourhood effects are likely to be non-linear, with increased concentrations of poverty linked to increasingly negative outcomes for individuals. The association between individual unemployment and the level of neighbourhood deprivation, for instance, supports this idea. However, associations between various factors is not the same as causation, and to understand the processes leading to assumed neighbourhood effects more fully, we must move beyond the use of associative measures.

If we are to reject the notion of neighbourhood effects then we must identify an alternative framework to account for the apparent effects of neighbourhood concentration. Acknowledging that neighbourhoods are different and that geography of place does matter, Cheshire (2007b) and others argue that the externalities that accrue to the residents of deprived neighbourhoods do not negatively alter their life chances above and beyond the level that their individual characteristics predict. Instead, concentrations of poverty are a consequence of unemployment, lower levels of education or structural deficiencies in the labour market. The concentration of these phenomena in deprived neighbourhoods is driven primarily by selection processes through which individuals and households enter neighbourhoods. Although Cheshire (2008) examines the role of economic access to neighbourhoods, whereby 'better' neighbourhoods cost more to access, there are other possible sorting mechanisms that include agglomeration effects and other social and cultural drivers that determine neighbourhood preference. Together these sorting mechanisms serve to create relatively homogeneous groups of individuals and households organised in what we have termed neighbourhoods. As more affluent neighbourhoods cost more to access, it follows that only those with relatively high incomes or high levels of wealth will be able to enter. Individuals and households with lower economic means will 'select' neighbourhoods within their budgetary constraints. It can be debated whether using the term 'self-selection' can be justified for those who are selected into concentrations of social housing, as they generally have very little choice. Ultimately, the selection processes lead to the concentrations of similar individuals in space. It is easy to understand that concentrations of poverty are the result of these sorting processes, but it is more difficult to see how real causal neighbourhood effects would work.

Methodological considerations

The key problem in the empirical investigation of neighbourhood effects is the (econometric) identification of causal relationships (Durlauf, 2004). As mentioned in the introduction to this chapter, ideally neighbourhood effects studies should use individual level longitudinal (quasi) experimental data. Unfortunately, such data are seldom available for research. Many studies use aggregated data for neighbourhoods (ecological data) instead of individual level data (see, for example, Graham et al, 2009). The problem with ecological data is that correlations between neighbourhood characteristics cannot automatically be translated into causal relationships for individuals. For example, there might be a high correlation between the percentage of social housing in a neighbourhood and the unemployment rate. It would be incorrect to conclude that concentrations of social housing cause people to be unemployed as this relationship might be spurious (this problem is known as the ecological fallacy; see Robinson, 1950). Using ecological data it is therefore not possible to gain useful insight into the causal effects of neighbourhood attributes on individual outcomes.

Many studies use individual level cross-sectional data (data collected for a single point in time). Although this data is a major improvement compared to ecological data, cross-sectional data does not allow the identification of the order of events, which is crucial for the identification of causal effects. For example, if cross-sectional data shows that individuals in deprived neighbourhoods are more likely to be unemployed than individuals in non-deprived neighbourhoods, this does not mean that deprived neighbourhoods *cause* people to be unemployed. It is more likely that unemployed people moved to deprived neighbourhoods because they could not afford to live elsewhere.

To establish whether living in a deprived neighbourhood causes people to be unemployed it is necessary to follow people over time while they are in a variety of employment statuses and living in a variety of neighbourhoods. Recently individual level longitudinal data has become available with sufficient geographical detail for the analysis of neighbourhood effects. Such longitudinal data still has its problems, but is more suitable for the analysis of causal relationships than cross-sectional data. Even with longitudinal data it is almost impossible to rule out selection bias. People sort into neighbourhoods based on measured and unmeasured characteristics, and this sorting process is typically non-random. The gold standard in neighbourhood effects research (and all social science research) is experimental data from randomised trials (see below for a discussion of randomised trials). In a randomised trial households are randomly allocated to neighbourhoods and then followed over a period of time. Such a design theoretically allows researchers to measure the real effects of living in deprived neighbourhoods.

The methodological neighbourhood effects literature has identified several econometric issues in the identification of neighbourhood effects (see Manski, 1993; Moffitt, 2001). The main issue is the simultaneity problem where neighbourhood composition is not only a cause of, but is simultaneously caused by, the characteristics of the individuals living there. A second problem is the endogenous membership problem that may lead to the misleading conclusion that neighbourhood effects really exist. The problem of omitted variable bias (OMV) can occur at both the neighbourhood and individual level. At the neighbourhood level important neighbourhood characteristics can be omitted from models and so any effect the neighbourhood context appears to have could be over- or under-estimated. A prime example of OMV comes from the related problem that households do not distribute themselves over neighbourhoods at random. Households select (themselves) into neighbourhoods based on a wide range of individual and household characteristics. It is likely that a number of these (hard to measure) characteristics will be unobserved and lead to biased model outcomes (Buck, 2001). At the individual level, OMV could refer to, for example, the willingness to take risks, or adaptability to new situations.

The econometric literature offers partial solutions for a number of the problems, mentioned above, using techniques such as the instrumental variable (IV) approach (Durlauf, 2004; Galster et al, 2008), fixed effects models and the use of longitudinal data (see work by Musterd and Andersson, 2005; Bolster et al, 2007; van Ham and Manley, 2010). However, these methods reduce but do not eliminate the possibility of alternative explanations of neighbourhood effects. The IV approach requires the identification of a variable that predicts an explanatory variable of interest (known as an instrument variable), say, the level of neighbourhood tenure mix, while being completely unrelated to the modelled outcome variable, say, employment. Only when there is complete independence between the instrument variable and the probability of being employed is there evidence that neighbourhood characteristics have an effect on the probability of being employed. While this theoretically offers a good method, in practice it is very difficult to identify true instruments for use in modelling. Despite the advances in modelling techniques, quantitative studies struggle to adequately identify neighbourhood effects. In this chapter, we argue that neighbourhood effects cannot be fully understood without a broad and deep understanding of the neighbourhood context, neighbourhood change and crucially the selective mobilities of individuals and households into and out of neighbourhoods. Given the awareness of the (self) selection processes, the neighbourhood effects literature pays surprisingly little attention to the literature on selective residential mobility into and out of neighbourhoods.

Empirical evidence: causal neighbourhood effects or selection effects?

Ecological and cross-sectional evidence

Within the context of neighbourhood effects evidence in Great Britain, cross-sectional ecological analysis has formed the basis for much of the empirical discussion over the last three decades. The only nationally representative quantitative investigation of the association between neighbourhood level tenure mix and a range of other neighbourhood characteristics has been carried out by Graham and colleagues (2009). Graham and colleagues explicitly focused on the question of what level of tenure mix provides the best outcomes by categorising neighbourhoods by several levels of mixing. Neighbourhoods with between 30 and 70% social renting were defined as mixed tenure (see also Tunstall, 2000). This approach is in line with the idea that thresholds exist and that neighbourhood effects might be non-linear (Galster, 2008). Thresholds are important to consider because prior to a given level a neighbourhood characteristic may not have a significant impact on individual outcomes. Above a critical level (the threshold) the characteristic could be thought to have a much greater and significant impact on individual outcomes. Consider an extreme example where an unemployment rate of 15% in a neighbourhood has no impact on the propensity of unemployed individuals to find a job, while at 30% there may be severe effects that result in unemployed individuals becoming very unlikely to find employment. The non-linearity issue is important as there is no reason to suspect that an increase in a neighbourhood characteristic (again, say, the neighbourhood unemployment rate) should lead to an equal decrease in the risk for an individual living in that neighbourhood to find a job. Galster (2008) argues that the relationship between neighbourhood characteristics and individual outcomes may be non-linear, taking the form of an exponential curve, or even a 'stepped curve'.

To address the question what is the most relevant spatial scale to study neighbourhood effects, Graham and colleagues used census geography to define two neighbourhood scales: wards, which are large neighbourhoods containing 5,000-6,000 people, and output areas, which are local neighbourhoods containing on average 150 people. The association between neighbourhood tenure mix and four neighbourhood level characteristics were investigated: unemployment and limiting long-term illness (derived from the census), and overall mortality and premature mortality (derived from vital registrations). Regression models were used to test if the predicted outcomes were significantly different (better or worse) than those observed in the data. Only for those wards with low levels of social renting (10-19%, 20-29%) were the observed correlations better than the expected correlations. For wards with high levels of social renting the positive effect gave way to an increasingly significant negative correlation for all outcomes (see Graham et al, 2009). Analyses at the output area level showed similar results. The results do not provide any evidence in favour of mixed tenure neighbourhoods as neighbourhoods with 30-70% social renting do not perform much better than neighbourhoods with higher percentages of social renting. Separate analyses testing the so-called 'pepper potting' hypothesis – that mixed tenure is most beneficial if social renters and owner-occupiers are thoroughly inter-mixed within neighbourhoods – did not show advantage. All in all, within a context of ecological data analysis, the evidence base for social mixing as a way to counter negative neighbourhood effects looks distinctly weak.

Longitudinal investigations in neighbourhood effects

The ecological analyses of Graham and colleagues, however, do not reveal anything at the level of the individual. Individual level data, and more specifically longitudinal individual level data, has the potential to move beyond identifying simple correlations and to identify causal effects of neighbourhood characteristics at the level of individual outcomes. Some of the best-known studies of neighbourhood effects have used data from the Gautreaux and Moving to Opportunity programmes in the US (Katz et al, 2001; Orr et al, 2003). These programmes offer a quasi-experimental setting for research. Under the Gautreaux programme households in some of the most deprived neighbourhoods in Chicago were able to use housing vouchers to move to more affluent neighbourhoods. The outcomes for these households could then subsequently be compared to outcomes for households who stayed behind in the deprived neighbourhoods. The individual outcomes for participants of the Gautreaux programme were largely positive, with improvement seen in labour market outcomes and child school attainment. However, a number of authors have warned that these results need to be interpreted with caution (see Moffit, 2001; Musterd et al, 2003; Clark, 2008). Initial selection was determined by a set of stringent criteria that removed problematic households, or those with problems in paying rent. In other words, it is likely that self-selection into the programme biased the outcomes. Also, confounding factors such as correlated environmental factors were not successfully removed from the studies so that while neighbourhood allocation may have been relatively random, a host of other important variables were not controlled for. These include varying labour market opportunities, school quality and the levels of crime. If any of these factors were correlated with the reported improved outcomes – and it is highly likely that they were – then evidence that the improved outcomes were the result of the improved neighbourhood context would be suspect.

The Moving to Opportunity programme had less stringent acceptance criteria. The outcomes of the programme were not as positive as those found for the Gautreaux programme. Four and seven years after the Moving to Opportunity programme started there was no evidence of improvement in adult earnings or employment levels and no reduction in public assistance required (Orr et al, 2003; Jacob, 2004). If the neighbourhood context really influences individual outcomes, then it would be reasonable to presume that those households that moved into the most affluent areas would experience improvements in their overall social well-being, including employment and income. The lack of positive results observed in the Moving to Opportunity programme, which came closest in design to a quasi-experiment in terms of selection and neighbourhood allocation mechanisms, provides additional material to question the neighbourhood effects evidence base. Unfortunately, quasi-experimental settings such as Gautreaux and Moving to Opportunity are rare, primarily due to the level of government intervention required and the costs associated with such programmes. As a result, most research on neighbourhood effects relies on secondary data from non-experimental observational studies.

The increasing availability of individual level longitudinal data provides potential to overcome some of the problems related to selection into neighbourhoods. One of the first studies using large-scale longitudinal data to analyse the effect of neighbourhood social mix on individual outcomes was by Musterd and Andersson (2005). They used data from Sweden addressing two questions: does tenure mix lead to a genuine social mix? – as suggested by many policy implementations; and does social mix in neighbourhoods benefit individual social mobility? The study included all Swedish residents aged 16 to 65, between 1991 and 1999, and characterised neighbourhoods based on three measures: housing mix, income and ethnic mix. Social mobility was measured using employment outcomes in 1991, 1995 and 1999. First, the modelling results showed that tenure mix does not directly lead to social mix. In Sweden a policy of social mixing has been pursued since the 1970s, and the fact that tenure mixing has not led to social mixing takes away part of the evidence base for tenure mix policies. Second, the modelling results did not show any negative effects of concentrations of neighbourhood poverty on the probability to stay in employment, after controlling for level of education. Finally, Musterd and Andersson did find an advantage for residents in homogeneously high-income areas.

Although Musterd and Andersson (2005) categorise neighbourhoods using tenure type and average household income, they do not differentiate between homogeneous social renting or homogeneous owner-occupied neighbourhoods. Evidence from other studies (see van Ham and Manley, 2010) evaluating the effects of tenure mix suggests that this omission is unfortunate, as living in these two types of neighbourhoods might lead to very different individual level outcomes. In addition, the selection of households into neighbourhoods is not controlled for in their models. In their conclusion, Musterd and Andersson are suitably cautious, noting that their 'findings are ... a warning to those who tend to focus too much on the neighbourhood as a source of problems' (Musterd and Andersson, 2005, p 786).

Moving the debate forward substantially, Oreopoulos (2003) used Canadian register data from Toronto for adults who grew up in various neighbourhoods. He compared employment outcomes for adults who lived in private housing and adults who lived in social housing in the same neighbourhoods. Because social housing was assigned primarily on a needs basis, the process of allocating households to neighbourhoods came close to that of a natural experiment. In contrast, households in private housing selected themselves into neighbourhoods, based on their preferences and resources within the choice set available. The modelling results showed significant neighbourhood effects on earnings, employment and welfare participation for adults who had grown up in private housing. By contrast, no effects were identified for the adults, from the same neighbourhoods, who had grown up in social rented housing. The absence of neighbourhood effects for those from social housing led Oreopoulos (2003) to the conclusion that the neighbourhood effects found for those in the private sector were in fact caused by neighbourhood selection processes.

Bolster and colleagues (2007) used data from the British Household Panel Survey (BHPS) to investigate the effect of neighbourhood disadvantage on income growth over a 1, 5 and 10-year period. Rather than using readily available administrative neighbourhoods, they created 'bespoke' neighbourhoods based on the residential location of each individual for a number of different spatial scales. This enabled them to control for the fact that it is likely that various neighbourhood effects, if present, do not necessarily operate over a single scale (also see Manley et al, 2006; Galster, 2008). After controlling for individual characteristics, Bolster and colleagues found no additional negative effect of neighbourhood deprivation on a range of individual outcomes. Running separate analyses for homeowners and social renters, they found that there was evidence of small positive neighbourhood effects only for households who owned their property, but not for social renters. These finding are in line with those of Oreopoulos (2003), and strengthen the idea that neighbourhood selection is an important component explaining neighbourhood 'effects' reported in many other studies.

In one of the most methodologically advanced attempts to eliminate the effects of omitted variable bias, Galster and colleagues (2008) used a fixed effects model to investigate the effect of the neighbourhood context on earnings for all working-age adults between 1991 and 1999 in Sweden. They concluded that there was evidence of substantial and significant neighbourhood effects on the earnings of individuals. Their findings are in stark contrast to other work presented in this chapter that emphasise the importance of selection mechanisms in explaining correlations of neighbourhood level characteristics and individual level outcomes. Galster and colleagues (2008) used a difference model in an attempt to eliminate all individual level OMV by controlling for all static individual characteristics. However, as Allison (2005) noted, such an approach (using a fixed effects model) still has the potential to over- or under-estimate the true magnitude and significance of any apparent neighbourhood effect. Therefore, it cannot be automatically assumed that such an approach will provide unbiased results. Allison expresses a preference for presenting the outcomes of both a fixed effects model *and* a traditional random effects model; he suggests that the true relationship between neighbourhood level variables and individual outcomes would probably lie somewhere within the range of the coefficients provided. Although the work by Galster and colleagues (2008) is technically very sophisticated, fixed effects models are not capable of controlling for unmeasured individual level variables that are not constant over time. We therefore also conclude that this work cannot claim to be fully unbiased.

The final study discussed in this chapter also uses individual level longitudinal data. Van Ham and Manley (2010) used data from the Scottish Longitudinal Study (SLS) to investigate the relationship between individual labour market outcomes and neighbourhood tenure mix and levels of deprivation. They combined several innovations from the studies discussed above. They modelled neighbourhood effects on multiple spatial scales and they presented separate models for social renters and homeowners. The SLS is based on the 1991 and 2001 Scottish Census and allows researchers to follow the same individuals over a 10-year period (Boyle et al, 2009). To assess the direction of causality in the models it is important to determine the ordering of events and therefore the study by van Ham and Manley used 1991 neighbourhood characteristics to predict 2001 individual labour market outcomes. The neighbourhood level variables were measured at two levels: consistent areas through time (CATTs) with an average of 5,000 people, and output areas with an average of 150 people. The dependent variables measured the transition from unemployment to employment and probability of staying in employment for those with a job in 1991.

Their models showed a clear negative correlation between the percentage of social housing in neighbourhoods, the level of neighbourhood deprivation and individual level labour market outcomes. The neighbourhood level coefficients were found to be larger for the smaller spatial units (output areas) than for the larger units (CATTs). This evidence is consistent with the results of Musterd and Andersson (2005) and Galster and colleagues (2008). Van Ham and Manley (2010) also found that neighbourhood level deprivation is a more significant predictor of labour market outcomes than neighbourhood tenure mix, a proxy for neighbourhood social mix. After controlling for a range of individual level characteristics, the negative effect of living in a neighbourhood with a high percentage of social renting disappeared (the effect even became positive in some models). Separate models for social renters and homeowners showed that neighbourhood characteristics only have a significant effect on labour market outcomes for owners. Those owners living in the most deprived neighbourhoods are also the most likely to remain unemployed or to lose their job. These findings are in line with the findings of Oreopoulos (2003) and Bolster and colleagues (2007). In all three studies, splitting the models by tenure caused the apparent negative neighbourhood effects for social renters to disappear.

Van Ham and Manley (2010) argue that in Scotland in the early 1990s housing applicants in social housing had very little choice in where to live as they were allocated a dwelling in a neighbourhood. Social housing was predominantly allocated based on needs without households having the option to express neighbourhood preferences (choice-based letting was not introduced until 2001). Although it is acknowledged that the allocation process was not completely random (housing officers are known to have made choices based on the individual characteristics of applicants; see Malpass and Murie, 1994), it can still be argued that the allocation process was quasi-random and that biases introduced by ethnicity, household size and age have been accounted for in the models presented by van Ham and Manley. The allocation process of homeowners to neighbourhoods was highly selective, as homeowners were able to express neighbourhood preference, constrained not by administrative procedures and government housing policy but by their budgetary means (Cheshire, 2008). In line with Oreopoulos (2003), van Ham and Manley (2010) conclude that neighbourhood *selection* and not causation are the driving forces behind the apparent neighbourhood effects.

Conclusion: constructing the evidence base

This chapter has investigated the evidence base for mixed tenure policies by asking the question whether neighbourhood effects found in the literature are the result of causation or selection. This is an important question as social mixing through creating mixed tenure neighbourhoods can only have the desired effect if causal neighbourhood effects exist in the first place. The chapter has highlighted some of the methodological problems in modelling causal neighbourhood effects and some of the inconsistencies found in the recent empirical literature on neighbourhood effects.

To make mixed tenure policies work, empirical studies first have to provide the evidence that living in mono-tenure social housing concentrations has a negative effect on individual life chances above and beyond the effect of individual characteristics. At best the evidence that living in social housing estates makes people poor(er) is very thin, and many studies show no effect of concentrations of social housing at all. In addition, there is no evidence that tenure mixing automatically leads to social mixing. In studies where significant negative neighbourhood effects have been identified, there are substantial methodological questions that make the findings at best inconclusive. The most apparent methodological problems are OMV and selection bias. The best strategy to control for selection effects is to use quasi-experimental data from programmes such as Gautreaux and Moving to Opportunity (Ludwig et al, 2001; Goering et al, 2002), or from randomised education studies (see Leventhal and Brooks-Gunn, 2004). In general these studies have provided little convincing evidence that neighbourhood effects exist for adults, although some effects for children were found. But even in the case of the quasi-experimental studies mentioned above, some (self) selection into the programmes – and therefore into more affluent neighbourhoods – took place, which is likely to have biased the outcomes of these studies. The bulk of the current neighbourhood effects evidence comes from non-experimental observational data and most of these studies are likely to suffer significantly from selection bias, especially studies based on cross-sectional data. Studies using longitudinal individual level data are more capable of controlling for selection effects as it is often possible to determine the order of events: do people first move into a deprived neighbourhood and subsequently suffer poor health and job loss, or did the fact that they lost their job cause them to move into social housing in a deprived neighbourhood? Recent studies using longitudinal data for Toronto, the UK and Scotland showed that it is unlikely that individual outcomes are affected by the neighbourhood where people live (see Oreopoulos, 2003; Bolster et al, 2007; van Ham and Manley, 2010). These studies concluded that selection effects are most likely responsible for the correlations found between neighbourhood characteristics and individual characteristics.

The consequences of the above conclusion for policy are significant. If there is no solid evidence that neighbourhood effects exist, there is no evidence base for mixed tenure policies, or more generally, social mix policies. Creating more socially mixed neighbourhoods is unlikely to create more opportunities in life for the original residents. Socially mixing neighbourhoods through tenure mixing will only change the population composition of neighbourhoods, increasing average incomes because more affluent (and employed) residents will move into the owner-occupied housing replacing social housing. The social renters who are subsequently displaced through tenure mix policies will most likely end up in other deprived social housing estates in the same urban area, and for them little will change for the good. The above does not mean that we see no reason to invest in neighbourhoods, but it does mean we do not see a reason to invest in neighbourhoods as a mechanism to directly improve the life chances of individuals. In line with Cheshire (2007b), we think it is better to invest in the skills and health of individuals if you want to improve life chances. Investment in deprived neighbourhoods is still important to create better and safer living environments for the most vulnerable in society, with little other choice than to live where they live.

What is the future for neighbourhood effects research? It is still important to show that there are correlations between neighbourhood characteristics and individual characteristics. Deprived neighbourhoods might not have an independent effect on individual outcomes, but that does not mean we should accept concentrations of poverty. Although existing quantitative research does not show conclusive evidence for neighbourhood effects, this does not mean that neighbourhood effects do not exist at all. Quantitative studies might not measure the right variables, or neighbourhood effects might only operate for certain groups, in certain areas, on certain spatial scales, or in certain national settings. One way in which neighbourhood effects might operate is through neighbourhood reputations where individuals are stigmatised based on the neighbourhood they live in (Permentier et al, 2007). Employers, for example, might not employ individuals from certain neighbourhoods because of where they live. Neighbourhoods with the same statistical characteristics might have very different reputations and quantitative studies are unlikely to pick up such subtle effects.

However, the fact that large-scale, quantitative, nationally representative studies do not pick up neighbourhood effects does show that even if they do exist, the effects are likely to be small compared to the effects of individual characteristics such as level of education. Also, those studies that produced some evidence for neighbourhood effects also showed that the effects found were relatively small compared to the effects of individual characteristics. The future for quantitative neighbourhood effects studies lies in the use of more sophisticated and tailored data that allows detailed geocoding of individuals and allows the modelling of selection mechanisms into neighbourhoods. Without information on how individuals sort into neighbourhoods it will be impossible to untangle the difference between causal effects and selection.

TWELVE

Meanings, politics and realities of social mix and gentrification – a view from Brussels

Mathieu Van Criekingen

Introduction

It is now a matter of fact that the spread of neoliberalism around the globe over the last three decades has been responsible for mounting social inequalities within and across national boundaries (see, for example, Landais, 2007; ILO, 2008; OECD, 2008). If only focusing on Western economies, numerous accounts provide detailed documentation connecting trends of rising income and broader social well-being inequalities to the wide range of political-economic neoliberal reforms enforced since the mid-1970s. Evidence in this respect brings out notably the role of these reforms in the gradual breaking of the post-war Keynesian social compromise, the steady fall in the share of unskilled workers and concomitant upswing in the share of skilled workers, the rise of mass unemployment as well as the general reduction of organised labour organisations' bargaining power (see, for example, Harvey, 2005). How these trends of rising social inequalities translate in changing urban socio-spatial configurations should be a basic underlying issue in any discussion of the meanings, politics and realities of 'social mix' in cities. Yet, in Brussels just as in many other cities, mainstream debates on social mix(ing) appear largely dissociated from any considerations of increasing social or spatial inequalities. The bulk of policy and media narratives tend rather to naturalise the desirability of social mix as a prime policy goal at whatever scale, hence depriving the notion of any proper political dimension and further inserting debates on urban development in the realm of the 'post-political" (Swyngedouw, 2008).

Looking at the Brussels case, social mix appears today as an undisputed policy *ideal*. As the *plan régional de développement* (regional development plan, that is, the city's main master plan) puts it:

> Contrary to the American city, the ideal type for the
> European city is based on a mix of functions and people.
> This ideal has to be found in a city that is able to regenerate
> itself and to create an added value by comparison with what
> the suburbs have to offer. (Government of the Brussels
> Capital Region, 2002, p 9 [author's translation])

However, the profusion of policy and media narratives unambiguously
putting forward the desirability of social mix(ing) offers a general sense
of social romanticism, which for these discourses appears at odds with
the harsh realities of a 'divided city' wherein the distribution of wealth
among social classes is highly uneven – and increasingly so (Kesteloot,
2000; Loopmans and Kesteloot, 2009). Today, 26% of Brussels'
inhabitants live at risk of poverty (compared to 15% in Belgium[1])
despite the fact that the city ranks among the wealthiest European
agglomeration in terms of gross domestic product (GDP) per capita
(Observatoire de la Santé et du Social, 2008). Moreover, about 50% of
the total taxable income is earned by the wealthiest 20% of the city's
population, whereas inhabitants in the lower quintile earn less than 5%
of this total; this gap has been widening since the early 1980s.[2] These
social inequalities translate in sharp spatial contrasts at the intra-urban
scale. Significantly enough, the difference in life expectancy at birth
between the city's poorest and wealthiest municipalities is today as
high as 5.7 years for women and 6.2 years for men. In such a context,
there is an urgent need to think beyond mainstream representations
of social mix as an unquestionable urban policy priority – rather than
fight against socio-spatial inequities.

This chapter is in two main parts. First, we tackle the proper
political dimension of social mix narratives in Brussels by shedding
some light on the politics behind the emergence of this notion as
an undisputed policy ideal. Moving back a little in the local history
of urban governance shows that the present-day broad consensus
among the city's political elites about social mix reflects the increasing
political power of the local, urban-oriented middle classes since the
late 1980s. Accordingly, the notion of social mix is intensively used in
reference to a policy orientation, laying emphasis on fostering a 'back-
to-the-city' (or 'stay-in-the-city') movement by local middle-class
households. In addition, looking at the latest developments in urban
governance and planning frameworks highlights that the meaning
attached to the notion of social mix can significantly change when the
composition or political agenda of the elite coalition in power – or
the type of urban regime – evolves. The adoption in December 2007

of the 'International Development Plan (IDP) for Brussels shows such a rearticulation of the strategic meaning associated with the 'social mix' notion. This rearticulation appears in line with the rise of a fully fledged neoliberal glocal growth coalition eager to capitalise on Brussels' image as imagined 'Capital of Europe'. The second aim in this chapter is to confront existing normative policy discourses promoting the reinvestment of inner working-class neighbourhoods by middle-class households in the name of an enhanced social mix with views on the actual processes reshaping Brussels' social geographies at the neighbourhood scale. Here, empirical findings derived from analysis of intra-metropolitan population migration dynamics suggest that the advance of state-sponsored gentrification in the central city goes hand in hand with increasing socio-spatial inequalities at the city scale – rather than increasing social mixing of population groups.

Social mix as policy ideal in Brussels: the rise of an urban revitalisation policy framework

The premise of social mix acts as a core value of the currently hegemonic vision of urban development in Brussels (Shaton, 2005; Baillergeau, 2008). It is not before the early 1990s, however, that an ideal-type of a socially – and functionally – mixed city has been formalised in regulatory and strategic planning frameworks at the national (that is city) scale, and further translated into various 'urban revitalisation' programmes focusing on inner working-class neighbourhoods. These programmes notably include the provision of renovation grants and tax cuts to homebuyers in these neighbourhoods, the sale of public-owned land at below market rates to private developers in order for them to build new middle-class housing schemes, and a variety of interventions on public spaces involving both beautification and surveillance measures (for example, redesigning pavements, installing new street lighting, furniture and CCTV systems, hiring of urban stewards and park keepers, organising festive events, and so on) (Dessouroux et al, 2009). All these actions share a strong desire to 'open up' inner-city neighbourhoods that were long kept out of the mental maps of the middle classes (Vandermotten, 1994; Kesteloot and Mistiaen, 1998; van Criekingen, 2009).

Looking back at dominant planning frameworks and policy orientations in post-Second World War decades returns a very different picture. National policy makers in the Belgian government primarily designed urban development strategies for Brussels. The main focus was on the reinforcement of the city's role as national capital and major place of transnational political centrality. This priority implied favouring the concentration in Brussels' core city of national administrations, international political bodies (the European Union [EU] first of all, since 1958) and whatever service functions linked to the EU presence (for example, cities' and regions' representation offices, law and consultancy firms, lobbies, non-governmental organisations [NGOs], etc). Moreover, middle-class households were strongly encouraged to settle down in suburban residential areas and commute daily by car or train. These options have notably led to the development of a large office market in the core city,[3] intense middle-class suburbanisation, and the displacement of numerous inhabitants, generally working-class and migrant households, from areas designated for redevelopment into office districts (for example. 15,000 people forced out of the Quartier Nord in the 1960s and 1970s– see Vanden Eede and Martens, 1994). Unlike in neighbouring countries, however, the Belgian post-war model of urban development has not included the production of a significant stock of public-owned housing units. In Brussels, social housing units account today for as little as 8% of the housing stock, and the production of new social housing units has dropped to extremely low levels since 2000 (28 units/year over the period 2000–05 – adapted from Zimmer, 2007), whereas 35,000 households are formally registered on waiting lists.

This model of urban development was backed by powerful coalitions of national and municipal politicians, and real estate developers. It was very much in line with the anti-urban values of the catholic-conservative bourgeoisie dominating then national governmental coalitions (Kesteloot and de Maesschalck, 2001). On the other hand, it was seriously harmful to the city's inhabitants, both the local middle class attached to central city living and – even more drastically – working-class households whose neighbourhoods were directly threatened with disinvestment or destruction. The former category played a key instrumental role in the emergence, from the late 1960s, of an anti-modernist urban social movement pushing forward a Jane Jacobs-like counter-model of urban rehabilitation, soon theorised as the 'Reconstruction of the European City' and backed by a myriad of local action groups campaigning against the destruction of the urban habitat (Aron, 1978).

Although this counter-model gained some political audience during the 1970s and 1980s (notably regarding the consultation of the local population affected by infrastructure projects), it was not before the institutionalisation of a new regional scale of governance in 1989, that is, the Brussels Capital Region, in the wake of the (still ongoing) federalisation of the Belgian state, that this advocacy of the rehabilitation of inner-city neighbourhoods was transcribed into an urban project backed by significant political and institutional power. Put shortly, the creation of the Brussels Capital Region has meant a rescaling of the urban regime, with planning options now being defined by regional political elites elected by the city's inhabitants. Owing to this political rescaling, the former counter-model of urban rehabilitation changed status, that is, it moved from opposition to power at the regional level.

Today, this model underpins a hegemonic 'urban revitalisation' policy framework set up in the early 1990s by the then newly elected first cohort of regional political elites. This policy framework rests on a broad range of programmes ultimately focusing on the enhancement of the quality of life in the city. First of all, 'revitalising' the city intends at altering the territorial imprints of the post-war urban development model which has established suburban municipalities as privileged residential environment for middle-class families (Vandermotten, 1994; Kesteloot, 2000).[4] Bringing middle-class households into central neighbourhoods is considered the best way to solve the 'urban crisis', the prime cause of the latter being attributed to the middle-class suburbanisation:

> The abandonment of these neighbourhoods results from … the fact that Brussels has lost its capacity to attract and settle inhabitants in the inner city, for upward social mobility has meant for many the opportunity to live in the suburbs. (introduction to the Revitalisation of Old Neighbourhoods Act 1992, Council of the Brussels Capital Region [author's translation])

Accordingly, middle-class home-owning families are regarded in mainstream policy narratives as the sole true 'saviours' of Brussels' regional institutions, simultaneously swelling the ranks of solvent taxpayer,[5] housing renovators, stable voters and 'decent' citizens deemed able to instil a new dose of social control in impoverished working-class and migrant inner neighbourhoods (see also Baeten, 2001a). For instance, this inclination is quite clearly expressed in the presentation of the rationale commanding the subsidisation by the federal and regional governments of the building of a new housing scheme in the neighbourhood next to Brussels' South Station:

> The production of the first housing units for middle-income groups would play an important role as 'starter' of the stimulation of this key neighbourhood alongside

> the country's biggest railways station ... Keeping [social
> and functional] mix at a reasonable level ... implies that
> housing for middle-income populations would not be
> forgotten. Unfortunately, the current sociological profile
> of the neighbourhood [i.e. working-class and migrant] and
> the still high land prices make this project difficult, if not
> impossible, unless public money is injected into it. Public
> money will be recovered in the long run thanks to the
> enhancement of the tax base associated with the attraction
> of new inhabitants into the neighbourhood, as well as with
> the attraction of new retail businesses and services which
> usually come with these new inhabitants. (Federal State
> and Brussels Capital Region, 'Beliris' Agreement, Annex
> 8, February 2003 [author's translation].

This is a quite explicit formulation of a state-sponsored gentrification strategy – or gentrification policy (Lees and Ley, 2008; Rousseau, 2008), and the promotion of social mix is given an indisputable priority in it. However, the notion is associated here with a limited, one-directional meaning. The Belgium's Court of Audit clearly emphasises this point in a recent assessment of policy programmes dedicated to 'neighbourhoods in crisis' in Brussels and nine other Belgian cities:[6]

> The promotion of social mixing is found in many
> programmes ...The notion of social mix is a very vague one
> ... Most often, however, it is about attracting middle-class
> households in impoverished neighbourhoods in order to
> create a social mix (it is rarely about promoting social mix
> in more affluent neighbourhoods). (Court of Audit, 2007:
> 47 [author's translation])

The social mix argument is indeed very rarely used in view of the opening up of the established bourgeois neighbourhoods to working-class households. However, in cities of advanced capitalist countries, the general level of social specialisation of residential spaces is generally highest in long-standing bourgeois neighbourhoods (see, for example, Pinçon and Pinçon-Charlot, 1989, 2007), and Brussels makes no exception in this regard (Debroux et al, 2007). In addition, the limited meaning attached to the notion of social mix also translates into the definition of the privileged instruments dedicated to achieve the desired 'revitalisation' of impoverished neighbourhoods. There is a general imbalance here between a very strong emphasis put on encouraging *spatial* mobility of new (that is, middle-class) inhabitants towards inner neighbourhoods (*via* renovation grants, tax cuts for homebuyers, production of new housing units, physical rehabilitation and animation of public space... etc) *versus* a weaker emphasis put on promoting upward *social* mobility of inner neighbourhoods' incumbent residents. Rather, social policies focused on incumbent populations in working-class neighbourhoods, albeit providing some highly welcome social benefits (for example. remedial teaching, training courses, etc), show a strong bias towards social control and surveillance of groups regarded as potentially troublesome, in view of a 'pacification' of these neighbourhoods (Réa, 2007). Finally, these social measures do not affect mechanisms of inflating rent levels and housing prices, hence leaving low-income incumbent residents at risk of forced relocation in case parallel revitalisation policies are actually successful in making the neighbourhood more attractive for wealthier newcomers.

In December 2007, a new strategic planning document was adopted by Brussels' regional government, named the 'International Development Plan for Brussels' (IDP).[7] In contrast to the vision of an urban revitalisation centred on the local middle classes, the IDP focuses on the attraction of international investors, foreign visitors, tourists or conference delegates, and whatever extra-local clienteles of consumers and (temporary or permanent) residents. The document's chief planning option amounts to the opening up of the remaining large pieces of vacant land located on the territory of the Brussels Capital Region for speculative real estate development projects (for example. a football arena, a concert hall, a shopping centre, a congress centre, an exhibition hall, etc). Moreover, the document also advocates the development of new office schemes and middle- to upper-class housing projects, notably in the EU district, as well as the construction of a EU-related landmark cultural centre which could act as a symbol of the city's international scope. These developments are thought to be conducted by public-private partnerships, and framed by ad hoc planning procedures (for example. speeding up the procedures for granting building permits). Accordingly, the IDP builds on a clear entrepreneurial rationale (Harvey, 1989): what is at stake here is the position of Brussels in the inter-urban competition for the attraction of mobile capital, beyond the city's already well-established position as political world city

The IDP is backed by economic elites pushing neoliberal agendas – that is, supporting strategies '[dedicated to] resuscitate cities as sites for capital accumulation' (Wilson, 2004, p 771), among which real estate businesses (that is. developers, investors, consultants) and federations of enterprises are predominant. In this sense, the recent adoption of the IDP points to the emergence since the early 2000s of a new glocal growth coalition, that is, an alliance between regional political elites eager to put forward Brussels' image as imagined 'Capital of Europe' and transnationalised economic elites operating in (or from) Brussels (Van Criekingen and Decroly, 2009 – compare Swyngedouw and Moyersoen [2006] commenting on the absence of such glocal growth coalition in the city *before* the realisation of the IDP). Significantly enough, the IDP was first presented to a panel of real estate and business leaders, and only afterwards to the regional parliament. By contrast, community groups traditionally advocating the middle-class urban revitalisation agenda have been consciously kept out of the elaboration of the plan. Furthermore, no single public debate or open discussion session dedicated to the general public has been held before or since the adoption of the IDP.

This new strategic planning document expresses a substantial re-conceptualisation of the meaning attached to the social mix notion. In substance, social mix is considered in the IDP one of the city's key assets, and one that should be insistently marketed towards extra-local clienteles of residents, investors, tourists and visitors. New city branding strategies articulated around the promotion of Brussels as a 'socially mixed' city – as well as a 'multicultural', 'cosmopolitan', and 'easy-to-live' one – are considered in the IDP as keys to alter common perceptions of Brussels as just the centre of EU bureaucracy, and foster instead new perceptions of a favoured place to live in, to visit and to consume in. Moreover, this new narrative of social mix goes hand in hand with a dramatic deepening of the option to open up inner working-class neighbourhoods to wealthier (local or extra-local) newcomers. The report used by the Brussels regional government as the basis for the redaction of the IDP is particularly unambiguous in this respect:

> ... [the plan advocates developing] a city marketing strategy at the neighbourhood scale ... notably for the most impoverished neighbourhoods, in order to increase their value as well as to prevent their negative image from transcending their boundaries and harming the international image of the city ('Bronx' effect).... Social mix must be a main thread of urban development in Brussels. One must enforce both out-going flows from priority zones [i.e. inner working–class neighbourhoods] in order to avoid the concentration of poverty in social ghettos, and in-going flows into these zones by stimulating the installation of

middle-class populations. (PricewaterhouseCoopers, 2007, pp 72-3 [author's translation])[8]

One could hardly find a more explicit, state-sponsored call for gentrification *and displacement!* This is also a rather violent expression of Neil Smith's (1996) revanchist urbanism thesis, for social mix is thought here to act *for* some (that is, incoming flows of middle-class newcomers) as well as *against* others (that is, out-going flows of incumbent residents). Put another way, promoting social mix is here simultaneously about attracting desired newcomers and excluding the undesirable locals, the latter deemed responsible for the negative image (that is, '*Bronx*') of the inner city. Eventually, this should, however, not obscure the intrinsic nonsense of the claim made here by the IDP promoters, for it is obviously impossible to get any mix of population groups if one argues for moving the incumbent ones out while simultaneously arguing for bringing others in.

To summarise, the recent introduction of the IDP shows that what is meant by social mix can change as the composition and political agenda of dominant elite coalitions evolves. There is an articulation between the type of elite coalition in power, that is, the type of urban regime, the kind of urban development agenda these protagonists push forward and the meaning attached to the notion of social mix. Once only used in reference to a (still vivid) policy orientation laying emphasis on fostering a 'back-to-the-city' (or 'stay-in-the-city') movement by local middle-class households, the notion of social mix is now also integrated as a core element of new city branding strategies, in line with the rise of a glocal growth coalition eager to capitalise on Brussels' image as imagined 'Capital of Europe'.

Social mix in discourses, gentrification in practice?

The above-mentioned report by the Belgium's Court of Audit also states that:

It is likely that the lowest categories of wage-earners which have the most severe difficulties to find a place to live will not benefit from the housing projects. Social mix is a goal put forward in many projects. In practice, it is often about attracting middle-class households in order to get a social mix. Within the framework of policies dedicated to impoverished neighbourhoods, one must take negative impacts into consideration. Rising prices can lead to the displacement of low-income people from these neighbourhoods. At the moment, such impacts are not taken into account. (Court of Audit, 2007, p 4 [author's translation])

Later on, the report even asserts that:

... within the framework of policies targeting impoverished groups, one must seriously take into consideration the negative effects of gentrification. (Court of Audit, 2007, p 47 [author's translation])[9]

As indicated by these quotes, this report makes a clear link between urban revitalisation policies framed in social mix narratives, the advance of gentrification processes and related displacement effects – in Brussels and other Belgian cities. In what follows, we intend to further build on this crucial articulation. After a presentation of the place-specific context in which gentrification processes are embedded in the Brussels case, I comment on previous empirical analyses (van Criekingen, 2008, 2009) dedicated to test whether gentrification-induced displacement processes fuelling broader patterns of increasing socio-spatial fragmentation could be identified at the city scale, using data on migrations to and from inner neighbourhoods.

In a city like Brussels, housing market mechanisms play an essential role in the remodelling of neighbourhoods' social geographies. The Brussels housing market has appreciably tightened up from the mid-1980s, showing a major increase of property values on both the homeowner market and the private rental market, far above the inflation rate (Zimmer, 2007; Bernard et al, 2009). About 50% of households in the city rent their home from private landlords – this proportion reaches two thirds in inner neighbourhoods – and the public housing sector is only residual. Accordingly, a majority of low-income households are accommodated as tenants of private landlords, typically in 19th-century houses divided up in multiple apartments offering poor-quality housing units. These households are highly vulnerable vis-à-vis escalating rent levels, since effective regulations on rent levels are lacking. How the new rent is worked out once a tenant leaves and a new lease is concluded is almost entirely left to the play of market forces through individualised negotiations between landlords and potential renters. Moreover, private landlords have ample opportunities for ending a lease before its term (for example, for self-occupation purposes or for the implementation of substantial renovation work;

see De Decker, 2001; Bernard, 2004). In this context, rising housing costs are now responsible for *in situ* deterioration of living conditions, as renters striving not to leave their neighbourhood have to devote a growing share of their earnings to paying the rent and therefore cut other budget items (education, healthcare, leisure, etc). Figures for 2006 indicate that 54% of renters in Brussels spend between 41% and 65% of their household budget on housing, while 25% is commonly seen as the admissible limit (Bernard et al, 2009).

The continuing internationalisation of Brussels has indisputably given housing market appreciation a major boost, as many landlords, homeowners and real estate investors intend to cash in on the influx of an expanding clientele of expatriate professionals working for the EU and other transnational public or private organisations. Nevertheless, this 'Europeanisation' of the city (Baeten, 2001b) has not (yet) been parallelled by a massive colonisation of working-class inner neighbourhoods by high-income expatriate households. Rather, most white-collar expatriates who opt for a residence in the core city favour long-established pericentral bourgeois neighbourhoods, hence further adding to the elite character of these neighbourhoods (van Criekingen and Decroly, 2003; Cailliez, 2004; see also Préteceille, 2007, on Paris). In parallel, white-collar expatriates who opt for more central locations, in or close to working-class areas, often end up in upmarket, secured residential schemes, including new-build premises and loft conversion projects in the historic core.

There is also ample evidence of central working-class neighbourhoods being recast in the mould of in-moving (lower) middle-class newcomers. The latter are mostly educated young adults (that is, between 25 and 34), living alone or in childless couples in apartments rented from private landlords. Survey evidence suggests that, for many among them, a presence in the inner city is associated with a pleasant yet transitional step in their residential career during which socially and culturally diversified inner-urban environments are strongly valued (Leloup, 2002). Accordingly, these households show generally high residential mobility rates. This implies a rapid turnover on the private rental market that acts in turn as a catalyst for rising rent levels, as it is quite practical for landlords to upgrade the pricing and characteristics of their properties in order to meet educated young adults' rising demand for non-luxury, yet comfortable rental units in the central city. This fuels a process of rental gentrification, that is, a trajectory of upward neighbourhood change basically associated with the reinvestment of the existing private rental market (van Criekingen, 2010). This therefore makes a notable difference from more classical stories of gentrification, whose key protagonists are affluent homebuyers in the inner city (Lees et al, 2007). In this context, the position of low-income households in the inner city is severely jeopardised, even in the absence of any significant transfer of private rental units to owner-occupation.

These housing market pressures, combined with changes in the local supply of retail and services framing expanding landscapes of 'trendy' consumption (van Criekingen and Fleury, 2006) and a general policy prioritisation of the attraction of middle-class newcomers to inner neighbourhoods, eventually affects incumbent residents in working-class neighbourhoods in various ways. Beyond direct considerations of mounting housing cost, displacement pressures also result from the dislocation of locally embedded social networks or the exacerbation of feelings of loss of a familiar sense of place. It is not surprising, in this context, that local community organisations in Brussels' inner neighbourhoods have now many personal stories of deteriorating housing conditions and displacement to relate (Béghin, 2006; Brussels Alliance for the Right to Housing, 2007). This strongly suggests that the current round of state-sponsored reinvestment in Brussels' inner neighbourhoods creates winners and losers, leaving the latter with few other options than staying put at the cost of deteriorating housing and living conditions, or moving away under constraint.

In a city like Brussels, empirical explorations of population migration dynamics directed towards or originating from inner neighbourhoods offers a relevant way to gain insights into the socio-spatial impacts of gentrification against which narratives advocating the revitalisation and enhanced social mixing of these neighbourhoods could be ultimately confronted (see Van Criekingen, 2008, 2009 for details on datasets and methodologies).

Quite unsurprisingly, multiple residential mobility patterns of a different nature are conflated in the set of migrants moving in or out of Brussels' gentrifying neighbourhoods. Educated young adults in non-family households, mostly tenants in the private rental sector, compose a prominent group among both in- and out-migrants to or from these neighbourhoods. Their residential trajectories are heavily focused on the densely built-up urban environment, that is, they move between different central neighbourhoods or between the latter and central areas in other urban agglomerations in the country – such as, for example, Ghent, Antwerp, Liège or Leuven. The prominence of this profile of migrants points to the above-mentioned rental gentrification dynamic associated with middle-class young adults generally opting for gentrifying inner neighbourhoods as temporary holding areas in their housing career.

Empirical treatments dedicated to trace the residential trajectory of out-movers from Brussels' gentrifying neighbourhoods also stress the permanence of a significant pattern of middle-class suburbanisation, involving higher-educated, family households with young children moving towards suburban areas, often remote ones. More importantly, however, findings derived from these treatments highlight a sizeable mobility pattern associated with low-status migrants, that is, less-educated individuals, unemployed people and workers, directed toward working-class and ethnic neighbourhoods in Brussels' western inner city or, to a lesser extent, beyond the city limits, either toward working-class municipalities in the suburbs or toward Wallonia's old industrial urban agglomerations. A large stock of old workmen's houses accounts for much lower housing prices in these municipalities severely hit by deindustrialisation in the past decades. These findings suggest therefore that a sizeable share of the migrants moving out of Brussels' gentrifying inner neighbourhoods are poorly resourced individuals moving towards economically depressed areas, within the city or beyond. However, the quantitative datasets providing the basic material for these empirical analyses do not enable us to conclude straightforwardly that these low-status migrants were forced out of their initial location because of the advance of gentrification. Rather, these findings indicate where the household types most vulnerable to gentrification-induced displacement pressures are most likely to relocate. In this sense, it is suggested here that most of the potential displacees are restricted to short-distance moves within the city, primarily directed towards impoverished working-class neighbourhoods in the western inner city, while some others move over longer distances and leave the city as a whole (Van Criekingen, 2008).

Eventually, these findings corroborate existing views on the mounting concentration of socially vulnerable groups in working-class and ethnic neighbourhoods through intra-urban migration. Earlier works on Brussels have empirically detailed such patterns of relocation of poorly resourced population groups (including, for example, unemployed people, low-qualified workers, migrant households from North African or Turkish origin) from gentrifying areas in the historic core and the eastern inner city towards impoverished working-class neighbourhoods in the western inner city (Kesteloot and De Decker, 1992; De Lannoy and De Corte, 1994; Van Criekingen, 2002). Furthermore, empirical findings also support appraisals by local community organisations (such as tenants unions and neighbourhood associations), stressing that part of the urban poor are now being 'exported' from Brussels' inner neighbourhoods towards other, generally depressed areas in the rest of the country, hence putting even more load on supportive services in destination areas.

In sum, exploring the migration dynamics associated with gentrification in Brussels brings out a pattern of rising socio-spatial fragmentation, both at the intra-urban scale (that is, between gentrifying neighbourhoods in the historic core or the eastern inner city, and further impoverishing working-class and migrant neighbourhoods in the western inner city) and at the inter-urban scale (that is, between Brussels' gentrifying core part, and working-class suburban municipalities or the country's old industrial agglomerations). Therefore, once looking beyond the limits of 'revitalised' inner neighbourhoods, one is confronted with evidence of rising socio-spatial inequality at the city scale – and even beyond – rather than with views of increasing social mixing.

Conclusion

> Social mix per se is neither good nor bad, just as working-class or migrant ghettos per se are neither good nor bad. One can argue a long time about the respective values of social mix and ghettos; one can praise the benefits of mixing social groups or on the contrary emphasize the risks of dispersal and division among working classes brought about by social mixing; one can highlight forms of neighbourhood solidarity in ghettos and even bring out the capacity of ghettos to act as centres of resistance or on the contrary insist on the problems created by housing overcrowding – but whatever the centre of the debate, a basic issue is left out: who takes part in this debate? Who decides? (Tevanian and Tissot, 2010, p 196 [author's translation]

In their insightful critique of French urban policy and dominant representations of the *quartiers sensibles*, Tevanian and Tissot (2010) vividly highlight the proper political dimension of contemporary policy narratives articulated around a social mix(ing) imperative. In this chapter, I have tried to shed some light on this issue in Brussels. Here, just as in many other places, and despite specificities in local social geographies or models of urban governance, social mix(ing) policy narratives refer to one-directional calls to open up working-class neighbourhoods to middle-class newcomers – either locals or extra-local clienteles – to lure into the city. Tackling the political dimension of recurrent calls for social mix therefore implies bringing to the fore underlying policy visions that see the middle classes as the only true 'saviours' of the city.

Opposing the advance of gentrification and related increase of socio-spatial inequalities first requires a radical reconsideration of such policy visions. One key implication for policy makers would then be to give priority to the promotion of upward *social* mobility of the incumbent population in working-class neighbourhoods, rather than the promotion of the *spatial* mobility of middle-class newcomers – that is, fighting poverty, discrimination and social insecurity rather than moving the poor.

Notes

[1] This means living with less than €860/month for a one-person household, or with less than €1,805/month for a household with two adults and two dependent children.

[2] FPS Economy, Statistics Division, data on living standards, own calculation.

[3] That is, 11.5 million m² of office space, excluding suburban office parks and about 2 million extra m² of vacant surfaces (Brussels Capital Region, 2009).

[4] Brussels' regional policy makers are largely powerless as far as the planning of the city's suburbs is concerned, for the boundaries of the Brussels Capital Region coincide with the extension of the core city (one million inhabitants), and not with the extension of the metropolitan area. About 1.4 million inhabitants live in the rest of the metropolitan area outside the region (that is, in Flemish or Walloon Brabant), among whom many are daily middle-class commuters and city users.

[5] The largest part of the region's receipts is due to residents' income taxes, registration fees paid by homebuyers and succession fees.

[6] Albeit this report is about programmes implemented by municipalities using funds provided by the Belgian federal urban policy (hence not about policies implemented by the Brussels regional government), its findings are instructive as far as Brussels' urban 'revitalisation' policies are concerned, for the goals and narratives of both policy frameworks are very similar. Actually, both policy frameworks have been designed under the patronage of the same politician (Mr Charles Picqué), Minister-President of the Brussels Capital Region between 1989 and 1999 and since 2004, and minister of the federal government in charge of urban policy between 1999 and 2003.

[7] See www.demainbruxelles.be (in French), www.brusselmorgen.be (in Dutch).

[8] These sentences have not been included in the official presentation of the IDP's 'road map', presented in January 2008.

[9] These conclusions were given quite a frosty reception by Brussels' regional authorities. As the head of the regional government put it in the press: 'The Court of Audit ... should better assess the legality of the procedures rather than talking politics by echoing the braying of some French sociologists' (*Le Soir*, 18 February 2007, p 10). The quite aggressive and very much anti-intellectual tone of this comment gives an additional sense of the importance of social mix as a key element for the legitimation of urban revitalisation policies in Brussels, as well as at the federal level. Linking revitalisation policies and narratives of social mix to the advance of gentrification is very much of a taboo in Brussels.

THIRTEEN

'Regeneration' in interesting times: a story of privatisation and gentrification in a peripheral Scottish city

Sarah Glynn

Introduction

When I first wrote about what was happening in Dundee, and the proposed demolition of council housing blocks that have dominated the city's skyline for almost 40 years, house prices were rising – though never as fast as in more fashionable places – and developers still had an unsatisfied appetite for land. That is the background of the first part of my story. But by the time I presented my work as part of the seminar series on which this book is based, the economy had turned, and even politicians seemed to be waking up to the importance of social housing (both council and housing association[1]). I was able to end my talk on two small sources of hope for Dundee: that it was not too late to stop some of the worst of the planned destruction of council housing; and that the forthcoming council by-election would bring a change of administration and just possibly a greater willingness to rethink past decisions. On 30 March 2009, Dundee got a Scottish National Party (SNP) council in place of a New Labour-dominated coalition,[2] and the new housing convenor responded to tenant pressure and the changed economic circumstances by agreeing to reconsider the demolition programme. The second part of this story looks at the last ditch campaign to save the blocks against the background of the post-crash economic crisis. I had hoped that the third part would give this story a happy ending, but the day after I completed the first draft of this chapter we learned that, despite all our campaigns and arguments, the council was going to proceed with the demolitions. We can now only try and ensure the buildings are well maintained to the end, and tenants are offered reasonable alternative accommodation – and that this story is told so that others can learn what is happening to social housing and be better equipped to fight for its survival. We will be spared the latest attacks on social housing being planned by the Conservative-Liberal Democrat Coalition Government in Westminster, but Scotland's hegemonic neoliberal consensus is far from accepting defeat.[3]

The era of 'regeneration': selling the city

I began working with Dundee council tenants angered by the potential demolition of their homes in 2004, when the demolitions were first proposed. I was not then a housing specialist but I could see that what was happening was both wrong in its effect on so many people's lives, and against common sense, and I wanted to uncover the mechanisms that were driving it forward. Along the way I got a three-year lectureship at the University of Edinburgh, allowing me to delve into the subject more thoroughly in what I hope was a symbiotic relationship between my academic research and my work with tenants in Dundee and other parts of Scotland.

Central to my research was the need to understand how our politicians and councillors have convinced themselves, and others, that the active promotion of policies that encourage gentrification and the displacement of lower income groups is for the common good. Using the example of what was happening in Dundee, I found that this involved: the (mis)use of popular consultation, the selective adoption of academic arguments, and the promotion of policy-driven research. The practices I exposed will be familiar to anyone who has been involved in community politics around the world, but it is important to continue to record and publicise what is happening.

What we are looking at is – in Europe – commonly carried out under the positive-sounding banner of 'regeneration', but it has been rather more accurately defined by Jason Hackworth and Neil Smith as 'third-wave gentrification': in other words, gentrification that is expanding into new areas, is carried out by large developers, and – crucially – is actively promoted by entrepreneurial urban governance (Harvey, 1989; Hackworth and Smith, 2001). Hackworth and Smith argue that this has become possible because of the turn away from the post-war social democratic consensus, which has involved both the dismantling of institutional structures designed to restrict such uneven development, and the dismantling of the physical structures of social housing and other low-cost housing that literally stood in its way. A lot of wealth has been created and, in the absence of previous constraints and redistributive mechanisms, so has exploitation, exclusion and a growing wealth gap. Gentrification's third wave has also been characterised by a decline in effective resistance as communities are dispersed and community organisers are incorporated into smoothing the progress of the new system. This dissipation of resistance is both symptom and further cause of the decline of the left more generally, and an important part of a wider manufacturing of consent.

This chapter focuses on plans for the demolition of two multi-storey blocks in Derby Street, at the top of the Hilltown in central Dundee, and for the subsequent redevelopment of the site. Dundee has little to offer the big league gentrifiers, but it competes with every other city to attract the globalised middle class, and it is these new citizens and their local counterparts, rather than the ex-industrial working class, that are regarded as the city's future. The 21st-century Dundonian has been envisaged as an aspirational homeowner, and schemes for regeneration in the city involve the demolition of thousands of council houses – over and above the more than 9,000 already demolished since 1990 (www. scotland.gov.uk/Resource/Doc/933/0056544.xls4). Under current plans, nearly 2,000 more homes are scheduled to go, including six multis in Hilltown (two in Derby Street and four in Alexander Street) and five in Menzieshill in the west end.[5] The regeneration plans were intended not only to replace council housing with private houses but to change the visual image of the city, especially for those arriving across the Tay Bridge. This is not, of course, promoted as gentrification, but, working with tenants and with Tony Cox and other housing activists, I found no evidence to back up the official reasons that have been given for demolition. At the same time, I found strong support for the argument that demolition is a damaging policy, in both the short and long term.

These conclusions made use of detailed surveys carried out by tenants in the affected multis, and an analysis of council documents. A crucial source of information was a report by the consultancy firm, DTZ Pieda, whose analysis provided the basis for the council's housing strategy (DTZ Pieda, 2005). Tenants were initially denied access to this report, and were only allowed to see it after an appeal to the Scottish Information Commissioner under the Freedom of Information Act. The grounds for the council's refusal were that the methodology used by the consultants was commercially valuable, so its disclosure would harm their commercial interests (Letter from the council's legal manager, 15 February 2005); an argument that shows a worrying attitude to the idea of objective research, as well as to concepts of consultation, democracy and accountability.

Although our criticisms of council policy have been covered in the local press, until the recent change in administration, debate was always

Photograph 13.1: Multis dominating the Dundee skyline

curtailed by an official response that, rather than engaging with the arguments, repeated the same discredited interpretation. Here is the official version of what was happening as set out in a letter to a tenant by the director of housing in May 2007:

> The continuation of population decline and changes in the housing market continue to generate a surplus of houses in the city, and there is strong, independent evidence that this will continue. Consequently, the Council has houses for which there is no expressed demand, which are blighting neighbourhoods and impacting on community social structures. Additionally there are houses with high investment needs which are unaffordable and uneconomic to retain…. This provides the city with the opportunity not only to remove poor quality stock, but to enhance the range and quality of housing opportunities in the city…. (Letter from Elaine Zwirlein to Tom Black, 3 May 2007)

In other words, and regardless of any evidence that was produced to the contrary, the problems were said to be 'surplus' council housing, council housing for which there was no demand, and high maintenance and improvement costs. These were the ostensible reasons for what was happening, but none of these claims bears much scrutiny.

Even before the economic crisis, homelessness was increasing and housing problems dominated MPs' surgeries.[6] Yet, the DTZ Pieda report had claimed, with no supporting data, that the city had surplus council housing. Dundee had seen a fall in population (though recent figures shows a light increase); however, the report predicted only a negligible fall in the number of households. Moreover, in a city with low wages and an ageing population, council housing was always likely to become more needed rather than less, but such considerations were not discussed. The report actually stated that only half the people who applied for a council house were allotted one (others, especially younger tenants, will not even bother to apply), and it acknowledged that Dundee Council was already finding difficulty emptying the buildings that had been scheduled for demolition because of lack of alternative accommodation.

It is at this point that we can see how policy-driven research is brought into play. When the Scottish Executive (as it was then called) commissioned researchers at Heriot-Watt University to devise a mathematical model that could be used to predict social housing need (Bramley et al, 2006), it was no doubt clear that what they were interested in were minimum figures. In fact the concept of 'need' in this context already implies that. The model responded to the policy agenda, and the two basic assumptions that underlie all the figures should raise the alarm for anyone who is hoping to be allotted social housing. The first is the assumption that social housing should only be made available as a last resort, with everyone else forced to rely on the market even if that leaves them just above benefit levels. The second is the completely arbitrary decision that councils should only have to meet one tenth of the backlog of housing need each year. So, taking the example of Dundee, although the report acknowledged that the city had a backlog need for 6,061 social rented homes – almost half due to overcrowding and sharing – this was translated into a backlog quota of 605 homes a year, which, with the restrictions on social housing eligibility, could be more than met by current turnover. That allowed the report to conclude that Dundee had a net *surplus* of social housing relets of 700 homes a year.[7]

The council claimed that, not only were the houses not needed, they were not wanted. There was no demand for so much council housing, and low demand for these particular homes. Academic theories about 'low demand' were originally developed to explain the decline and deterioration of areas of housing; however, 'low demand' housing has come to be seen not just as a symptom of area decline, but as a cause. Research in this field remains a relatively speculative attempt to make sense of a wide range of interconnecting variables, but it has been invested with an unwarranted authority by councils anxious to divest themselves of the costs of public housing, and to promote developments that will attract a new wealthier class of people. Glen Bramley, together with Hal Pawson, has noted with approval how arguments about low demand have been used by councils to justify diversion of investment away from the worst areas of public housing, which were portrayed as fit only for demolition, enabling them to reduce their housing stock (Bramley and Pawson, 2002); and DTZ Pieda commented in a report for the Office of the Deputy Prime Minister in England that the reduction of social housing was an important by-product of such demolitions (DTZ Pieda, 2000). Architectural determinism can be used to gloss over more fundamental social problems, and may itself contribute to neglect and spiralling decline. However, more critical academic assessment (Gough et al, 2006) has generally been ignored in favour of these ostensibly pragmatic models.

In Dundee, even after decades of minimal maintenance of council stock, there were, as we have seen, still twice as many people applying for council houses as were allotted them; and, even before the recession, there were clearly many more people who could have benefited from council homes but, for various reasons, had not applied. Some houses and areas are, of course, more popular than others, but, as with any other product, demand is not a fixed number waiting to be discovered: it will increase if the housing is improved or otherwise made more desirable. Graphic evidence of this was provided by two groups of medium-rise flats in Lochee in West Dundee, which were built to identical plans. One group had become very run down, and few residents objected to being moved out to allow its recent demolition. The other received an injection of money and a makeover some years ago, and the flats are much sought after.[8]

In order to demonstrate the unpopularity of the specific homes proposed for demolition – and also their commitment to consultation – the council's housing department carried out surveys of the affected tenants. These were done very rapidly and with minimal supporting information: the buildings were described (ambiguously) as 'at risk', and the £1,500 Home Loss payment was emphasised. The surveys produced the desired results – 57% in favour of demolition in the case of Derby Street – and the councillors speedily and unanimously supported the demolition proposals, despite an impassioned plea from tenants' representatives and a packed gallery of protestors.

As unease and anger grew among the tenants, I worked alongside housing activists and tenant campaigners to produce alternative independent surveys. These were able to give a more realistic assessment of tenants' views after anti-demolition campaigns had generated discussion of the issues in the local media and in the buildings concerned, and there had been time for people to understand what was involved and the lack of other options available.

The picture that emerged was very different from that portrayed by the council, and I think that the tenants involved in carrying out the surveys were themselves surprised at the extent of the opposition to demolition (Glynn, 2005). In the two Derby Street multis, we found that 71% of those surveyed wanted to remain in the buildings.[9] Only 18% wanted to leave, and several of those told us that they needed to find somewhere without stairs for medical reasons, or somewhere cheaper. Only 9% supported the idea of demolition. We also found that 30% of the households surveyed said they had not received the council ballot paper on demolition.

The council argued that demolition made economic sense, freeing up money for essential investments in its 'core stock' so as to bring it up to the new mandatory Scottish Housing Quality Standards by the 2015 deadline. In fact, the housing department's plan assumed that by that date a further 1,300 homes would have been declared 'surplus' and emptied for demolition so that they would not need investment in improvements. The crucial DTZ Pieda report for Dundee hinges on economics: it is a 'Financial Viability Study'. However, the figures given in that report suggest that demolition could, in fact, be a hugely more expensive option than repair and improvement. Demolition may have made economic sense for the council, but only, it seems, because they expected to receive vast amounts of subsidy in various forms from the Scottish Executive, or as it is now called, the Scottish Government. It should be noted that then, as now, there was virtually no subsidy available for the management, maintenance and refurbishment of council housing, and that councils' housing revenue accounts were and are expected to be self-supporting. However, there was subsidy for demolition, and for grants towards limited numbers of new housing association, although not council, homes.[10] According to DTZ Pieda (who give no explanation for, or breakdown of, their figures), demolition of 4,630 homes would require an additional sum of £32 million, plus a further £60 million of grant subsidy towards 1,350 new housing association homes. Can we assume that such subsidies were considered a price worth paying to get rid of a large amount of social housing, boost private developers and woo middle-class incomers?

A further abuse of economic logic is found in the arguments about which buildings to demolish. The DTZ Pieda report for Dundee made clear that, despite all the talk about popularity, when it came to choosing targets for demolition, they were largely influenced by maintenance costs.[11] Although the multis were in good condition, with a likely minimum life of 30 years, they have higher electrical and mechanical costs, including lift replacement. But what are never mentioned are the many savings associated with vertical living in matters such as public transport and the maintenance of roads and pathways – savings that would, of course, benefit different budgets.

Tenants were also told that one reason for demolitions was that the buildings did not comply with new, greener, statutory insulation standards. However, insulation can be improved relatively easily, and a serious environmental policy would welcome the multis' compact planning with minimal travel distances, and would reject unnecessary demolition.[12] We are being asked to recycle yoghurt pots by the same authorities that promote the wasteful destruction of whole buildings. (We discovered much later that the majority of the Derby Street flats actually already met the minimum insulation requirement, but the council had never done any calculations.[13])

After we had finally managed to get access to the DTZ Pieda report, some of these criticisms were covered in the local paper. They were followed by the usual response from the council's then housing convenor, who told their reporter,

> We make no apology for taking away the type of housing
> people no longer want in a bid to regenerate communities
> and to saving hard-earned rentpayers' money on property
> that incurs needless costs. (*The Courier*, 28 April 2006)

Six years after demolition was agreed, 50 out of 374 flats in the Derby Street multis are still occupied (October 2010). It is taking much longer to empty the buildings than planned because people did not want to move, and because of the very real lack of alternative housing.

Many people have been put through high levels of stress. Moving is always stressful, and a sense of powerlessness and an inability to control events only increases stress. It is known that taking older people away from the places with which they are familiar can have serious affects on their psychological – and consequently physical – health.[14] There were disproportionate numbers of older people in all the buildings scheduled for demolition, and quite early on, we were already being told of people being made ill with worry.

At the time the multis were built, slum clearance schemes were being accused of destroying communities. Now another generation of linkages is being pulled apart. In most places today, community ties are not seen to be as strong as they were at that earlier time, but that does not mean that they are not there, or are not important. There are families in which two or even three generations lived in different flats in the same multi, and many people have other family members in the area. There are also people who have maintained long-term friendships with their neighbours.

People have been put under a lot of pressure, tempting them to accept places they might not be happy with, in areas where they have no links, for fear of something worse. There are many stories of people who regret having moved and who miss their multi – the security, location, friends, generous-sized rooms and panoramic views. Several people have a housing history of moving from flat to flat ahead of different regeneration schemes – and some from Derby Street have gone to the adjacent sheltered housing scheme, which itself is now being considered for demolition.

Photograph 13.2: View from the Derby Street multis

Some households will have found themselves forced into peripheral estates, away from the services they are used to, and with few services altogether, dependent on the bus for everything. What's more, the people who lived in the multis formed a significant proportion of those who used local shops, and other amenities. As they left, these have become less viable. Already in January 2007, the council was becoming concerned about commercial decline in the Hilltown (*The Courier*, 9 January 2007), and local shopkeepers were very supportive of our recent anti-demolition campaign.

Many tenants will have ended up in homes with higher rents and service charges run by housing associations, or even in much more expensive and less secure private tenancies. Almost all new social

Photograph 13.3: The Derby Street multis and local shops – several of which have closed!

housing has been built by housing associations rather than the council, so although the council said it would respect the consultation that showed Dundee tenants did not want stock transfer of council housing to housing associations, it then carried out policies that have resulted in transfer by the back door. The Scottish Executive tried to rebrand stock transfer as 'community ownership', but there is widespread understanding that transferred housing is less democratic, as well as more expensive to run – and consequently to rent.[15]

The statutory £1,500 Home Loss payment (set back in 1989; see *Statutory Instrument 1989 No 47 [S.2]*) was intended as compensation for the stress and upset of a forced move. Although the Land Compensation (Scotland) Act 1973 stipulates that tenants are also eligible for 'disturbance payments' to cover 'reasonable expenses', these are ill defined and have been interpreted differently by different councils. Dundee City Council has got away with providing nothing more than vouchers to help with, but by no means meet, decoration costs.[16] Tenants have to pay removal costs, and many have invested considerable amounts of money, time and energy in improving their homes, which they are now expected to do all over again. This can leave them seriously out of pocket.

Photograph 13.4: A much-loved multi flat

Those still living in the emptying multis initially welcomed the relative quiet, but new difficulties soon materialised. As the buildings emptied out, repairs were kept to a minimum and vandalism spread. People found themselves the only ones left on an otherwise empty landing, and vital concierge systems were cut back. Flats where all the surrounding homes are empty can become unbearably and unhealthily cold and damp – and very expensive to heat. Some households in Menzieshill and Alexander Street had to endure three winters in these conditions before being found alternative homes. Derby Street tenants have described wrapping up in extra layers or even staying in bed to ward off the cold, and our May 2009 survey showed that many had spent over £40 a week on heating (Glynn, 2009b). (For the winter of 2009-10 – after repeated demands – tenants were provided with some financial assistance through the fuel poverty scheme, and similar arrangements have been made this winter.)

The demolitions are affecting not only tenants in the buildings being knocked down, but also many other existing and would-be tenants, as the number of houses available has decreased. Good flats have been sealed up while homelessness continues to rise, and while recession is increasing the need for affordable rented homes. Level entry flats in Menzieshill have been left empty (and are now being demolished), while people with limited mobility remain stuck in upper floor tenements. And, with so many flats unused, the council is receiving fewer rents, forcing it to impose substantial rent increases on remaining council tenants.[17]

And what of the plans for the sites? The regeneration strategy document for the Hilltown, produced in 2008, disguised the plans to remove a large section of the area's existing population under the usual rhetoric about consulting with 'community groups', creating 'a place where people would want to live' and 'planning for strong and stable communities' (Dundee City Council, 2008, pp, 8, 12, 10, 7). No account was taken of the views of existing tenants being forced to leave their homes, for whom these developments are "fancy houses for somebody else to buy on my plot" (interview with tenant, 28 July 2006). On the sites occupied by over a thousand council houses in the multis and adjacent buildings, the document proposed an increase in the percentage of 'affordable' private housing, through mixed-tenure developments of around 420 new homes, of which less than a quarter would be socially rented. For the whole of the Hilltown, the council's housing strategy for 2004-09 gave a short-term (five-year) target of just 98 new social-rented units, which was planned to rise to 250 units by 2034 (Dundee City Council, 2004, p 27). Clearly, only a fraction of tenants having to leave their homes will be able to be accommodated in the area. Is this what the director of housing meant by 'enhanc[ing] the range and quality of housing opportunities'?

An internal council discussion document on 'affordable housing', leaked to housing activists in the summer of 2006, presented the development of private housing on the demolition sites as improving the quality and choice of *private* housing in the city, and as bringing 'regeneration benefits through encouraging more balanced communities with more diversity of tenure' (Dundee City Council, 2006). Here we see another example of the selective use of academic research. Tenure mix – and implied social mix – is being promoted simply as an unquestioned good, ignoring the growing body of evidence that questions this assumption.[18]

While Dundee Council has made no attempt to record what has happened to those households displaced by demolition, it could not claim to be unaware of some of the knock-on consequences of its policies. The leaked document also noted that registered social landlords [RSLs] (generally housing associations) were 'reporting difficulties in competing with private developers to acquire land ... for new housing development' and that '[t]here is a danger that RSLs are only able to secure land in locations that are least attractive to the private sector' (Dundee City Council, 2006). The demolitions, as we have seen, were leading to a substantial reduction in low-cost rented housing in the centre of the city and in the west end, and new housing association homes were being forced out to cheaper land on the margins.

Despite this internal acknowledgement that all was not well, the effect of the way housing policy is currently presented – of which Dundee provides just one example – is to shift debate away from fundamental questions. As with other aspects of neoliberalism, structures that were generated in accordance with the hegemonic political agenda have been credited with the neutrality of scientific facts, and major policy shifts have been accepted as somehow inevitable. Discussion has been restricted to the mechanics of implementation, and bureaucrats drive policy forwards in compliance with centrally audited targets. Elected representatives are portrayed as powerless to resist these 'natural' forces, and have become disengaged from the policies they are nominally responsible for. This was brought home to Derby Street tenants when one of the councillors came to meet them, and confessed to never having seen the crucial DTZ Pieda report, at which point they felt like helping him unceremoniously out of the multi window. I doubt if most other councillors had seen the report either, yet they all voted for demolition with hardly a question asked.

After the crash: struggling to get out as the juggernaut ploughs on

In the last three years so much has changed – and also so little. The construction of an economy around property speculation has proved as unstable as any other pyramid selling scheme, and much of the mechanism of 'regeneration' has been brought to an abrupt halt. However, belief in the free-market economics that created the speculation has proved rather more resilient. Politicians of all hues are attempting to take on the crisis from within the same neoliberal paradigm that brought it about. While some have used the crisis as an excuse for a stronger dose of neoliberalism, in line with what Naomi Klein labelled disaster capitalism (Klein, 2008), no mainstream politicians have shown willing to do much more than tinker with the edges of existing systems.

After the crash there appeared to be a growing recognition of the importance of social rented housing, as increasing numbers of families saw other options disappear, and private developers stopped building new homes. But there was more talk than political action. Money for new social housing was announced with great fanfare, but the amounts do not begin to match the scale of the problem. Scottish housing policy is devolved and social housing has generally been treated better here than south of the border; however, the total Scottish budget is dependent on funding from Westminster, and Housing Benefit is not devolved, so scope for a radically different approach would anyway be limited.

By the spring of 2008, the situation in Dundee was so bad that the local paper ran features on the city's housing crisis (and the council's denial of its existence) for over two weeks.[19] In response to this, I worked with other activists to organise a public meeting and street stalls. No member of the council administration accepted our invitation to the meeting, and the Dundee Federation of Tenants' Associations, which is funded – and much quoted – by the council, refused too, on the grounds that such a meeting was 'political'.[20] We were also told that we could not hold a stall in the city square as we did not have public liability insurance and someone might trip over it – a tactic increasingly used to clamp down protest. In the event (and to the disappointment of the waiting press cameraman) we were not stopped, presumably because the council wanted to avoid more bad publicity. We had won our small battle in the fight to reclaim public space and prevent the suppression of dissent, but the council took little heed of our arguments. And up on the hill, the Derby Street tenants were still facing a war of attrition, which is a very hard war to win.

While refusing to accept that the city had a housing crisis, Dundee Council did acknowledge the need for more affordable rented homes, and they were one of the first councils to buy up unsold privately built houses. Such policies were being widely promoted as a way of bailing out private developers; however, this gained the council only 15 homes, and was balanced by a reduction in their target for future social house building (*The Courier*, 7 August 2008). At the same time, most of the developers that might have been expected to build on cleared regeneration sites had stopped building – and Dundee had its share of half-finished aborted developments. But still the council would not reconsider its policy on demolitions.

Then, at the end of March 2009, following a council by-election and subsequent political dealing, a new SNP administration was formed, with one of the Hilltown councillors as housing convenor, and Derby Street tenants began to hope that this could herald a new approach to the future of their homes.

The changed economic situation was central to these hopes. After all, the previous decision to demolish had been supported by the SNP along with all other councillors, and even though Jimmy Black, the new housing convenor, seemed sympathetic to their position and had not been a councillor at the time of the earlier vote, he needed the support of his SNP group. The tenants' association had, of course, always argued that the decision to demolish was ill-founded, but now it was more manifestly so, and councillors would have ample public justification for a change of policy. In a long interview with Dundee's *Evening Telegraph*, Black stated:

> We have about 14,000 council houses, with around 8,000 people on the waiting list, 2,500 homeless applications every year and some 600 homeless families and individuals waiting to be housed at the moment. On that basis, the idea that we have a surplus of housing is just daft, which is why I want to look again at the demolition programme. (9 April 2009)

While Black might also have liked to rethink the demolition of the Menzieshill multis, these had had a less active tenants' campaign, were more nearly empty, and – crucially – were less expensive to demolish and on more valuable land.

For the Derby Street tenants, this second stage of their campaign was very different from the first. Whereas, before, all approaches to the council had been peremptorily dismissed, they now found themselves working alongside the new housing convenor in an attempt to make the case for refurbishment robust enough for him to have both the confidence and the ammunition to take it to his colleagues. I worked with the tenants, helping in the organising of the group and the gathering of evidence.

One of the first things we did was carry out another survey among remaining tenants, which found a very similar proportion wanting to stay in the buildings as before (Glynn. 2009b). It also looked in some detail at what people liked, or did not like, about the flats and the local area. The responses showed strong appreciation of the central location, local shops and good bus services, and of the security of the buildings with their concierge system. People also appreciated the spacious layout of the flats, and, of course, the views; and we included some comments from people who regretted leaving and would like to return. The suggested improvements – better heating, insulation and window seals, rewiring, new kitchen and bathroom fittings, improvements to public areas, and reinstatement of concierge manning levels – would be standard components of a refurbishment scheme; and our report noted that these would have to be combined with better building management.

Figure 13.1: From the cover of the Second Tenants' Survey challenging demolition

Next, I looked at the several million pound question of refurbishment costs. To ensure a realistic estimate for the construction costs, I used comparisons with other refurbishments, and budget costs available via the web. Council officers responded with their own calculations, coming up with a figure that was two thirds as much again as mine (PowerPoint by Jimmy Black, 30 September 2009). Unimpressed – and with the convenor's consent – we invited a private contractor, Wates Construction, who had done similar work in Glasgow and other cities, to look at the buildings. Their price of £7.8 million (including £2.4 million for full insulated external cladding) was a bit lower than my original calculations. In addition, refurbishment would have obviated the need to pay the substantial demolition costs, which the council estimated as between £2.5 and £4.4 million.

Then followed long discussions with Jimmy Black and officers from the housing department, where we argued over financial projections and disputed the assumptions on which they were based. We questioned the assumed void level of 10% (when it had only been 6.4% without refurbishment) and the requirement to pay back any loan within 15 years, and we pointed out possible instances of double counting of maintenance costs and the need to factor in inflation and its impact on the real value of interest payments. (We also pointed out that they had miscounted the number of flats!) Long-term projections will always have a large margin of error, and relatively small changes in basic variables can be used to give very different conclusions. The conclusion of the council officers was that the sums did not add up, and without their support it became clear that the elected representatives were not going to be persuaded to take on what was being presented as a huge and costly risk. People tend to be more concerned about being blamed for doing something that goes wrong than about not doing something right.

By this time we felt like the hero in a fairy story who at each turn is set an ever more impossible task. Reluctantly, we had to accept that we had reached the end of the line in our pursuit of council investment, and, in spite of all our concerns about stock transfer, we asked if we could approach housing associations to see if they might be interested in taking the buildings on and retaining them as social housing. We put together a description of the buildings (including plans, photographs and sketches of possible improvements) and sent it to the five housing associations active in the city, together with a supporting letter from the housing convenor. Although they found such an approach from a tenants' group rather unorthodox, four of the associations were sufficiently interested to send senior people to meet us and look at the buildings, and one went on to initiate funding discussions with the banks.

Figure 13.2: Proposals for improvements to external areas from the brochure we sent to housing associations (1)

Figure 13.3: Proposals for improvements to external areas from the brochure we sent to housing associations (2)

The issue then became the council's willingness to demonstrate its commitment to make the scheme work, and to do a deal that did not transfer unsupportable risk to the housing association. To the intense frustration of the association, as well as the tenants, this last hope was dashed when the SNP group agreed not to rescind the original demolition decision. The councillors' position clearly responded to that of the unelected housing bureaucrats, who had always demonstrated an extreme reluctance to backtrack on their plans or admit that they had made a mistake in their assessment of the buildings. Keeping the multis would have had knock-on implications for their regeneration plans, and any successful scheme would not have reflected well on those who had tried to write the buildings off. Throughout these negotiations, the housing department continued to plough ahead with policies geared towards demolition, and a council officer told the chair of the Derby Street tenants' group that they intended to pick off remaining tenants one by one. Maintenance was allowed to deteriorate and one couple was even sent an eviction notice that had to be stopped by the housing convenor.

It did not help, either, that, in the middle of our discussions, the council received the results of its latest 'housing need' study. Although Black publicly disputed the conclusion that there was a 'surplus' of social rented housing, and accused the formula of giving 'distorted results' (*The Courier*, 3 October 2009), this new report helped to strengthen

quarter rose from 136 in 2004 to 313 in 2006. Over the first three quarters
of 2009 it averaged 446 (www.scotland.gov.uk/Topics/Statistics/Browse/
Housing-Regeneration/qrtrefmarch2010).

The figures for Glasgow are even more worrying. A backlog *need* for 29,603
social rented homes was translated into a backlog quota of 2,960 homes a year
and a claimed *surplus* of social housing relets of 4,590 homes a year, which
has been used to justify demolitions on a vast scale.

oggeyley Gardens is now largely demolished. Nearby Dryburgh Gardens
owned by a housing association, but the differences can be attributed to
estment and maintenance rather than tenure.

he survey had a 48% response rate.

dget tightening has meant that there is no longer money available for
olition, but Dundee City Council received and spent £3.4 million of
ish taxpayers' money on demolition related programmes. (Figure for
nditure given by Jimmy Black to a meeting of Derby Street tenants, 22
2009.)

have since been told that there were also higher than average management
due to high turnover (meeting with Jimmy Black, 15 June 2009). There
many reasons for this, but it would not be unreasonable to expect a
turnover in flats than in family houses, and there are always people
ed short-term accommodation. Besides this more transient group, there
any tenants who had been in the multis a long time, and our May 2009
of remaining tenants showed a broad spread of length of residence.

nne Power's arguments for improving older housing (Power, 2008).

we got refurbishment priced by Wates Construction, Wates carried
eat-loss calculations.

t think it is an exaggeration to argue, as Bob Dumbleton has done,
me cases the disruptions of demolition can be fatal, although of
is is very difficult to prove (Dumbleton, 2006).

, the National Audit Office in London calculated that investment
ransfer cost the public purse an extra £1,300 per house, and the
counts Committee commented that this was an underestimate
Commons Council Housing Group, 2005). The DTZ Pieda report

official thinking and encourage officers' fears that either the Derby
Street multis would be hard to let, or that they would take tenants
away from other council multis. (It also discouraged at least one of the
housing associations.) This approach is consistent with a wider culture
of governance that emphasises risk-minimising auditing at the expense
of progressive social change (Cowan and McDermont, 2006).

There remains just one positive note. The council has promised that
there will be no more mass demolitions, and that the 1,300 further
homes that had been planned to go before the new standards became
mandatory will be kept and improved. As Black pointed out, there is
no where else for tenants to go – but our long campaign must have
made his decision easier.

Meanwhile, at a national level, after three-and-a-half years in power
the SNP government is still patching together its policy towards
housing. Subsidies are still being given to support home ownership,
housing associations are being told they should rely less on public
funding, there are proposals for new partnerships with the private
sector, and money for refurbishment of council housing has hardly
even made it onto the agenda. Despite articulating support for social
housing, the Scottish Government is still pushing a version of the
Bramley 'housing need' model (which was used in Dundee Council's
recent reassessments) and encouraging an increased reliance on private
renting (Scottish Government, 2010, p 3). However, they have ended
the Right to Buy for new social housing tenants – though not for
existing tenancies; the social housing budget has been increased – but
as a short-term measure taken out of future budgets; and some money
has been given for new council housing – though only a fraction of
what is needed. In 2009 a Shelter report observed that the number
of social rented homes in Scotland was the lowest it had been in 50
years (Shelter, 2009).

I have tried to use this case study to intervene in the developing
policy debate, and I would like to end this section with a summary
of the arguments for refurbishment of council housing that I wrote
for the Scottish Tenants' Organisation to give to the Scottish Housing
Minister in April 2009:

> The Scottish Government recognises the need for more
> social housing. It also wants to get the most housing it can
> for its investment. Improving existing housing is generally a
> lot cheaper than building new. It is also much greener. And it
> can avoid the destruction of communities and forced moves
> that were so rightly condemned in the redevelopments of

the 60s and 70s. The underlying reason for most demolitions has been a deliberate reduction in the amount of social housing. If government now recognises the need for more social housing rather than less, then it needs to re-look at the case for demolitions. It is commonly argued that the homes that are demolished are those for which there is no demand. Our research with tenants in Dundee shows that this is by no means always the case. On top of this, demand for a house, as for any other product, will go up if that house is improved. Government has recognised the importance of improved standards for social housing, but unless more money is made available for improvements then the new standards will force councils to get rid of the homes they can't afford to do up – and many tenants will be forced into poor quality private rented housing. Much existing council housing that is currently scheduled for demolition has the potential to become good quality homes for a relatively small investment. To make that happen the Scottish Government needs to work with local councils to make the money available for upgrading existing stock. If not, millions of pounds worth of assets and thousands of potentially good homes will just be destroyed.

Back to an uncertain future

As the remaining tenants vacate the multis – slowly, as there are few places for them to go – there are as many unanswered questions about the future of the Hilltown as there are about the futures of those who are leaving it. Dundee was always the poor cousin of other gentrifying cities, and it has little to fall back on to attract developers in times of recession. (The city's most successful company would appear to be Safedem, which, in 2009, was named World Demolition Contractors of the Year; *The Courier*, 6 October 2010.) However, as we have seen, this did not stop Dundee Council from adopting, unquestioningly, the standard 'regeneration' paradigm and attempting to replace social housing with 'social mix'. Dundee's ability to attract gentrifiers may be limited,[21] and the nature of the resulting Hilltown 'community' will not be clear for many years; however, the impacts of the destruction of social housing are already being felt. Other tenures are less expensive in Dundee than many places, but the city has large numbers of households on very low income. The demolitions are affecting not only those forced to leave their homes but everyone who needs somewhere to live. Even

as we campaign to ensure that those displaced by t offered decent homes, we are aware that each hom from the multis makes one less for others on the same time, and contrary to all the 'social mix' rhe poorer households from the centre of the city t actually promote segregation rather than decrea is not only geographical, it is also political. Des intentions of some individuals, the political syster disregard for the clearly articulated requiremen most in need of its help. It has been made cle to have no stake in the future of the city. This encouraging social interaction; it is social exc

Acknowledgements

With thanks to the tenants and housing activists six years. A longer version of the first part was *and Practice* (2008, vol 1, no 2).

Notes

[1] The greater part of British public housing wa local councils. Recent decades have seen a po to 'third sector' non-profit housing association of existing council stock, but in Dundee ten initial consultative phase. The term 'social council and housing association homes.

[2] The previous administration was a Labou support from the Conservatives.

[3] Since Devolution in 1997, housing in of the Scottish Executive – now Goverr

[4] These demolition statistics do not giv majority will have been public rented,

[5] 1,898 homes were declared 'at risk' – – by the council's housing committee demolish the Derby Street multis w

[6] Meeting with Shona Robison MSP 6 October 2006. The average numb

[7] s a h

[8] is in

[9] T

[10] B dem Scot expe Apri

[11] We costs can b higher who n were n survey

[12] See A

[13] Wher out full

[14] I do n that in s course th

[15] In 2003 via stock Public Ac (House of

for Dundee observed that an increase in supervision and management costs per unit from £495 to £595 would be a 'reasonable cost for an alternative landlord in stock transfer' (DTZ Pieda, 2005, para 4.16).

[16] Instead of vouchers, the council is now making sure relets are in good decorative order, but tenants still need to pay for curtains and floor coverings as well as more personal changes.

[17] With each of the (approximately) 4% rent rises introduced in 2006, 2007 and 2008, the director of housing commented on the fall in rental income due to council house sales and demolitions (*The Courier*, 17 January 2006 and 2007 and 22 January 2008).

[18] Although, in the different context of their response to the Scottish Government's 2007 housing Green Paper, council spokespeople themselves noted that 'some of Britain's most sustainable and stable communities are single tenure' (www.scotland.gov.uk/Resource/Doc/214031/0056981.pdf, answer to question 23).

[19] See *Evening Telegraph* from 25 March 2009 onwards. This is the sister paper to *The Courier.*

[20] For an analysis of the role of officially supported tenants' organisations such as the Federation, see Glynn (2010). Funding for the Federation comes from the Housing Revenue Account, and so, ultimately, from tenants' rents.

[21] The council's hopes now rest on the 'Bilbao effect' of the proposed Dundee V&A Design Museum, which will move the city centre further from the Hilltown.

FOURTEEN

HOPE VI: calling for modesty in its claims

James Fraser, James DeFilippis and Joshua Bazuin

Introduction

There is little question that the goals and policies of mixed-income housing in US cities are fundamentally about the transformation of urban space. And yet, despite the centrality of this goal, there are only a few studies to suggest that the transformation of urban space envisioned by its supporters and decried by its opponents is of any great magnitude (GAO, 2003; Holin et al, 2003; Zielenbach, 2003; Turbov and Piper, 2005; Castells, 2010). While these point towards benefits of the spillover effects of HOPE VI (Home ownership and Opportunity for People Everywhere) mixed-income projects, there is variation even within HOPE VI developments in the same city. Many of these empirical studies, as well as more conceptual accounts of the factors which would support neighbourhood transformation, suggest that development pressure, that is, the existence of neighbourhood desirability in relation to other areas of potential investment, are the strongest correlates to change. Studies have not concluded that mixed-income itself has been the cause of neighbourhood change; the two most recent studies on the effect of HOPE VI mixed-income housing development on neighbourhood change have concluded that other development pressures, market dynamics and a host of other amenities (that is, transportation, commercial retail, employment opportunities) may be necessary to transform low-income areas of cities. These factors tend to come together in economically strong cities (Castells, 2010; Zielenbach and Voith, 2010). Further, Goetz (2010) finds that the degree of neighbourhood change is not correlated with positive changes for individual-level outcomes for low-income families.

Based on these and other studies on the effects of HOPE VI for neighbourhood change and individual-level outcomes including the everyday experiences households have in HOPE VI redevelopments, we suggest a call for modesty regarding the impacts of the actual 'mixed–income' component of these revitalisation and poverty amelioration initiatives. Notwithstanding non–HOPE VI mixed–income initiatives that may only use 'mixed–income' as a veil for market penetration into, and subsequent gentrification of, targeted low–income neighbourhoods, we contend that many cities that are not 'economically strong' may show less pronounced HOPE VI effects as measured by people or place–based outcomes. These changes, as previous work has suggested, may be unevenly distributed when examining multiple HOPE VI initiatives in the same city. Our study of four HOPE VI developments in Nashville, Tennessee, examines both place–based change as well as changes experienced by residents in these developments. We examine the narratives of 120 households within these developments to understand the perspective of people actually living in four of these environments. Prior to the case study, we briefly review mixed–income housing policies and how the 'mixed–income' component is purported to operate.

Policies and practices of mixed-income housing

In general, mixed–income housing is done in one of two closely interrelated but not synonymous ways. The first is through the dispersal of poor people who are geographically concentrated. The second is through the redevelopment of formerly poor areas or housing developments. These two ways can roughly be thought of as people–based and place–based mixed–income policies respectively. Or they can be thought of as two different ways in which the urban geography of poverty is being remade. The first is a deliberate spatial strategy of dispersal and deconcentration of poor people away from a poor area in which the fate of the area from where they are dispersed is of secondary concern, if it is of any concern at all. The second is a deliberate spatial strategy that remakes the spaces in which poor people reside. In so doing the bulk of the poor are inevitably displaced, but what happens to them is of secondary concern. And while they are distinct from each other, they have significant overlap – if for no other reason than the fact that poor people are dispersed from areas that are redeveloped. There are several policies or sets of policies associated with each of these strategies. We discuss the policies associated with dispersal before proceeding to those associated with redevelopment.

Since the early 1970s, and increasingly since the early 1990s, there has been a decided shift in the form that federally subsidised housing takes, and that shift has been away from the project–based subsidised stock and towards the voucherisation of subsidised housing. While vouchers were not originally meant to promote mixed-income housing or neighbourhoods, they have become strongly associated with this goal, and therefore they have grown in support among mainstream housing policy analysts. As the project-based subsidised stock opt out of the affordable housing programmes and convert to market housing, the tenants within them receive vouchers that they can use *in situ* or they can take with them wherever they decide to live. This slow drip of the conversion of housing from project-based to vouchers has not received the attention of the more dramatic demolitions associated with HOPE VI, but has impacted far more affordable housing units, as more than a quarter of a million units have been lost, with most converting the tenants to vouchers (see DeFilippis and Wyly, 2008).

The second set of dispersal policies are Gautreaux and Moving to Opportunity. The Gautreaux programme began in 1976 and was the result of a US Supreme Court decision against the Chicago Housing Authority for concentrating public housing in black neighbourhoods in the city. The programme gave selected residents counselling, and other assistance, to help them move into whiter neighbourhoods. The Moving to Opportunity programme has generated significant attention among academics and policy makers, more than is perhaps suggested by the experimental programme's very modest size of fewer than 5,000 people in just five cities (see, for instance, Briggs et al, 2010). The programme placed people in project-based subsidised properties into one of three groups: (1) a group that simply stayed where they were; (2) a group that received vouchers that could only be used in low-poverty neighbourhoods; and (3) a group that received regular Section 8 vouchers. The point of the programme was to measure the outcomes for the people in the three different groups. While Moving to Opportunity was modelled on Gautreaux, the big difference is that Gautreaux was race-based and Moving to Opportunity was income-based.

Policies that focus on the transformation of poor neighbourhoods or housing developments take several forms. Perhaps the best known, and most studied, is HOPE VI. HOPE VI is the demolition of public housing and its rebuilding as mixed-income housing, often with New Urbanist design principles. The specific dimensions of HOPE VI have been outlined in numerous studies, but one of the central goals of this programme is to create physical and social environmental conditions that will enable those defined as lower income to pull themselves up from poverty into a higher socioeconomic status and experience an increased quality of life as it relates to the places they live (see Joseph et al, 2007, for an excellent overview of HOPE VI's stated underpinnings and goals). While many critics of HOPE VI show that the absolute numbers of subsidised housing units in these developments decrease in comparison to the pre-existing public housing development on which they were built, other studies have demonstrated that mixed-income housing neighbourhoods have not produced the intended economic, or quality of life, goals, even for those who have been able to relocate into the completed HOPE VI developments (Joseph et al, 2007; Fraser and Nelson, 2008). Joseph et al (2007) suggest that there is a 'need to lower expectations' for what HOPE VI might accomplish for lower-income populations because the conceptual underpinnings and routes by which low-income people might achieve their goals in the context of HOPE VI are either underspecified or not operating as conceived. We add that this current state of affairs may be due to an under-appreciation of the relationships between home, neighbourhood and work. For example, while HOPE VI-inspired improvements in housing stock, architectural design and aesthetics are seemingly desirable, public housing authorities, social service providers and even HOPE VI communities all operate in the context of social forces – such as the production of labour markets and public policy – which are beyond their immediate power to change.

Finally, there is the issue of gentrification. Whether or not policy makers, public officials or private sector supporters of mixed-income housing explicitly endorse gentrification as a potential outcome of mixed-income housing implementation, the reality is that the creation of desirable housing markets can have that effect. Goetz (2005, p 70), citing Bennett and Reed (1999) as an example, notes, 'that private investors are now bidding up property values in the vicinity of public housing projects', as a way to accrue profit from speculative increases in land rent. Neil Smith (2002) notes that gentrification is a general strategy engaged by public and private sectors to revitalise their cities to be competitive places for other forms of economic investment. The confluence of housing policy and broader urban economic development strategies tends to promote place as an amenity for new economy workers (that is, those with more disposable income). What is remarkable about this trend is not that developers have pushed for new markets to invest their capital in, but rather that public policy, via academia (Florida, 2005), has fostered this sense of creating a common good that, like the Reagan years, promises to trickle down to those in the most vulnerable position but rarely does. While some observers have demonstrated that HOPE VI-styled mixed-income housing pushed people out of their home spaces, for the more capitalised members of society, the parallel non-HOPE VI – public–private ventures to reclaim low-income neighbourhoods for higher socioeconomic status populations – simply devastate opportunities for those who are less privileged (Fraser and Kick, 2007).

Why mixed-income housing, and does it work?

The fundamental goal of mixed-income housing in the US is a reorganisation of the relationship between poor people and urban space. We have discussed the two different ways in which these respatialisations occur. But the questions remain, why are such policies being pursued, and what kind of evidence is there to support or critique such efforts? There are various reasons why mixed-income housing is a goal, but all share a core belief about the deleterious 'neighbourhood effects' of poor people living together. And all the justifications, or at least those stated anyway, inevitably come back to the issue of helping the poor by having them live in proximity to the rich (or at least middle class). These effects are thought to play out in four different ways (see Joseph et al, 2007; DeFilippis and Fraser, 2010): the improved social networks/social capital of the poor people that live in mixed-income neighbourhoods; the increased social control and improved social organisation the poor will have if living near middle and upper-class people; the importance of middle class and wealthy people on the behaviour of the poor – in terms of presenting role models for the poor; and the improved services and goods available to the poor once upper-income people live nearby (the political economy of place).

The first of these four has its roots in Putnam's (2009) understanding of social capital, the thinking being that poor people lack social capital and placing them in proximity to the wealthy will increase the quality and quantity of their social networks, thereby enabling them to improve their incomes and quality of life. The second and third have their roots in Wilson's 'underclass' perspective (Wilson, 1987) and Lewis's 'culture of poverty' (Lewis, 1959) – any distinction between the two being increasingly irrelevant from the point of view of policy. This is the idea that, as Brophy and Smith (1997, p 6) bluntly put it, 'physical concentration of poor households in multifamily projects causes severe problems for the residents, including joblessness, drug abuse, and welfare dependency ... a mixture of income levels will reduce the social pathology caused by concentration'. Finally, the last reason, the political economy of place, is rooted in the recognition that public services and the goods of collective consumption are better provided in middle-class and wealthy neighbourhoods than in poor ones.

When examining the impacts of these policies, it is clear that these programmes do not produce their hypothesised results and there is little evidence that the expected benefits will be realised. Simply put, poor people do not seem to benefit much from mixed-income housing. Goetz, in an article summarising the literature on mixed-income housing, states, 'the degree of improvement in quality of life reported by the residents is mixed, being quite modest in most cases and frequently nonexistent' (Goetz, 2010, p 5).

The failure of mixed-income housing neighbourhoods to improve life for poor people is not particularly difficult to understand. There are several reasons that seem clear to us. These policies – particularly those that promote mobility – often leave poor people in places without the social networks and informal social support of prior neighbourhoods. Similarly, such mobility-based policies often leave poor people without the institutional services and support of their prior neighbourhoods, and locates them in new places which lack the institutional capacity to provide those services (Goetz, 2010). Finally, mixed-income policies have also failed to create social mixing, networks and interaction – that is, social capital. This is because the mixed-income housing neighbourhoods leave the larger social cleavages unaltered. For example, HOPE VI developments – and the organisations that govern them – typically sort people based on subsidised versus market rate status. Thus, social sorting occurs based on classed, and in many cases, raced and gendered identities.

There are a wide range of urban redevelopment efforts that purport to use mixed-income housing strategies as a way to deconcentrate poverty and improve neighbourhood conditions by attracting higher income populations to targeted low-income areas of cities (see Fraser and Nelson, 2008, for an overview). These efforts have been marked by a large degree of variation of people and place-based outcomes (A. Smith, 2002), and this heterogeneity has posed a challenge for researchers to make generalisations about the people and place-based effects of mixed-income housing strategies as a whole. While we report that most studies find little, if any, direct effects for low-income residents, there have been more pronounced place-based outcomes. Indeed, this edited volume usefully asks the (possibly rhetorical) question 'Is mixed-income housing yet another route towards urban gentrification?', to which we respond 'Sometimes'. A host of studies on HOPE VI have emerged that find 'positive' place-based changes related to urban revitalisation and accompanying increases in housing values (Zielenbach, 2003; Kleinhans, 2004; Bair and Fitzgerald, 2005), and there are a wide range of treatments that focus on routes toward these place-based outcomes highlighting the importance of location, management and 'appropriate' income mix (Brophy and Smith, 1997; Finkel et al, 2000; Wexler, 2001; Varady et al, 2005). While these enabling conditions to transform public housing and nearby neighbourhoods may come together to produce pronounced urban revitalisation, in some cases gentrification, in many cases HOPE VI mixed-income housing initiatives produce more modest spatial outcomes. This does not mean that these outcomes are trivial, as some segments of society may experience very real advantages while others experience the effects as deeply disadvantaging.

Our case study draws on historical documents and interviews ($n = 120$) with households from four HOPE VI sites in Nashville, Tennessee, as well as housing authority staff, social service providers and city officials. These data tell a story of mixed-income housing development that has a range of effects on people and place that fall somewhere in between the status quo and complete neighbourhood/ development transformation. Nashville is in some ways a unique case, but it does demonstrate well our key theme: HOPE VI outcomes are often modest, and the mixed-income component may provide relatively little to the dynamics of limited change. We are intentionally placing ourselves between people who sing the praises of the programme and those who condemn it, to create a more nuanced story, one in which the important successes in transforming people and places are noted but their limited scope and reliance on dynamics other than income mix are acknowledged. Context always matters in geography, and our examination of HOPE VI in Nashville demonstrates that there is a lot more to HOPE VI than just its mixed-income structure.

HOPE VI in Nashville, Tennessee

The Metropolitan Development and Housing Authority (MDHA) in Nashville has received a total of four HOPE VI grants to rehabilitate four distressed public housing complexes in the city. The agency's applications to the Department of Housing and Urban Development catalogue a litany of deficiencies and problems with the physical plant, high crime rates and extreme poverty levels at the now rehabilitated complexes. The barracks-like construction and high density that characterised these sites prior to redevelopment were criticised as fitting in poorly with the surrounding neighbourhoods, which were rapidly deteriorating themselves due to disinvestment.

MDHA received its first HOPE VI grant in 1997 and received subsequent grants in 1999, 2002 and 2003 to rehabilitate Vine Hill,

Preston Taylor, Sam Levy and John Henry Hale Homes respectively (Figure 14.1 shows the locations of the sites in Nashville). Like many HOPE VI projects across the country, the programme involved a significant reduction in the number of units available at the sites; only 800 subsidised rental units remain at the four sites, from more than 1,800 original units (see Table 14.1 for details). MDHA was quite intentional in structuring eligibility requirements for the units to radically alter the residents' income diversity; it was an explicit goal of the programme that less than 50% of residents would fall into the 'very low income' category, whereas 100% of pre-HOPE VI residents fell into this category.

Figure 14.1: Public housing complexes in Nashville

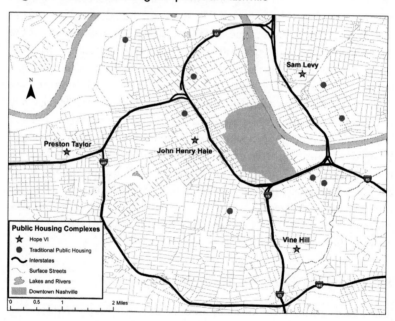

Efforts to include market rate residents in Nashville's HOPE VI redevelopments have been mixed at best. Only 10% of rental units at Preston Taylor, the largest HOPE VI site, are reserved for market rate tenants; the rate rises to 20% for John Henry Hale and Sam Levy. Market rate rental units are physically identical to subsidised units and are dispersed throughout the complexes. Only Preston Taylor has on-site homeowner units, expanding the resident mix from renters to owners, but even here the majority of units built for sale – incidentally, almost all of which were priced for low-income families – were located off-site.

Table 14.1: Changes to site-based housing at four HOPE VI complexes in Nashville

Complex name	Original number of units (bedrooms)	New subsidised rental units	New market rate rental units	New onsite home ownership units	Total new units (bedrooms)
Vine Hill	280 (590)	152	16	0	168 (420)
Preston Taylor	550 (1,437)	280	30	40	310/40 (732)
Sam Levy	480 (1,256)	181	45	0	226 (562)
John Henry Hale	498 (1,176)	188	40	0	228 (547)
Total	1,808 (4,459)	801	131	40	916 (2,261)

Mixed-income living and opportunities in HOPE VI communities

Many of the residents with whom we spoke were able to identify many advantages and opportunities inherent in living in HOPE VI communities as opposed to living either in other forms of public housing or in market rate rentals. By virtue of policy, to be eligible for a unit residents must be either working or pursuing an educational qualification. Those who are working towards either a General Educational Development (GED) certificate or degree are generally quite happy with the opportunity to do so and the support they receive through HOPE VI in the pursuit of that opportunity. Consider this woman, a single mother with two young children, who was studying to become a nurse:

> Interviewer (I): "So when you moved [to HOPE VI] were you already in nursing school?"

> Respondent (R): "No, when I first moved in here I was not in nursing school. I was doing tech work at Bordeau [nursing home], and I had another part-time job. I was working at a daycare. Then they had these papers coming around saying who wants to go back to school to be an LPN [licensed practical nurse], so I was like I'll try it, just give it a shot.... They offer some other type of programs too, but I know it's not just nursing."

I:"And so you knew about the nursing school through the site manager?"

R:"Through the site manager, uh-huh."

I:"And have any of your neighbours said there is a hospital in Franklin that is going to be hiring soon and you should put in your resume? Is there any of that kind of networking that happens here?"

R: "No, cause everybody's just like in and out over here. Cause I can sit here all day long, and I can just watch how my neighbours are ... everybody is in and out. We got kids, some of us work at night, some of them work during the day, some work part time, full time.... Other than my two neighbours on each side of me, I'm going to say hey as they are going down the street or as they are coming in I might just say hey...."

I:"So when it comes time for you to find a job do you think that you will be able to get help with like your resume or something with the services that are here?"

R: "Uh-huh, uh-huh, they have classes. They always send these papers around like now they are offering a free computer class. They do free GED courses up here ... free resume writing, free classes for all of this different stuff, so yeah they do."

I:"So generally you think that living here has been a boost to your goals?"

R: "Uh-huh. But not only that, I can afford to do it. I don't have to pay like six hundred dollars in rent. I can go to school, work a little part time and still be able to afford my home, and not worry about getting evicted, so I think it has benefited me a lot."

This woman was only a few months away from graduating and had a plan that when she had a job as an LPN she would move out of the city to find better schools for her children and housing that was still of high quality but cost less. In our discussion around how HOPE VI had helped her achieve her goal of becoming an LPN, she explicitly denies that links with her neighbours had played any role. Rather, she says that people's busyness in trying to maintain their current status through work or to get ahead through education were an obstacle to meaningful interaction that could provide the networking that could potentially help neighbours identify new opportunities. This theme appeared in a number of interviews: neighbours are constantly in and out at all hours of the day, taking care of their children or going to work, and do not have compatible schedules or the time to be particularly neighbourly. This woman attributes her success in moving towards her goals to two things, specifically vocational programmes offered either by site management or by social service providers and the opportunity to live in housing that was affordable as she pursues the goal. She found out about the opportunity for LPN training through information provided by site management and will be able to use formal career services provided in the neighbourhood to assist in the search for a permanent position after she graduates if she needs to; her neighbours play no role in the means by which she finds and accesses these opportunities. Furthermore, she describes her affordable rent as a significant advantage that provides her with more stability so that she can continue to pursue her studies without interruption. This is a feature of *affordable* housing policy, not mixed-income housing policy.

Residents also report that HOPE VI provides them with the opportunities to take risks in their lives, such as opening their own business or changing careers. Consider this woman, who has just finished her culinary education and is beginning to open a catering service:

> I: "If there is anything particular about Sam Levy versus any other place that you might have lived that is particularly helpful for you in meeting your goals, or maybe challenging or maybe some obstacles?"

> R: "I think, well with me really I think it's just because of the income part of it, it's allowing me to save and it's helped me that way, because if I was living somewhere else where I had to pay about eight hundred dollars a month I honestly wouldn't be able to afford some of the things that I do have for my business and pay some things off that I was able to pay. I was actually able to pay my truck off since I've been here because I haven't had to pay as much as I would somewhere else. Financially it has allowed me to better

myself, and I don't think my business would have grown as much over the past two years because I wouldn't have had the money to make it grow like that. And it gives you an opportunity, you can still have somewhere nice to live, but you can still put your money into, you know, furthering business, education, whatever. I've finished school since I've been here, you know, it's allowed me to do a lot of things financially that I don't, I can't honestly say I would have done had I not been here."

I: "Okay, do you think that uh, that if you were living somewhere else that you might not have finished school?"

R: "Maybe not. The last apartment that I was living in before my sister's house, it was about the size of this downstairs and I was paying seven hundred dollars a month, and the utilities were much higher – we get a break on the utilities over here. Being here allowed me to pay for that, so financially I don't think I would have been done with school now. I don't think we would be having another baby right now either. I mean a lot of things factored into the finances and being over here allows you to financially get yourself together. I don't think anybody should just use it, people who might say, hey I don't have to pay as much let me go spend that extra money. It has allowed us to save and do other things and get out of debt and all that."

This woman's HOPE VI experience has helped her both to finish school, start and expand her own small business, pay off some debts and improve her overall financial situation – she says elsewhere that she is also taking advantage of the escrow account which accumulates money towards a down payment for a house and has used credit counselling classes to improve her credit score. Increased financial stability and capacity has also allowed her to expand her family without worrying how to pay the bills. She is, in many ways, a posterchild for the outcomes that the people who initially drafted the HOPE VI legislation had envisioned, but she is also extraordinary, for she is among a handful (four or five) of individuals in our sample who have similar levels of achievement and optimism for the future. Most tellingly, however, she attributes none of her success to the mixed-income nature of the neighbourhood. Her neighbours are not booking her for parties or referring her to potential clients, nor is she providing networking services to them. Instead, like the woman finishing up her LPN coursework, she has taken advantage of programmes offered by site management or community partners. Most crucial to this process of achievement has been the affordable rent, indicating again that the subsidised rent at HOPE VI is perhaps the most important component in promoting upward mobility. Unlike the previous example, however, this woman was pursuing this trajectory even before she moved to HOPE VI. She outlines an education process that took 11 years to complete as motherhood, changing schools and financial challenges created delays. She had nearly completed her degree prior to moving to HOPE VI and had a clear plan to start a business; HOPE VI provided the financial stability to accelerate her achievements. A significant number of people in our sample had similar narratives: they had a clear agenda for personal growth and identified HOPE VI as a means of achieving their goals. They pick HOPE VI as a place to live because it provides safe, clean and relatively cheap accommodation, combined with structural support for the self-improvement process, which they cannot find on the private rental market for affordable prices. The mixed-income nature of HOPE VI seemingly plays no consideration in these choices, nor are residents able to articulate how the diversity of income in their communities enhances the opportunities for self-improvement.

Over and over again, residents told us that they were pleased with the calm, quiet and safe environment that HOPE VI provided. For the most part, they felt confident raising their children here, felt confident walking around the community at night, and felt safe in their homes. So says a former resident who was moved to another public housing complex during the redevelopment and then returned to his mixed-income site:

> I: "So could you compare Sam Levy now to where you used to live, I guess the one before?"
>
> R: "Well before they tore it down and rebuilt it, it was violent. They were shooting and killing up each other, and it's just peaceful now. Before the rebuild, I wouldn't sit outside and stuff. I would stay in the house and try to stay calm, and now I can sit outside and have peace of mind at night so it's a great here."

These changes are drastic, and the anecdotal evidence provided by residents is confirmed by MDHA analysis, which shows that the

HOPE VI sites went from being the public housing complexes in Nashville with the highest crime rates to having the lowest crime rates in their portfolio post-redevelopment. But how are these changes sustained? Does the presence of a mix of incomes in the neighbourhood automatically lead to less social disorder? We have very little empirical data with which to form any opinion, but some of the residents appear to have been asking themselves similar questions. This man, a single father and a medical student at a nearby university, summed it up as follows:

> R: "I knew of a person who lived in another HOPE VI. I didn't know them personally; it was a friend of a friend who had explained to me basically what HOPE VI was all about, the premise behind it. I know my concern was I didn't grow up in public housing. Before this place was built it was the projects. When they knocked down the projects they gave the old residents an opportunity to come back.... Before I thought about moving into public housing it was my concern as to the type of people I would be living around, not that I think I'm better or nothing of that nature, [but] it's just a legitimate concern of mine. When I sat down with the manager she explained to me you know what they were doing. You know they were only looking for people that were in school or working which you know when you pull in a group of people like that, it changes the dynamics of you know everyday living and it was true."

This man attributes the changes to a qualitatively different type of person being allowed to live in the neighbourhood. Intentionally, access to this housing has been restricted to people who are working or pursuing education; in addition, people with felony convictions, poor rental histories with MDHA, and other records of misdeeds can also be excluded. Site management made a claim to this man that this new type of person who would be allowed to live in the neighbourhood would change the dynamic of the place compared to the previous dynamics present in the projects, and he affirms that the change has taken place. But could this change have taken place without constructing HOPE VI sites as mixed-income communities? Does a high concentration of poverty necessarily lead to increased social disorder? Is it not possible to ensure that it is the most needy individuals and families who receive high quality subsidised housing, and then ensure that the communities in which they live remain safe?

Although theoretical claims do not necessarily connect to residents' experience in the way imagined by policy makers, we cannot discount the effect, in the discursive sense, of living in a mixed-income environment. The question, again, is not whether or not mixed income means anything to residents, but rather how it is made to mean. So, while many of the benefits of living in HOPE VI may be attributable primarily to affordability, or to site improvements above any claims to the effect of income mix, the fact that these are mixed-income sites remains significant. The mixed-income aspect makes it evident to residents, particularly those in market rent units, that HOPE VI is not only concerned with the provision of housing. When asked to compare living in a HOPE VI site with her experience renting in the private market, one resident reported:

> "I've been in the private market before and this is nothing like private market at all. And I don't see them acclimating us to be able to adjust to a private market because private market is nothing like the way that they are trying to run this."

Another resident explains:

> "I think people feel like ... it's just a part of being on public assistance, I think, to a certain extent. You don't have full control ... because you're under a programme, you know?"

Residents are aware, then, of mixed income in terms of each site representing a mix of housing and programmatic aspects. Mixed income serves to differentiate residents in terms of who is, as this resident put it, "under a programme", and who is simply a tenant. Living under a programme, however, means more than service utilisation, or fulfilling one's contractual obligation to the housing authority under the terms of QWHRA (Quality Work and Housing Responsibility Act). As a perceived benefit of a mixed-income environment, living under a programme can also mean having one's own opportunity structure revitalised in a process parallelling the redevelopment of the site. A number of residents, in subsidised and market rate units alike, summarise mixed income in this way. As one market rate renter explains:

> "If you have someone like me and my neighbour, who are market rate, it kind of takes away the stigma of, 'Oh, this is just for people, Section 8 people, or this is just for people

who left the projects, so it's going to be the same thing'. If you can say, 'Well, now we have people that are' ... that society would say are successful, or people who are working people, then you have people will say 'OK', and they have no problem with that over here, if you have a mixture ... you are not saturated with people who have a Section 8 mentality."

The income mix is interpreted as having an intercessory effect, improving relationships between residents at each site, as well as between the sites, given their history as traditional public housing, and the community-at-large. Mixed income is the new face of the projects. As a resident in a subsidised unit states:

"[The presence of market rate tenants] helps the neighbourhood to bring value because of the people that come in. If they are paying market rent, they aren't hanging out with hoodlums. To me, it makes me feel that I'm not just living in the projects."

Another resident makes clear that opportunity is the product of aesthetic improvements that have been designed principally to attract tenants of higher socioeconomic status:

"You can see how the neighbourhood is going up over here, it makes people just want to do more, and you can, you know, anticipate better things happening in the neighbourhood. I mean like ... this neighbourhood grocery store that looks run down, they are finally actually redoing it on the outside, where it kind of goes with the neighbourhood, and you can see some of the street signs now ... and they are doing the lampposts and, I mean, when you do that for neighbourhoods I think it gives people hope that it's going to be better."

There may be agreement between theory and practice as to the role of aesthetic improvements in attracting higher income tenants, but we find after this point that there is a parting of ways. In practice, aesthetics is not the precursor to economic mobility in the way that it may be hypothesised. Rather, it is made to be the very substance of mobility, or at least, perceived mobility. It is possible, even likely, that if HOPE VI were designed only to make site improvements and did not include the mixed-income model, that residents might make a similar connection between aesthetics and opportunity, but this is not the HOPE VI that we have. The policy as it is has the discursive function of making site improvements presuppose income mix such that the two are interpreted as equivalent; the physical spaces are made nicer because middle-class people live there.

Beyond the fences: mixed-income complexes and neighbourhood change

Resident interviews also provide some information on how HOPE VI might change a neighbourhood. One resident noted that there were early signs of gentrification around Sam Levy, as white residents started moving into a predominantly African American neighbourhood:

> "I've gone and talked to the neighbours who are buying and redoing the houses. I would say that they're neighbours you don't normally expect. I will admit that this is a predominately black neighbourhood. Now it is kind of weird because you see white people. That's what people are starting to do over here. It's not just a black neighbourhood any more."

Certainly there are signs of neighbourhood change around Sam Levy, but it is limited in scope. Our own neighbourhood audits have identified three blocks directly adjacent to the complex where a number of homes have been refurbished, but we estimate that there are no more than approximately 30 homes that show outward signs of significant investment, despite Sam Levy having been rebuilt five years ago. Certainly the neighbourhood is changing, but it has not substantially changed.

This respondent identified that higher-income residents are often able to demand change from governmental and other authorities, but noted that the change she saw around Sam Levy was limited in scope:

> R: "I'm very familiar with the neighbourhood. The only problem I would say over here is because of the way the neighbourhood was before this, I think people are just stuck that they only have to provide simple services to cater to the people who were here before. And I just don't feel like because you live in low income housing that everything around you has to cater to low-income people. You know,

not saying that you are better than anybody like that, but
a lot of the work that I do is in Brentwood and Franklin
so when you are around other people and you see a better
quality of life and that's what I'm used to even though I
can't afford it. That's what I'm used to so when I try to
find services around here you see that they still cater to
what was here before and that's just kind of hard for me
to deal with....''

She compares the services and amenities available at Sam Levy to
Brentwood and Franklin, two areas of the city that are quite wealthy.
While she herself would like to have some of the same services available
to her, she notes that that the neighbourhood currently houses services
and amenities for a low income population – perhaps because the
number of middle-income residents in this neighbourhood is still too
low to provide sufficient demand for different services and amenities.

Conclusion

Examination of the HOPE VI sites in Nashville challenges one of the
major theoretical justifications for mixed-income developments, namely
that the lower-income residents will benefit from the social and cultural
capital of the higher-income residents. While we have documented
a willingness on the part of both lower-income and higher-income
HOPE VI residents to participate in such exchanges (a willingness, it
must be said, which has been untested by their actual participation in
such an exchange), we have found very little evidence to suggest that
they actually do. The narratives of personal success and improvement
that are present in our interviews with residents attribute success to
the provision of affordable housing and programmatic supports like
credit counselling, savings programmes and occupational training. What
is remarkable in these sites is a systemic lack of resident interaction,
particularly in regard to networking towards opportunity.

There are a number of reasons for this lack of interaction around
opportunity. Residents themselves frequently cite the obligations of
their pre-existing job or schooling commitments, combined with the
need to raise their families, as precluding wider contact with their
neighbours. As such, the very requirements of residence at HOPE VI,
namely that one must work or be enrolled full time in an educational
programme, preclude the possibility of self-improvement through
networking with one's neighbours. Some residents also feel hostile
towards their neighbours, in some cases a class-oriented antagonism

based on the fact that residents receive similar housing despite vastly different rent payments or perceptions that the scarce spaces reserved for the very poor are being invaded by higher-income residents who are unable or unwilling to understand their needs and wants. Other residents are suspicious of their neighbours, worried that their behaviour is being constantly monitored and infractions reported to management, which then endangers their tenancy. Management itself promotes a culture that simultaneously discourages resident interactions beyond sanctioned (and perhaps controlled) social events while wanting residents to survey each other's behaviour.

It is clear from these communities that, in pursuit of promoting personal improvement among lower-income residents, it is not sufficient to simply sprinkle a limited number of higher-income residents in a historically poor community and then expect that the lower income residents, either through indirect observation of their more affluent neighbours' behaviours or through direct mentoring, will somehow become more like the higher income residents. What is less clear, however, is where the fault lies in the programme model. One could argue that there are simply not enough higher-income residents in the four Nashville HOPE VI communities, where the maximum concentration of market rate renters never exceeds 20%. Many residents reported that they interacted most with their two or three immediate neighbours, and the probability of having a market rate renter in that mix is less than 50%. Another possibility is that site management has not promoted a structure in which residents know how to find the neighbours, which could be most useful in providing resources. While residents reported participating in social events and meetings around neighbourhood problems (primarily infrastructure and nuisance concerns), opportunities for career networking through a neighbourhood directory which includes people's occupations, through formal mentoring mechanisms or through panel presentations in which successful residents talk about how they pursued their educational or career goals seemed to be non-existent.

Our study finds that living in a mixed-income environment, at least in the case of HOPE VI, has provided low-income residents with benefits, although the vast majority of these are not directly related to the income mix. Rather, in the case of public housing transformation – which has certainly had pernicious effects on displaced populations and those who cannot access the rebuilt housing – residents have benefited in a myriad of modest, yet important, ways. Alternatively, one could conclude that there was a lack of intentionality on the part of HOPE VI administrators in Nashville to promote better outcomes for residents by leveraging neighbour-based assets and creating the enabling conditions for spillover effects. A different reading of this might be that mixed income, as it has been deployed to promote urban transformation of public housing sites around the US, has occurred in places where other development pressures do not exist, and HOPE VI administrators were aware that even modest improvement as measured by a range of people and place-based indicators would be sufficient. This does not deny that HOPE VI, or mixed-income models in general, are deeply disadvantaging to some, especially very low-income people. Mixed-income housing development may very well be neoliberal in intent by seeking to recreate urban space in a manner that increases the economic 'entrance' requirements to targeted neighbourhoods and in non-HOPE VI efforts it is likely that gentrification might occur, but mixed income as a discourse and practice is not autonomous and it operates under already existing conditions that moderate what it can produce.

Over the past 20 years there has been an urban policy emphasis on creating 'mixed-income' neighbourhoods out of ones that 'experts' have characterised, largely, as unhealthy environments. The use of mixed income to justify the wholesale displacement of former public housing residents is problematic in a variety of ways that scholars and activists alike have documented. In tandem, building on other critiques of mixed income promoting 'gentrification by stealth', our previous work highlights the ways in which people living in poverty are marginalised in mixed-income development schemes, primarily through the tendency of policy makers to conflate harsh neighbourhood conditions with the dominant discourse that concentrations of the poor are the problem. This conceptual slippage, in our estimation, is not surprising because virtually none of the literature hints at how low-income people have value in mixed-income housing development initiatives (DeFilippis and Fraser, 2010). The findings we present do not discount the possibility that many stakeholders in the city would like to see the HOPE VI, mixed-income, areas gentrify. Our goal has been to show that the narratives of those residents who were able to gain entrée to the new HOPE VI developments speak of the tangible – if modest – benefits they have experienced as a result of being able to live in quality housing; yet, these benefits have come at a cost to the 'truly disadvantaged'. Our respondents, in parallel form to promoters of HOPE VI in Nashville, largely support the displacement or exclusion of former public housing residents who once lived in the area by constructing these prior inhabitants as the problem, as rational actors who somehow could have singlehandedly improved their public housing development even in the face of decades of government neglect and negative public sentiment toward allocating the needed resources to address systemic poverty.

It would be difficult to make the case that these new residents, or the population shifts in neighbourhoods surrounding these redeveloped housing estates, constitute gentrification. This is because the socioeconomic 'mix' that HOPE VI has generated is truly modest. We suggest that the more significant aspect of these initiatives to transform urban space is the hegemony of mixed-income policies. Even in the face of growing evidence that mixed-income housing development does not ameliorate poverty for very low-income households, policy makers enthusiastically support it as a strategy. More importantly for our case study, low-income residents who have been able to move into these redeveloped areas (whether they be market rate or subsidised units) provide narratives suggesting that the mixed-income component of their new environment is inoperative in any sense of providing a public good that individuals can access. Alternatively, the effectiveness of using mixed-income approaches to frame the transformation of urban space is evidenced in the ways in which the same residents distinguish themselves as being different from the prior residents. Their accounts suggest an alignment with the state in that current residents view themselves as legitimate rights-bearers to this improved housing and environment, and many of them identify the prior residents in much the same way as the prior housing, out of place. While gentrification may be the desire and outcome of many urban redevelopment efforts operating under the banner of mixed-income, context is important to recognise the multitude of ways that it operates to provide advantage for some while erasing the citizenship rights of others.

Part 5
Experiencing social mix

FIFTEEN

The impossibility of gentrification and social mixing

Mark Davidson

Introduction

Social mixing, less segregation and more 'socially balanced' neighbourhoods all seem like inherently positive policy ambitions. Why, then, have a raft of urban policy programmes that have placed the goal of social mixing at their core been subject to, at times, condemning criticism (N. Smith, 2002; Slater, 2006; Lees, 2008)? The answer proposed here is that the current policy-led push to generate social mixing and socially mixed neighbourhoods through 'social upgrading' has contained a deeply problematic understanding of class dynamics and politics. This, it is argued, is symptomatic of a wider treatment of the question of class in the neoliberal period (Peck and Tickell, 2002a, 2002b), where a utopian kernel embedded within the intellectual project of Hayek and his followers (see Harvey, 2005) has been – not always exactly – translated into a multitude of policy visions, notably including Richard Florida's influential creative city (Peck, 2005).

Given that class remains an antagonistic social relation in critical theory, it is unsurprising that some, if certainly not all (see Slater, 2006), gentrification scholars have been critical of social mixing policy agendas in Europe and North America (see Lees, 2008, for a review). As Slater et al (2004) have argued, the term 'gentrification' refers 'to nothing more or less than *the class dimensions of neighbourhood change* – in short, not simply changes in the housing stock, but changes in housing class' (p 1144, emphasis in original). For most gentrification scholars, then, the analytical focus on pro-social mixing policy agendas has centred on socioeconomic dimensions (that is, not racial or ethno-cultural dimensions). In terms of the instruments used within these policy agendas, such a focus does not represent a problematic bracketing of the object (Zizek, 2006). For example, housing tenure requirements (that is, affordability requirements) have driven social mixing via socioeconomic characteristics, even if this inevitably carries other social dimensions. In addition, the spatial planning dimensions of the UK governments' Urban Renaissance and Housing Renewal programmes have been premised on 'rebalancing' socioeconomic mix, via attracting the 'respectable' middle classes back to problematised (inner-city) neighbourhoods. For the most part, policy programmes have not been focused on rebalancing other modes of social difference, although various identity politics are certainly intertwined in neighbourhood change.

If we therefore focus on the question of social mixing in its socioeconomic dimensions, pro-social mix urban policy agendas pose a particular question: can the juxtaposition of different social classes generate the intended policy outcomes? In order to answer this question we must first examine how the intentions of pro-social mix urban policy programmes are set out. In this chapter, I focus on the policies of the UK Labour government dating from the launch of Urban Renaissance (DETR, 2000), although similar policy frameworks have been installed elsewhere (see Lees, 2008). With this thesis sketched out, the rest of the chapter approaches the question of spatial proximity and class. Drawing on recent gentrification scholarship that has examined cross-class neighbourhood relations, a theoretical understanding of what Butler and Robson (2003) have described as 'social tectonics' is developed. The intention here is to signal both the politics inherent to currently in-vogue social mix agendas and the particularity of the question of socioeconomic mixing.

Social mix prescriptive

From its very inception, the New Labour government of Tony Blair, and subsequently continued under Gordon Brown, premised its (urban) social policy thinking around a very particular understanding of socioeconomic difference. Established soon after election in 1997, the Social Exclusion Unit (SEU) was charged with implementing a cross-departmental programme of poverty alleviation. In doing so, specific understandings of socioeconomic difference were installed through the New Labour agenda (Fairclough, 2000). Colley and Hodkinson (2001) have argued this understanding has been primarily premised on viewing the poor as morally irresponsible, self-excluding and anti-social: 'Deep-seated structural inequalities are rendered invisible, as social exclusion is addressed through a strongly individualistic strategy based on personal agency' (p 335). For some, then (see also Powell,

2000), the lexicon of the SEU erased key structural concerns and a related claim for redistribution.

In response to such claims, Anthony Giddens (2002) stated:

> A focus upon social exclusion has nothing to do with trying to sweep poverty under the carpet. Social exclusion is not just about poverty, but about living in neighbourhoods that are crime-ridden and lack access to shops, transport, decent schooling and job opportunities. Many of the excluded are, to some degree, casualties of the welfare state itself, caught up in a negative spiral of dependency. (www.independent. co.uk)

Here, Giddens starkly illustrates the spatial dimension placed on social exclusion. In differentiating this key policy concept from plain-old poverty, it is space – problematic neighbourhoods – that generate social (and spatial) exclusion. And certainly, Giddens' thinking is present in the SEU's work. In *A new commitment to neighbourhood renewal* released by the SEU in 2001 (SEU, 2001), they located the problem of poverty in the neighbourhood setting. In the document's foreword, Tony Blair states:

> The job of renewing and revitalising poor neighbourhoods has consistently been a top priority for this Government. In my first speech as Prime Minister, I set out our new approach to social exclusion.... It made clear that [these] neighbourhoods suffered from serious multi-faceted problems that would require action on all fronts. (SEU, 2001, p 5)

Blair's message is echoed throughout the document, as it identifies 'economic ghettoisation', the 'erosion of social capital', 'the failure of core services in deprived areas' and 'the lack of clear strategy or concerted joint action' as the various spatial qualities of social exclusion.

This thinking has been directly reflected, if with some mutations, in New Labour's urban policies since the release of the urban White Paper in 2000. And while there has been extensive debate over New Labour's policy programmes – notably Urban Renaissance (Imrie and Raco, 2003), Housing Renewal (Allen, 2008) and Sustainable Communities (Raco, 2007) – it is worth stressing one particular point here: that the discursive and conceptual reworking of poverty (in its various guises) that has taken place under third way governments has been closely tied to a particular set of spatial ideas about causation and solution. As Lupton and Power (2002) argue:

> Poverty and social exclusion in Britain are spatially concentrated. This is not a new pattern ... the concentration of problems in particular neighbourhoods is not coincidental; [...] the nature of neighbourhoods actually contributes to the social exclusion of their residents. (p 118)

The intuitive solution that emerges from this framing of poverty unites the UK government's urban policy programmes: the deconcentration of problematised people from problematised neighbourhoods.

We therefore see the Urban Task Force (DETR, 1999) – architects of the Urban Renaissance (DETR, 2000) – proclaiming that we must implement reform that 'brings people back to the city' and enables these to 'take back control of them'. We see Housing Renewal demolishing vast tracts of housing to disperse the poor and reinstall a newly composed neighbourhood community (see Allen, 2008). Similarly, the Sustainable Communities (ODPM, 2003; also see Raco, 2007) programme has focused on addressing a complex set of housing delivery and standards problems with the objective that 'It will take us towards successful, thriving and inclusive communities, urban and rural, across England. Communities that will stand the test of time and in which people want to live' (ODPM, 2003, p 3). Social mixing has therefore become a desired outcome of urban policy. It is perceived to offer a way in which 'damaging' socio-spatial agglomerations can be eliminated. The fix for poverty is therefore intimately spatial, as Lees (2008) argues in the global context: 'Socially mixed urban communities created by the in-movement of middle-class people into poor, marginal areas of the inner city are being posited, under the rubric of urban renaissance, as the desegregating answer to lives that are lived in parallel or in isolation along class, income, ethnic and tenurial fault lines' (p 2463).

Social tectonics and the prospects of mixing

What, then, have been the implications of pro-social mixing policy programmes? Have they proven capable of addressing socioeconomic disparities? In terms of new (gentrifying) residents mixing with incumbent (the working-class) residents, the gentrification literature has been quite unanimous: there is little mixing between these groups and even fewer signs that social class divisions are eroded by the generated spatial proximity. Indeed, it would seem the left-leaning liberal gentrifier of the 1960s and 1970s who actively seeks out social diversity – moving into the inner city to seek out social diversity and reject suburban middle-class sterility (see Caulfield, 1994; Ley, 1996; Butler and Lees, 2006) – is now a rare being, perhaps only present within the imagery of urban policy.

Most accounts of cross-class relations in gentrifying neighbourhoods now correspond to Butler and Robson's (2003) idea of 'social tectonics'. Drawing on their examinations of gentrification and the practices of gentrifiers in neighbourhoods across London, Butler and Robson argue that, for the most part, gentrifiers and incumbent communities tend to pass each other by; they simply co-habit proximate spaces, having few social relations. These findings have been echoed elsewhere in London (Davidson, 2008) and across the globe (Rose, 2004; Slater, 2004). Within the gentrification literature and beyond, there are various reasons offered for such disconnection. Influentially, Smith's (1996) 'revanchist city' thesis has been used to contrast divided gentrified neighbourhoods to the image of the emancipatory gentrifier. Smith argues:

> The revanchist city represents a reaction to an urbanism defined by recurrent waves of unremitting danger and brutality fuelled by venal and uncontrolled passion. It is a place, in fact, where the reproduction of social relations has gone stupifyingly wrong […], but where the response is a virulent reassertion of many of the same oppressions and prescriptions that created the problem in the first place. (p 212)

Beneath Smith's graphic language, it is not difficult to see the presence of the urban policy thinking that underlies pro-social mixing policies (see Uitermark, 2003): dangerous places where the reproduction of social relations has gone wrong. Is this not the imaginary for the Urban Renaissance? We might therefore draw more from Smith's thesis, particularly in terms of the built form of the latest 'third wave' (Hackworth and Smith, 2001) of gentrification. For N. Smith (2002), the revanchism he identifies has become manifest in new collections of actors implementing gentrification, alongside new built forms:

> Retaking the city for the middle classes involves a lot more than simply providing gentrified housing. Third-wave gentrification has evolved into a vehicle for transforming whole areas into new landscape complexes that pioneer a comprehensive class-inflected urban remake. These

> new landscape complexes now integrate housing with shopping, restaurants, cultural facilities [...], open space, employment opportunities – whole new complexes of recreation, consumption, production, and pleasure, as well as residence. (p 443)

For Atkinson (2006), the residential form of this mode of gentrification is the gated development. He argues:

> Gentrification provides an example of what can be seen as both insulation and incubation strategies by upper-income groups.... Policy-makers seem to have understood these preferences as a route into remaking and boosting central-city spaces by facilitating enclave-style new-build and a wider promotion of gentrification. Buyer confidence is achieved through the scale and relative secession of new development which facilitates a sense of privacy, status and withdrawal that connects with middle-class patterns of sociation. (p 826)

While pro-social mixing urban policies may, in some sense, rely on the imaginary of the emancipatory gentrifier, in the post-1993 third wave of gentrification, this figure is largely absent. Instead, an excluding and exclusive form of gentrification has expanded (Atkinson and Bridge, 2005). It has featured social practices that actively avoid cross-class social mixing and has been increasingly characterised by the construction of built environments that inhibit the very possibility of mixing (Atkinson, 2006; Davidson, 2008).

There is therefore little doubt that as a tool for the promotion of cross-class social mixing, gentrification has been a total failure, not least because the process inevitably displaces those lower-income groups who are the very focus of policy (Davidson, 2008). Why, then, has this form of inclusion been so difficult to achieve? Of course, part of the answer to this question has been the decline in tenure security of many low-income groups; the ability of many to remain (that is, not displaced) in gentrifying housing markets has diminished over the past 30 years as various protections have been eroded by neoliberal reforms (Newman and Wyly, 2006). However, we require an explanation as to why the spatial proximity of different social classes, engendered by policy-led gentrification, has failed to create 'a' community. In the following sections, a theoretical explanation is developed which claims it is the very question of social class, and the particularities of the demand of socioeconomic 'inclusion', that causes social tectonics.

Social distance

Gentrification's emancipatory spectre – that which is embedded within pro-social mix, gentrifying policy agendas – emanates largely from the prospect that because people of different social classes are living together in the same neighbourhood, this will generate reduced social difference and/or greater levels of understanding/tolerance. It is therefore concerning that the gentrification literature continues to document both the particular lifestyle practices of gentrifiers (Bridge, 2001; Butler with Robson, 2003; Ley, 2003) and how the cohabitation of gentrifiers with working-class communities tends not to result in any sense of cohesive collective identity (Watt, 2006; Davidson, 2008). In short, there is little evidence, particularly within recent scholarship, that gentrification operates in an emancipatory mode.

Scholarship that has employed Bourdieu's habitus concept has been particularly effective in explaining the continued social distance between gentrifiers and the communities they move into and, indeed, how this is recreated through everyday practice. For Bourdieu, habitus represents the system of dispositions (and by extension, practices and perceptions) that incorporates the subject into a set of objective social structures. As Bourdieu (1984) states:

> Taste classifies, and it classifies the classifier. Social subjects, classified by their classifications, distinguish themselves by the distinctions they make, between the beautiful and the ugly, the distinguished and the vulgar, in which their position in the objective classifications is expressed or betrayed. (p 6)

As a method through which to articulate and practice their socio-cultural dispositions, gentrification has been recognised as a significant mode of contemporary class practice. Bridge (2006a) has argued that this takes two forms:

> ... there is a spatial and a temporal deployment of cultural capital. The spatial deployment is classic gentrification involving overt housing aesthetic, neighbourhood politics and distinctive consumption in public – as part of a symbolic reordering of the central city. "Temporal" deployment

involves capital accumulation that is not necessarily so
rapidly materialised (or convertible into economic capital).
It is less visible and aligns much more with traditional
middle-class strategies of distinction through education.
(p 726)

While the full implications of Bourdieu's understanding of class
remain debated, its use within the gentrification literature has brought
theoretical reasoning to the fact that gentrifiers have mostly remained
distinct from their working-class neighbours. In this sense, we can
return to the phenomenology of Edmund Husserl that influences
Bourdieu's work (see Robbins, 2005; also see Coole, 2007, on Merleau-
Ponty). Robbins (2006) has claimed that much of Bourdieu's work
was focused on an examination of how the lifeworld experience – the
pre-given for Husserl – generates intellectual difference and distinction.
For Husserl, the lifeworld emphasised the centrality of perception for
human experience (see Moran, 2005). It proposes the pre-conscious as
the route to establish science via the essential features of consciousness.
Importantly here, Husserl's lifeworld is the individual's horizon of
meaning, the plane of perception and cognition that conditions choice
and reaction. It is the 'natural standpoint' with which we insert ourselves
into 'the concrete world' (Brand, 1973). Bourdieu therefore shares with
Husserl a key concern with the ways in which individuals 'construct'
perception and intentionality:

Bourdieu was interested in understanding how far cultural
tastes are biologically determined or how far individuals
inherit a natural culture which circumscribes their choices
of artificial cultural products or symbols. (Robbins, 2005,
p 16)

Bourdieu's habitus therefore offers a sociological interpretation (and
extension) of the lifeworld. It shares Husserl's emphasis that the lifeworld
remains, by definition, an inter-subjective entity: 'The constitutive
element of the life-world is inter-subjectivity, not the Ego' (Brand,
1973, p 158). The lifeworld, particularly in Husserl's later work (Moran,
2005), becomes something that is defined in a social sense through the
shared 'we'. In particular, Husserl emphasises the prefabricated meaning
that is circulated through time and space via language – the lifeworld
as cultural creation. Just as Bourdieu's later concept of habitus pivots
around the differentiated structuring of socio-cultural dispositions,
so, then, Husserl's understanding of the lifeworld is shaped by an

appreciation of how social action structures communities. However, Bourdieu's sociological approach places much greater emphasis on the hierarchical structuring of the inter-subjectively defined lifeworld. As Browitt (2004, p 1) puts it:

> *Habitus*, however, is much more constraining than lifeworld in that forms of "symbolic domination", that which situates us as either the submissive or the dominant in social hierarchies, radically limit our practical capacity as agents to transform the social world.

The question of gentrification's emancipatory potential – via the generation of social mix(ing) – therefore takes on a more radical dimension when Bourdieu's emphasis on hierarchy is highlighted. While it may be generally accepted that the localised perceptions and practices of gentrifiers and their working-class neighbours are different, existing, in Butler and Robson's (2003) terms, as parallel worlds that simply rub past each other, what Bourdieu's concept of habitus highlights is the inherent processes of class differentiation and structuring that are at play. Not only are the lifeworlds of gentrifiers and working-class residents different, but they are necessarily so for Bourdieu:

> The habitus is not only a structuring structure, which organises practices and the perception of practices, but also a structured structure: the principle of division into logical classes which organises the perception of the social world is itself the product of internalisation of the division into social classes. Each class condition is defined, simultaneously, by its intrinsic properties and by the relational properties which it derives from its position in the system of class conditions, which is also a system of differences … social identity is defined and asserted through difference. (1984, p 172)

Here, then, the prospect of the liberal gentrifier, the individual(s) who move(s) 'back to the inner city' and engages with the existent community – eats the same things in a similar manner, participates in the same leisure activities, enjoys shared conversation – represents a truly radical injunction.

If we follow Bourdieu, it is therefore of little surprise that gentrification has such a poor record of generating social mixing between the social classes:

> The most fundamental oppositions in the structure (high/ low, rich/poor etc) tend to establish themselves as the fundamental structuring principles of practices and the perception of practices. (Bourdieu, 1984, p 172)

For example, it has long been recognised that landscape change, the revision and re-inscription of urban aesthetics, has played a central role in the gentrification process. As Jager (1986) argues with respect to the classical gentrification process: 'the aesthetics of gentrification not only illustrate the class dimensions of the process but also express the dynamic constitution of social class of which gentrification is a specific part ... etched into the landscape in the decorative forms of gentrification is a picture of the dynamics of social class' (p 78). Jager, drawing on Bourdieu, is talking here of the expression of class identity 'through the appropriation of history, and the "stylization of life" as Victorian gentility' (p 80). The same usage of architectural aesthetic to signify class identity is evident across the many different forms of gentrification today.

In the rural context, Phillips (1993, 2002) has illustrated the ways in which local community and planning disputes have played out in the context of a 'back to the country movement' that has constituted social distinction through quite different sets of architectural practices in both renovated and new-build constructions. Furthermore, a literature on new-build gentrification (see Mills, 1988; Davidson, 2007) has demonstrated the ways in which modern urban aesthetics have been incorporated into systems of social signification. Describing the gentrified Fairview Slopes neighbourhood in Vancouver, Caroline Mills (1988) argued: '... Fairview developments display a more pointed postmodern sensibility, each so self-conscious in its play of codes and symbols, its attempt at distinction' (p 175). She goes on to argue that as a result, 'any sense of an integrated landscape is overwhelmed' (p 175). The key point here is that gentrification has featured the articulation of difference, for example via architectural aesthetic, but also through consumption practices and political activities, which maintains social distance. In this sense, gentrification is unlikely to ever feature the radical emancipatory figure who might act outside of the structuring practices that Bourdieu emphasises as central to the construction and recreation of class. In this sense, the lifeworlds of gentrifers and working-class communities are persistently demarked and separated.

Of course, we might want to insert some caveats to this Bourdieuian interpretation. In particular, I want to make two points here. The first concerns what Bridge (2001) calls 'Bourdieu's oversocialized conception of human action' (p 207). Here, Bridge draws attention to the fact that Bourdieu's concept of habitus leaves little space for human agency. Drawing on Elster (1983), he states,

> Bourdieu's move to a conception of class utility maximization, regardless of the conscious actions of individuals, leaves his analysis devoid of any causal mechanism between dispositions and what people actually do. (Bridge, 2001, p 208)

In response, Bridge proposes the insertion of Rational Action Theory into a Bourdieuian interpretation of gentrification, primarily through a claim that the gentrifier represents a particular manifestation of the middle classes: 'This new class fraction is defined to some extent by their self-consciousness. The new middle class is a reflexive class. Whereas the dispositions of the traditional bourgeoisie are unschooled, tacit, unreflexive – the aesthetic practices of the new middle class are public, discursive and self-conscious' (Bridge, 2001, p 211). As opposed to being a fixture of class structuring, Bridge argues that the gentrification process:

> ... provides an example where the class habitus is adapted to a new field as a result of the existing habitus and the articulation of prior dispositions. It also involves conscious choices involving the physical and social environment exercised by a few members of the "urban" middle class. (Bridge, 2001, p 213)

While Bridge (2001) critiques Bourdieu's emphasis on class circumscriptions, he continues to note that '[T]he gentrification aesthetic is deployed to obtain distinction from the conventional middle-class suburbs and from working-class taste in the central city...' (p 214). In this sense, both individual choice and social predispositions are (still) orientated around the maintenance and cultivation of social class difference.

The second caveat required concerns the occurrence of socio-structural disruption, the actual blurring of economic position and socio-cultural disposition. While it is generally acknowledged that gentrification has failed to generate social mixing – and any envisaged reductions in inequalities – there is evidence that some (if limited) cross-class relations take place. Notably, Caulfield's (1994) Toronto-based gentrification research found that:

> ... respondents reported that there had not previously
> been a conspicuously high degree of close contact between
> working- and middle-class residents, but in each case a
> substantial number of residents of both groupings turned
> out at community meetings to discuss the issues and try to
> take mutual action. (p 174)

While Caulfield's findings are not repeated throughout the
gentrification literature, they do represent a significant disruption to a
Bourdieuian interpretation since social practice is not orientated around
maintaining difference, but rather building mutual understanding and
objectives. In the policy arena, such an observation remains important
since it transforms 'social tectonics' (Butler with Robson, 2003) from
a necessary feature of a capitalist urban society (Bourdieu, 1984) to a
multiplication challenge. In short, the problem is not presented in any
way as structural, but rather it is one of fostering neighbourhood-based
communitarianism (see Fairclough, 2000).

But does the socio-cultural interaction of social classes represent
a potentially radical injunction? In Rancière's (2005) critique of
Bourdieu's static reading of class, we find a questioning of this prospect.
For Rancière (2005), Bourdieu's reading of social class – via his concept
of 'field' – fails because it provides an account of domination and, in
parallel, narrates the same domination's inevitable reproduction:

> If the social machine captures us, it is because we do not
> know how it captures us. And if we do not know it captures
> us even though it is right before our eyes, it is because we
> do not want to know it. All recognition is a misrecognition,
> all unveiling a veiling. (Rancière, 2005, p 170)

The possibility of emancipation is, for Rancière, therefore absent from
Bourdieu's sociology: 'The sociologist needs only to show each time
the sufficient reason organizing the universe of judgements – simple
distinction.... There must be no mixing, no imitation. The subjects
of this science, like the warriors of *The Republic*, must be unable to
"imitate" anything else than their own dye' (p 189). Rancière therefore
urges us to consider the political implications of Bourdieu's class
schema through a critique of what he describes as the 'division of
the sensible'. By this, Rancière articulates his view that emancipation
(for the working classes) does not come through gaining (reflexive)
knowledge – becoming incorporated into certain modes of perception

– but rather through redefining the world view in a way that transcends current hegemonic installations.

Rancière (2005) therefore diagnoses a particular absence of transcendent possibility within Bourdieu's interpretation of social class. He states: 'The great strength of the opponents of freedom is that they show it to be inapplicable on the grounds of the inequality of competences and social capacities – the gulf separating working class brutality from bourgeois civility' (p 198). Drawing on his historical portrait of Louis Gabriel Gauny, a Parisian carpenter writing to Saint-Simonian workers in the 1830s, Rancière describes the politics he sees as absent in Bourdieu. He describes Gauny's account of himself laying on a parquet floor, gazing at the décor around him, a décor that positions his servitude. Rancière describes how, in Gauny's account, his writings demonstrate a transcendence of any trappings of habitus:

> The acquisition of this aesthetic gaze, the paradoxical philosophy of asceticism that this dispossessed worker draws from it, this torsion of habitus that he imposes upon himself and proposes is also the claim of a human right to happiness that extends the rhetoric of proletarian recruiters, the battle of cottages and castles. (2005, p 199)

Rancière is describing how Gauny, the working-class carpenter writing his diary, operates outside of Bourdieu's schema, how Gauny's own philosophising presents a 'cutting up' (Rancière, 2001, 2005) of any deterministic, un-thought, sense of habitus.

What both these caveats add to the dominant Bourdieuian understanding of gentrification's relationship to social mixing is that, not only does an account of habitus as necessary socio-cultural disconnection lack an understanding of choice and temporality (Bridge, 2001), but – and most importantly – it also mirrors the current pro-social mix urban policy in that it lacks emancipatory potential (Rancière, 2005). By this, I mean that a perceived common route to progressive reform is shared: the inclusion of working-class people into dominant (middle-class) modes of being. Hierarchical divisions are both based on those 'who know' and those who don't, the 'ignorant'. This, I argue below, must be understood as a key element of currently hegemonic thinking centred on the symbolisation of middle-class identity.

The paradox of middle-class inclusion

In this final section, I want to make the point that the consistent absence of social mixing from gentrifying neighbourhoods is not simply a policy failure or simple function of class reproduction, but rather that this absence is symptomatic of a wider politics. Indeed, the absence of mixing *and* its continued promotion within pro-gentrification policy circles are two sides of the same coin. As Ranciere's (2005) critique of Bourdieu informs us, the prospect of mixing – in UK policy terms, the generation of social inclusion – is a false one within current social articulations – what Ranciere calls 'division of the sensible'. Ranciere sees emancipation not in the moralistic middle classes, who offer the prospect of a hand up, but rather with the political agency of the working classes, the very group he accuses Bourdieu of assigning to the role of blind victim. A programme of inclusion (for example, New Labour's Urban Renaissance) premised on a process that is constitutive of middle-class identity (that is, gentrification) – and the current 'division of the sensible' – is therefore antithetical; the prospect of emancipation is trapped within Bourdieu's habitus.

We must therefore locate the politics of pro-social mixing, gentrifying urban policy agendas. What does this policy vision, one that presents the prospect of incorporating the 'excluded' into 'mainstream' (that is, middle-class) society, represent? This is particularly so when this mainstream society, or rather with respect to gentrification, a particular gentrifying fragment of it (Bridge, 2001), is necessarily defined inter-subjectively, through hierarchical difference. For Slavoj Zizek (2000a), such policy visions represent an ideological distortion of the key social antagonism. He states: 'The [...] distortion is discernible in the fact that, today, the only class which, in its "subjective" self-perception, explicitly conceives of and presents itself as a class is the notorious "middle-class" which is precisely the "non-class"' (p 186). Here, the middle class is the non-class because it is defined 'not only by their allegiance to firm moral and religious standards, but by a double opposition to both "extremes" of the social space' (Zizek, 2000a, p 186). For Zizek (2000a), then, the vision of a middle-class inclusive city (and society) is precisely a hegemonic distortion because it denies the economic and socio-cultural inter-subjectivity that defines it:

> The 'middle class' grounds its identity in the exclusion of
> both extremes which, when they are directly counterposed,
> give us 'class antagonism' at its purest ... the "middle class'
> is, in its very 'real' existence, the *embodied lie*, the denial of

antagonism – in psychoanalytical terms, the 'middle class' is
a *fetish*, the impossible intersection of Left and Right which,
by expelling both poles of the antagonism into the position
of antisocial 'extremes' which corrode the healthy social
body ..., presents itself as the neutral common ground of
Society. (2000a, p 187, emphasis in original)

In his political resolution, Zizek turns to Rancière's (1999)
understanding of 'politics': 'political conflict designates the tension
between the structured social body in which each part has its place,
and "the part of not part" which unsettles this order on account of the
empty principle of universality' (p 188).

We can think about this in terms of the Parisian carpenter Gauny, laid
on the parquet floor. For Rancière, Gauny's written accounts represent
an attempt to think beyond the structured social body, to step outside
of the 'division of the sensible', to think of 'the principled equality of
all men *qua* speaking beings' (Zizek, 2000a, p 188). It also, for Rancière,
represents the actual occurrence of a working-class being operating
outside of their habitus (Bourdieu, 1984). Of course, Bourdieu's concept
of symbolic violence may be used to counter Rancières criticisms here.
Symbolic violence, a concept not often attached to that of the much-
used habitus within the gentrification literature, is defined by Bourdieu
and Wacquant as: 'the violence which is exercised upon a social agent
with his or her complicity' (Bourdieu and Wacquant, 2004, p 272).
However, this is not meant to signify pure passivity or acquiescence;
rather, it is argued 'social agents are knowing agents who, even when
they are subjected to determinisms, contribute to producing the
efficacy of that which determines them insofar as they structure what
determines them' (Bourdieu and Wacquant, 2004, p 272). For Bourdieu,
then, the cognitive structures of the agent are necessarily created by
the very structures of the world around them, and, as such, there is a
fundamental misrecognition, a doxic acceptance of the (social) world.
This constitutes a violent self-perpetuation of habitus for Bourdieu.
Yet, in terms of overcoming this repressive politics, Rancière's critique
must still stand: that we must not, as Bourdieu and Wacquant state
(2004, p 273), ignore 'the *illusio* that leads one to engage in the central
games of society', but rather seek transformative integration. As Zizek
(2000a, p 188) states:

This identification of the non-part with the Whole, of the
part of society with no properly defined place within it (or

resisting the allocated subordinated place within it) with the Universal, is the elementary gesture of politicization.

The promise of social mixing (and, consequently social inclusion) via gentrification therefore appears nonsense. An urban process that operates to hierarchically structure society, through the articulation of distinction, is being asked to do the exact opposite. But, of course, the spatial imaginary of 'socially mixed neighbourhoods' remains an enticing policy vision: who is against social mixing? Through appealing to the moral consciousness of the enlightened middle classes, all structuring functions are denied. The necessity of socioeconomic difference is excluded. What we are left with is a vision of a middle *classed* society, whereby the middle classes are the agents of change, civilising the socially excluded through various means – sharing social capital, providing informal employment opportunity, providing 'good' role models etc. Gentrification's poor record of generating social mixing, its social tectonics, can therefore tell us that the spatial, neighbourhood-based imaginary of the policies that promote it do not contain an adequate social imaginary. Put simply, a socially inclusive society will not be achieved through any attempt to include people into a society that, by definition, relies on excluding social differences.

Conclusion

Of late, the association between gentrification and social mixing has been largely generated by policy makers. This has involved the spatial thinking of social policy problems, one where the physical segregation of different communities/classes is seen as the barrier to inclusion (see Lees, 2008). In the UK, this has involved problematising both the (spatial) barriers to the poor being 'included' in mainstream society and the barriers to the middle classes 'helping' – a moral obligation often associated with New Labour – those not 'included'. Of course, within the rhetoric of social inclusion we encounter the problem of which aspect of identity is to be subject to inclusion. I have argued above that gentrification and the policies that now promote inclusion via gentrification are intimately connected to social class. However, there are aspects of current urban policies that engage with other identities. We must therefore briefly address the relationship between various social fractures and the notion of inclusion. Furthermore, we must also guard against the simple problematisation of segregation, as Young (2002) argues: 'Group-differentiated residential and associational clustering is not necessarily bad in itself, inasmuch as it may arise from legitimate desires to form and maintain affinity grouping' (p 197). Here, Young forwards the notion of 'differentiated solidarity', where largely cultural differences may result in residential clustering; however, this, it is argued, should only occur when it is recognised that all exist 'within a set of problems and relationships of structural interdependence that bring with them obligations of justice' (p 196). Here, Young's correction of an overarching multicultural liberalism is pivotal, since it highlights how different calls for 'inclusion' must be articulated at different scales and, therefore necessarily, between different 'communities'.

It is therefore necessary to conclude by situating the particularity of the question of inclusion with respect to gentrification. Gentrification's emancipatory potential emanates from the fact it has become one of very few 'voluntary', market-based processes that brings different groups together in the same neighbourhood. This offers a powerful (spatial) metaphor for policy makers because the breaking down of socio-spatial segregation is commonly viewed as a potentially effective mechanism for overcoming exclusion. However, and as Young (2002) warns, we should be wary of simply proposing an all-encompassing programme of inclusion. Indeed, this is exactly what Zizek (2006) sees as being a key component of contemporary technocratic, liberal multiculturalist politics. For Zizek, liberal multiculturalism represents an impotent political space, where the 'Other' (for example, religious minorities, the poor) is tolerated, but only to the extent that they are not really the 'Other'. In Rancière's (1999) terms, the 'Other' is tolerated until they become truly political. Inclusion, in this sense, is only offered so long as the 'Other' remains symbolically ordered. When this ordering does not accompany inclusion, exclusion is re-inscribed. As Dean (2007) provocatively argues:

> White Leftist multiculturalists, even as they encourage the flourishing of multiple modes of becoming, find themselves in a similar bind (one in which class difference is inscribed): their support of differentiated cultural traditions means that they oppose the racism, sexism, and religiosity that bind together some poor whites. Just as the superego imperative operates in conservatism to encourage hate, so can it be found in liberalism and Left multiculturalism as well. (p 28)

But Zizek (2000b) goes further than the problematising of inclusion, claiming that the question is transformed in the context of social class. Class, Zizek (2000b) argues, is not another facet of identity politics. Disagreeing with Laclau, he argues that unlike struggles over gender, 'race' or religion, the political claim around class is not simple inclusion. It is not a demand to get along, to be accepted or to be respected. Rather, its politics must necessarily be transformative. It is about, in both economic and cultural capital terms, transforming the very social structures that generate this 'difference', removing the types of structuring structures of domination that are captured in Bourdieu's concept of habitus. The mode of spatial inclusion – the neighbourhood cohabitation of different social classes – promoted in pro-gentrification urban policy programmes therefore becomes inadequate not only because gentrification has a dismal record of generating social mixing (and any consequent reductions in inequality), but also because it is not inclusion that is at question. Rather, any politics/policy must be concerned with the excluding and differentiating processes that give rise to gentrification in the first place. If we promote gentrification as a fix to poverty, we are, metaphorically, treating a drug overdose with yet more drugs.

To conclude, it is necessary to make one final point. Throughout this chapter I have taken the relationship between gentrification and social mixing seriously in terms of considering its emancipatory potential, considering its utility as a tool to address socioeconomic inequality and resulting problems. It is therefore imperative that we do not lose sight of the fact that gentrification has consistently shown itself to be an exacerbator of social inequity (Slater, 2006). Our understanding of state-led gentrification would therefore not be complete without recognising that in order to promote it, the injustices that gentrification has consistently inflicted have had to have been overlooked/displaced. In doing so, we might certainly apply Zizek's (2003) understanding of postmodern (un)ethics:

> On today's market, we find a whole series of products deprived of their malignant property: coffee without caffeine, cream without fat, beer without alcohol.... And the list goes on: what about virtual sex without sex, the Colin Powell doctrine of warfare with no casualties (on our side, of course) as warfare without warfare ... up to today's tolerant liberal multiculturalism as an experience of the Other deprived of its Otherness [...]? (p 96)

Might we add 'gentrification without class or displacement' to this list? It would certainly seem like that is indeed where urban policy is at. And if it is, perhaps we should be talking not about social mixing and inclusion, but rather about social ethics and a city without gentrification.

SIXTEEN

Not the only power in town? Challenging binaries and bringing the working class into gentrification research

Kirsteen Paton

Introduction

The contributions in this collection confirm the pressing need to move beyond conventional wisdom on gentrification processes in order to advance our understanding of the contemporary 'third model' of gentrification in which public policy is a crucial driver (Cameron and Coaffee, 2005). However, the relationship between gentrification and public policy has not been a primary focus of gentrification research (Lees and Ley, 2008), and consequently our understandings are not fully theoretically developed. Explanations offered are often beset by the same binaries of older orthodox explanations: culture/consumption versus capital/production explanations and a dichotomisation of social groups – working class/middle class, with a bias towards the experience and role of the latter. More sociological approaches to gentrification, which one would expect to capture the tensions between structural and agential processes and groups, frequently attend to the lifestyles of only the middle class (Butler with Robson, 2003; Rofe, 2003; Savage et al, 2005). Deeming meaningful place-based attachment and ontological insecurity a middle-class concession forecloses the possibility of a similar working-class association, and serves to reify the middle-class role in the justification and delivery of social mix policy rather than problematise it. The working class tends to be omitted from gentrification research while current representations of, and conceptual language used to describe, working-class lives have waned within mainstream sociology in general. Yet, paradoxically, they are the key targets of gentrification as social mix policy. Moreover, it is not only this social group that is obscured; the wider neoliberal agenda that heralds privatisation and the end of social housing and social welfare more broadly is not brought to the fore nor connected with working-class experiences in a theoretical or conceptually meaningful way.

In this chapter, I attend to these shortcomings and overcome the binaries in explanations of gentrification.[1] I offer a sociological perspective on the working-class experiences of state-led gentrification. This begins by problematising gentrifiers' sovereignty within the context of public policy and social mix. N. Smith (2002, p 445), in his critique of state-led gentrification, suggests that 'probing the symptomatic silence of who is to be invited back into the city begins to reveal the class politics involved'. Scrutinising gentrifiers' practices offers a means of assessing the efficacy of social mix policy. However, this is only a precursory step in what needs to be a wider agenda that explores how gentrification is received, negotiated and resisted by working-class groups – the supposed key beneficiaries of this public policy process (Paton, 2009). The chapter title is a reference to Watt's (2008) article, 'The only class in town: gentrification and the middle class colonisation of the city and urban imagination'. My title, first, infers that there is another class group, the working class, whose agency and presence has a significant but overlooked role in gentrification. Second, it infers that there is another driving power – that of the state which colludes with the private sector to support and promote gentrification via a broader neoliberal agenda. In this chapter I bring these issues together by suggesting that they are inextricably linked as part of a wider gentrification hegemony. 'Hegemony' refers to a form of rule relevant to how transformations in social relations are managed while the capitalist system is maintained overall (Gramsci, 1971). This involves a mix of consent and coercion that combine structural and agential processes, highlighting the reciprocal relationship between the material and the cultural. Within this, gentrification is conceived as a political strategy. Gentrification is more than just an economic intervention used to develop private housing to 'improve' traditionally working-class and industrial areas; it is also a cultural intervention to 'improve' the behaviours and practices of working-class residents in these neighbourhoods. Practices that relate to traditional forms of welfarism and industrial ways of life need to be realigned in order to fit with the neoliberalisation of the neighbourhood. Put differently, gentrification not only seeks to create space for the more affluent user (Hackworth, 2002); it also seeks to, consensually, create the more affluent user via the working-class subject which, in the context of neoliberalism, relates to a moral and financial economy (Paton, 2009). The outcome of gentrification is not simply displacement: rather than being evicted or excluded, the working class is asked to participate in these processes in their neighbourhoods as consumer citizens. This sociological perspective on gentrification combines cultural and material understandings while making working-class communities and their everyday lives the centre point of analysis.

My discussion is organised in four parts. First, I problematise gentrifiers' sovereignty in relation to social mix. I argue against the focus on gentrifiers' sovereignty via identity-making consumption, arguing that they are not the sole power in town. Calls for social mixing and the focus on gentrifiers' practices reinforce binaries in the gentrification debate between social groups and between explanations. Second, I challenge the binary thinking that characterises the debate. Most gentrification literature alludes to the idea that there are essential cultural differences between the working class and middle class. This view lacks a necessary articulation of the role of the working class and of policy and governance in contemporary gentrification processes. I demonstrate the link between these (groups and explanations) in the third section by advancing an alternative perspective to the debate: understanding gentrification as a hegemonic shift. This reading helps transcend the misleading binaries. It provides a cultural-material basis for both the working class and gentrifiers' preferences and identity-making as linked to policy and urban restructuring. I furnish this empirically in the fourth and final part of my chapter. I draw from ethnographic research including interviews with 49 residents, which explores everyday working-class lives in a gentrifying neighbourhood, Partick, Glasgow from 2005 to 2009. This area has undergone social and economic change through deindustrialisation, then the subsequent transformation of former shipyards and grain mills into a luxury housing development, Glasgow Harbour. This has been accompanied by an increase in house prices, changes to shops and the broader neoliberalisation of neighbourhood services and provisions. I show how state-led gentrification is received and negotiated by residents, and draw from this to challenge present one-dimensional understandings of gentrification. I illustrate that the working class often have similar values and behaviours to the middle class as cosmopolitans and even gentrifiers, yet, importantly and in contrast to the middle class, they are *simultaneously* excluded and included.

Problematising the sovereignty of gentrifiers

In orthodox readings of gentrification, gentrifiers have generally been given a central role. In culture-based explanations, the middle class are seen as pivotal to this process as consumers. They are awarded sovereignty in the sense that they initiate the process through their expression of a postwar identity and consumption practices which are manifested in a proclivity for inner-city living (Caulfield, 1994; Ley, 1996). In capital-based explanations, gentrifiers are also awarded a significant role as initiators of displacement and segregation within the urban housing setting and disruptors of existing communities and neighbourhoods (Marcuse, 1985; N. Smith, 2002). This has led some writers to leap to the defence of gentrifiers, claiming that they are, in fact, the saviours of the city. Hamnett (2008) suggests that middle-class locational choices have been at the heart of transforming cities over the past 15 years, saving neighbourhoods that planners had given up on. Hamnett is not alone in his belief that their settlement is a tool of regeneration (Lambert and Boddy, 2002; Freeman, 2006). The case for social mix within policy is made on the basis that a greater degree of mix has beneficial consequences. It is said to increase social interaction between different classes and ethnic groups that results in social and cultural assimilation and an improvement of values and attitudes. Mixing is believed to mitigate potential negative 'area-effects' that are conceived to be the additional negative effects of being 'poor' and living in a 'poor' area, that is, working class. However, the benefits of social mix are based on assumptions rather than certainties, as illustrated in the tentative findings in the Joseph Rowntree Foundation report *Creating and sustaining mixed communities: A good practice guide*:

> Mixed income areas may be able to attract and support a higher level of local services, leisure activities, shops and related facilities.

> The potential for negative area affects, such as low aspirations, low educational attainment and low-level crime is reduced.

> Higher average levels of disposable income *may* create additional employment opportunities for local residents. (Bailey et al, 2007, p 21; emphasis added)

The success and benefits have yet to be empirically validated. This warrants further discussion. It is not simply that gentrifiers are being blamed for too much (that is, the cause of gentrification); rather, I suggest, they are awarded too much responsibility within public policy. They are charged with a huge task: their settlement is said to bring about economic and cultural transformation to the lives of working-class residents. To understand this it is essential that we look more critically at their role within policy prescriptions and investigate the assumption that the middle class *can* be the saviours of the city. It is my position that this ideology is fundamentally questionable in the sense that it offers a cultural solution to fix economic and structural issues of poverty, unemployment and the decline of the built environment. Even those impervious to such political arguments cannot deny the more practical anomalies in using gentrification as a form of regeneration.

Some research findings challenge policy assumptions around social mixing based on the settlement of middle classes (Butler with Robson, 2003; Davidson, Chapter Fifteen, this volume). Examinations of gentrifiers' behaviours in relation to whether they do or do not, in fact, mix in a socially meaningful way have found that the middle class *enjoy* the mix but tend not to mix socially with their 'Other' working-class neighbours (Butler with Robson, 2003; Paton, 2009; Davidson, Chapter Fifteen, this volume). This disposition, then, seems incongruous with social mix: if middle-class locational choice involves creating social distinction, the possibility of social mix and cohesion is thereby foreclosed. Rather, their move into working-class neighbourhoods constitutes what Skeggs (2005) calls 'asset stripping' – a form of class cultural consumption which allows the middle class to sample the 'exotic' and experience 'edginess' but from safe enough distance away. This begs the question: what does social mix actually mean in practice? Much work looking at middle-class housing choices demonstrates that gentrification is part of a wider process of globalisation and ontological insecurity (Giddens, 1991; Butler with Robson, 2003; Rofe, 2003; Savage et al, 2005). Here middle-class self-making is deemed a response to ontological insecurity wrought by restructuring of social positions and class relations. The distinctions that people seek to make are often predicated on consumption of, and meaningful relationship to, place. Savage et al's (2005) study of middle-class neighbourhoods in Manchester demonstrates how social identities relate to place and a locally articulated sense of belonging. Using a Bourdieuvian framework, they illustrate how connections to space and place are embodied and used to mark out distinctions in relation to the class cultural field and location. In this way, gentrification is then only part of the wider 'ethic' and interest in place-making and territoriality via what they term 'elective belonging' (Savage et al, 2005). This refers to how location in residential space is used by residents as a marker of their identity and social position. This resonates with much literature on cosmopolitanism as a form of spatialisation and distinction (Hannerz, 1992; Werbner, 1999; Binnie and Skeggs, 2004). Definitions of cosmopolitanism are intrinsically connected to space and place, as a philosophy of global citizenship that rejects citizenship based on the nation (Binnie et al, 2006), and as an expression of attitudes and aptitudes that uphold cultural diversity and openness towards 'Otherness' and difference (Hannerz, 1992). Cosmopolitans are often conceived as mobile elites, juxtaposed to the fixed local (Hannerz, 1992). This suggests that gentrifiers are not easily amenable to policy desires. If gentrification is part of a wider ethic then it is not underpinned by rationality or altruism.

This challenges the efficacy of attempting to harness gentrifiers' residential settlement as part of public policy. Ultimately, the middle classes' higher income accords them sovereignty and the ability to move location, which not only undermines the philosophy of social mix, it also creates additional 'area effects', such as an increase in expensive shops and services catering for incoming groups. It can also impact on the distribution of area-based funding as an increase in the affluent population skews the measurement of levels of deprivation since it is collected at a spatial level. This can disqualify neighbourhoods from receiving funding as they no longer fit the criteria needed to receive community regeneration funds. This suggests that, contra to policy wisdom, being 'poor' in a socially mixed neighbourhood can have negative 'area effects'. Nonetheless, the danger is that in proclaiming the benefits of social mix we reify the 'area effects' debate. It is not wholly accurate to blame middle-class settlement for causing inequality nor is their settlement an antidote – it is neither cause nor solution. It is only a mitigating effect that compounds existing structured inequality within an increasingly privatised housing system. This foregrounds gentrifiers' autonomy which not only helps evaluate social mix policies, it begins to elucidate how their practices actually impact on working-class communities – the supposed beneficiaries of their arrival. There is a tendency within gentrification research to depict two discrete and oppositional social groups with essentially different desires and practices. However, this may set up too simple binaries. There is a danger of giving too much weight to the relationship that gentrifiers have with place identity, over and above that of other groups. This brings me to the second part of my discussion in which I undermine the crux of my argument so far by asserting that there is too much focus and responsibility awarded to the middle class in explanations of gentrification. They are, unjustifiably in my view, given autonomy over and above the working class and public policy.

Challenging the binaries of social groups

Gentrification research has tended to refer to homogeneous, fixed categories. Conceptual and theoretical accounts uphold a notion of diametrically opposed groups relating to the role of the working and middle classes in gentrification processes. Some of these are outlined in Table 16.1.

Table 16.1: Actors in gentrification processes as fixed category binaries

The mobile	The fixed
The incomer	The born and bred
The middle class	The working class
The cosmopolitan	The local

This raises several issues; first, much research on stratification demonstrates the changes to these 'fixed' categories and positions due to deindustrialisation. Subsequent challenges to the occupation model and the 'cultural turn' have seen a shift away from economically delineated categories (Crompton and Scott, 2005). Second, and related to this, it is important to exercise caution over exactly how we delineate the social groups involved in these processes and social groups more generally, and instead ask whether they are essentially different. Young (2007) suggests that the predominance of binary thinking about 'us and them' permeates public and official discourses and is utilised in the construction of 'Other' cultures, countries and nationalities. This is not just limited to policy; binaries are commonplace throughout social science discourse, as outlined in Table 16.2.

Young (2007) identifies these binaries in relation to the dualism of social exclusion that he believes is fundamentally misconceived and often operationalised in uncritical ways. The term 'social exclusion' implies that there is a binary that divides an inclusive and largely satisfied majority and an excluded and despondent minority (Young, 2007). It is assumed that this contented majority has better values, behaviours, interests or, put differently, higher stocks of social capital (Putnam, 2000). Social exclusion does not grasp the dynamic nature of processes and actors. Barriers, divisions and separateness exist, but their solidness is overstated with hard lines imposed on demarcations that are blurred in reality (Young 2007). Similarly, the 'dual city thesis', which posits the idea that there are discrete urban social worlds, has been criticised by Mooney and Danson (1997); on the basis of their research in Glasgow, these authors argue that the 'tale of two cities' is a misrepresentation.

Table 16.2: The binaries of social exclusion

Society at large	The underclass
The unproblematic	The problematic
Community	Disorganisation
Employment	Worklessness
Independence	Welfare dependency
Stable family	Single mothers
The natives	The immigrants
Victims	Criminals

Source: Young (2007, p 20)

The depiction of peripheral council housing estates as a homogeneous mass does not match the reality since they are often diverse within themselves, and mixing always occurs in some form. Mooney and Danson's research demonstrates that the working class, often depicted as an underclass, is not as culturally or as physically or economically corralled as conceived. Rather, the affluent and the working class are inextricably linked, and their lives are often enmeshed. The key difference is that the working class tends to be *simultaneously* excluded and included, which Young (2007) refers to as a 'bulimic society'. This has ramifications for social mix since it is premised on the idea of combating social exclusion. The persistence of such binary thinking reinforces the merit of social mixing based on the assumption that we are socially dichotomised with essentially different values and desires.

Challenging this dichotomised depiction of values and behaviours leads us to question whether ontological insecurity and claims to place and identity-making are a stratified experience. This recalls Newman's (1999) realisation when she first ventures into Harlem:

> Standing at the bus shelters were lines of women and men dressed for work, holding the hands of their children on their way to day care and the local schools. Black men in mechanic overalls, women in suits – drinking coffee from Dunkin' Donut cups, reading the *New York Post*, fussing with their children's backpacks – tapped their feet on the ground, waiting for the buses trying to manoeuvre towards them, caught in the same maddening traffic. The portals of the subways were swallowing up hoards to commuters who had given up their buses. Meanwhile people walking purposefully to work were moving down the sidewalks flowing around the bus shelters, avoiding the outstretched

arm of the occasional beggar, and ignoring the instant calls of the street vendors selling clothing and videotapes from tables set up along the edge of the sidewalk. It was Monday morning in Harlem, and as far as the eye could see, thousands of people were on their way to work. (Newman, 1999, pp ix–x)

This excerpt foregrounds the wider decline in contemporary representations of working-class lives within social science research that has compounded the denigration of working-class culture within contemporary media and policy discourses more generally. It also demonstrates how we create over-exaggerated cultural differences when the key differentiations are material ones. Werbner's (1999) conceptual contribution of 'working class cosmopolitan' echoes this idea. Werbner (1999) coins this term to invert the idea that cosmopolitanism is strictly stratified. Instead, it express how working-class groups are often more mobile and transnational and more likely to engage with 'Other' cultures and ethnicities as migrant labour than the traditionally conceived middle-class or elite cosmopolitan figure. The intellectual efficacy in challenging the ideas of essentialised class dispositions is clearly evident. Middle-class attachment to place is often fetishised and subsequently reified, which helps advance and legitimate policy promotion of middle-class settlement and the benefits it brings. Ontological expressions of individuality have a clear material basis. Just as places are made through place-marketing, they are 'unmade' by affixing problems to them. Working-class places and people are denigrated and devalorised by policy discourses. Target problems become targeted places but also targeted lives (Haylett, 2003). The next section considers how we might bring these distinctions together more coherently to elucidate the use of gentrification as social mix policy.

Challenging the binaries of explanations of gentrification

As I have previously claimed, gentrifiers' sovereignty is by no means the only power in town, and suggesting so reactivates another binary – of consumption versus production – which has long plagued the debate. Broadly speaking, structure and agency have been considered in a static, non-reciprocal way. Table 16.3 depicts some of the binary interpretations of gentrification processes.

The biggest difference between the contemporary forms of gentrification and older forms is the advanced role of the state in

Table 16.3: Binaries of explanations of gentrification

Consumption	Production
Agency	Structure
Emancipatory	Revanchist
Misunderstood saviour	Vengeful wrecker
Good	Evil
Cultural	Economic

Source: See Ley (1996); Smith (1996); Atkinson (2003); Lees (2004)

implementing the process, most notably as a form of governance (Wyly and Hammel, 2005; Lees and Ley, 2008) that relates to increasing neoliberalism:

> More than ever before, gentrification is incorporated into public policy – used either as a justification to obey market forces and private sector entrepreneurialism, or as a tool to direct market processes in the hopes of restructuring urban landscapes in a slightly more benevolent fashion (Wyly and Hammel, 2005, p 35)

The specific use of gentrification as urban public policy is still conceptually and theoretically undeveloped. While there are exceptions, like Marcuse (1985) and N. Smith (2002), these do not engage with notions of the working-class subject. Further still, rather than making the debate more cohesive, interpretations of gentrification now coalesce around opposing perspectives: rational policy accounts, some of which are pro-gentrification, uphold the benefits of social mix and its use in urban renewal strategies (Lambert and Boddy, 2002; Freeman, 2006); and more polemic critiques of neoliberal governance and anti-gentrification sentiments, which uphold the significance of displacement (Wyly and Hammel, 2005; Slater, 2006; Watt, 2008). The focus tends to be on material outcomes rather than working-class experiences. It is important that we capture both economic and cultural processes since Haylett (2003) claims we have entered a particular urban policy moment whereby places are pathologised with discrete denigrated identities that are classed as well as racialised and gendered. Haylett (2003, p 56) asserts that within regeneration policy, inequality is considered almost exclusively in relation to place rather than structure:

[…] policies designed to bring about changes in economically disadvantaged lives constitute a cultural process through which class positions and identities are partly created. That process signals inextricable relations between cultural and economic aspects of the way society works, expressed in the daily practices of social life and in observable social differences and inequalities.

Similarly, Uitermark et al (2007) argue that our understanding of policy-led gentrification and its effects must become more sophisticated since it is used to restructure both people and places. Uitermark et al (2007) attempt to enhance present thinking within gentrification research by conceiving it as the state's attempt to reassert its grip on social life. Their research examines gentrification as a governmental strategy that exerts social control through the guise of social cohesion in Rotterdam. They demonstrate that state-led gentrification is not simply part of a programme to improve neighbourhood facilities and the urban environment; rather, it acts as the primary 'means through which governmental organisations and their partners lure the middle classes into disadvantaged areas with the purpose of civilising and controlling these neighbourhoods' (Uitermark et al, 2007, p 127). Gentrification created through socially mixed housing does not create an immediate profit. The value added lies in using gentrification to govern the behaviours of 'problem' populations. Thus we can take from this that displacement is not their immediate goal; rather, public policy seeks to encourage working-class participation in these processes.

The concept of hegemony (Gramsci, 1971) can conceptually strengthen the gentrification heuristic in a number of crucial ways in this respect. It offers a more complex explanation of the use of gentrification within urban policy. Hegemony refers to a form of rule relevant to how transformations in social relations are managed while the capitalist system is maintained overall. It is a critical strategy during periods of change, such as the shift away from industrial towards more post-industrial forms of production and from a broadly Keynesian-style political economy to a neoliberal one. This is secured by the diffusion and popularisation of the view of the ruling class throughout the rest of society. This distillation involves a mix of consent and coercion which combine structural and agential processes, highlighting the reciprocal relationship between material and the phenomenological levels (Gramsci, 1971). This expresses the idea that cultural and economic processes are inextricably linked. Hegemony captures structural processes in a Marxist sense but includes the role of the subject, agency and everyday life often overlooked in traditional Marxist analysis, both in gentrification research and within sociological research more broadly. Within this understanding, gentrification can be conceived as a political strategy which not only seeks to create space for the more affluent user (Hackworth, 2002); it also seeks to, consensually, create the more affluent user which, in the context of neoliberalism, relates to a moral and financial economy (Paton, 2009). By promoting home ownership while deconstructing formerly fixed positions such as working-class support for social housing, it is used to attach this group to the 'new' set of ideas on increased privatisation of housing and neighbourhood space in general. This expresses the interests of the neoliberal national and local state that attempt to promote consumerism, responsiblism and individualism. This is evident in the increasing privatisation of social housing and the shift of emphasis from tenant to that of consumer (Flint, 2006; McKee, 2008). Gentrification in working-class neighbourhoods signals the effective end of traditional social and municipal provisions replaced by state partnerships with private and public, which is quite different to the seemingly philanthropic goal of social mix.

The use of the hegemonic framework problematises the notion of gentrification as 'good' or 'evil'. It allows studies of gentrification to be inclusive of working-class agency and to explore how and why gentrification is both resisted and negotiated by this group, since hegemony is achieved as much consensually as it is coercively. Residents are encouraged to participate in gentrification processes in their neighbourhood and those who do not are treated punitively, vilified or even displaced. This goes some way in explaining the lack of resistance to these processes in the UK compared to the US: the latter having adopted a more coercive, aggressive approach compared to the former consensual, 'partnership' 'community ownership' style. There are perceivable cultural and material benefits of gentrification as much as there are disadvantages for working-class groups. Studies of gentrification often fail to grasp this due to a misconception that working-class people have an instrumental relationship to place and their neighbourhoods. This is compounded by research on the middle classes (Butler with Robson, 2003; Savage et al, 2005), and by Allen's (2008) research on working-class neighbourhoods that claims the working class have a 'bricks and mortar' relationship to home ownership. A new sociological perspective on gentrification that combines cultural and material understandings can put working-class communities and their everyday lives at the centre point of analysis. It would enable an exploration of how working-class residents may at times enjoy and support gentrification but perhaps not in the way policy intended. However, to explore this we need to shift perspective.

Bringing the 'Other' into research

Inverting the research focus challenges the gentrification orthodoxy that many researchers agree is outmoded. Methodology plays an important part. The local case study approach has come under some criticisms as partly contributing to the lack of critical perspectives (Slater, 2006). While a comparative method of analysis is essential in understanding gentrification at a national and international level, locality studies and community studies should not be rendered inward-looking or parochial. Watt (2008) and Slater (2006) suggest that the antidote to the loss of critical edge in gentrification research is inversion of the focus, forming a 'bottom-up' or 'backstage view'. I strongly advocate this approach because shifting perspective helps bring out the autonomy and agency of the working class and uncover vitally important processes such as the role of social housing in increasingly promoting gentrification. Without empirical work on the ground, such pivotal processes are overlooked. In what follows I draw on work undertaken in Partick to substantiate some of these claims about the importance of including the working class in studies of gentrification.

In this study I interviewed 49 local working-class residents[2] of Partick in Glasgow. Historically Glasgow has been characterised as a working-class city. More recently, just as post-devolution Scotland presents itself as post-industrial, 'Smart successful Scotland', so Glasgow too is repositioned as cosmopolitan: 'it has shaken off its shroud of industrial soot and shimmied into a sparkling new designer gown' (Lonely Planet, 2009). Scotland's housing tenure has changed significantly: the number of people owning their own homes has doubled over the past 20 years while social housing has hit a 50-year low (Shelter, 2009). Partick is a traditionally working-class neighbourhood, formerly home to shipyards and working-class leisure and social reproduction. It is situated close to the salubrious and fashionable West End. The former sites of industry have been transformed into luxury high-rise housing development, Glasgow Harbour, which is home to an estimated 5,000 new residents and covers 49 hectares and over 3km of waterfront. Glasgow Harbour began as a joint venture between Clydeport Plc and the Bank of Scotland but was acquired by Peel Holding Plc in 2003. The land has been purchased by Glasgow Harbour Ltd, a private sector company and wholly owned subsidiary of Clydeport and part of Peel property and transport group. Glasgow City Council envisages the project as having 'hugely beneficial economic, tourist and social implications for both Glasgow and Scotland' (Clyde Waterfront, 2007). Currently, seven years after work began, there are no shops, services or amenities on the site, only luxury flats. It has led to the creation of a wealthy ghetto, contra to the policy goals of social mix. Mix is physically prohibited by an expressway that separates the new incoming affluent residents from the rest of Partick. The following section outlines some of the findings from this research. I couch my discussion in the conceptual language of cosmopolitanism, re-appropriating the term to examine the effects of social mix. Beck (2000, p 100) notes that: 'cosmopolitan society means cosmopolitan society and its enemies' – there are always cosmopolitan losers and winners. However, implicit in this is the continued use of the 'us and them', suggesting the experience of cosmopolitanism is strictly stratified rather than 'bulimic' (Young, 2007). My findings show that, complexly, gentrification was not a zero sum game for working-class residents.

The winners?

Glasgow Harbour did not add value in the way that Glasgow City Council proclaimed it would, such as creating affordable housing and jobs, but many Partick residents still supported it as adding value to the area, which, in their opinion, was a barren, disused 'eye sore'. A small number of those I spoke to 'loved' the regeneration of the Harbour and thought it was beautiful. This positive view was more common among men who had experienced the sharp end of deindustrialisation, such as Brian, Tim and Steve, and who rejected what the undeveloped site represented – the death of industry and the defeat of workers who had fought against closures. Although outwardly excluded through lack of resources, some residents actively challenged this and used the site in different ways – for dog walking, cycling, or, in subversive ways, drinking alcohol or, in the case of one resident, who was renting a Glasgow Harbour flat which he had paid for by Housing Benefit.

Partick's close proximity to the West End, home to the University of Glasgow and Kelvingrove Art Gallery, gives the neighbourhood cosmopolitanism by association, which working-class residents enjoyed and partook of. Indeed, it was important to them in identity-making and forming local attachment. The following residents were 'incomers' to Partick – David from Ibrox in Glasgow and Natasha from London. Both rented their houses from Partick Housing Association:

David: "This side is more cosmopolitan, it's a bit more integrated. You meet all sorts of walks of life in Partick. It's a sort of self-contained town within itself. It's got every pub you need, every shop you need and people just accept you."

Natasha: "As a Londoner if I went to somewhere like Drumchapel, and I don't mean this in a bad way, I think that there is a racist problem in Glasgow, right? [...] When I first moved up here the West End would be the only place where you saw someone who was black or Jewish or someone who was gay. There was that cosmopolitan mix that has spread out into Partick and I've never experienced any racism from anyone within this area."

It is argued that the working class, since they are forced to engage with the 'Other', are more cosmopolitan than the middle classes who can retreat or stay a safe enough distance away. This resonated with one resident, Sean, who was renting out his spare room and sofa to Polish workers. Like gentrifiers, working-class residents made strong claims to place with the phrase 'I belong tae Partick' often used. Place attachment was particularly meaningful for ontologically insecure residents in this changing neighbourhood and city, more generally. Further, provided they had the resources, they could act as gentrifiers. One resident, Bea, considered herself a true working-class Partick resident, having lived there all her life. Her family scrambled together money to buy homes in Partick as the council tried to decant working-class families to peripheral estates in the 1970s and 1980s.

Bea: "When we realised that we were not all going to get houses, my granny said that we are going to have to buy them as they came up to stay in Partick. It was the only way. Most of us all did that, most of us so that we could live here rather than schemes like Arden.[3] That's where we would have ended up. It was so we could stay together. I can remember her saying 'I am not going to have my family scattered to the wind'."

This was an act of security against being displaced. Bea later bought a new-build home in Partick, becoming a gentrifier in this respect, but it was underpinned by financial imperatives – her family fixed themselves to place to gain control and security from being displaced. Gordon's family made substantial gains from the increase in property prices. This 24-year-old barman's grandparents bought a flat cheaply many years ago. This was split into two properties and was subsequently inherited by his parents:

> Gordon: "It was valued at £60,000 then and now it's £250,000. That's mad. That much in that time."

But this consumption of private housing exceeded financial imperatives. Participating in gentrification in this way gave Bea ontological meaning. She was consuming and preserving her own history, as she bought a new-build property on the site of the 'steamie', laundry and washhouse traditionally used by local women:

> Bea: "[...] I look out my kitchen window and I look across the luxury car park and I see my granny and the poorer women who were there in the 'steamie' but I also see the better off ones that I even see today who are 70 years old. [...] I can stand at night and dream."

The point to make here is that the same behaviours exist across classes, and the majority of people in Partick, working and middle class, often want similar things for their neighbourhood, such as security, a close-knit community, successful social reproduction and a sense of belonging. Importantly, there is working-class support for regeneration. Indeed, the working class can be gentrifiers and take pleasure and gains from participating in this process. However, there are also limits to this cosmopolitanism.

The losers?

Not everyone can participate in this cosmopolitanism, and indeed, as Young (2007) makes clear, working-class residents were often simultaneously included and excluded from processes. There is no question that displacement was occurring in Partick. Table 16.4 shows the house price increases in Partick.

With such changes, local residents' fixity to place was increasingly embattled and precarious. Natasha accounts for the changes taking place in her neighbourhood:

> Natasha: [...] "Middle class, more affluent people coming in, buying their own properties, keep to themselves and there's an aloofness. For example, when we lived in Dumbarton

Road, it was all housing association all up the close and we did talk to each other whether it was 'hello' or anything like that. When I moved up to this close it was bought houses and there is only one couple who speak, you know? It's very much like my kids 'are cheeky', not in a right way but in a snobbery way, like 'your child is too loud' or 'drawing on the wall'. […] I really think that is part of it, you know what I mean, the ownership? And it's not just about owning properties it's about their values and stuff obviously would be different to mine."

Table 16.4: Increase in house price sales at intermediate geography[a], city and national levels, 1997 and 2007

House sales, median price	Partick	Glasgow Harbour and Partick South	Glasgow City	Scotland
1997	£47,850	£36,000	£40,000	£44,000
2007	£125,000	£172,495	£102,000	£100,000

Note: [a] The intermediate zones are aggregations of data zones within local authorities and are designed to contain between 2,500 and 6,000 people. Partick comprises of three intermediate geography zones. Only the two listed 'Partick' and 'Glasgow Harbour and Partick South are representative.

Source: Scottish Neighbourhood Statistics (2009)

This suggests that the working class reject the middle-class 'Other' because they are first rejected by this more powerful 'Other'. It exemplifies the relationship between property and propriety – as social renters they are problematic and their children are deemed unruly. Natasha suggests that their values are fundamentally different. However, this was challenged later in the interview. The conversation turned to Glasgow Harbour, which provoked reaction from Natasha and her partner Jimmy who live next to the underpass that connects the two neighbourhoods:

Jimmy: "They've got those cameras up specifically because of the Harbour. The tunnel has been redone, all fancy lights, trees at the side, all because they folk have forked out the money for these flats and I think that it's disgraceful. Disgraceful. We've been crying out for stuff for years and have never got it."

Security is a 'positional good' that can be amassed by residents at the Harbour. It became clear that Partick residents wanted this security themselves. Harbour residents have the opportunity and the means to buy safety, which Natasha and Jimmy cannot. They want security as a public good, to keep their children safe:

> Jimmy: "[We want] Aesthetic stuff, parks, trees, but practical stuff. I mean growing up, luckily the eldest kids are alright but they have grown up with groups of people where there has been fighting and stuff and there needs to be some sort of intervention for young people so they are not labelled and not stigmatised."

The gentrifiers could secure their social reproduction via purchasable and positional goods, whereas Natasha and Jimmy were left to worry about the safety of their children in their neighbourhood. Fundamentally the problem is that gentrification involves a form of hegemony which endeavours to shift the social contract, encouraging privatisation rather than social welfarism. This couple cannot become the consumer citizens that gentrification promotes. They have fewer resources and freedom of mobility or fixity than middle-class homeowners. Yet they invest their time and resources into the neighbourhood, and maintain the public provisions that remain, including saving a park from being turned into houses. They negotiated and sold off a small proportion of the park to developers and used the money to upgrade the remaining park facilities. However, while their neighbourhood is regenerated, not everyone is able to enjoy the benefits of this. This simultaneous exclusion and inclusion, in both cultural and economic terms, is encapsulated by the following incidents recounted by Lisa and Mhairi. Lisa describes the local Organic Farmers' Market in Mansfield Park:

> "It was your West End types going initially but a couple of times I've went recently there was a real mix of Partick punters and from outside the West End. I was having a conversation with this old wifey the other day about carrots she says 'these carrots actually taste of carrots, it's great', you know? So folk are using it."

This 'old Partick wifey' enjoys these organic carrots over the mass-produced, cheaper supermarket variety. However, as Mhairi notes, as much as local people may enjoy the organic food, they do not have the material means to consume, and are therefore excluded:

"They are trying to make the place more interesting, Polish delis and Delizique but I guess that's where the divide is up there that attracts the middle class or people with money or too lazy to cook paying through the nose. I was up there [Delizique] and there was an old lady there and she was arguing and she was saying to me 'Bloody £6 for carrots! I could get that round the corner for £1.50!'."

Conclusion

Through recent research we have developed a keener understanding of gentrifiers, their sovereignty and what informs their locational choices. This partly, although not fully, problematises their role in social mix strategies. However, focusing on middle-class hegemony in gentrification partly propagates the hegemonic mission of gentrification, that strong distinctions exist as essential differences between the working class and middle class. This legitimates the use of social mix policy and yet, ironically, middle-class desires to draw distinctions mean that social mix does not take place. Analysing the use of gentrification as social mix policy in relation to the effects it has on working-class lives begins to reveal the complexity of this process. Used this way, gentrification involves the decimation of public provisions borne out of social welfarism in neighbourhoods and the creation of space for, and creation of, the more competent consumer. We are witnessing the effective end of social housing which has, historically, been a lifeline against displacement for many residents in working-class neighbourhoods. Neoliberalism has reshaped housing and this marketisation permeates social housing which increasingly has to be 'income-generating'. This has serious ramifications for marginalised and poorer social renters. Yet this hegemonic shift has been achieved both consensually and coercively. The accentuation of differences between the working class and the middle class is essential to the ratification of this neoliberal hegemony. More worryingly is that the present Conservative-Liberal Democrat Coalition government deems that the current housing problems are not due to the failure of neoliberalism but rather that neoliberalism has not been correctly implemented, which they hope to rectify by minimising the role of the state further.

We cannot foreclose on the fact that a gentrification discourse or elective belonging (Savage et al, 2005) is part of working-class subjectivity. Moving the analytical focus to the working-class experience drives the debate on, both theoretically and conceptually. Considering working-class experiences when examining gentrification and when set within the context of hegemony helps us to problematise the relationship between structure and agency. Working-class residents are not always displaced, they do not always resist gentrification; some enjoy it since gentrification brings new pleasures. However, this is in addition to new inequalities and this is an important issue to examine. From these insights, it is clear that the differences between the working class and middle class in the neighbourhood are not essential; they are material. They both wish for similar things for and from their local area, but working-class residents have less opportunity to participate; they are flawed consumers because they are not in a powerful enough material position to consume. The key differential in the binary is the degree of control residents hold. Middle-class residents displayed more control over their movement in and out of the neighbourhood. They did not need to invest in the area; they could afford to secure activities to ensure their social reproduction and lifestyles outside of the neighbourhood. Working-class residents have less control and, therefore, less choice. That is not to deny that they have any choice. Through regeneration, residents find that choice is extended, but their capacity to make choices is constrained. This is an important research trajectory to pursue further. The concept of control over fixity to place offers a critical insight into gentrification in relation to displacement but also stratification research. This could invigorate present conceptual readings of class identities and inequalities. This offers an extension to traditional structuralist Marxist readings of gentrification, which are increasingly resonant in the present financial crisis, to include the agency, experience and identity of the contemporary working-class subject.

Notes

[1] This chapter was originally presented as a discussant paper at ESRC seminar 1, 'Gentrification and social mix', 22-23 May 2008, King's College London. It was a response to some papers on the role of gentrifiers in gentrification and public policy that have not been included in this collection, and I have adapted the paper accordingly including by drawing on my own empirical research in Glasgow.

[2] I have a broadly Marxist understanding of class as a structured relationship, materially based but not determined, although this is cross-cut by issues of ethnicity and gender. A Marxist reading of class has major analytical shortcomings in the context of this research principally because it does not analytically capture the struggles of cultural and material differentiation between working and middle-class groups and the material basis for these. This is crucial to the process of restructuring and to how hegemony is achieved.

I employed the National Statistics Socio-economic Classification framework that is the primary social classification in the UK, first used in the 2001 Census, only because it was useful for gathering data on the neighbourhood. It is an imperfect but valuable guide. I took a purposive and heterogeneous approach. Residents were sampled from different sites in Partick, using techniques such as flyers and posters and snowball sampling. All respondents' names have been changed to pseudonyms.

[3] Arden is a SSHA (Scottish Special Housing Association) built estate on the outskirts of Glasgow designed to re-house families from the overcrowded inner-city tenements.

SEVENTEEN

From social mix to political marginalisation? The redevelopment of Toronto's public housing and the dilution of tenant organisational power

Martine August and Alan Walks

Introduction

Canada's largest landlord, the Toronto Community Housing Corporation (TCHC), is in the process of revitalising the country's oldest and largest public housing community, Regent Park. The 15-year 'revitalisation' of the community will transform 70 acres of rent-geared-to-income (RGI) subsidised housing into a mixed-use, mixed-income neighbourhood, with new market housing and a New Urbanist-style redesign. The proportion of RGI-subsidised units will decline from 100% to only one quarter, in order to accommodate the community's new 'social mix'. The TCHC is executing a similar redevelopment approach in two of its other public housing communities, Don Mount Court (now called 'Rivertowne'), and Lawrence Heights. Both of these areas, like Regent Park, are in sought-after areas, sited on potentially valuable urban real estate. While the social and economic benefits promised by socially mixed public housing redevelopment have received much attention in the academic literature and local media, very little has been written about how such 'revitalisation' may affect residents' political networks and ability to influence governance decisions. Indeed, even if benefits do result from the forced imposition of social mix on public housing communities (a claim we find highly dubious; see August, 2008), redevelopment stands to create significant power imbalances between the new majority of residents paying market rent for their housing, and the minority of tenants in subsidised housing. Focusing on the redevelopment underway in Toronto, this chapter explores the implications of socially mixed public housing redevelopment for tenant participation, organisational structure and political capital.

Social mix in Canada

Canada has no nationally driven social mix policy, or even any national housing policy. The Canadian federal government devolved its responsibility for housing to the provinces in the 1990s (in Ontario, housing was then further devolved to municipalities). As such, current attempts to promote social mix in Canada are the result of locally based decisions made by individual municipalities, local public housing agencies, and in some cases, the provinces, in the absence of federal funding. Despite this lack of any nationally driven agenda, the social mix ideal has, since the 1990s, been cemented into mainstream Canadian notions of what constitutes 'good planning' (August, 2008).

Social mix became popular among progressive planners and policy makers in Canada in the late 1960s and 1970s. Although public housing had been federally funded since 1949, programme changes in 1964 resulted in a ten-fold increase over the next decade in the construction of public units. While predominantly small-scale and disproportionately housing senior citizens (Sewell, 1994, p 138), enough public housing was in large, high-rise communities and built via slum clearance and urban renewal that it began to attract attention for disrupting stable neighbourhoods and ghettoising the poor. By the late 1960s pressures were mounting to halt urban renewal and make public housing less homogeneous. Support for social mix was boosted by anti-urban renewal sentiment coming from academics, professionals and citizens, who were inspired by the writings of urbanists like Jane Jacobs, and by the leftward shift in the political spirit of the times (August, 2008). In the early 1970s, this shift was reflected in dramatic changes in the country's political landscape. The federal liberal minority government, supported by the social democratic New Democratic Party, approved funding for non-profit and cooperative social housing projects with social mix as a key objective in 1973 (van Dyk, 1995). In 1972 'liberal reformist' city councils were elected in Toronto and Vancouver, and large-scale socially mixed development projects were approved for False Creek, an 1,800-unit community built on an industrial site in central Vancouver, and for the St Lawrence neighbourhood, which featured a mix of 3,500 co-ops, affordable rental and private homes built on formerly industrial land in central Toronto.

Despite enthusiasm for social mix in Canada during the progressive heyday of the 1960s and 1970s, most on-the-ground city building did little to break from conventional practices and typical postwar suburban development continued to dominate the landscape. It took two decades for 'social mix' and its associated ideas to fully displace modernist planning as the new conventional planning wisdom, during which time sweeping economic restructuring was playing out in Canada and at the global scale. By 1985 mixed-income social housing had come under fire for providing subsidies to higher-income Canadians, and was ideologically out of step with the objectives of the new Conservative government (Pendakur, 1987). Federal policy changes targeted assistance towards households in 'core need', making higher-income units in 'mixed' communities ineligible for federal assistance and significantly discouraging mixed-income social housing development. In 1993 the federal government's involvement in any new social housing was terminated, and responsibility for housing was fully devolved to the provinces.

In Ontario the 1995 election of the Mike Harris Progressive Conservative government, largely on the basis of the suburban vote, ushered in an intense round of neoliberal restructuring in the province. This included drastic welfare cuts, the implementation of a 'Safe Streets Act' targeting marginalised groups, the introduction of workfare, legalisation of the 60-hour work week, downloading of provincial responsibility, attacking and weakening public sector unions, dismantling and underfunding public education and monitoring and harassing civil society organisations (Keil, 2002; Walks, 2004). Harris also merged hundreds of local governments, including the amalgamation of seven municipalities into a new City of Toronto. This move tipped the balance of electoral power to Toronto's suburbs, resulting in the 1997 and 2000 elections of a Mayor whose policies focused on law and order, tax cuts and crackdowns on unions and marginal populations (Boudreau, 2000; Keil, 2002, p 594). Finally, the Harris government made good on their promise to get the Province 'out of the housing business' (Hackworth, 2008, p 13). Under the 2000 Social Housing Reform Act municipal 'housing service providers' in Ontario were given all responsibility for social housing, with imposed governance structures forcing them to become entrepreneurial and 'more like businesses' (Hackworth and Moriah, 2006, p 516). Two effects of this change have been to make the administration of public housing more complex and confusing and to intensify Ontario's affordable housing crisis (Hackworth and Moriah, 2006). Pressure to be entrepreneurial has led to uneven outcomes, favouring larger housing service providers with valuable land resources and bigger city governments to depend on, while the majority of providers worry deeply about their ongoing ability to survive. What constitutes 'success' in this entrepreneurial model is questioned by housing providers who argue that 'privatizing resources is not a sign of success when it threatens the future accessibility of a housing unit' (Hackworth and Moriah, 2006, p 522).

It was in this context of neoliberal restructuring and declining support for social housing that the ideal of social mix re-emerged and wedged itself into mainstream principles of 'good planning' in Canada (see August, 2008).[1] Critiques of modernist postwar planning models originating in the debates of the 1960s and 1970s gained steam over the next two decades and won institutional acceptance by the 1990s and 2000s. Movements for smart growth, new urbanism, sustainable development, transit-oriented development and 'creative cities' policy shared a vision of a mixed-use, higher-density, socially diverse urban realm. By the late 1990s these ideas were vigorously adopted in Canada, influencing policy debates at academic conferences and professional meetings, and inspiring the re-write of city plans across the country (Grant, 2002, p 72). While social mix is a goal associated with these movements, *explicit* support for social mix in practice tends to arise only to justify projects of renewal or revitalisation in areas dominated by marginalised people (August, 2008, p 92). This is certainly the case in Toronto, where social mix is billed as a key planning objective for only a few projects: TCHC's public housing redevelopments, the redevelopment of Canada's largest Centre for Addictions and Mental Health and as a justification for anti-rooming house legislation in the gentrifying South Parkdale area (see Slater, 2004).

Contemporary pro-social mix sentiment is quite different than in former decades. At that time, Pendakur (1987) argued that it represented a compromise between social reformers on the left and conservative politicians on the right, who opposed public housing entirely. Introducing social housing construction as 'socially mixed' in 1973 was accepted as the lesser of two evils by the right, while it achieved the left/liberal goal of creating new social units in mixed communities. In the current context, the situation is reversed. Little social housing is being built across most provinces, and the language of social mix functions now to appease left/liberals (who are attracted by its progressive connotations), while in practice social mix projects allow for private sector incursions into public housing communities and the privatisation of publicly held land assets.

Public housing redevelopment in neoliberal Toronto

In 2002 the Toronto Community Housing Corporation was created; it inherited an ageing, neglected, twice-downloaded stock of 60,000 housing units and limited revenue streams to take care of it. TCHC's first act was decisive and symbolic – a plan to demolish and rebuild Canada's first and largest public housing community. Built between 1947 and 1958 on the razed site of a low-income downtown community, Regent Park typified modernist urban renewal-style development, consisting of exclusively subsidised housing without through-streets or spaces for businesses (see Photographs 17.1 and 17.2). The redevelopment plans promise to eradicate the vestiges of high modernist design, creating new streets and ground-floor retail opportunities, and re-orienting buildings to the street. TCHC's planning rhetoric and design rationale is heavily influenced by the US HOPE VI programme (Home ownership and Opportunity for People Everywhere), which had existed for a decade by 2002. Redevelopment planners promise that changing the design in Regent Park will reduce crime and social problems and address the 'isolation' allegedly experienced by the residents. Redevelopment also promises to 'improve the lives and living environment' for residents, leading to 'better access to training, employment and economic development opportunities, more immediate retail choices, and enhanced coordination of community services' (Regent Park Collaborative Team, 2002, p 5). As with HOPE VI, a key objective for TCHC's redevelopment is poverty deconcentration. The lead revitalisation planner explained that: "It was clear to the people at the TCHC that a concentration of poverty like that in one area was not healthy for the people who were living there … or from a city building perspective" (personal communication, 1 February 2007). Thus, redevelopment in Toronto is presented as a solution to the problems ostensibly arising from concentrated poverty and outdated urban design, instead of the impact on social housing of reduced government support, downloading and neglect.

Socially mixed redevelopment is also under way in two other TCHC communities, both located on potentially valuable real estate (see Figure 17.1). The much-smaller Don Mount Court is located just east of Regent Park (across the Don River Valley) in the South Riverdale neighbourhood (for a history of gentrification in this area, see Walks and August, 2008).[2] Now called 'Rivertowne' and refashioned as a New Urbanism-inspired low-rise condo townhouse community, the original 252 RGI-subsidised units were demolished in 2002 and rebuilt on site alongside 187 new market units. Tenants began returning to the first phase of the redevelopment in July 2008, with the community expected to be completely re-settled by early 2011. TCHC's third foray into socially mixed redevelopment is still in its planning stages. The low-density Lawrence Heights community is located well north

Photograph 17.1: North Regent Park: the northern half of Regent Park (built between 1948 and 1957) consists largely of red-brick, cruciform-style walk-up buildings

Photograph 17.2: Regent Park South (built between 1957 and 1959) consists of apartment towers and low-rise townhouses, surrounded by mature trees, walking paths and play areas

of downtown in Toronto's inner suburbs, near a regional shopping mall and a major highway, and adjacent to the City's subway transit network. The plans for this community involve replacing its 1,208 RGI-units on site with a redeveloped community that will include 5,500-6,000 housing units when complete. Thus, the proportion of subsidised units is decreasing with each TCHC redevelopment: from 57% of all units in the redeveloped Don Mount Court, to 25% in Regent Park, to 18% (or less) in Lawrence Heights.

Figure 17.1: Map of Toronto, showing the three social housing redevelopment sites

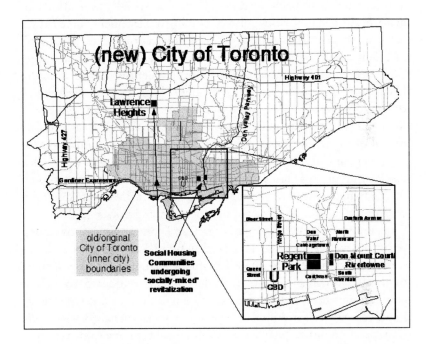

Despite drawing on HOPE VI for inspiration, the Toronto model of social housing redevelopment is marked by a number of distinguishing features. First, there is no Canadian voucher programme, so tenant-based subsidies, which are a key element of the US HOPE VI poverty deconcentration and public housing redevelopment strategies, are not part of the model. In Canada, the subsidies are administered via rents being geared to income. Second, one-for-one unit replacement is required for all public housing units demolished in Ontario. In Toronto, there are also requirements that all units be replaced on site, which means that substantial increases in density are required if market housing is going to be built. The culture of accepting density in Toronto makes it different from many US jurisdictions where high-density redevelopment is much less likely to be tolerated. A third difference is that there is no federal funding for redevelopment in Canada, and housing providers must operate according to provincial mandates. As a result, redevelopment efforts (in Ontario) are market-oriented, prioritising projects that can attract private sector interest rather than those with the greatest social need.

The political impacts of revitalisation?

While much has been written about the social implications of gentrification in its various guises, including displacement, there has yet to be a sufficient focus on the political implications of 'revitalisation', including effects on political capital and influence. The mainstream view, as echoed by TCHC, implies that political benefits will flow from the heightened levels of social capital brought about by concentrations of the middle class. The assumption is that the arrival of more politically influential middle-class newcomers will enhance the social and political capital of the marginalised, as the middle class help them to fight for improvements in local infrastructure and services. Joseph (2006), for instance, argues that under this sort of social housing redevelopment 'homeowners will have greater stability, participation in community organizations, likelihood of voting, and spending power' (p 221).

The empirical research on social capital and community bonds among tenants, however, suggests that social networks may be damaged, not strengthened, by redevelopment. US studies examining the experiences of public housing tenants who have been relocated to mixed communities have not found any evidence that tenants experience improvements via 'bridging' or 'leveraging' social capital (Briggs, 1998; Clampet-Lundquist, 2007; Keels, 2008). Tenants in one study reported *reduced* informal social control post-relocation (Clampet-Lundquist, 2007), and tenants at a Philadelphia HOPE VI site reported lower levels of trust post-redevelopment (Popkin et al, 2000). A loss of friends (Clark, 2002; Clampet-Lundquist, 2004; Sullivan and Lietz, 2008), of connections to church (Hanratty et al, 1998), of supportive social ties (Curley, 2006; Clampet-Lundquist, 2010) and of a 'sense of community' (Gibson, 2007) are also cited as resulting from poverty deconcentration strategies in public housing. These findings suggest that as redevelopment takes place, the power of tenants to develop or maintain an influential political voice and remain connected to one another in their community is diminished. Physical relocation of tenants throughout the process can quickly amount to 'political displacement'. Middle-class newcomers moving into market-based housing, with their 'greater ... participation in community organizations' (Joseph, 2006, p 221) can easily step in and usurp what little political influence tenants are able to build.

The little research that has examined this question concurs with this hypothesis. Martin (2007), for instance, examined how gentrification led to 'political displacement' in several gentrifying Atlanta neighbourhoods, and a weakening of political organising power for long-term residents, which worked to the benefit of the interests of the gentrifying middle class. Bentancur (2002) found that resident opposition and resistance to gentrification is often dominated by a 'politics of suppression' in gentrifying areas, as more powerful newcomer groups silence the political voice of dissident long-term residents in neighbourhood-based organisations, at local council meetings, through their ability to elect local councillors and the influence they have over local development decisions (p 783). Likewise, Gibbs Knotts and Haspel (2006) found that gentrification led to lower electoral turnout among long-term residents in Atlanta.

When gentrification occurs in public housing via socially mixed redevelopment schemes there may be even more potential for the suppression of tenant political voice. In the mixed-income HOPE VI redevelopment of Maverick Gardens in East Boston, for example, Graves (2010) found that a clear power differential emerged between subsidised tenants and market residents. The latter were given preferential treatment by the management, since it was they who were depended on for the financial viability of the project. A housing management company has control over many aspects of tenants' lives, and can use this to limit independent tenant organising and expressions of dissent.

The political realities of social mix in Toronto

Toronto's experience to date with the imposition of social mix in low-income communities provides a window into the political realities of redevelopment policy. Instead of better access to resources, amenities and political capital, there is a real danger that tenants will find themselves in the minority and become politically marginalised from their community. We interrogate the impacts of social housing redevelopment on the political influence of tenants, tenant experiences with community consultation, channels for opposition and resistance and the impact of higher-income newcomers. Our analysis derives from semi-structured interviews with 12 stakeholders from tenant- and community-based organisations working in the study communities, participant observation at local events and reports from tenant organisations, news media and the TCHC itself. Since social housing redevelopment is still underway in Toronto, any conclusions regarding its ultimate outcome are by definition speculative. As such, we focus on the politics related to tenant representation, tenant organisations and social mix as it continues to unfold in the redevelopment of these communities. The evidence points to a future of political marginalisation and exclusion, rather than the social harmony promised by normative discourses of social mix.

1. Avant mix: manipulating 'choice' and marginalising tenant voices

Tenant consultation and engagement has been an important part of the planning for all of TCHC's revitalisation projects. Once the plan to redevelop these communities had been hatched, the new entrepreneurial TCHC moved to sell it to a number of constituencies – including tenants. TCHC claimed that their system of tenant participation would give tenants 'a say in the decisions that affect their home, building, neighbourhood, and community' (TCHC website: www.totontohousing.ca/tenantlife/tenantparticipationsystem). It soon became clear, however, that TCHC was mostly interested in having acquiescent tenants who could be counted on to support development decisions already made. Among these was the model of a socially mixed neighbourhood with a majority middle-class population, a decision that tenants soon found was not up for discussion.[3] Thus, from the outset, broader critiques of socially mixed redevelopment and concerns about social and political dilution were marginalised.

Representing who? 'Tenant' organisations in Regent Park

In Regent Park, two organisations officially exist to represent tenant interests. The first is the tenant council comprised of 'tenant representatives' who are elected by residents in each TCHC building to take part in its 'tenant participation system' (TCHC, 2007a). Tenant representatives are also involved in the TCHC's participatory budgeting system which allows residents to prioritise how to spend 'money set aside for tenant decision making' and choose which capital priorities should receive funding (TCHC website: www.totontohousing.ca/tenantlife/tenantparticipationsystem). Although reps are elected by tenants, their ability to meaningfully represent tenant interests is severely circumscribed by the housing company. To begin with, the range of issues over which reps preside is quite limited, preventing them from becoming involved in redevelopment-related discussions. Reps are not supposed to meet on their own or organise independently of TCHC, and the Corporation has been known to select and groom candidates prior to tenant elections. In selecting pliant representatives, TCHC can control the perceptions of how tenants view the development process.

The second organisation that officially represents tenants is the Regent Park Neighbourhood Initiative (RPNI). Created by the TCHC in 2002 out of an existing residents' organisation 'to advocate and protect the interests of residents', RPNI serves 'as a social planning body in Regent Park over the course of redevelopment, a convener of working groups on various arising issues, and a change promotion agent for community services' (TCHC, 2007c, p 15). The RPNI is positioned to represent not only tenants but also the new condo residents and businesses in the community (TCHC, 2007c, p 94), and includes redevelopment-related issues in its mandate.

Despite its billing as a 'voice of residents' (TCHC, 2007a, p 2), RPNI is staffed and run by non-residents, and has a clear mandate to support the redevelopment. As such, RPNI cannot be a 'voice' of those residents who might be critical of TCHC's plans. The director of RPNI put it this way: "if people have concerns, they can come to us. We'll try to get them addressed. But if they were an 'opposition organization', they'd be on their own. If they were opposing redevelopment, it wouldn't fit" (Catherine Goulet, personal communication, 15 September 2008). In addition, with its mandate to represent both tenants and new condo residents, RPNI is structurally organised in the interests of the new middle-class residents. Demonstrating that RPNI is far from 'tenant-led', the RPNI director explained that "[unlike tenants] middle-class folks have pointy elbows, we throw our weight around". A number of respondents pointed out that because RPNI was established by TCHC in order to advocate for both redevelopment and the new middle-class residents, they are not likely to take seriously tenant complaints about the redevelopment process. And because some of RPNI's funding and all of their office space is provided by TCHC, the Corporation can exert enough control to prevent RPNI from evolving into an avenue for tenant protest.

Unfortunately for tenants, the two organisations ostensibly set up to represent them are fundamentally incapable of presenting opposition to the redevelopment. As such, residents who have problems with the revitalisation have no easy way of connecting with others of like mind, and no easy way of making their voices heard. When tenants bring concerns to RPNI, these are chalked up to a misplaced 'fear', and easily dismissed. RPNI's director explained that: "there is a lot of fear. People's housing is being torn down. There is fear about the sense of community – that it will get lost in the process ... even people who wanted this, they were at the demolition crying because their home was being demolished". Characterising tenant opposition as 'fear' presents tenants as un-sophisticated and irrational, suggesting that if they only understood what was going on they would embrace it. This discursive act works to undermine and dismiss legitimate opposition as temporary, unreasonable and resulting from a lack of emotional control. In this way, planners working for TCHC justify their paternalistic imposition of 'social mix' as the victory of logic over emotion, a form of tough love. Miriam Nazar (not her real name), a tenant activist opposing redevelopment, found herself up against this attitude, noting that the TCHC "addressed us in many ways – unreasonable, irrational, trouble makers ... they'd say 'what we are doing is common sense, this is what is happening with all public housing now'" (personal communication, 17 November 2008). Tenants have furthermore been characterised as 'abnormal', and in need of the influence of higher-income neighbours. According to a representative from a community agency working with TCHC, revitalisation was necessary to 'normalise' Regent Park because "it has not been a normal community" (comment at the Regent Park 'Roundtable on Affordable Housing', Reunion Panel Discussion, 14 October 2010). Selling the revitalisation as 'normalisation' brands the prior community and its residents as deviant and untrustworthy, serving to justify paternalistic treatment.

Manipulating choice

In Toronto, the concept of a newly designed, socially mixed community has been presented as the only alterative to the degeneration and under-maintenance of public housing, mirroring the 'false choice' between gentrification and neighbourhood decline often promoted by advocates of the former (DeFilippis, 2004). This discursive logic is accepted by many working on revitalisation, who believe not only that socially mixed redevelopment is the remedy for public housing decline, but even that the idea originated from tenants. The director of RPNI argued that "residents wanted this [redevelopment] to happen", and that "the community was very clear. They wanted mixed income. They want the streets back".

In reality, the degree to which residents might want redevelopment is highly constrained by the severe state of neglect suffered by social housing within the context of a neoliberalised Toronto and an entrepreneurial TCHC. John Clarke, of the Ontario Coalition Against Poverty, explained that the poor state of living conditions in Regent Park has constrained the meaningful choice of tenants in the consultation process. In selling the redevelopment to tenants, Clarke explained that TCHC "played on the fact that it was already run down [and] since the housing was in such bad shape, tenants are at a point where they are thinking 'anything but this'" (personal communication, 29 May 2008). Adonis Huggins, who runs a media arts centre for young people in Regent Park, explained that "housing has deteriorated because of neglect. The number one complaint of residents was maintenance. So people were happy once the redevelopment was announced" (comment at the 'Panel on Revitalisation', Regent Park Film Festival [RPFF], 7 November 2007). A similar trend was recognised by tenant organiser Steve Da Silva, who noted that: "a lack of maintenance and repairs were serious issues in Lawrence Heights, [but] when people complain about this, it plays into TCHC's argument that it needs to be demolished" (personal communication, 20 November 2008). As one Lawrence Heights tenant remarked: "Nobody got to vote on [redevelopment]. It's not a choice and that's what disturbs me. Being a person that is marginalised already and the TCHC with their approach as 'community based' and 'tenants have rights', when in fact we don't, and can't even express the fact that we don't want to move" (Amal, cited in BASICS *Newsletter*, 12 June 2007). The lack of meaningful choice was even admitted to by the director of RPNI, who explained that: "absolutely there were those who were opposed, but not as many as you think. The quality of housing was so bad, most people saw it as an opportunity to get other housing".

The Corporation's tenant engagement process has permitted little meaningful involvement for tenants, serving primarily to manufacture the impression of tenant consent, and its control over the only existing avenues for tenant organisation has prevented oppositional movements from emerging. In addition, TCHC appears not to tolerate any opposition to its chosen development model and has cracked down on opposition in ways that are both subtle and overt. Community organisations operating in Regent Park hesitate to publicly criticise redevelopment for fear that they will lose their space, funding, or both. One organisation, the Regent Park Film Festival, was forced out of its TCHC-owned space after hosting a 'Panel on Revitalisation' at its annual festival, in which attendees were provided with the rare opportunity to voice critical thoughts on redevelopment. The very next day a TCHC representative told RPFF to vacate their space, claiming "we don't owe you an explanation" (Nazar, 17 November 2008). The marginalisation of the political voice of tenants during the process of redevelopment planning reveals one way social mix policy can lead to social exclusion, as those who question, criticise or oppose the plans are excluded from the process of planning for their community.

2. Après mix, le dilution: pointy elbows and the prospects for tenant power

As redevelopment moves forward in Regent Park the composition of the community will be significantly altered. Occupying just over one quarter of post-redevelopment units, subsidised tenants will forfeit their monopoly over the footprint of Regent Park as new condo dwellers move in and alter the social landscape. In a community currently dominated by recent immigrants and visible minorities, the TCHC predicts that as redevelopment proceeds, the one group to experience demographic growth will be English-speaking adults aged 25-50 with household incomes over $60,000 (2007a, p 29). As local governance structures representing this group gain power in the area, the voice of tenants is likely to be submerged and subordinated to those of the incoming middle-class homeowners.

Loss of community

Despite the limitations put on tenants in consultations and the lack of outlets for tenant resistance to redevelopment, Regent Park tenants have a long history of political activism. In the late 1960s tenants marched on City Hall to protest provincial control of public housing, and actively fought against the 'slum' label that was being used by the media to describe their community. Tenants created organisations to raise money to build a swimming pool, to fight for improved maintenance and agitated for 'fair' rent policies (Purdy, 2004). In the not-so-recent past, tenants have fought for the construction of a community centre and approved a rent levy to finance it. The emergence of this political activism, and the ability of a marginalised group to develop a collective political voice, is rooted in the reality of concentrated poverty in Regent Park. The rather obsessive treatment of concentrated poverty as a problem in sociological and planning literature overlooks the fact that benefits to concentration do exist. Tenants in Regent Park and other TCHC communities have developed a strong sense of community and attachment to the place where they live. Nazar described her concern that deconcentration strategies may destroy this:

> "We've lived around each other for some time. We still want to live around each other. We want to continue the way we were. TCHC sees us as 'problem tenants'. This means that friends, neighbours, relatives – people we've lived side-by-side with for many years – may not come back."

Tenants in Lawrence Heights expressed similar concern about the loss of community:

> "The number one fear, personally, is our sense of family that we have developed over such a long period of time, is now going to be broken. The security of knowing – we all know each other here in Lawrence Heights – is going to be broken up. Because we will all be sent to different areas in Toronto and our community won't be as tight-knit as it is now and has been." (Tanisha, cited in BASICS *Newsletter*, 12 June 2007)

The presence of a distinctively different new population affects how comfortable tenants feel in their own community. John Clarke argued that "there is a strong sense of community in Regent Park, a sense of pride [which] will be affected by the process of out-and-out dispersal. [Redevelopment] will break that". Once tenants become "minorities in a new condo community they will feel a sense of inferiority and judgement ... like they are being monitored by social workers, cops, and new homeowners". Clarke predicts "a disastrous social environment [with] a lot of resentment involved" between both the new condo owners and tenants. Nazar envisions a similar outcome: "for low-income people, they see themselves as being looked down on – they get pity they don't want. They are [viewed as though] they are not capable of pulling their own weight" (17 November 2008). Tanisha, from Lawrence Heights, expressed concern over the potential clash of values that a mixed community might bring:

> "Here in Lawrence Heights, because many of the members have known each other for such a long time, we know our neighbours, we know our neighbours' children, we have a common set of values where we all kind of think alike or we experience the same issues as other members of our community. And I just feel, with revitalisation, having so many different people coming in from so many different areas, from so many socioeconomic backgrounds, there's

gonna be too many people with too many sets of values. And the issues that we might be facing – the new people may not have faced those issues – and vice versa." (cited in BASICS *Newsletter*, 12 June 2007)

Viewpoints like these challenge the assumption that low-income people benefit from having middle-class 'role models' in their communities. When low-income communities are concentrated, they can develop a sense of community in an environment of support and non-judgement.

From dilution to marginalisation

Enhanced political activism and local political influence emerged in Regent Park from an extended situation of concentrated poverty. John Clarke noted that while "politically, there is no independent structure of public housing or tenancy organizations", as long as tenants are concentrated in place "they are at least a community that can politically organise". Having a monopoly over this space also ensures that tenants have a role in local politics. Elsa Pratt (not her real name), director of a community-serving organisation in the area, explained that "right now there are two community centres in Regent Park. Nobody other than tenants use these places ... tenants use them and have a lot of input. Community residents are hired to work there" (personal communication, 26 November 2008). After revitalisation these spaces will 'belong' to a broader group than just tenants, and this will affect their political influence. According to Pratt: "now it's going to be a community centre for the entire area. People are concerned [that they will be excluded]. So while there is some negativity about isolation [from the middle class], here is also some safety in it".

The redevelopment will also affect the make-up of political constituencies and potentially the outcome of electoral politics in Regent Park. Since tenants account for a good portion of constituents in their area, Pratt described how they have become politically savvy and "know how to engage with politicians at all three levels of government". Yet, she feels tenant influence will decline as the demographics in the area change: "in terms of availability to have impact on the political system with a vote, there will be a smaller proportion of rent-geared-to-income [people]". In addition, Pratt noted that "once it is diluted, there will be fewer public housing units. With density doubling, there is a sense that [tenants] won't have the ability to influence politicians because there will be more of the people who don't want them there". John Clarke elaborated on what he thinks this will mean for tenants:

"to be a part of a minority in a condo neighbourhood, the potential for organising is much weaker, there is a real challenge to [tenants] having a say". This issue has been given very little priority by those working on the redevelopment. An author of the original *Regent Park revitalisation study* (Regent Park Collaborative Team, 2002) revealed a paternalistic and derogatory attitude towards tenant needs and concerns: when asked how revitalisation will affect tenant political influence, his response was: "it doesn't really matter – they don't vote anyway" (personal communication, 1 February 2007).

In light of such attitudes, it may not be surprising that many tenants believe revitalisation is proceeding in the interests of the wealthy. In Regent Park Pratt noted that "there is anger and frustration that all this is being done for the middle-income. There are real fears that while the intent is to make Regent Park 'less Regent Park' and to integrate, there is a huge potential for it to segregate people even more". According to Nazar, "the priority will now be people with higher income, people who bring revenue to the owner". In her opinion, "integration is another way of saying clean up the area, get rid of the have-nots; the less low-income the better". In Lawrence Heights, Steve Da Silva noted that "people are concerned that with a mixed-income community, their voices will be less effective, and that class-privileged people will have more of a say". There is widespread concern that once middle-class residents arrive, the interests of tenants will be over-ruled: "When we get that lovely mix people are talking about", explained the director of in important tenant-serving centre, "the white middle-class will have a much stronger voice politically than people living in poverty and with mental health issues ... how long until [this centre] is no longer a voice of these people?" (personal communication, 15 September 2008).

Between a rock and a pointy elbow

In addition to dilution, redevelopment and the imposition of social mix have the potential to create a polarised community where the interests of public housing tenants and new property owners clash. There is little acknowledgement, in either the TCHC's promotional material or among mainstream planners, that these groups might have different interests. Incoming middle-class residents are discursively constructed as saviours of low-income communities; with their political skills and money, they bring new services, amenities and recognition to the redeveloped communities. The director of RPNI expressed this sentiment, as noted above, with regard to how the middle class are the ones with the 'pointy elbows': "We throw our weight around.

Many low-income people don't do that. Particularly here, with new immigrants, people don't do it. So RPNI is asking, how do we build pointy elbows?". This thinking fails to address the reality that low-income public housing residents are most likely to be *on the sharp end* of these 'pointy elbows', and that the superior political influence of the middle class often manifests in an assault on the poor. Tensions between existing tenants and higher-income newcomers have been reported in other socially mixed public housing redevelopments. In a Tampa, Florida HOPE VI redevelopment, middle-class neighbours tried to use 'nuisance abatement' legislation to prevent the construction of more low-income housing (Greenbaum et al, 2008, p 216). Tach (2009) reported that in a Boston HOPE VI mixed-income community, higher-income neighbours have actively resisted interacting with public housing residents. In a Chatanooga, Tennessee mixed-income redevelopment, Fraser and Kick (2007) reported 'deep divides' between the two groups.

The existing evidence of relations between low-income and middle-class neighbours in Toronto does not suggest a harmonious future. Residents' associations near Regent Park are surprisingly vicious, and galvanise around the demonisation of poor people and the insistence that they be 'removed' from the community. The Corktown Residents' and Business Association (CRBA) represents the area directly south of Regent Park.[4] The CRBA's chief activities involve campaigns aimed at local, provincial and federal politicians to protest the existence of homeless shelters, housing for refugees and harm reduction programmes in the area. The CRBA claims that their community is 'the dumping ground for programs and services that other communities refuse' (CRBA, 2005a). Public housing falls into their category of unwanted neighbours, and in 2005 the Association protested the construction of Regent Park relocation housing on an undeveloped site slated to be part of the 'West DonLands', a new residential community nearby, on the grounds that it would hamper their property values. CRBA argued that 'parachuting' public housing onto this site 'provides short-term expediency to the Regent Park programme and is detrimental to both the Corktown community and the West DonLands in the long term' (CRBA, 2005a). In the same month, CRBA made the following argument in its newsletter:

> The [CRBA Board's] concerns are not only feel good topics but also bottom line matters that affect property values. If certain types of housing are expanded, like Regent Park, or additional social service facilities move into the area,

> not directly today, but the day after tomorrow, your house values, the rent you pay, the safety of your streets and parks, and your quality of life, limb, and the pursuit of happiness are affected. (CRBA, 2005b)

This (unfortunately all too typical) ratepayers group, which stated that harm reduction would come to the area 'over Corktown's dead body', has also appealed to the concept of a socially balanced community (CRBA, 2005c). In a letter to City Council protesting homeless shelter placements in Corktown, the CBRA argued:

> It is essential for our community to have the opportunity to revitalize. There must be a more *proportionate balance* across the entire *diverse* range of residents within Corktown. In the case of Corktown, the city must act immediately to relocate some facilities to other areas than this clearly overloaded community. (CRBA, 2002, p 2; emphasis added)

The language of social mix is used by CRBA to justify the removal of community members who are not valued by white, middle-class gentrifiers. By cloaking exclusionary sentiments in progressive clothing, the concept of 'social mix' reveals itself to be malleable indeed. Nick Blomley (2004) recognised a similar use in Vancouver's Downtown Eastside, where property owners 'deployed a language of balance in the service of exclusion' (p 99). Another Toronto group, Action 4 Balanced Communities Downtown East (A4BCDE), exemplifies this contradiction. In 2004 A4BCDE joined with other residents' associations to protest the expansion of a Salvation Army shelter near Regent Park, an action that saw middle-class residents march in front of the shelter with placards. Prior to the protest, the president of the organisation was quoted as shouting "this is why we don't want you people here" to supporters of the shelter who came to an A4BCDE meeting (Smith, 2004).

The Garden District Residents' Association (GDRA) claims to represent the area northwest of Regent Park.[5] This group is motivated by a strong sense of entitlement to aggressively expand on the area's incipient gentrification. On their website, they explain how new lofts and investment have been moving in, and that 'encouraged by this new direction, local residents and businesses have joined forces to *reclaim* our parks and streets for all members of our community ... we must *heal* this neighbourhood' (GDRA, 2004; emphasis added). Regent Park residents are clearly not included in this vision of the 'healed' neighbourhood. Indeed, people without money are blamed squarely for the problems in the area: 'high concentrations of *residents without disposable income* are behind the flight of the retail sector, professional and financial services, and educational institutions' (GDRA, 2004; emphasis added). Public housing falls under the category of 'problematic' for the GDRA, and public housing locations in the neighbourhood are mapped on the organisation's website, along with the shelters, social agencies, rooming houses and drug use facilities that the association would like to see removed.

Following the announcement that Regent Park would be redeveloped, many residents' associations expressed disappointment that the public housing would be rebuilt, rather than simply demolished or at least significantly reduced. According to the RPNI director, an association from the area west of Regent Park demanded that the proportion of subsidised units be lowered to 15% in the redeveloped community. In Don Mount Court, the local Riverside Area Residents' Association (RARA) took TCHC to court to stop redevelopment.[6] Their key demand was that the public units be rebuilt *elsewhere*. RARA testified that 'the old Don Mount Court was a haven for drug dealers and other undesirables who preyed on its residents and neighbours' (Ontario Municipal Board, 2005, p 4). Not all residents' associations are opposed to redevelopment. The RPNI director explained that residents north of Regent Park "saw the advantage, that redevelopment would be positive for them". Indeed, the promise of poverty dilution in east downtown Toronto is raising property values and attracting real estate investment. The developer of two condos in the nearby area explained that, 'what was attractive to us coming in here was that the Regent Park revitalization program was under way' (quoted in van de Ven, 2008).

Community organisers in Regent Park are worried about the dynamic that will develop between new condo dwellers in Regent Park and returning residents. Elizabeth Schaeffer of SCAARP (the School Community Action Alliance – Regent Park) worries that "social cohesion and mixing is going to be where there's going to be the most problems.... When we see people coming in, middle-class people in condos, I think it is going to cause a real power imbalance. You can see it happening already" (personal communication, 30 January 2009). Schaeffer described how representatives from local residents' associations dominate the proceedings at police–community liaison meetings with complaints about Regent Park: "every single problem that emerges, [they say] 'it's Regent Park'". Despite hopes for social inclusivity, Schaeffer worries this polarised dynamic will be 'reproduced' and intensified post-redevelopment. These fears are shared by Elsa Pratt, who copes with NIMBY (not in my backyard) attitudes from residents in recently developed condos near her agency. Promises of social mix aside, she explains that the incoming condo residents "do not want to see diversity and difference in the city". John Clarke's predictions for the area are similar and based on what he has watched unfold as gentrification expands across the east downtown:

> "I can tell you what's going to happen in Regent Park. Condo owners in the newly-built condos will form residents' associations. These will be dominated by residents from the condos and may have a few, token, conservative people from RGI housing. The Association will develop a rapport with the [police], and then … a war will be unleashed on RGI people…. In a market-driven economy, homeowners are not going to want to live in an area near social housing. [Social mix] is not a recipe for amicable diversity, it's a recipe for class war."

A post-redevelopment picture of tenant politics

Given the character of middle-class residents organising in the area, there is little reason to suspect vocal newcomers to Regent Park will use their political muscle to help out public housing tenants. In fact, local residents worry their political voice will be effectively muted by newcomers. According to the TCHC's Social Development Plan (SDP):

> Consultations with tenants in Regent Park throughout the redevelopment period show their deep concern about their representation in decision making in the future community. Tenants have consistently spoken of fears of being marginalized and sidelined by their more affluent neighbours. (2007c, p 18)

The TCHC's plans for post-redevelopment tenant representation are not likely to allay these fears. The SDP promotes socially mixed local governance structures in the revitalised community, ideally with equal representation from subsidised tenants and newcomers. Given the existing community dynamics, Elizabeth Schaeffer is sceptical about the plan: "the reality is that no matter how hard they try they're going to end up with a completely imbalanced situation where the new people have more power". TCHC's plan is to create a community-wide residents' association called the 'Neighbourhood Forum' in which tenants, condo dwellers, homeowners and business owners would come together and discuss neighbourhood issues. The Forum would include tenant representatives from RGI-buildings and non-tenant representatives from condo and homeowner associations. The SDP states that 'Regent Park already has structures in place that support the expression of tenant priorities in their community' and these structures will form the basis of tenant representation in the new community (TCHC, 2007c, p 17). The structures that the plan refers to are the RPNI and the tenant participation system, discussed above, which, we noted, are presently not capable of meaningful tenant representation on many matters related to the redevelopment.

Even before redevelopment is complete, the SDP privileges the voice of the middle-class newcomers, by placing 'tenant voice' in the hands of the RPNI and tenant council and providing 'equal' representation to players with unequal power. In addition, TCHC has prioritised the demands of future condo residents, arguing that tenants should not be able to influence decision making if it affects homeowner interests,

> Homeowners in East Downtown expressed a *willingness* to be involved in associations with tenants to jointly guide the future of the community. They hesitated, however, to give tenants enough voice to make decisions that might affect the way their homes are run and that might affect their property values. (TCHC, 2007c, p 18; emphasis added)

Martin Blake, vice president of the Daniels Corporation, the main developer building market housing in Regent Park, was upfront about the need to control the political representation of tenants in the community. In response to a question about the lack of social mix in the condo buildings which have already been sold, he explained that it would be difficult to sell any units if potential buyers thought that TCHC tenants were "in control" (comment at the Regent Park 'Roundtable on Affordable Housing', Reunion Panel Discussion, 14 October 2010). Quite unfortunately for tenants, residents' associations in east downtown perceive the presence of social housing as detrimental to their property values, and tenant power is perceived as a threat to the marketability of the new private housing in the redeveloped community.

Conclusion

By reducing low-income tenants to a minority of the population, socially mixed public housing redevelopment in Toronto will have a significant impact on the social landscape and political dynamics of the affected communities. Justified on the grounds that it will eliminate concentrated poverty and its associated ills, redevelopment will also eliminate important *benefits* that have been struggled for and nurtured, partly as a response to concentrated poverty. In Regent Park, such benefits include a strong sense of community, a history of political activism in the face of unsupportive housing management, a significant degree of political influence in local decision making, and in turn, a dense network of tenant-led and tenant-serving organisations. It is difficult to imagine that tenants will be able to maintain their sense of community and shared political voice, when clear attempts are being made to eliminate these as part of the revitalisation process. The marginalisation of tenant voices is not an accidental side-effect of redevelopment, but is built into both the structures of the official tenant organisations meant to serve the new community. An organised and politically active tenant presence in public housing is potentially dangerous to new property owners, threatening both the public image of the TCHC and the rising property values that the private sector developers, incoming homebuyers and the TCHC are depending on.

The undoing of the tenant political gains and sidelining of tenant voices is the result of a strategy to impose social mix on the Regent Park community. While planners and policy makers may not have seen inherent value in this community, it is not surprising that some tenants have been resistant, sceptical and suspicious of the justification for the demolition of their homes. One tenant from Don Mount Court used a rare public forum to express her dismay at the 'renewal' of her community during the 2007 RPFF 'Panel on Revitalisation':

> "Most of the things I saw happening in those films happened in Don Mount ... I lived in Don Mount Court for 22 years and no one could show me a community where people were more caring for each other. As a true community should be, it was there.... [Now] They even changed the name! They changed the name to 'Rivertowne'. It's like Africville."

This tenant's reference to the destructive urban renewal programme and the racially motivated demolition of Africville[7] belies a very different perspective than the one promoted by urban policy makers – presenting the redevelopment process as a process of racially motivated community erasure from which new white homeowners would benefit. Such is the legacy of social mix in Toronto. Even more unsettling, perhaps, is that it was the day after these statements were made that the TCHC evicted the community group that had provided this rare space for political engagement.

Toronto's early experiences with socially mixed urban renewal raise serious questions about the impacts of public housing redevelopment on the political voice of low-income tenants. Despite its celebrated process of tenant engagement, TCHC's consultations have provided very little space for meaningful tenant input, and debate on the 'big' questions surrounding redevelopment remains off limits. Beyond official consultation, tenants in Regent Park have no legitimate channels for expressing criticism of or opposition to revitalisation. The two self-described 'tenant organisations' are not independent of the TCHC and do not have the trust of tenants. This is not an accident. In order for redevelopment to be financially successful it must attract the middle classes and to do this middle-class interests must be prioritised. As redevelopment continues in Toronto, higher-income residents and homeowners' associations will move into the territory of public housing tenants, and in turn will dominate local political debates and decisions. If the existing attitudes of residents' associations nearby Regent Park offer any hint at what is to come, tenants can expect an increasing assault on their political voice and their community supports as redevelopment unfolds. Based on this evidence, the politics of social mix point to social polarisation, political marginalisation and exclusion rather than social harmony and inclusion.

Notes

[1] In Montreal, Rose (2004) argues that recent social mix policies are not associated with a neoliberal agenda and that the Québec welfare state has been less affected by neoliberal influences than elsewhere in Canada. Thibert (2007) notes that post-1993 the Québec government continued to fund social housing, focusing on acquiring and renovating existing buildings (p 24). In 2001, new commitments to social housing were made in Montreal. While Toronto was coping with the Social Housing Reform Act, Montreal signed a housing agreement with the provincial and federal governments to build social and affordable housing on infill sites, with social mix articulated as a key component of the policy (Rose, 2004, pp 288-9).

[2] The Don Mount Court redevelopment actually preceded Regent Park by about six months, making it the first socially mixed public housing redevelopment project in Canada.

[3] The early engagement process included workshops to identify 'strengths, weaknesses, opportunities and threats' and to develop planning principles 'to guide the remainder of the process'. Less than one month later, four 'alternatives' were presented to the community. The only differences between them were the location and sizes of parks, and some minor design differences. Tenants had no opportunity to choose how socially mixed redevelopment would work, how many market buildings would be built or whether or not social mix was desirable at all (see Regent Park Collaborative Team, 2002, pp 12, 22).

[4] Their boundaries run from the Don River to Berkeley Street, and from Shuter Street to Lakeshore Street.

[5] GDRA was created in 2001 out of the existing TEDRA (Toronto East Downtown Residents' Association) and TEDNA (Toronto East Downtown Neighbourhood Association) groups. Its area is bounded by Carlton, Sherbourne, Yonge and Queen Street East.

[6] This case was taken before the Ontario Municipal Board, a quasi-judicial body that settles planning appeals. In the case of Don Mount Court, RARA appealed the Official Plan Amendment and Zoning By-Law amendment that were sought by TCHC in order to pursue redevelopment.

[7] Africville is the name of an African-Canadian community near the edges of the Halifax metropolitan area. The community's land was expropriated, and the community was evicted, demolished and re-located to the Uniacke Square social housing project in inner Halifax in the late 1960s under the urban renewal programme (Clairmont and Magill, 1974).

EIGHTEEN

Mixture without mating: partial gentrification in the case of Rotterdam, the Netherlands

Talja Blokland and Gwen van Eijk

Introduction

Since Ley (1986) showed convincingly that gentrification is not simply a matter of the market, especially not in developed welfare states, showcases of state-led neighbourhood improvement have been found in many European states (Cameron, 2003; see also Hackworth and Smith, 2001). In the Netherlands, the specific history of the housing policy, based on a principle of accessible rental for everyone in an inclusive scheme, has long defined housing as part of general social policy (cf van Kempen and Priemus, 2002). It therefore comes as little surprise that there has been a strong tradition in the Netherlands of state intervention in neighbourhood improvement (see Horak and Blokland, 2011: forthcoming). On the waves of neoliberalism and a retreating welfare state since the 1990s, strategies for neighbourhood improvement have moved away from simply trying to improve the quality of life for current residents (cf Uitermark et al, 2007). Stirred by fears about ghetto formation and poverty concentration, and concerns that immigrant enclaves could hamper integration, areas classified as disadvantaged are now to be 'improved' through altering their demographic make-up. As a result, state-led gentrification has become a common strategy in the Netherlands for 'improving' deprived neighbourhoods, surrounded by a public aura of positive meanings unknown in other European countries (see, for example, Häussermann and Siebel, 1987; Slater, 2006; Holm, 2010). The positive expectations are held not only by policy makers, but are more generally shared by political actors across the right–left spectrum.

The Dutch context is particularly interesting because it stalls gentrification in various ways. First, the strong presence of state-controlled housing associations caps rent increases of the overall housing stock in most urban areas while ensuring that a certain degree of mixture will continue to exist at the neighbourhood level. Moreover, the historically broad provision of good quality social housing and high private rent levels have produced so-called *scheefhuurders*: residents who have grown more affluent but who still live in very cheap housing of adequate quality. They do not want to leave because, if they did, they would have to leave the area, move into a commercial, much more expensive rental, or buy – if there was anything around to buy. Hence such state-led gentrification, where blocks of apartments are being demolished to make way for houses, where parts of the housing stock are being upgraded and then sold, or where people get an opportunity to buy their current apartment, produces mixed neighbourhoods but does *not necessarily* create displacement.[1] One may argue that the process may not stop here and state-led gentrification will lead to full-blown gentrification and eventually the homogeneity of middle and upper class neighbourhoods. There is, however, as yet, no evidence that supports this claim. And for our purposes here, if there was, it does not matter. We look at the case of the Netherlands in this chapter because it serves as a laboratory to assess the value of residential mixture through partial gentrification.

More precisely we look at the expectations that politicians across the political spectrum have embraced over the last few decades. These are, first, the idea that residential mixture produces social mixing, and second, that it encourages ties between residents who differ in socioeconomic status and/or ethnic background. Such ties are intended to provide the means to access resources (following the idea of ties as 'social capital') that would otherwise have remained closed to them. For such effects to occur, residents of a mixed neighbourhood who have easy access to resources should have more ties across socioeconomic and ethnic or racial boundaries than their counterparts living in a homogeneous affluent neighbourhood. We investigate this using original data on the personal networks of nearly 200 middle-class residents living in two differently composed urban neighbourhoods: Cool and Blijdorp (both in Rotterdam, the second largest city of the Netherlands). The inner-city neighbourhood of Cool is mixed in class, 'race' and ethnicity, while the urban neighbourhood Blijdorp is fairly homogeneously composed of mainly middle-class, native Dutch residents (we introduce the areas in more detail below).

While Cool changed quickly in the 1990s, for the past decade the demographic make-up remained more or less the same, making Cool a good site to study state-led gentrification where it produced a stable mix of residents of various categories. Yet, as we will show, the statistical and spatial mixture in demographic data does not produce a social mixture. This chapter aims to explore explanations for the lack of social mix which go beyond simply saying that similarity is what people like.

Our argument

There are various arguments in the literature suggesting why this might be. The simplest argument, or even a simplistic one, is that people *like* to interact with people who are like them, or, in its more structural formulation, it is their 'habitus'.[2] This argument has often been used to explain segregation and absence of inter-racial or inter-ethnic ties. It assumes that likeness is defined beforehand through categorical ascription, not through encounters in which one learns the (un)likeness of the other. Put sharply, we expect people to ascribe stereotypical categorical distinctions to others, then pick those who are like oneself, and then start building ties. Experiments may produce such outcomes. But urban life is not an experiment: we do not scan other urbanites systematically, then rank them according to some scale of 'same as me' or 'not the same as me', and then walk up to the ones we have classified as 'same' and start to interact.

What needs to be explained, in our view, is the limited number of local ties in mixed Cool *compared to* homogeneous Blijdorp, and, second, the limited social mix in such networks when compared to the statistical probability of meeting others unlike ourselves. Even if birds flock according to their feathers by simple categorisations and personal preferences for sameness, our case of Cool remains a fascinating one because a good share of the middle-class residents consciously moved in there seeking diversity and expressed a preference for difference, not sameness, among their neighbours.

We think it is useful to take homophily – the tendency for ties to form between similar people, rather than between different people (Lazarsfeld and Merton, 1954; McPherson et al, 2001) – as a phenomenon that needs an explanation as opposed to simply being used as a descriptive device. The tendency points to an empirical pattern, not to individual tendencies to behave in a certain way. Moving beyond this tendency to accept individualistic preferences as given, we explore the alternatives that the literature provides, discuss their limitations and then use our empirical data in order to try to develop two other arguments, focusing on, first, the institutional development of neighbourhoods, and second, the organisational structure of social inequalities.

First, we argue that the historically changing role of neighbourhood and local institutions has affected their capacity as spatial sites to bring different segments of the population together (see Blokland and Rae, 2008). People from different backgrounds may share a place of residence, but other perhaps than on the streets and in local shops, they do not meet. The 'rubbing shoulders' through superficial encounters may bring about more tolerance towards difference (Sennett, 1970), but just as much may contribute to a *blasé* attitude of distancing (Simmel, 2006 [1908]): rubbing shoulders in the urban spaces of mixed city neighbourhoods does not necessarily, and surely not automatically, translate into boundary-crossing personal ties – or even ties at all. Second, and strongly associated with the first argument, class, ethnic and racial relations are so strongly interwoven with existing organisational structures (Tilly, 1998) that spatial integration cannot *in itself* initiate changing relations. Similar to Tilly's notion of 'durable inequalities' (1998), segregations are durable – choosing to live in a diverse neighbourhood will do little to change social boundaries of class, ethnicity and 'race', as such boundaries are created through processes far beyond neighbourhood life. Acting out boundaries may happen there in all sorts of tiny experiences on streets and squares. On occasions, such boundaries may be challenged or even overcome, but some *other* event or occasion is needed for this to happen. Spatial proximity may at best increase the chances that such an event or occasion occurs, but does not bring it about.

Research sites and data

Cool, a centrally located 19th-century neighbourhood with both original redeveloped housing as well as newer structures, close to the main museums and downtown centre, was chosen as a neighbourhood for the survey in the initial phase in 2002 for its gentrification. That is, Cool was a relatively disadvantaged area but its demographics altered due to an influx of more people with a higher socioeconomic status. This was connected to a modest increase in rent and property prices and degree of homeowning occupants, as well as some commercial gentrification of its main shopping street (Meulenbelt, 1994). Blijdorp, by contrast, is a leafy neighbourhood with brick buildings from the 1920s and 1930s with generally spacious apartments, inhabited by residents with a more traditional professional background (school teachers, office clerks and the like) and for most of its parts has been and still is a stable middle-class area. Table 18.1 shows some key statistics on the composition of the two neighbourhoods, compared with Rotterdam.

Table 18.1: Composition of the two research neighbourhoods, compared with Rotterdam

	Cool	Blijdorp	Rotterdam
Socioeconomic composition			
Average annual income (€)	18,900	22,600	18,800
% below poverty line	19	7	17
% high income	17	28	15
% out of work	58	75	58
% receiving unemployment benefits	19	5	17
Ethnic composition			
% of native Dutch origin	45	78	54
% of Western, non-Dutch	18	12	9
% of non-Western origin	37	10	38

Notes: 'Poverty line' refers to a standardised income level used by Dutch authorities; 'high income' refers to the income level of the top 20% of the total Dutch population; 'native Dutch origin' refers to people who are born in the Netherlands and whose both parents are born in the Netherlands; 'Western, non-Dutch' refers to (parents) born in Europe (except Turkey), North America, Oceania, Japan and Indonesia; 'non-Western origin' refers to (parents) born in all other countries.

We draw on data here from a survey conducted first by Blokland and a team of field researchers in 2002 in Cool and then by van Eijk and her team in 2007 in Blijdorp (see van Eijk, 2010a, for details on research methods and sampling). We interviewed with a structured questionnaire, using a sample stratified by streets, as different streets had different types of tenure and were thus likely to reflect the diversity of the residents. After an introductory letter, we sampled through 'cold calling' every third residence in Cool and every sixth residence in Blijdorp, simply ringing door bells, returning twice or if possible making contact by telephone when we got no answer. When we could not contact any inhabitant, we moved next door. In total, we interviewed 210 residents in Cool and 100 residents in Blijdorp. In this chapter we examine only those respondents we have classified, based on their (former) occupation, as 'middle class'; this includes in total 194 respondents (106 in Cool, 88 in Blijdorp).[3]

The interviews gathered data on people's everyday lives and social and political participation within and outside the neighbourhood and generated network data. For the social networks we followed the 'exchange method' (Völker, 1999, p 135; see also McCallister and Fischer, 1978; Völker, 1995) of collecting names through asking interviewees about certain types of support. Our primary goal was not to map entire ego-centred networks, but to gain information about relationships that may provide social capital. We used 15 'name generators' in Cool and 18 in Blijdorp. We asked, for instance, whether someone helped the interviewee to get a job, or house or supported with small tasks in or around the house. We asked whether interviewees had anybody specific to talk to and to confide in. As the overall project focused on social and political participation, we also asked with whom people participated in the social and political activities that they had mentioned. For each network tie, we collected data on age, gender, ethnicity, place of residence, level of education, relationship type, duration of relationship and contact frequency.

A taste for different feathers: existing explanations

As elsewhere, up to the late 1980s many affluent Dutch people settled in the suburbs. While suburban lifestyle ideals were widely shared, certain segments of the middle classes did (re)settle in the city. At the end of the 1980s the first efforts were made to change the housing variety and tenure structure in cities (van der Wouden et al, 2006). City life left its predominantly negative image behind (Machielse, 1989), as manifested in a growing demand for urban dwellings (see also Ebels and Ostendorf, 1991). People did not necessarily move back into cities, but university graduates stayed (Karsten, 2003; cf Smith, 1979; Butler with Robson, 2003), a process possibly also related to the rising number of female college graduates, female labour market participation in a more service-oriented economy, dropping birth rates and increased traffic congestion around cities. As pointed out by Bondi (1991), there is a gender dimension to gentrification. Next to changes in economic and housing structures, gentrification is hence also an expression of changing lifestyles,[4] or the 'ultimate expression of consumption' (Butler with Robson, 2003, pp 76-7; cf Ley, 1986, 1994; Bridge, 2006b). This consumption distinguishes gentrifiers from the affluent who buy ready-made dwellings in homogeneous, mono-functional suburbs. They differ also in their choice for 'diversity' rather than for suburban sameness.

Elsewhere (Blokland and van Eijk, 2010), we compared the personal networks of these 'diversity seekers' – those residents for whom neighbourhood diversity was an important reason to move into Cool – and other residents living in Cool. As residents who would adhere less to the rule of homophily – that is, preferring difference rather than sameness – diversity seekers should have social ties across boundaries of 'race', ethnicity and class more often than residents who did not value diversity. But they did not.

Our study is not alone in pointing to the lack of mixed ties in demographically mixed neighbourhoods. Various studies have been very critical about the extent to which people who *like* diversity also *practice* diversity (Ley, 1986; Zukin, 1987; May, 1996; Butler with Robson, 2003, pp 110-13; Reijndorp, 2004; Rose, 2004; Karsten et al, 2006). Others have argued that the better off even employ 'strategies of disaffiliation' (Atkinson, 2006) by avoiding public transport and contact with 'others'. Furthermore, by displacing the original residents (Smith, 1996; Slater, 2006; Lees, 2008), gentrifiers turn what could be mixed neighbourhoods into homogeneous privileged areas. While they choose to live in the city, it is argued, they struggle with insecurity and disorder, and express a wish to 'purify' public places or withdraw from public places altogether. Through state-led gentrification, policy makers would aim not to mix but to 'cleanse' the streets from everything disorderly and marginal, an argument captured by the idea of urban revanchism (Smith, 1996; Wacquant, 2008; cf Uitermark et al, 2007).

Yet, here Cool becomes an interesting case: if revanchism would be the lens through which to understand the absence of mixed networks, as, ultimately, all the middle classes would want is to cleanse the city, then it would be difficult to explain that gentrification did not continue. The state should have supported private investors to completely turn over the area, which they have not done. Maybe they had other, politically not necessarily neoliberal, aims such as social integration (see van Eijk, 2010b). Revanchism presumes motivations by policy makers that are hard to disprove.

Equally, we need to consider the option that those people seeking diversity but failing to practice it do so *not* because they are not revealing their real motives, or are even unaware of their real motives, but because their motives are genuinely progressive (just like those of the social scientists writing critically). If we assume that these diversity seekers *are* the exceptions to the homophily rule, then we have to look somewhere else to explain the gap between what they think and what they do. We should then look at the extent to which urbanites in mixed neighbourhoods form mixed social networks, and how mixed their networks are, *compared to* urbanites and their networks in homogeneous areas.

Another frame of explanation is offered by the thesis of 'elective belonging' (Savage et al, 2005). Practices, Savage et al (2005, p 10) argue, which rely on 'spatial fixity', are automatically more exclusive than practices that are accessible to anyone. So places are 'as significant as ever in generating cultural distinction' and perhaps even gain significance in a world where everything is mobile (Savage et al, 2005, pp 11-13).

Thus, *where* and *among whom* one lives have increasingly become markers of distinction (see also Butler and Watt, 2007).

Savage and colleagues (2005b) further argue that the depiction of members of the new middle class as 'cosmopolitans' who are detached from their neighbourhood needs modification. Cosmopolitans may move around more than the locality-bound; this does not mean that they never feel they 'belong' to their residential area once they moved there. Savage and colleagues hence speak of 'elective belonging'. Yet, the experience of belonging is not necessarily the same as that of people who live in a certain area because they have no choice or who express belonging through 'nostalgia' for (a fictitious) cohesive and unified community – which may actually never have existed (Blokland, 2001, 2003; Savage et al, 2005b). Elective belonging emphasises instead a choice for individuality's sake: 'their choice ... confirms their identities, their sense of themselves' (Savage et al, 2005b, p 152). Choosing a neighbourhood as part of identity construction may imply another relation to fellow residents. While nostalgia and a sense of community indicate an experience of neighbourhood through (past) social identification and personal relationships with others, elective belonging rather suggests an experience of neighbourhood through distinction – which in turn implies distance rather than engagement. This may explain that they may like diversity as a stage for their individuality, while not aiming to develop a diverse network. There, it becomes interesting to compare Cool and Blijdorp: if elective belonging is a general urban middle-class phenomenon, then the localness of networks in both areas should not differ and nor should the mixture of their networks.

The notions of urban revanchism and elective belonging are both important caveats against the idea that because new urban middle classes *choose* diversity, they will therefore also *socialise* with a variety of people. But while most research has focused on establishing a lack of mixture and then trying to explain it, we still need to ask whether these *residents of mixed areas actually do differ in these respects from people who live in homogeneous urban neighbourhoods.*

Measuring mating

Diversity in personal networks

Let us therefore look at our data. For the degree of homogeneity of the networks, we include educational level and ethnic category. We asked respondents about their highest educational achievement. For all network members of respondents we asked whether they had any education after secondary school. We could thus estimate what proportion of the networks was made up of 'like' people and of people who were 'different' – independent of whether respondents and their network members themselves would feel this way. Following Bourdieu (1984), we assume that levels of cultural and economic capital are associated with lifestyles and that educational difference can serve as a proxy for difference here. We assume that someone, say, with a university degree, is likely to experience a tie with someone who left school at 8th grade as a tie of difference.

We did the same for ethnic and racial background. We here followed the categories 'autochthonous' and 'allochthonous' that are common in the Netherlands, more or less comparable with, respectively, 'native Dutch' and '(non-Western) ethnic minority'. We estimated whether respondents had only 'alike' network members or also members who were 'different'. Table 18.2 shows the average network heterogeneity of respondents' networks in our samples.

Table 18.2: Network heterogeneity

	All	Cool	Blijdorp	Significance
Educational level				
Proportion with 'different' ties	0.25	0.29	0.20	$t=2.232$*
% of respondents with at least one 'different' tie	65	70	58	ns
Ethnic category				
Proportion with 'different' ties	0.13	0.16	0.09	$t=2.328$*
% of respondents with at least one 'different' tie	39	47	30	Cramer's $V=0.166$*
n	186	103	83	

Note: *$p<0.05$.

As the average level of network heterogeneity is low, this means that most networks are composed mostly of 'like' people. Many of the networks are 100% homogeneous, meaning that people did not report any member of different educational level or ethnic category. Because the network data are highly skewed towards full homogeneity, they are unsuitable for linear regression analyses. Therefore, we measure the likelihood that respondents have *at least one network member* who is different from them in terms of educational level or ethnic background. This variable shows the most variation and can be used in a logistic regression analysis. Many respondents mentioned at least one network tie with a different educational level, while not even half of the respondents mentioned a tie that crosses ethnic category (Table 18.2).

As noted above, many studies have concluded that gentrifiers in mixed neighbourhoods 'rub shoulders' with different people without socialising with them, but do not examine the *relative* homogeneity of their networks – that is, compared with networks of people who live in a homogeneous neighbourhood. They may indeed hardly form such relationships but refrain from these *regardless* of whether they live in a homogeneous or mixed neighbourhood. On the other hand, it is possible that those who live in a mixed neighbourhood have few of such relationships but still *more* than those who live in a homogeneous neighbourhood (Blokland, 2004).

Table 18.2 shows that, on first sight, Cool residents indeed seem to have more mixed networks than Blijdorpers. For educational level, the difference is nearly 10% of the network; for ethnic category the difference is 7%. Although small, these differences are statistically significant. The two residential categories also differ in whether they reported at least one 'different' network member: on both measures, Cool residents are more likely to report such a tie (only statistically significant for ethnically different tie).

Can we then immediately argue that the social mixture in Cool does produce mixed networks more than a non-mixed area like Blijdorp may do? However attractive that might be for policy makers trying to achieve change through spatial mix, this would be to rush towards a conclusion too quickly. While we do find a difference between the neighbourhoods at first, this is not necessarily produced *by* the neighbourhood. Let us therefore, first, have a closer look at the middle-class residents of both areas. While they may be similar in educational background and all be members of an urban middle class in that they live in the city and have incomes and jobs that make them middle class, they could well be very different in lifestyle.

Differentiating the metropolitan habitus

At times, the literature seems to ascribe a rather stable, undifferentiated habitus to 'the urban middle class' or 'the gentrifiers', and here it may be necessary to differentiate the 'metropolitan habitus' (Butler with Robson, 2003, p 9; also Butler and Watt, 2007, pp 90–1): a disposition that prefers living in the 'metropolis' above life in the suburbs, deploying combinations of (sometimes less) economic capital and (more) cultural capital in shaping a 'distinctive' lifestyle (see Bridge, 2001; Butler, 2002).

Such differentiation would do justice to the broadly shared view, that current cultural and economic developments have made classes so segmented (Savage, 1995; Crompton, 1998). While classes may still broadly be differentiated, boundary work within social classes, especially of a symbolic kind (Lamont and Molnar, 2002), is common practice. Is there, then, any indication that living in either Cool or Blijdorp is part of a *different articulation* of the metropolitan habitus? Differences in personal networks may then reflect or follow from this difference.

Table 18.3 shows the socioeconomic and sociodemographic characteristics of the middle-class Cool and Blijdorp residents. Cool residents fit the description of the 'new urban middle class' better than Blijdorpers: they are significantly more often single, without children and younger. They are also more likely to be of non-Western origin. The two groups are similar in employment status, but not in job sector. Cool residents work more in professional services (that is, financial, legal, insurance and real estate sector, including high-skill IT and technical work) and slightly less in public sector jobs (that is, civil servants, welfare, health care, and social workers, teachers and lecturers). Cool residents are *not* more likely to work in the cultural industry (jobs in, for example, arts, media, design), which suggests that Cool does not attract more members of the 'creative class' (Florida, 2002) than Blijdorp. Some sociodemographic characteristics show two different middle-class categories.

Mixed networks as a neighbourhood effect?

As we now know that Cool residents differ from Blijdorpers on several accounts, we need to include sociodemographic and socioeconomic variables simultaneously in our analyses if we are to find out whether living in a mixed neighbourhood goes together with a greater likelihood to have cross-category ties in one's network. The results are shown in Tables 18.4 and 18.5.

We now see that where one lives or in which sector one works is not significantly associated with greater network heterogeneity. Cool residents are as likely as Blijdorp residents to report a tie that is different from them. What matters, however, are respondents' ethnic backgrounds and educational levels. Dutch residents, in both neighbourhoods, are *less* likely to have a lower-educated network member, while people of a minority ethnic background are more likely.

The second model adds two variables that may indicate whether the neighbourhood context matters at all for the formation (or maintenance) of interclass ties: network localness (the proportion of local ties, including neighbours, friends, colleagues and so on) and neighbourhood use.[5] The analysis shows that both network localness and neighbourhood use are *not* significantly associated with network heterogeneity, indicating that even those who have a relatively high number of local ties are forming ties with 'alike' fellow residents. The neighbourhood is, in other words, not the first place where ties are formed, and even when the neighbourhood is, it is not a place where interclass relationships develop. Considering the Nagelkerke R^2, much of the variation between residents remains unexplained.

Table 18.3: Socioeconomic and sociodemographic characteristics of Cool and Blijdorp respondents

	Cool	**Blijdorp**	**Significance**
Paid job	89	82	
Native Dutch	81	96	Cramer's V=0.218**
Age			
20-34	45	25	Cramer's V=0.231*
35-49	34	51	
50-64	16	15	
65+	5	9	
Household			
Single	53	36	Cramer's V=0.165*
Children under age 13	13	31	Cramer's V=0.223**
Educational degree			ns
University	34	43	
Higher vocational	32	38	
Medium vocational	18	9	
Lower	17	10	
Job sector			ns
Professional services	47	37	
Cultural industry	17	15	
Public sector	37	48	
Social/political participation			
Membership organisation	80	92	Cramer's V=0.166*
Active membership	50	48	
n	106	88	194

Notes: *$p<0.05$, **$p<0.01$.

Table 18.4: Results of logistic regression analysis on network heterogeneity for educational level

	Model 1		Model 2	
	Wald	**Exp(B)**	**Wald**	**Exp(B)**
Job sector				
Professional services	0.278		0.463	
Cultural industry	0.186	1.241	0.085	1.162
Public sector	0.016	0.955	0.215	0.841
Native Dutch/Western	4.315	*0.198	5.350	*0.141
Has a paid job	0.564	0.681	2.045	0.447
Has education after secondary school	4.815	*0.099	4.980	*0.092
Lives in Cool	0.786	1.345	0.092	0.877
Network localness			3.536	0.179
Neighbourhood use			1.629	1.347
Constant	10.737	79.056	12.728	200.401
−2 LL	210.543		202.940	
Nagelkerke R^2	0.154		0.182	
n	177		174	

Notes: *p<0.05, **p<0.01.

Table 18.5: Results of logistic regression analysis on network heterogeneity for ethnic category

	Model 1		Model 2	
	Wald	**Exp(B)**	**Wald**	**Exp(B)**
Job sector				
Professional services	0.219		0.976	
Cultural industry	0.212	0.799	0.748	0.644
Public sector	0.058	0.917	0.576	0.754
Native Dutch/Western	6.305	*0.257	9.706	**0.132
Years in neighbourhood	2.257	0.832	2.186	0.824
Age	0.445	0.989	0.036	0.997
Has education after secondary school	0.642	1.614	0.684	1.728
Lives in Cool	1.693	1.553	0.123	0.862
Network localness			4.327	*0.109
Neighbourhood use			2.810	1.469
Constant	2.189	4.231	3.277	7.054
−2 LL	216.937		205.764	
Nagelkerke R^2	0.143		0.200	
n	176		173	

Notes: *p<0.05, **p<0.01.

Table 18.5 shows the results of the analysis of network heterogeneity in terms of ethnic category. Again, Dutch residents are less likely to form an inter-ethnic tie. Interestingly, when we add network localness and neighbourhood use to the equation (Model 2), we find that *higher* the proportion of local ties, the *less* likely one is to report an inter-ethnic tie. Ties formed and/or maintained in the setting of the neighbourhood are therefore more likely with 'alike' people than with people of a different ethnic category. Further analysis shows that those respondents who have relatively more local ties, more often moved into the neighbourhood to be close to family members or friends – these ties are apparently less likely to bridge ethnic difference.

To summarise the results, there is no difference in network heterogeneity between the two residential categories. Differences that appear at face value are associated with educational level and ethnic background. This means that middle-class residents living in mixed Cool and their counterparts living in Blijdorp are equally likely to have at least one network member who is 'different' from them. Furthermore, higher network localness is negatively associated with having an inter-ethnic tie, which suggests that inter-ethnic relationships do not develop in neighbourhood settings but *elsewhere*. These findings support earlier studies that found that the urban middle class in mixed neighbourhoods are not likely to express their liking for diversity in their personal network. Moreover, our study shows that the urban middle class in a mixed area as Cool are not more likely to do so than their counterparts in a homogeneous middle-class area such as as Blijdorp.

Towards an explanation: some suggestions

As argued above, a possible explanation of the finding that those who chose to live in a neighbourhood of diversity, as Cool, did not have more diverse networks than those for whom this was not a consideration may be that the middle-class residents seeking an urban way of life in Cool understand that urban life differently than the residents of an also urban, but not mixed area, like Blijdorp. While we have discussed various differences between the two groups already, the differences of public sector families in Blijdorp and private sector service professional singles and couples in Cool are also linked to what Hunter (1974) has called 'local status'. If belonging is elective, the two groups elect different ways.

Table 18.6 shows various indicators of local status. Several differences, again, appear between the two residential groups. First, Blijdorp residents are more likely to own their home and on average live longer in their neighbourhood than Cool residents. They have not lived in their current dwelling much longer, so when they move, they move locally. This may make it easier to maintain established relationships with fellow residents – who are likely to be similar in socioeconomic status and ethnic background. Blijdorpers are slightly more likely to be a member of an organisation, but when it comes to active membership (attending meetings, volunteering for activities), there is no difference between the two groups (more Blijdorpers report 'cheque book membership' of charity organisations). Very few Blijdorpers and Cool residents are actively involved in local organisations such as neighbourhood groups or homeowners' associations (on average about 3% for both respondent categories). More Blijdorpers do attend activities of the residents' association, but for many respondents this involves seeing an annual parade and not much more. Cool residents go out more in the area, which is largely a consequence of its bars and restaurants with a citywide clientele, which are mostly lacking in Blijdorp.

Middle-class residents of Cool are more likely to work at home, in the neighbourhood or in Rotterdam, while Blijdorpers more often work outside Rotterdam. The first could therefore be more visible and accessible on streets and squares or even in the hallway of their building for fellow residents who could meet them there. At least, that is what a theory of mixing and then mating would hope for. However, the geographical dispersion of the personal networks (see Table 18.6) suggests that even though Cool residents may spend more hours of their day there and travel less far, this does not involve interaction with fellow residents. It may thus be that when Blijdorpers do local things, they do things that produce ties, while the things that Cool residents do in their neighbourhood (leisure, work) do not produce local ties.

Indeed, Blijdorpers have relatively *more* local ties in their personal networks, while their counterparts in Cool have more ties elsewhere in Rotterdam.[6] This is not due to a difference in neighbouring – the proportion of ties described as 'neighbours' is similar for both categories (5 and 6% for Cool residents and Blijdorpers respectively). Rather, there is a difference in other types of local ties: friends, people met through (local) associations, (former) colleagues and so on. This supports our suggestion that Blijdorpers' local activities go together with forming and/or maintaining ties with fellow residents. Cool residents, on the other hand, have relatively more ties with people living elsewhere in Rotterdam. That Cool residents work at home or in the neighbourhood thus seems associated with forming and maintaining ties in the city, not the neighbourhood.

Table 18.6: Local status of Cool and Blijdorp respondents

	Cool	Blijdorp	Significance
Owner-occupant	40	71	Cramer's V=0.304***
Years in neighbourhood			
0-2	35	32	Cramer's V=0.299*
3-5	25	10	
6-10	18	25	
11+	22	33	
Years in dwelling			
0-2	21	14	
3-5	31	32	
6-10	26	26	
11+	22	29	
Attend social act in neighbourhood	13	30	Cramer's V=0.201**
Neighbourhood meeting ever	12	9	
Go to park in neighbourhood	82	50	Cramer's V=0.341***
Go to bars and restaurants in neighbourhood	85	15	Cramer's V=0.698***
Index neighbourhood use (0-3)	1.8	1.0	T-test=7.255***
Work at home sometimes	50	28	Cramer's V=0.227**
Place of work			
At home/neighbourhood	30	15	Cramer's V=0.281**
Rotterdam	47	36	
Elsewhere	23	49	
Geographical dispersion network			
Proportion with ties in neighbourhood	0.13	0.23	t=3.130**
Proportion with ties in Rotterdam	0.37	0.28	t=2.162*

Notes: *p<0.05, **p<0.01, ***p<0.001.

This, then, suggests that only looking at people and their lifestyles and individual preferences is helpful in understanding quite a few things about people's liking of diversity and how they practice it, but it is not sufficient. Residents of Cool show a pattern of urban life in which consuming urban facilities plays an important role, but participating in the neighbourhood does not, not even as a neighbourhood of limited liability. This is *not* because they are only consumers not doing their civic duties: they are just as likely to participate in organisations, associations and the like and just as likely to be politically active as are residents in Blijdorp. They do the things by which one only rubs shoulders in their neighborhood (shopping, travelling and the like), and the things where one deliberates, builds ties, exchange telephone numbers and shares worries some place else. The only difference is that they do not do such things locally. If they did, *then*, may be, there would be some effect of the socioeconomic and ethnic mixture.

In short, the picture that emerges is one that shows that the differentiation of metropolitan habitus is needed, and that both areas attract different sections of what may appear to be the same group. Changing some features of Cool – more neighbourhood activities to give residents a chance to participate, or more home ownership – will not make a difference here, because the metropolitan habitus of the groups is a product of individual preferences, structural positions and the peculiarities of the locality. This, then, brings us to the point being made at the beginning of our chapter.

The relevance of neighbourhoods as sites of local institutions has changed; to give but one example of Cool, what once was a Catholic parish church in Cool is now a Hispanic Catholic church serving the Hispanic community in the broader metropolitan region. When urbanites become more mobile, lifestyles more differentiated and rules of conduct less strict (cf Blokland, 2003, pp 160ff), their options to affiliate with organisations and institutions far beyond the borders of their neighbourhood increase – in principle. While middle-class Cool residents use their home as the starting point for organising the rest of their metropolitan life, their neighbourhood as a social frame of reference hardly seems to exist; by contrast, for Blijdorpers it appears to be the place to where they return, where they make and maintain relationships – especially with 'people like us'.

The urban revanchism thesis brings us very little here: we should have found active involvement to 'cleanse' Cool rather than barely any local engagement. The theory of elective belonging does not bring us very far either, because both can be said to use their neighbourhood as a marker of distinction – it does help us understand that place of residence has not ceased to have relevance to the middle classes and that it helps them to form individuality, but *not* how this process is then linked to networks and why these local networks would, as a consequence, not differ *more* than they actually do. Identity is, after all, as Jenkins (1996) has argued, something we do through practices with others.

The homophily thesis understood as individual preference for sameness, then, cannot be of much help either. If this thesis was correct, people should always be looking for those similar to them – and we have found that they do not. The apparent difference between Cool and Blijdorp turned out not to be a neighbourhood effect, but an effect nevertheless: ethnic and racial minorities were more likely to build bridges across class and ethnic boundaries. As categorical inequalities persist, it may be much more likely that we need a theory of exclusion and how exclusion boils down to the level of personal networks rather than one of a general psychological law of preference that can be removed from the laboratory context and applied as explanation in real social life. In short, we build ties through what we do, not through what we think, and through whom we encounter while doing things – alongside or with one another. This necessitates the study of how social ties come about, and in what contexts they do so. Neighbourhood, then, may be the least important of all of these.

Conclusion

'Choosing diversity' may be a way for a segment of the urban middle class to distinguish themselves from suburbanites, but this habitus does not indicate a tendency to cross boundaries between themselves and their underprivileged urban fellows. If choosing diversity is indeed about identity formation and distinction, then this may rather indicate the formation of new 'within-class boundaries' and consolidating existing 'between-class boundaries'. In this way, the state-sponsored strategies of partial gentrification will not result in a more 'integrated' or equal society.

Where 'neighbourhood effect studies' on networks stress the effects of spatial constraints (that is, the constraints that spatial segregation poses on meeting opportunities), gentrification studies concerned with networks usually focus on different housing choices and lifestyles. There is thus more room for 'agency' in such an approach, whereas neighbourhood effect studies emphasise the (possible) effects of 'structures'. Starting from such a viewpoint, we may thus assume that changes are brought about by different predispositions ('habitus'). But while we then have some grip on structured agency, as the habitus is related to class-based tastes and hence not free to be chosen, we may get too far, and by saying 'it is the habitus' eventually have not achieved anything – either theoretically or empirically.

After all, we would have to ascribe an understanding to the people we interview that they themselves have not. Let us, as a final thought/

game, think of a progressive, middle-class activist woman committed to help the worse-off in her area change their lives, and let us assume we know her well enough to *know* that she is sincerely engaged. If she lived in Blijdorp, she would not be able to bring her political activism into practice in the neighbourhood, but if she lived in Cool, she would not either. She could pick a conversation in the store, or at the playground near the school, but she would need an incident or an event for such everyday superficial interactions to turn it into durable social ties. As Lofland (1998) and others have shown incontrovertibly, the characteristic of urban life, if there is such a thing, is that floating interactions *do not turn into network ties* (cf Soenen, 2006; Blokland, 2009).

Because things in 'people's heads', whether distinctions or ideals, cannot 'do' alone, we have to study how these differences – assuming that they exist – are embedded in different practices. What is it that people *do* that actually gets them involved in durable ties with people from different walks of life? The results of this study suggest that it has little to do with what people do *in their neighbourhood*. The search now is for settings that do matter, or for the value of brief interactions that *do not* turn into durable ties.

Notes

[1] Of course, displacement is not only a matter of affordability of housing but can also take place along cultural lines, where some will no longer feel welcomed in a world of café lattes and Bugaboos. Precisely because groups with limited resources living in rent-controlled apartments have also limited options of moving, symbolic exclusion alone is, in the Dutch housing market, unlikely to produce much moving out.

[2] As an analytical concept, Bourdieu may have introduced 'habitus' with other aims, but in empirical studies, it runs the risk of being nothing but another term for a set of preferences that are considered fixed.

[3] Respondents were classified as middle class based on their (former) occupation. We followed the Standard Occupation Classification 1992 (2001 edition) of Statistics Netherlands in classifying occupational levels (linked to education and skills needed for the job). Middle-class occupations include 'medium', 'higher' and 'academic' occupations that would typically require, respectively, at least medium vocational training, higher vocational training and academic education or comparative experience.

[4] Although this position has, of course, evoked a debate on how gentrification comes about, where authors like Smith (1979) and Marcuse (2010 [1986]) have argued for structural explanations, but we are not intending to explain gentrification: all we want to do here is show that the literature broadly suggests that cultural preferences and lifestyles of gentrifiers have specific characteristics that links them to urbanism 'as a way of life'.

[5] This is an index ranging from 0 to 3, counting whether respondents did any, none or all three of the following activities in their neighbourhood: visit the local park, visit local bars and restaurants and attend meetings of the neighbourhood association.

[6] We cannot tell from the survey data whether these are formed in the neighbourhood or rather formed elsewhere and now maintained (also) through local proximity. We can therefore not establish a causal relationship.

Afterword

Gary Bridge, Tim Butler and Loretta Lees

This book has explored social mix policies in a number of countries and in terms of policy expectations and outcomes. In spite of the differences in national policy contexts, housing systems, city and neighbourhood characteristics, the overwhelming conclusion of this review is that social mix policies are largely ineffective in enhancing the welfare of the poorest urban residents, and in some cases detrimental to the welfare of the urban poor. A senior policy figure on mixed communities in the US – Bruce Katz – voiced that he had no idea why they had gone for mixed communities policy in the US and that it should not have been applied in Europe![1] Why, then, have governments continued with this policy? There are three reasons: first, it coincided with a neoliberal climate; second, mixed communities is a faith-based policy (Cheshire, 2009) and has assumed the status of a mantra (Bolt and van Kempen, 2008); and third, once a policy or programme gains momentum, it is hard to step back from it, although maybe the current financial crisis will mark a turning point here.

So where do we go from here in policy[2] and theory terms? As van Criekingen argues at the end of his chapter (see Chapter Twelve), policy should concentrate on 'the upward social mobility of the incumbent population in working-class neighbourhoods, rather than the promotion of the spatial mobility of middle-class newcomers – that is, fighting poverty, discrimination and social insecurity rather than moving the poor'. It will be a challenge to persuade policy makers to do this given that (as Ley argues in Chapter Six) the interventions in liberal welfare states in the 1960s and 1970s have given way to a more marketised neoliberal environment, but it is a challenge we must take up. In so doing we are not saying that large spatially segregated concentrations of poverty (the starting concern of social mix policies historically) do not exacerbate the problems of poverty; rather we are saying that such problems are tackled more fruitfully through a more direct connection to power and investment of resources. This connection can be at the level of the neighbourhood itself. This is shown, for example, by Fung's (2006) work on grassroots mobilisation in a southside Chicago ghetto neighbourhood which was connected to new institutional mechanisms through which residents turned around a failing school and changed the nature of neighbourhood policing. But connection also has to be at the scale of the (nation) state and the social contract more widely (as Cheshire's work has long argued). As numerous chapters in this volume suggest, social mix policies by contrast have a tendency to represent nothing more than the rhetoric of intervention and mobilisation, for which the reality of tangible outcomes is often lacking. One explanation for this, suggested by a number of the chapters, is that there is very little social mixing in socially mixed neighbourhoods. Indeed neighbourhood social mix might exacerbate divisions with the louder voices and sharp elbows of the middle classes monopolising local services and schools, for example. Whether or not there is social interaction across social groups, the evidence of the presumed rub-off effects of having middle-class incomers as neighbourhood advocates seems extremely limited, or might be limited to the advocacy of their own interests. Again, as Fung's (2006) study suggests, direct access to power and resources for all groups in a neighbourhood is likely to be more effective than the lobbying efforts for resources (however well intentioned) of any single group.

Aside from the evidence now emerging on the failures of mixed communities policy with respect to the social mobility of the poor, some of which is presented here, there is also much evidence from the gentrification literature that market processes can result in a particular form of social mix (over a range of timescales), but that they too do not enhance welfare overall, and in fact often severely undermine the interests of the working class and the poor (Lees, 2008). The end result is more often than not some form of gentrification. There are also many examples of social mix in neighbourhoods as a result of past public policy and planning (such as social housing initiatives) that were not aiming for social mix but where neighbourhood social mix was the result, again with no real evidence of welfare gain from that mix. It seems, then, that social mix is a difficult mix (Bretherton and Pleace, 2011). Moreover, any form of planned or policy-led social mix is not self-sustaining and will need continued support over time, something that policy makers have thought little about. Social mix might well be desirable for all kinds of reasons (as the opposite of segregation, as a possible antidote to prejudice, to enhance civility) but, to reiterate, as the chapters in this volume suggest, as an aim of public policy, the evidence to date suggests the results are, at best, unconvincing, more often negative, and at worst, enact gentrification by stealth. The policy focus needs to move towards welfare adjustments, not population adjustments.

A second significant set of questions raised in this book is both theoretical and methodological. There is a tendency when talking about mixed communities policy to view it in terms of a singular form of neoliberalism, something that Peck (2010) takes David Harvey and others to task for. As a number of the chapters in this book attest to, there are different neoliberalisms being rolled out (and indeed rolled back and around) in different cities around the world. Theoretically we need to get to grips with this, and one way may be through a more informed comparative urbanism (Lees, forthcoming). There is also a tendency for some critical social scientists (both in this collection and elsewhere) to forget that the origins of the mixed communities policies (especially in the US and the UK) that they are discussing occurred in eras that were not neoliberal (as Ley's chapter shows – see Chapter Six). This is a significant misreading – mixed communities policy is being operationalised in neoliberal times but its origins are quite different. Drawing on, and extending, the new policy mobilities literature (see McCann, 2010), much more research needs to be done not just on the origins of these policies but on their mobility and transformation through time. Indeed the problems of social inequality and poverty that US and British policies in particular are addressing, are the result of much earlier rounds of national urban policies that had unforeseen consequences, consequences that countries have as yet failed to deal with properly.

Methodologically, we would argue, there is some scope for building on and combining the different quantitative and qualitative approaches to investigating social mix that have been outlined in chapters in this book. Future studies might also benefit from an explicit discussion of the appropriate spatial scale at which analysis of social mix should take place in different national, regional and urban contexts. Context is likely to be significant and a systematic acknowledgement of its importance would be valuable. Understandings of scale have long been acknowledged in the analysis of urban social segregation and so should be applied to social mix. This also relates to the analysis of sources of quantitative data and this is likely to become more important as small area statistics and other quantitative data (from official censuses and surveys, through to, appropriately interpreted, geodemographic data) become more readily available. Most of the qualitative data reported here is the result of in-depth interviews with residents usually of one or other social group. It would be good to build on this work through more direct comparisons of the perceptions and understandings of different class or social groups within neighbourhoods (gentrifiers and long-term residents, for example). Furthermore, the mapping of social mix (or otherwise) could be developed through social network analysis (building on the approach discussed by Blokland and van Eijk, for example, see Chapter Eighteen), of which there is a longstanding tradition in sociology and anthropology. Both quantitative and qualitative social network analysis could be used to help understand the degree and significance of social contacts, while bracketing the spatial patterns. A social network approach could be combined with a functional analysis of what gets done and how people get it done through networks and how these are confined to socially circumscribed or more broadly socially mixed realms. The ethnographic side of network analysis could be developed in this context to look at the points of critical interaction in public forums (such as council meetings, local neighbourhood meetings, school meetings) to assess the degree to which any class/social differences in the performative and discursive aspects of the situation have impacts on who gets to speak and who is heard. This last point brings us to one other important arena of discussion in social mix policy, and that is the institutional context itself. Several of the chapters in this book rightly deal with the discursive aspects of policy (and provide powerful critiques of policy discourse, see also a review by Smith, 2011). It is also important to map (especially in a comparative sense) the institutional mechanisms and the design (and possible points of intervention and redesign) of these mechanisms to produce better outcomes in neighbourhoods where, up to now, their results have only increased social divisions, rather than enhancing welfare based on the ideal of social mix.

Finally, it is important to underline that it is a tragedy that social mix policies have almost never led to greater social mobility for the urban poor nor to urban social justice. This is a sad indictment of a policy that has been massively state funded and our ability to influence it. In a world where evidence-based policy seems to be moving into conviction-based policy, academic commentators and those involved in policy formation, formulation and implementation have a moral obligation to work together towards a better solution to social segregation, urban poverty and social immobility. To that end we hope that this book will move debates and people in the right direction.

Notes

[1] Katz made this personal observation to a British policy analyst at a mixed communities seminar.

[2] Compare with Galster (2007a, 2007b, and 2011a, 2011b: forthcoming).

References

Abu-Lughod, J.L. (2005) 'Commentary: what is special about Chicago?', *City and Society*, vol 17, no 2, pp 289–303.

Allen, C. (2008) *Housing Market Renewal and social class*, London: Routledge.

Allen, C., Camina, M., Casey, R., Coward, S. and Wood, M. (2005) *Mixed tenure, twenty years on: Nothing out of the ordinary*, York: Joseph Rowntree Foundation.

Allison, P. (2005) *Fixed effect regression methods for longitudinal data*, Cary, NC: SAS Institute Inc.

Amin, A. (2002) 'Ethnicity and the multicultural city: living with diversity', *Environment and Planning A*, vol 34, no 6, pp 959–80.

Amion Consulting Ltd (2010) *Evaluation of the National Strategy for Neighbourhood Renewal: Final report: Summary*, London: Communities and Local Government.

Andersson, R. (2006) 'Breaking segregation', *Urban Studies*, vol 43, no 4, pp 787–99.

André-Bechely, L. (2005) *Could it be otherwise? Parents and the inequities of public school choice*, New York: Routledge.

Andreotti, A., Moreno Fuentes, F. and Le Galès, P. (2011: forthcoming) 'Upper middle classes in European cities: the game of distance and proximity', *International Journal of Urban and Regional Research*.

Anyon, J. (2005) *Radical possibilities*, New York: Routledge.

Applied Research Center (2007) *Facing race: Legislative report card on racial equity*, Chicago, IL: Applied Research Center.

Aron, J. (1978) *Le tournant de l'urbanisme bruxellois*, Brussels: Fondation Jacquemotte.

Arthurson, K. (2002) 'Creating inclusive communities through balancing social mix: a critical relationship or tenuous link?', *Urban Policy and Research*, vol 20, no 3, pp 245–61.

Arthurson, K. (2004) 'Social mix and disadvantaged communities: policy, practice, and the evidence base', *Urban Policy and Research*, vol 22, no 1, pp 101–6.

Arthurson, K. (2010) 'Operationalising social mix: spatial scale, lifestyle and stigma as mediating points in resident interaction', *Urban Policy and Research*, vol 28, no 1, pp 49–63.

Atkinson, R. (2006) 'Padding the bunker: strategies of middle-class disaffiliation and colonisation in the city', *Urban Studies*, vol 43, no 4, pp 819–32.

Atkinson, R. and Bridge, G. (eds) (2005) *Gentrification in a global context: The new urban colonialism*, London: Routledge.

Atkinson, R. and Kintrea, K. (2000) 'Owner occupation, social mix and neighbourhood impacts', *Policy & Politics*, vol 28, no 1, pp 93-108.

Atkinson, P. and Kintrea, K. (2002) 'Area effects: what do they mean for British housing and regeneration policy?', *European Journal of Housing Policy*, vol 2, no 2, pp 147-66.

Atkinson, A. and Piketty, T. (eds) (2010) *Top incomes: A global perspective*, Oxford: Oxford University Press.

August, M. (2008) 'Social mix and Canadian public housing redevelopment: experiences in Toronto', *Canadian Journal of Urban Research*, vol 17, no 1, pp 82-100.

Australand (2009a) 'ASX announcement: Australand and St Hilliers JV to undertake $300 million urban renewal project in Carlton, Victoria', 10 June, Rhodes, New South Wales: Australand.

Australand (2009b) Marketing brochure.

Authier, J.Y. (2003) 'La gentrification du quartier Saint-Georges à Lyon', ['The gentrification of Saint-Georges, Lyon'] in C. Bidou (ed) *Retours en ville, [Return to the city]*, Paris: Descartes et Cie, pp 107-26.

Bacqué, M.-H. (2005) 'Action collective, institutionnalisation et contre-pouvoir: action associative et communautaire à Paris et Montréal', *Espaces et Sociétés, [Space and Society]*, no 123, pp 69-85.

Bacqué, M.-H. and Fol, S. (2003) 'Les politiques de mixité sociale en France: de l'injonction politique nationale aux contradictions locales', in D. Fée and C. Nativel (eds) *Crises et politiques du logement en France et au Royaume Uni*, Paris: Presses de la Sorbonne Nouvelle, pp 117-35.

Baeten, G. (2001a) 'Clichés of urban doom: the dystopian politics of metaphors for the unequal city – a view from Brussels', *International Journal of Urban and Regional Research*, vol 25, no 1, pp 55-69.

Baeten, G. (2001b) 'The Europeanisation of Brussels and the urbanisation of "Europe": hybridising the city, empowerment and disempowerment in the EU district', *European Urban and Regional Studies*, vol 8, no 2, pp 117-30.

Bailey, N., Haworth, A., Manzi, T., Parangamage, P. and Robert, M. (2007) *Creating and sustaining mixed income communities: A good practice guide*, Chartered Institute of Housing Scotland, Edinburgh: Joseph Rowntree Foundation.

Baillergeau, E. (2008) 'La promotion de la mixité sociale dans l'habitat à Bruxelles', [Promoting mixed communities in urban Brussels], in E. Baillergeau, J.W. Duyvendak, P. van der Graaf and L. Veldboer (eds) *Les politiques de mixité sociale dans l'Europe du nord Belgique, Pays-Bas, Suède*, [Mixed communities policies in northern Europe's Belgium, Netherlands and Sweden] Paris: PUCA, pp 69-84.

Bair, E. and Fitzgerald, J.M. (2005) 'Hedonic estimation and policy significance of the impact of HOPE VI on neighborhood property values', *Review of Policy Research*, vol 22, no 6, pp 771-86.

Ball, S.J. (2003) *Class strategies and the education market: The middle classes and social advantage*, London: RoutledgeFalmer.

Banks, J.A. and Banks, C.A.M. (eds) (2004) *Multicultural education: Issues and perspectives* (4th edn), Boston, MA: Allyn and Bacon.

Barlow, A.L. (2003) *Between fear and hope: Globalization and race in the United States*, Lanham, MD: Rowman & Littlefield.

BASICS (2007) 'Lawrence heights redevelopment: residents speak out', *BASICS Free Community Newsletter*, issue 5, p 3, 12 June.

Batty, E., Beatty, C., Foden, M., Lawless, P., Pearson S. and Wilson, I. (2010) *The New Deal for Communities experience: A final assessment*, London: Communities and Local Government.

Bayer, P., Ross, S.L. and Topa, G. (2005) *Place of work and place of residence: Informal hiring networks and labour market outcomes*, NBER Working Paper No 11019, Cambridge, MA: National Bureau of Economic Research.

Beck, U. (2000) 'The cosmopolitan perspective: sociology of the second age of modernity', *British Journal of Sociology*, vol 51, pp 79-105.

Becker, J. (2010) 'Anerkennung – Annäherungen an eine sozialwissenschaftliche Schlüsselkategorie', [Appreciation - Approaching a key category in social sciences], in M. Becker and R. Krätschmer-Hahn (eds) *Fundamente sozialen Zusammenhalts*, [Foundations of social cohesion], Frankfurt am Main: Campus Verlag, pp 85-100.

Becton Corporation (2008) Marketing brochure.

Beghin, J. (2006) (ed) *Armoede in Brussel / Pauvreté à Bruxelles*, Berchem: EPO.

Bennett, L. (2006) 'Downtown restructuring and public housing in contemporary Chicago: fashioning a better world-class city', in L. Bennett, J.L. Smith and P.A. Wright (eds) *Where are poor people to live? Transforming public housing communities*, Armonk, NY: M.E. Sharpe, pp 282-300.

Bennett L. and Reed A, Jr. (1999) 'The new face of urban renewal: the Near North redevelopment initiative and the Cabrini-Green neighborhood', in A. Reed Jr (ed) *Without justice for all: The new liberalism and our retreat from racial equality*, Boulder, CO: Westview Press, pp 175–211.

Bennett, L. and Reed, A. Jr (1999) 'The Near North Development Initiative and the Cabrini Green Neighborhood', in A. Reed Jr (ed) *Without justice for all: The new liberalism and our retreat from racial equality*, Boulder, CO: Westview Press, pp 175-211.

Bennett, L., Hudspeth, N. and Wright, P.A. (2006a) 'A critical analysis of the ABLA redevelopment plan', in L. Bennett, J.L. Smith and P.A. Wright (eds) *Where are poor people to live? Transforming public housing communities*, Armonk, NY: M.E. Sharpe, pp 185-215.

Bennett, L., Smith, J.A. and Wright, P.A. (eds) (2006b) *Where are poor people to live? Transforming public housing communities*, Armonk, NY: M.E. Sharpe.

Bentancur, J.J. (2002) 'The politics of gentrification: the case of West Town in Chicago', *Urban Affairs Review*, vol 37, no 6, pp 780-814.

Bernard, N. (2004) 'Clefs pour appréhender la crise du logement à Bruxelles', *Les Echos du Logement*, vol 5, pp 197-202.

Bernard, N., Zimmer, P. and Surkin, J. (2009) 'Housing, control over land use and public space', Brussels Studies, Citizens' Forum of Brussels, Synopsis no 6, pp 1-13 [French, Dutch and English version available online at www.brusselsstudies.be].

Bernt, M., Grossmann, K. and Kabisch, S. (2010) 'Shrinking housing estates and booming speculations: global games and their local consequences in East Germany', Paper delivered to the International Sociological Association Conference RC21/RC43, Gothenberg, Sweden, 12-17 July.

Berube, A. (2005) *Narrowing the gap? The trajectories of Britain's poor neighbourhoods 1991-2001*, CASE Census Brief 4, London: Centre for the Analysis of Social Exclusion, London School of Economics and Political Science.

Biddle, B.J. and Berliner, D.C. (2002) 'Unequal school funding in the United States', *Educational Leadership*, vol 59, no 8, pp 48-59.

Bidou, C. (1984) *Les aventuriers du quotidian: Essai sur les nouvelles classes moyennes*, Paris: Presses Universitaires de France.

Binnie, J. and Skeggs, B. (2004) 'Cosmopolitan knowledge and the production and consumption of sexualized space: Manchester's gay village', *The Sociological Review*, vol 52, pp 39-61.

Binnie, J., Holloway, J., Millington, S. and Young, C. (eds) (2006) *Cosmopolitan urbanism*, Routledge: London.

Blanc, M. (2010) 'The impact of social mix policies in France', *Housing Studies*, vol 25, no 2, pp 257-72.

Blau, D. and Robins, P. (1992) 'Job search outcomes for the employed and unemployed', *Journal of Political Economy*, vol 98, pp 637-55.

Blokland, T.V. (2001) 'Bricks, mortar, memories: neighbourhood and networks in collective acts of remembering', *International Journal of Urban and Regional Research*, vol 25, no 2, pp 268-83.

Blokland, T.V. (2003) *Urban bonds: Social relationships in an inner city neighbourhood*, Cambridge: Polity Press.

Blokland, T.V. (2004) 'Buren als bruggen? De betekenis van burenrelaties voor sociaal kapitaal in een Rotterdamse gemengde wijk', *Sociale wetenschappen*, vol 47, no 2, pp 31-48.

Blokland, T.V. (2009) *Oog voor elkaar*, Amsterdam: Amsterdam University Press.

Blokland, T.V. and van Eijk, G. (2010) 'Do people who like diversity practice diversity in neighbourhood life? Neighbourhood use and social networks of "diversity seekers" in a mixed neighbourhood', *Journal of Ethnic and Migration Studies*, vol 36, no 2, pp 313-32.

Blokland, T.V. and Rae, D. (2008) 'The end to urbanism: how the changing spatial structure of cities affected its social capital potentials', in T.V. Blokland and M. Savage (eds) *Networked urbanism: Social capital in the city*, Aldershot: Ashgate, pp 23-40.

Blomley, N. (2004) *Unsettling the city: Urban land and the politics of property*, New York: Routledge.

Blume, L. and Durlauf, S. (2001) 'The interactions-based approach to socioeconomic behaviour', in S. Durlauf and H.P. Young (eds) *Social dynamics*, Cambridge, MA: The MIT Press, pp 15-45.

BMVBS (Bundesministerium für Verkehr, Bau und Stadtentwicklung) (ed) (2010) *Entwurf Weißbuch Innenstadt. Starke Zentren für unsere Städte und Gemeinden*, Berlin/Bonn: BMVBS.

Board of Education (2007) *Establish renaissance schools: Chicago public schools policy manual*, Section 3027, Board Report 07-0627-PO4, adopted 27 June (http://policycpsk12ilus/documents/3027pdf).

Bolster, A., Burgess, A.S., Johnston, R., Jones, K., Propper, C. and Starker, R. (2007) 'Neighbourhoods, households and income dynamics: a semi-parametric investigation of neighbourhood effects', *Journal of Economic Geography*, vol 7, pp 1-38.

Bolt, G. and van Kempen, R. (2008) De mantra van de mix: ideeeën, idealen en de praktijk [*The mantra of the mix: Ideas, ideals and practices*], Utrecht: Forum, Institute for Multicultural Development.

Bolt, G. and van Kempen, R. (2010) 'Dispersal patterns of households who are forced to move: desegregation by demolition: a case of Dutch cities', *Housing Studies*, vol 25, no 2, pp 159-80.

Bondi, L. (1991) 'Gender divisions and gentrification: a critique', *Transactions of the Institute of British Geographers*, New Series, vol 16, no 2, pp 190-8.

Boudreau, J.A. (2000) *The MegaCity saga: Democracy and citizenship in this global age*, Montreal: Black Rose Books.

Bougras, M. (2008) 'Les ventes immobilières à la Goutte d'Or 2000-2005', *Mémoire de Master*, Université Paris 7.

Bourdieu, P. (1984) *Distinction: A social critique of the Judgement of taste*, London: Routledge.

Bourdieu, P. and Wacquant, L. (2004) 'Symbolic violence', in N. Scheper-Hughes and P. Bourgois (eds) *Violence in war and peace: An anthology*, Malden, MA: Blackwell, pp 272-4.

Boyd, M. (2005) 'The downside of racial uplift: the meaning of gentrification in an African American neighborhood', *City & Society*, vol 17, no 2, pp 265-88.

Boyle, P.J., Feijten, P., Feng, Z., Hattersley, L., Huang, Z., Nolan, J. and Raab, G. (2009) 'Cohort profile: the Scottish Longitudinal Study (SLS)', *International Journal of Epidemiology*, vol 38, no 2, pp 385-92.

Bramley, G. and Pawson, H. (2002) 'Low demand for housing: incidence, causes and UK national policy implications', *Urban Studies*, vol 39, no 3, pp 393-422.

Bramley, G., Noah, K.K. and Watkins, D. (2006) *Local housing need and affordability model for Scotland – Update (2005 based)*, Edinburgh: Communities Scotland.

Brand, G. (1973) 'The structure of the life-world according to Husserl', *Man and World*, vol 6, no 2, May, pp 143-62.

Brenner, N, and Theodore, N. (2002b) 'Cities and the geographies of "actually existing neoliberalism"', *Antipode*, vol 34, no 3, pp 349-79.

Bretherton, J. and Pleace, N. (2011:) 'A difficult mix: issues in achieving socioeconomic diversity in deprived UK neighbourhoods', *Urban Studies*, vol 48, no 4, pp 1-11.

Bridge, G. (2001) 'Bourdieu, rational action and the time-space strategy of gentrification', *Transactions of the Institute of British Geographers*, vol 26, pp 205-16.

Bridge, G. (2005) *Reason in the city of difference: Pragmatism, communicative action and contemporary urbanism*, London: Routledge.

Bridge, G. (2006a) 'Perspectives on cultural capital and the neighborhood', *Urban Studies*, vol 43, no 4, pp 719-30.

Bridge, G. (2006b) 'It's not just a question of taste: gentrification, the neighbourhood, and cultural capital', *Environment and Planning A*, vol 38, no 10, pp 1965-78.

Briggs, X. (1998) 'Brown kids in white suburbs: housing mobility and the many faces of social capital', *Housing Policy Debate*, vol 9, no 1, pp 177-221.

Briggs, X., Popkin, S. and Goering, J. (2010) *Moving to Opportunity*, New York: Oxford University Press.

Brophy, P.C. and Smith, R.N. (1997) 'Mixed income housing: factors for success', *Cityscape: A Journal of Policy Development and Research*, vol 3, no 2, pp 3-31.

Browitt, J. (2004) 'Pierre Bourdieu: homo sociologicus', in J. Browitt and B. Nelson (eds) *Practising theory: Pierre Bourdieu and the field of cultural production*, Newark, DE: University of Delaware Press, pp 1-2.

Brown, T., Lishman, R. and Richardson, J. (2005) *Implementing and developing choice-based lettings*, London: Office of the Deputy Prime Minister.

Brown-Saracino, J. (2009) *A neighborhood that never changes: Gentrification, social preservation and the quest for authenticity*, Chicago, IL: University of Chicago Press.

Bruns-Berentelg, J. (2010) 'HafenCity Hamburg: public urban space and the creation of the public sphere', in J. Bruns-Berentelg, A. Eisinger, M. Kohler and M. Menzl (eds) *HafenCity Hamburg: Places of urban encounter between metropolis and neighborhood*, Vienna: Springer-Verlag, pp 424-55.

Brussels Alliance for the Right to Housing [Rassemblement Bruxellois pour le Droit à l'Habitat] (2007) 'Que peuvent les travailleurs sociaux devant l'avancée de la gentrification?', *Article 23*, vol 28, no 1, pp 29-32.

Brussels Capital Region (2009) *Review of office property: Vacancy 2008 and hidden vacancy*, Brussels: Administration of Planning and Housing and Brussels Regional Development Agency.

Buck, N. (2001) 'Identifying neighbourhood effects on social exclusion', *Urban Studies*, vol 38, pp 2251-75.

Burgess, G., Monk, S., Whitehead, C. and Crook, T. (2008) *The provision of affordable housing through Section 106: An update*, York: Joseph Rowntree Foundation.

Buron, L. and Popkin, S.J. (2010) *After Wells: Where are the residents now?*, Washington, DC: Urban Institute.

Butler, T. (2002) 'Thinking global but acting local: the middle classes in the city', *Sociological Research Online*, vol 7, no 3.

Butler, T. (2003) 'Living in the bubble: gentrification and its "others" in London', *Urban Studies*, vol 40, no 12, pp 2469-86.

Butler, T. and Lees, L. (2006) 'Super-gentrification in Barnsbury, London: globalization and gentrifying global elites at the neighbourhood level', *Transactions of the Institute of British Geographers*, vol 31, no 4, pp 467-87.

Butler, T. with Robson, G. (2003) *London calling: The middle classes and the remaking of inner London*, Oxford: Berg.

Butler, T. and Watt, P. (2007) *Understanding social inequality*, London: Sage Publications.

Cailliez, J. (2004) *Schuman-City des fonctionnaires britanniques à Bruxelles*, Louvain-la-Neuve: Academia Bruylant.

Cameron, S. (2003) 'Gentrification, housing redifferentiation and urban regeneration: "going for growth" in Newcastle upon Tyne', *Urban Studies*, vol 40, no 12, pp 2367-82.

Cameron, S. and Coaffee, J. (2005) 'Art, gentrification and regeneration: from artist as pioneer to public arts', *European Journal of Housing Studies*, vol 5, no 1, pp 39-58.

Castells, N. (2010) 'HOPE VI neighborhood spillover effects in Baltimore', *Cityscape: A Journal of Policy Development and Research*, vol 12, no 1, pp 65-98.

Catalyst Chicago (2007) *Special report: School autonomy all over the map*, February (www.catalyst-chicago.org/news/index. php?item=2141&cat=23).

Caulfield, J. (1994) *City form and everyday life: Toronto's gentrification and critical social practice*, Toronto: University of Toronto Press.

Cernetig, M. (2009) 'Olympic Village: social housing to cost $595,000 a unit', *Vancouver Sun*, 23 February, p A1.

Chalvon-Demersay, S. (1984) *Le triangle du 14ème: De nouveaux habitants dans un vieux quartier de Paris*, [*The triangle of the 14th arrondissement: Of new inhabitants in an old Paris borough*], Paris: Editions de la Maison des Sciences de l'Homme.

Chamboredon, J. and Lemaire, M. (1970) 'Proximité spatiale et distance sociale: les grands ensembles et leur peuplement', *Revue Française de Sociologie*, ['Spacial proximity and social distance: The great ensembles and their people', *French Sociology Review*], vol 11, pp 3-33.

Cheshire, P. (2006) 'Resurgent cities, urban myths and policy hubris: what we need to know', *Urban Studies*, vol 43, no 8, pp 1231-46.

Cheshire, P. (2007a) *Are mixed communities the answer to segregation and poverty?*, York: Joseph Rowntree Foundation.

Cheshire, P. (2007b) *Segregated neighbourhoods and mixed communities: A critical analysis*, York: Joseph Rowntree Foundation.

Cheshire, P. (2008) 'Policies for mixed communities: faith-based displacement activity?', Paper Given at ESRC Seminar, King's College London, 22-23 May.

Cheshire, P. (2009) 'Policies for mixed communities: a faith-based displacement activity?', *International Regional Science Review*, vol 32, no 3, pp 343-75.

Cheshire, P. (2010) 'The evidence for and policy implications of urban spatial equilibrium: or why nice neighbourhoods cost more – implications for cities, citizens and welfare', Plenary lecture to 50th European Regional Science Association Congress, Jönköping, Sweden, August.

Cheshire, P, and Sheppard, S. (2004) 'Capitalising the value of free schools: the impact of supply constraints and uncertainty', *The Economic Journal*, vol 114, issue 499, November, pp 397-424.

Cisneros, H. and Engdahl, L. (eds) (2009) *From despair to hope: HOPE VI and the new promise of public housing in America's cities*, Washington, DC: Brookings Institution Press.

City of Ottawa (1975) *The Sandy Hill Development Plan*, Ottawa: Community Development Department.

City ofVancouver (2007) *The Vancouver Agreement: Economic development* (www.vancouveragreement.ca/EconomicDevelopment.htm).

Clairmont, D.H. and Magill, D.W. (1974) *Africville:The life and death of a Canadian black community*, Toronto: McClelland and Stewart.

Clampet-Lundquist, S. (2004) 'HOPE VI relocation: moving to new neighbourhoods and building new ties', *Housing Policy Debate*, vol 15, pp 415-47.

Clampet-Lundquist, S. (2007) 'No more "Bois Ball": the effect of relocation from public housing on adolescents', *Journal of Adolescent Research*, vol 22, no 3, pp 298-324.

Clampet-Lundquist, S. (2010) '"Everyone had your back": social ties, perceived safety, and public housing relocation', *City & Community*, vol 9, no 1, pp 87-108.

Clark, E. (2005) 'The order and simplicity of gentrification – a political challenge', in R.Atkinson and G. Bridge (eds) *Gentrification in a global context:The new urban colonialism*, London: Routledge, pp 256-64.

Clark, G., Huxley,J. and Mountford, D. (2010) *Organising local economic development:The role of development agencies and companies*, Paris: OECD.

Clark, S.L. (2002) 'Where the poor live: how federal housing policy shapes residential communities', *Urban Anthropology*, vol 31, no 1, pp 69-92.

Clark, W.A.V. (2008) 'Re-examining the Moving to Opportunity Study and its contribution to changing the distribution of poverty and ethnic concentration', *Demography*, vol 45, pp 515-35.

Clarke, J. and Newman, J. (1997) *The managerial state*, London: Sage Publications.

Clyde Waterfront (2007) (www.clydewaterfront.com).

Cochrane, A. (2007) *Understanding urban policy: A critical approach*, Oxford: Blackwell.

Cole, I. and Flint, J. (2007) *Housing affordability, clearance and relocation in the Housing Market Renewal pathfinders*, London: Chartered Institute of Housing.

Cole, I. and Goodchild, B. (2001) 'Social mix and the "balanced community" in British housing policy – a tale of two epochs', *GeoJournal*, vol 51, pp 351-60.

Colley, H. and Hodkinson, P. (2001) 'Problems with bridging the gap: the reversal of structure and agency in addressing social exclusion', *Critical Social Policy*, vol 21, no 3, pp 335-59.

Commonwealth of Australia (2004) *Productivity Commission Inquiry Report*, No 28, March, Canberra: Productivity Commission.

Coole, D. (2007) *Merleau-Ponty and modern politics after anti-humanism*, Lanham, MD: Rowman & Littlefield.

Court of Audit (2007) *La politique fédérale des grandes villes: Examen des contrats de ville et des contrats de logement 2005-2007*, Brussels.

Cowan, D. and McDermont, M. (2006) *Regulating social housing: Governing decline*, Abingdon: Routledge-Cavendish.

CRBA (Corktown Residents' and Business Association) (2002) Letter to the East York Community Council Re: Meetings of community councils to consider the enactment of a municipal shelter by-law, Per Chris Hutcheson, President.

CRBA (2005a) Letter to President of the Toronto Revitalization Corporation Re: The McCord Site, Per Suzanne Edmonds, President.

CRBA (2005b) *Newsletter*, April.

CRBA (2005c) *Meeting Minutes*, April.

Crompton, R. (1998) *Class and stratification: An introduction to current debates*, Cambridge: Polity Press.

Crompton, R. and Scott, J. (2005) 'Class analysis: beyond the cultural turn', in F. Devine, M. Savage, J. Scott and R. Crompton (eds) *Rethinking class: Culture, identities and lifestyle*, Basingstoke: Palgrave, pp 186-202.

Crump, J. (2002) 'Deconcentration by demolition: public housing, poverty and urban policy', *Environment and Planning D: Society and Space*, vol 20, no 5, pp 581-96.

Curley, A. (2005) 'Theories of urban poverty and implications for public housing policy', *Journal of Sociology and Social Welfare*, vol 32, no 2, pp 97-118.

Darling-Hammond, L. (2004) 'What happens to a dream deferred? The continuing quest for equal educational opportunity', in J.A. Banks and C.A.M Banks (eds) *Handbook of research on multicultural education* (2nd edn), San Francisco, CA: Jossey-Bass, pp 607-30.

Davidson, M. (2007) 'Gentrification as global habitat: a process of class formation or corporate creation?', *Transactions of the Institute of British Geographers*, vol 32, no 4, pp 490-506.

Davidson, M. (2008) 'Spoiled mixture – where does state-led "positive" gentrification end?', *Urban Studies*, vol 45, no 12, pp 2385-405.

Davidson, M. (2010) 'Love thy neighbour? Interpreting social mixing in London's gentrification frontiers', *Environment and Planning A*, vol 42, no 3, pp 524-44.

Davidson, M. and Lees, L. (2005) 'New build "gentrification" and London's riverside renaissance', *Environment and Planning A*, vol 37, no 7, pp 1165-90.

Davidson, M. and Lees, L. (2010) 'New-build gentrification: its histories, trajectories, and critical geographies', *Population, Space and Place*, vol 16, pp 395-411.

De Decker, P. (2001) 'Jammed between housing and property rights: Belgian private renting in perspective', *European Journal of Housing Policy*, vol 1, pp 17-39.

Dean, J. (2007) 'Why Žižek for political theory?', *International Journal of Zizek Studies*, vol 1, no 1, pp 18-32.

Debroux, T., Decroly, J.-M., Deligne, C., Galand, M., Loir, C. and van Criekingen, M. (2007) 'Les espaces résidentiels de la noblesse à Bruxelles (XVIIIe-XXe siècle)', *Belgeo*, vol 4, pp 441-52.

DeFilippis, J. (2004) *Unmaking Goliath: Community control in the face of global capital*, New York: Routledge.

DeFilippis, J. and Fraser, J. (2010) 'What kind of mixed-income housing and for what reasons?', in J. Davies and D. Imbroscio (eds) *Critical urban studies: New directions*, Albany, NY: SUNY Press, pp 135-47.

DeFilippis, J. and North, P. (2004) 'The emancipatory community? Place, politics and collective action in cities', in L. Lees (ed) *The emancipatory city: Paradoxes and possibilities*, London: Sage Publications, pp 72-88.

DeFilippis, J. and Wyly, E. (2008) 'Running to stand still: through the looking glass with federally-subsidized housing in New York City', *Urban Affairs Review*, vol 43, no 6, pp 777-816.

de Lannoy, W. and de Cortes, S. (1994) 'De migraties van Marokkaanen en Turken binnen het Brusselse Gewest in de periode 1988-1992', in M. Goossens and E. van Hecke (eds) 'Van Brussel tot Siebenbürgen. Liber Amicorum Prof. Dr Herman Van der Haeghen', *Acta Geographica Loveniensa*, vol 34, pp 63-9.

Dessouroux, C., van Criekingen, M. and Decroly, J.-M. (2009) 'Embellissement sous surveillance: une géographie des politiques de réaménagement des espaces publics au centre de Bruxelles', *Belgeo*, vol 2, pp 167-84.

DETR (Department of the Environment, Transport and the Regions) (1999) *Towards an urban renaissance: Final report of the Urban Task Force*, chaired by Lord Rogers of Riverside, London: Spon Press.

DETR (2000) *Our towns and cities: The future – Delivering an urban renaissance*, London: The Stationery Office (*www.communities.gov.uk/documents/regeneration/pdf/154869.pdf*).

DHS (Department of Human Services) (2002) *Tender for Kensington Estate Redevlopment Social Impact Study*, Melbourne: DHS.

Dikeç, M. (2007) *Badlands of the republic: Space, politics and urban policy*, Oxford: Blackwell.

Dorling, D., Rigby, J., Wheeler, B., Ballas, D., Thomas, B., Fahmy, E., Gordon, D. and Lupton, R. (2007) *Poverty and wealth across Britain 1968 to 2005*, York: Joseph Rowntree Foundation.

Driant, J. and Lelévrier, C. (2006) 'Le logement social, mixité et solidarité territoriale', in H. Lagrange and M. Oberti (eds) *Emeutes urbaines et protestations*, Paris: Presses de Sciences Po, pp 177-95.

DTZ Pieda (2000) 'Demolition and new building on local authority estates', Summary of report commissioned by the Office of the Deputy Prime Minister, Freedom of Information request – not published.

DTZ Pieda (2005) *Dundee City Council – Financial viability study Phase 2: Final report*, Freedom of Information request – not published.

Duffrin, E. (2006) 'Promise of new schools not met', *Catalyst*, vol 17, no 6, p 11.

Duke, J. (2009) 'Mixed income housing policy and public housing residents' "right to the city"', *Critical Social Policy*, vol 29, no 1, pp 100-20.

Dumbleton, B. (2006) *'Help us somebody': The demolition of the elderly*, London: The London Press.

Dundee City Council (2004) *Local Housing Strategy 2004–2009*, Dundee: Dundee City Council.

Dundee City Council (2006) 'Affordable housing and housing choice issues in Dundee', Consultation paper.

Dundee City Council (2008a) *The Hilltown physical regeneration framework*, Dundee: Dundee City Council (www.dundeecity.gov.uk/dundeecity/uploaded.../publication_616.pdf).

Dundee City Council (2008b) *Local housing strategy: 2004-2009*, Dundee: Dundee City Council (www.dundeecity.gov.uk/dundeecity/uploaded.../publication_617.pdf).

Durlauf, S. (2004) 'Neighborhood effects', in J.V. Henderson and J.F. Thisse (eds) *Handbook of regional and urban economics*, Vol 4, *Cities and Geography*, Amsterdam: Elsevier, pp 2173-242.

Ebels, H.J. and Ostendorf, W.J.M. (1991) *Achter de schermen van de gentrification de bewoners van dure woningen in de centra van Amsterdam en Den Haag*, Amsterdam: Instituut voor Sociale Geografie.

Edin, P.-A., Fredriksson, P. and Åslund, O. (2003) 'Ethnic enclaves and the economic success of immigrants – evidence from a natural experiment', *Quarterly Journal of Economics*, vol 118, no 1, pp 329-57.

Elster, J. (1983) *Sour grapes: Studies in the subversion of rationality*, Cambridge: Cambridge University Press.

Epstein, R. (2011) *Rénovation urbaine, mixité et nouvelle gestion des territoires, à paraître*, [*Emerging urban renovation, mixed societies and new territorial policies*], Paris: Presses de Sciences Po.

Fainstein, S. (2005) 'Cities and diversity: should we want it? Can we plan for it?', *Urban Affairs Review*, vol 41, no 1, pp 3-19.

Fairclough, N. (2000) *New Labour, new language?*, London: Routledge.

False Creek Study Group (1972) *Report 3*, Vancouver: City of Vancouver.

Fenton, A. (2010) *The contribution of housing, planning and regeneration policies to mixed communities in Scotland*, Edinburgh: Scottish Government.

Fijalkow, Y. and Préteceille, E. (2007) 'Gentrification, discours et politiques', *Sociétés Contemporaines*, ['Gentrification, discourse and politicies', *Contemporary Societies*], vol 63, pp 5-13.

Fincher, R. and Jacobs, J. (eds) (1998) *Cities of difference*, New York: Guilford Press.

Finkel, A.E., Lennon, K.A. and Eisenstadt, E.R. (2000) 'HOPE VI: a promising vintage?', *Review of Policy Research*, vol 17, nos 2-3, pp 104-18.

Finney, N. and Simpson, L. (2009) *Sleepwalking to segregation? Challenging myths about race and migration*, Bristol: The Policy Press.

Fleming, J., Greenlee, A., Gutstein, E., Lipman, P. and Smith, J. (2009) *Examining CPS' plan to close, phase out, consolidate, turn-around 22 schools*, Paper No 2, Data and Democracy Project: Investing in Neighborhoods, Chicago, IL: Collaborative for Equity and Justice in Education, College of Education, University of Illinois-Chicago and Nathalie P.Voorhees Center for Neighborhood and Community Improvement, College of Urban Planning and Public Affairs, University of Illinois-Chicago (www.uic.edu/cuppa/voorheesctr/DataAndDemocracyRelease.pdf).

Flint, J. (2006) 'Housing and the new governance of conduct', in J. Flint (ed) *Housing, urban governance and anti-social behaviour*, Bristol: The Policy Press, pp 19-36.

Florentin, D. (2007) 'La Goutte d'Or au gré des rues Evolution du parc privé et analyse des mutations du quartier', Mémoire de Master, Université d'Evry Val d'Essonne (ss la direction de M.-H. Bacqué).

Florida, R.L. (2002) *The rise of the creative class and how it's transforming work, leisure, community and everyday life*, New York: Basic Books.

Florida, R.L. (2005) *The flight of the creative class: The new global competition for talent*, New York: Harper Business.

Forrest, R. and Kearns, A. (1999) *Joined-up places? Social cohesion and neighbourhood regeneration*, York: Joseph Rowntree Foundation.

Fraser, J. and Kick, E. (2007) 'The role of public, private, non-profit and community sectors in shaping mixed-income housing outcomes in the US', *Urban Studies*, vol 44, no 12, pp 2357-77.

Fraser, J. and Nelson, M. (2008) 'Can mixed-income housing ameliorate concentrated poverty: the significance of a geographically-informed idea of community', *Geography Compass*, vol 2, no 6, pp 2127-44.

Fraser, N. (2009) 'Zur Neubestimmung von Anerkennung', in H.-Chr. Schmidt am Busch and Chr.-Z. Zurn (eds) *Anerkennung*, Berlin: Akademie Verlag, pp 201-12.

Freeman, L. (2006) *There goes the 'hood: Views of gentrification from the ground up*, Philadelphia, PA: Temple University Press.

Fried, M. (1963) 'Grieving for a lost home', in L. Duhl (ed) *The urban condition*, New York: Basic Books, pp 151-71.

Friedrichs, J. (1998) 'Do poor neighborhoods make their residents poorer? Context effects of poverty neighborhoods on their residents', in H. Andress (ed) *Empirical poverty research in a comparative perspective*, Aldershot: Ashgate, pp 77-99.

Friedrichs, J. (2010) 'Welche soziale Mischung in Wohngebieten?', in A. Harth and G. Scheller (eds) *Soziologie in der Stadt- und Freiraumplanung*, [*Sociology in city and open space planning*], Wiesbaden: VS Verlag für Sozialwissenschaften, pp 319-34.

Friedrichs, J. and Blasius, J. (2003) 'Social norms in distressed neighbourhoods: testing the Wilson hypothesis', *Housing Studies*, vol 18, pp 807-26.

Fujitsuka, Y. (2005) 'Gentrification and neighbourhood dynamics in Japan: the case of Kyoto', in R. Atkinson and G. Bridge (eds) *Gentrification in a global context: The new urban colonialism*, London: Routledge, pp 137-50.

Fulford, R. (2006) 'How we became a land of ghettos', *National Post*, 12 June.

Fullilove, M.T. (2005) *Root shock: How tearing up city neighborhoods hurts America, and what we can do about it*, New York: One World Books.

Fung, A. (2006) *Empowered participation: Reinventing urban democracy*, Princeton, NJ: Princeton University Press.

Galster, G. (2007a) 'Neighbourhood social mix as a goal of housing policy: a theoretical analysis', *European Journal of Housing Policy*, vol 7, pp 19-43.

Galster, G. (2007b) 'Should policy-makers strive for neighbourhood social mix? An analysis of the Western European evidence base', *Housing Studies*, vol 22, no 4, pp 523-45.

Galster, G. (2008) 'Quantifying the effect of neighbourhood on individuals: challenges, alternative approaches, and promising directions', *Schmollers Jahrbuch*, vol 128, no 1, pp 7-48.

Galster, G. (2011a: in press) 'Neighborhood social mix: theory, evidence, and implications for policy and planning', in N. Carmon and S. Fainstein (eds) *Planning for/with people* (wwwclaswayneedu/multimedia/usercontent/File/Geography%20and%20Urban%20Planning/GGalster/Galster_Neighborhood_Social_Mix_Israel_paper_1-2010pdf).

Galster, G. (2011b: in press) 'The mechanism(s) of neighbourhood effects: theory, evidence, and policy implications', in M. van Ham, D. Manley, N. Bailey, L. Simpson and D. Maclennan (eds) *Neighbourhood effects research: New perspectives*, Dordrecht: Springer.

Galster, G., Cutsinger, J. and Lim, U. (2007) 'Are neighbourhoods self-stabilising? Exploring endogenous dynamics', *Urban Studies*, vol 44, pp 167-85.

Galster, G., Andersson, R., Musterd, S. and Kauppinen, T.M. (2008) 'Does neighborhood income mix affect earnings of adults? New evidence from Sweden', *Journal of Urban Economics*, vol 63, pp 858-70.

Gans, H. (1961) 'The balanced community: homogeneity or heterogeneity in residential areas', *Journal of the American Institute of Planners*, vol 27, no 3, pp 176-84.

Gans, H. (1962) *The urban villagers*, New York: Free Press.

GDRA (Garden District Residents Association) (2004) *Who, what, where, when, why: Healing the neighbourhood*, Toronto: Garden District Residents' Association (www.gardendistrict.ca).

Gibbs Knotts, H. and Haspel, M. (2006) 'The impact of gentrification on voter turnout', *Social Science Quarterly*, vol 87, no 1, pp 110-22.

Gibson, K. (2007) 'The relocation of the Columbia Village community: views from residents', *Journal of Planning Education and Research*, vol 27, no 5, pp 5-19.

Giddens, A. (1991) *Modernity and self-identity: Self and society in the late modern age*, Cambridge: Polity Press.

Giddens, A. (2002) 'There is no alternative – the Third Way is the only Glasgow Harbour (2007) (www.glasgowharbour.com).

Glass, R. (1963) *Introduction to London: Aspects of change*, London: Centre for Urban Studies.

Globe and Mail (2009) 'Our nation's slum: time to fix it', 14 February, A1, A10.

Glover, R.L. (2005) *Making a case for mixed-use, mixed-income communities to address America's affordable housing needs* (wwwamericanprogressorg/kf/gloverpdf).

Glynn, S. (2005) *More time for Butterburn and Bucklemaker Courts? The tenants' survey* (wwwsarahglynn.net/images/Butterburn%20and%20Bucklemaker%20Tenants%27%20Surveypdf).

Glynn, S. (2009b) *Ed Butterburn and Bucklemaker Tenants' Survey – Four years on* (www.sarahglynn.net/images/Butterburn%20and%20Bucklemaker%204%20years%20on.pdf).

Glynn, S. (2010) 'The Tenants' movement: incorporation and independence', in A. Emejulu and M. Shaw (eds) *The Glasgow papers: Critical perspectives on community development, Community Development Journal*.

Goering, J., Feins, J.D. and Richardson, T.M. (2002) 'A cross-site analysis of initial Moving to Opportunity demonstration results', *Journal of Housing Research*, vol 13, no 1, pp 1-30.

Goetz, E. (2005) 'Comment: public housing demolition and the benefits to low income families', *Journal of the American Planning Association*, vol 7, no 14, pp 407-10.

Goetz, E. (2010) 'Better neighborhoods, better outcomes? Explaining the relocation outcomes in HOPE VI', *Cityscape: A Journal of Policy Development and Research*, vol 12, no 1, pp 5-31.

Goldblum, C. and Wong, T.-C. (2000) 'Growth, crisis and spatial change: a study of haphazard urbanisation in Jakarta, Indonesia', *Land Use Policy*, vol 17, pp 29-37.

Goodchild, B. and Cole, I. (2001) 'Social balance and mixed neighbourhoods in Britain since 1979: a review of discourse and practice in social housing', *Environment and Planning D: Society and Space*, vol 19, no 1, pp 103-22.

Gough, J., Eisenschitz, A. and McCulloch, A. (2006) *Spaces of social exclusion*, Abingdon: Routledge.

Government of the Brussels Capital Region (2002) *Plan régional de développement*, Brussels.

Government of Victoria (1999) Media release: 'Support for Kensington redevelopment report', 20 August, Melbourne: Office of the Minister for Housing.

Government of Victoria (2007) *Melbourne planning scheme amendment C117*, Panel report, February, Melbourne: Independent Planning Council.

Graham, E., Manley, D., Hiscock, R., Boyle, P. and Doherty, J. (2009) 'Mixing housing tenures: is it good for social well-being?', *Urban Studies*, vol 46, no 1, pp 139-65.

Gramsci, A. (1971) *Selections from the Prison Notebooks* (edited and translated by Quintin Hoare and Geoffrey Nowell-Smith), London: Lawrence and Wishart.

Grant, J. (2002) 'Mixed use in theory and practice: Canadian experience with implementing a planning principle', *Journal of the American Planning Association*, vol 68, no 1, pp 71-84.

Graves, E. (2010) 'The structure of urban live in a mixed-income housing "community"', *City & Community*, vol 9, no 1, pp 109-30.

Greenbaum, S. (2002) 'Report from the field: social capital and deconcentration: theoretical and policy paradoxes of the HOPE VI program', *North American Dialogue*, vol 5, no 1, pp 9-13.

Greenbaum, S., Hathaway, W., Rodriguez, C., Spalding, A. and Ward, B. (2008) 'Deconcentration and social capital: contradictions of a poverty alleviation policy', *Journal of Poverty*, vol 12, no 2, pp 201-28.

Gregg, A. (2006) 'Identity crisis: a twentieth-century dream becomes a twenty-first century nightmare', *Walrus Magazine*, March.

Grenville, S. (2010) 'ADB outlook background paper: the evolving post-crisis world', *Working Papers in International Economics*, vol 1, no 10, Sydney: Lowy Institute for International Policy.

Güntner, S. (2007) *Soziale Stadtpolitik*, Bielefeld: transcript Verlag.

Gwynne, J. and de la Torre, M. (2009) *When schools close: Effects on displaced students in Chicago public schools*, Chicago, IL: Consortium on Chicago School Research.

Hackworth, J. (2002) 'Post-recession gentrification in New York City', *Urban Affairs Review*, vol 37, pp 815-43.

Hackworth, J. (2007) *The neoliberal city: Governance, ideology, and development in American urbanism*, Ithaca, NY: Cornell University Press.

Hackworth, J. (2008) 'The durability of roll-out neoliberalism under Centre-Left governance: the case of Ontario's social housing sector', *Studies in Political Economy*, vol 81, pp 7-26.

Hackworth, J. and Moriah, A. (2006) 'Neoliberalism, contingency, and urban policy: the case of social housing in Ontario', *International Journal of Urban and Regional Research*, vol 30, no 3, pp 510-27.

Hackworth, J. and Smith, N. (2001) 'The changing state of gentrification', *Tijdschrift voor Economische en Sociale Geografie*, vol 92, no 4, pp 464-77.

HafenCity, Hamburg (2006) *The masterplan.*

Hamnett, C. (2003) *Unequal city: London in the global arena*, London: Routledge.

Hamnett, C. (2008) 'The regeneration game', in 'Comment is Free', *The Guardian*, Wednesday 11 June (www.guardian.co.uk).

Hannerz, U. (1992) *Cultural complexity: Studies in the social organisation of meaning*, New York: Columbia University Press.

Hanratty, M., McLanahan, S. and Pettit, B. (1998) *The impact of the Los Angeles Moving to Opportunity program on residential mobility, neighbourhood characteristics, and early child and parent outcomes*, Working Paper No 98-18, Princeton, NJ: Princeton University Woodrow Wilson School of Public Affairs, Centre for Research on Child Well-being.

Harvey, D. (1989) 'From managerialism to entrepreneurialism: the transformation in urban governance in late capitalism', *Geografiska Annaler B*, vol 71, pp 3-17.

Harvey, D. (2001) *Spaces of capital: Towards a critical geography*, London: Routledge.

Harvey, D. (2005) *A brief history of neoliberalism*, Oxford: Oxford University Press.

Hasson, S. and Ley, D. (1994) 'The downtown Eastside, one hundred years of struggle', in S. Hasson and D. Ley (eds) *Neighbourhood organizations and the welfare state*, Toronto: University of Toronto Press, pp 172-204.

Häussermann, H. and Kronauer, M. (2009) 'Räumliche Segregation und innerstädtisches Ghetto', ['Spacial segregation and inner city ghetto'], in R. Stichweh and P. Windolf (eds) *Inklusion und Exklusion: Analysen zur Sozialstruktur und sozialen Ungleichheit*, [*Inclusion and exclusion: Analyses of social structures and social inequality*], Wiesbaden: VS Verlag für Sozialwissenschaften, pp 157-73.

Häussermann, H. and Siebel, W. (1987) *Neue Urbanität*, [*New urbanity*], Frankfurt/Main: Suhrkamp Verlag.

Haylett, C. (2003) 'Culture, class and urban policy: reconsidering equality', *Antipode*, vol 35, no 1, pp 33-55.

Haymes, S.N. (1995) *Race, culture and the city*, Albany, NY: SUNY Press.

He, S. (2007) 'State-sponsored gentrification under market transition: the case of Shanghai', *Urban Affairs Review*, vol 43, no 2, pp 171-98.

He, S. and Wu, F. (2009) 'China's emerging neoliberal urbanism: perspectives from urban redevelopment', *Antipode*, vol 41, no 2, pp 282-304.

Heartland Alliance (2006) *Illinois Poverty Summit*, Chicago, IL: Author.

Hilber, C.A.L. (2010) 'New housing supply and the dilution of social capital', *Journal of Urban Economics*, vol 67, no 3, pp 419-37.

Hills, J., Brewer, M., Jenkins, S., Lister, R., Lupton, R., Machin, S., Mills, C., Modood, T., Rees, T. and Riddell, S. (2010) *An anatomy of economic inequality in the UK: Report of the National Equality Panel*, London: Government Equalities Office.

Holin, M.J., Buron, L.F. and Baker, M. (2003) *Interim assessment of the HOPE VI Program: Case studies*, Bethesda, MD: Abt Associates.

Holm, A. (2010) *Wir Bleiben Alle! Gentrifizierung – Städtische Konflikte um Aufwertung und Verdrängung*, Münster: Unrast-Verlag.

Horak, M. and Blokland, T. (2011: forthcoming) 'Neighbourhood and civic practice', in S. Clawe et al (eds) *Handbook of urban politics*, Oxford: University Press.

House of Commons Council Housing Group (2005) *Support for the 'fourth option' for council housing: Report on the enquiry into the future funding of council housing 2004-2005*, London: House of Commons.

Hulse, K., Herbert, T. and Down, K. (2004) 'Kensington estate redevelopment social impact study', Prepared for the Department of Human Services, Institute for Social Research, Swinburne University of Technology, Melbourne.

Hunter, A. (1974) *Symbolic communities: The persistence and change of Chicago's local communities*, Chicago, IL and London: University of Chicago Press.

Hyra, D. (2008) *The new urban renewal: The economic transformation of Harlem and Bronzeville*, Chicago, IL: University of Chicago Press.

Hyra, D. (2010) 'The new urban renewal, part 2: public housing reforms', in J. Brown-Saracino (ed) *The gentrification debates*, New York: Routledge, pp 305-18.

IDS (Institute of Development Studies) UK (2009) *Accounts of crisis: Report on a study of the food, fuel and financial crisis in five countries, Report on a pilot study in Bangladesh, Indonesia, Jamaica, Kenya and Zambia*, Brighton: IDS.

ILO ([International Labour Organization)] (2008) *Income inequalities in the age of financial globalization, World of Work Report 2008*, Geneva: International Institute for Labour Studies.

Imbroscio, D. (2008) '"United and actuated by some common impulse of passion": challenging the dispersal consensus in American housing policy research', *Journal of Urban Affairs*, vol 30, no 2, pp 111-30.

Imrie, R. and Raco, M. (eds) (2003) *Urban renaissance? New Labour, community and urban policy*, Bristol: The Policy Press.

Ioannides, Y. and Loury, L. (2004) 'Job information networks, neighbourhood effects and inequality', *Journal of Economic Literature*, vol 42, no 4, pp 1056-93.

Ion, J. (1997) *La fin des militants*, [*The end of the activists*], Paris: Editions de l'Atelier.

Iossifova, D. (2009) 'Negotiating livelihoods in a city of difference: narratives of gentrification in Shanghai', *Critical Planning*, vol 16, pp 99-116.

Jacob, B. (2004) 'Public housing, housing vouchers, and student achievement: evidence from public housing demolitions in Chicago', *American Economic Review*, vol 94, no 1, pp 233-58.

Jacobs, J. (1961) *The death and life of Great American cities*, New York: Random House.

Jager, M. (1986) 'Class definition and the aesthetics of gentrification: Victoriana in Melbourne', in N. Smith and P. Williams (eds) *Gentrification of the city*, London: Unwin Hyman, pp 78-91.

Janssen, P. (2009) 'Phuket's Chinatown on the road to gentrification', *Jakarta Globe*, 6 August (www.thejakartaglobe.com/lifeandtimes/phukets-chinatown-on-the-road-to-gentrification/322481#).

Jansson, A. (2005) 'Re-encoding the spectacle: urban fatefulness and mediated stigmatisation in the city of tomorrow', *Urban Studies*, vol 42, no 10, pp 1671-91.

Jekel, G. and Frölich von Bodelschwingh, F. (2008) 'Stadtpolitik und das neue Wohnen in der Innenstadt – Wohnungsangebot, Anbieterstrukturen und die Bedeutung neuer Wohnformen für die Stärkung des Wohnstandortes Innenstadt', *Deutsche Zeitschrift für Kommunalwissenschaften*, ['City policies and new living in the centre – Housing supply, offerer structures and the meaning of new forms of housing for strengthening city centre habitats', *German Journal for Community Sciences*] vol 47, no 1, pp 13-35.

Jenkins, R. (1996) *Social identity*, London and New York: Routledge.

Jones, C. and Murie, A. (2006) *The Right to Buy*, Oxford: Blackwell/ Royal Institution of Chartered Surveyors.

Joseph, M.L. (2006) 'Is mixed-income development an antidote to urban poverty?', *Housing Policy Debate*, vol 17, no 2, pp 209-34.

Joseph, M.L. (2008) 'Early resident experiences at a new mixed-income development in Chicago', *Journal of Urban Affairs*, vol 30, no 3, pp 229-57.

Joseph, M.L. and Chaskin, R. (2010) 'Living in a mixed income development: resident perceptions of the benefits and disadvantages of two developments in Chicago', *Urban Studies*, vol 47, no 1, pp 2347-66.

Joseph, M.L., Chaskin, R. and Webber, H. (2007) 'The theoretical basis for addressing poverty through mixed-income development', *Urban Affairs Review*, vol 42, no 3, pp 369-409.

Kahlenberg, R.D. (2001) *All together now: Creating middle-class schools through public school choice*, Washington, DC: Brookings Institution Press.

Karsten, L. (2003) 'Family gentrifiers: challenging the city as a place simultaneously to build a career and to raise children', *Urban Studies*, vol 40, no 12, pp 2573-84.

Karsten, L., Reijndorp A. and van der Zwaard, J. (2006) *Smaak voor de stad Een studie naar de stedelijke woonvoorkeur van gezinnen*, Den Haag: Ministerie van VROM.

Katz, B. (2009) 'The origins of HOPE VI', in H. Cisneros and L. Engdahl (eds) *From despair to hope: HOPE VI and the new promise of public housing in America's cities*, Washington, DC: Brookings Institution Press, pp 15-29.

Katz, L., Kling, J. and Liebman, J. (2001) 'Moving to Opportunity in Boston: early results of a randomized mobility experiment', *Quarterly Journal of Economics*, vol 116, pp 607-54.

Katz, M. (1989) *The undeserving poor: From the war on poverty to the war on welfare*, New York: Pantheon Books.

Kearns, A. (2002) 'Response: From residential disadvantage to opportunity? Reflections on British and European policy and research', *Housing Studies*, vol 17, no 1, pp 145-50.

Keels, M. (2008) 'Neighborhood effects examined through the lens of residential mobility programs', *American Journal of Community Psychology*, vol 42, pp 235-50.

Keil, R. (2002) '"Common-sense" neoliberalism: progressive conservative urbanism in Toronto, Canada', *Antipode*, vol 34, no 3, pp 578-601.

Kensington Management Company (2008) *KMC community development model* (www.kmcnetau/community/).

Kesteloot, C. (2000) 'Brussels: post-Fordist polarisation in a Fordist spatial canvas', in P. Marcuse and R. van Kempen (eds) *Globalizing cities: A new spatial order?*, Oxford: Blackwell, pp 186-210.

Kesteloot, C. and de Decker, P. (1992) 'Territoria en migraties als geografische factoren van racisme', in E. Desle and A. Martens (eds) *Gezichten van het hedendaags racisme*, Brussels: VUB-Press, pp 69-108.

Kesteloot, C. and de Maesschalck, F. (2001) 'Anti-urbanism in Flanders: the political and social consequences of a spatial class struggle strategy', *Belgeo*, vol 1/2, pp 41-62.

Kesteloot, C. and Mistiaen, P. (1998) 'Les limites de l'usage de la mixité sociale', *Cahiers Marxistes*, ['The limits of mixed communities', *Marxist Writings*] vol 211, pp 35-47.

Kintrea, K. (2007) 'Policies and programmes for disadvantaged neighbourhoods: recent English experience', *Housing Studies*, vol 22, no 2, pp 261-82.

Klein, N. (2008) *The shock doctrine: The rise of disaster capitalism*, London: Penguin.

Kleinhans, R. (2004) 'Social implications of housing diversification in urban renewal: a review of recent literature', *Journal of Housing and the Built Environment*, vol 19, no 4, pp 367-90.

Kling, J., Liebman, J.B. and Katz, L.F. (2007) 'Experimental analysis of neighbourhood effects', *Econometrica*, vol 75, no 1, pp 83-119.

Kling, J., Ludwig, J. and Katz, L.F. (2005) 'Neighbourhood effects on crime for female and male youth: evidence from a randomised housing voucher experiment', *Quarterly Journal of Economics*, vol 120, no 1, pp 87-130.

Knapp, M.S. and Woolverton, S. (2004) 'Social class and schooling', in J.A. Banks and C.A.M. Banks (eds) *Handbook of research on multicultural education* (2nd edn), San Francisco, CA: Jossey-Bass, pp 656-81.

Kotlowitz, A. (1992) *There are no children here: The story of two boys growing up in the other America*, New York: Anchor Books.

Kronauer, M., Noller, P. and Vogel, B. (2006) 'Hamburg: contradicting neighbourhood effects on poverty', in S. Musterd, A. Murie and C. Kesteloot (eds) *Neighbourhoods of poverty*, New York: Palgrave Macmillan, pp 70-86.

Krupka, D.J. (2007) 'Are big cities more segregated? Neighbourhood scale and the measurement of segregation', *Urban Studies*, vol 44, no 1, pp 187-97.

Lambert, C. and Boddy, M. (2002) *Transforming the city: Post-recession gentrification and re-urbanism*, CNR Paper 6, Bristol: ESRC Centre for Neighbourhood Research.

Lamont, M. and Molnar, V. (2002) *The study of boundaries in the social sciences*, Princeton, NJ: Princeton University Press.

Landais, C. (2007) *Les hauts revenus en France (1998-2006): Une explosion des inégalités?*, Mimeo, Paris: Paris School of Economics.

Läpple, D., Mückenberger, U. and Oßenbrügge, J. (eds) (2010) *Zeiten und Räume der Stadt – Theorie und Praxis*, [*City times and city spaces - Theory and practice*], Opladen and Farmington Hills, MI: Verlag Barbara Budrich.

Lascoumes, P. and Le Galès, P. (2008) *Sociologie de l'action publique*, Paris: Colin.

Latham, A. (2003) 'Urbanity, lifestyle and making sense of the new urban cultural economy: notes from Auckland, New Zealand', *Urban Studies*, vol 40, no 9, pp 1699-724.

Lazarsfeld, P. and Merton, R.K. (1954) 'Friendship as a social process: a substantive and methodological analysis', in M. Berger, T. Abel and C.H. Page (eds) *Freedom and control in modern society*, New York, NY: Van Nostrand, pp 18-66.

Lees, L. (2003) 'Visions of "urban renaissance": the Urban Task Force Report and the Urban White Paper', in R. Imrie and M. Raco (eds) *Urban renaissance? New Labour, community and urban policy*, Bristol: The Policy Press, pp 61-82.

Lees, L. (ed) (2004) *The emancipatory city: Paradoxes and possibilities?*, London: Sage Publications.

Lees, L. (2008) 'Gentrification and social mixing: towards an inclusive urban renaissance?', *Urban Studies*, vol 45, no 12, pp 2449-70.

Lees, L. (2010) 'Planning urbanity?', *Environment and Planning A*, vol 42, no 10, pp 2302-8.

Lees, L. (forthcoming) 'Revisiting the "geography of gentrification": thinking through comparative urbanism', *Progress in Human Geography*.

Lees, L. and Ley, D. (2008) 'Introduction to a special issue on gentrification and public policy', *Urban Studies*, vol 45, no 12, pp 2379-84.

Lees, L., Slater, T. and Wyly, E.K. (2007) *Gentrification*, London: Routledge.

Lelévrier, C. (2007) 'Mobilités et ancrages des familles en Ile-de-France: les changements de la rénovation urbaine', *Informations sociales*, ['Mobility and anchoring of families in Ile-de-France: The changes of urban renovation', *Social Information*], no 141, pp 98-109.

Lelévrier, C. (2008) *Mobilités et trajectoires résidentielles de ménages relogés lors d'opérations de renouvellement urbain, synthèse de travaux menés entre 2004 et 2007*, Paris: PUCA/DIV/DREIF.

Leloup, X. (2002) *La ville de l'autre*, [*The other's city*] Louvain-la-Neuve: Presses Universitaires de Louvain.

Lemann, N. (1992) *The promised land: The great black migration and how it changed America*, New York: Vintage Books.

Leventhal, T. and Brooks-Gunn, J. (2004) 'A randomized study of neighborhood effects on low-income children's educational outcomes', *Developmental Psychology*, vol 40, pp 488-507.

Lewis, O. (1959) *Five families: Mexican case studies in the culture of poverty*, New York: New American Library.

Ley, D. (1983) *A social geography of the city*, New York: Harper & Row.

Ley, D. (1986) 'Alternative explanations for inner-city gentrification: a Canadian assessment', *Annals of the Association of American Geographers*, vol 76, no 4, pp 521-35.

Ley, D. (1987) 'Styles of the times: liberal and neo-conservative landscapes in inner Vancouver, 1968-1986', *Journal of Historical Geography*, vol 13, no 1, pp 40-56.

Ley, D. (1993) 'Co-operative housing as a moral landscape', in J. Duncan and D. Ley (eds) *Place/culture/representation*, London: Routledge, pp 128-48.

Ley, D. (1994) 'Gentrification and the politics of the new middle class', *Environment and Planning D: Society and Space*, vol 12, no 1, pp 53-74.

Ley, D. (1996) *The new middle class and the re-making of the central city*, Oxford: Oxford University Press.

Ley, D. (2003) 'Artists, aestheticisation and the field of gentrification', *Urban Studies*, vol 40, no 12, pp 2527-44.

Ley, D. (2010) 'Multiculturalism: a Canadian defence', in S. Vertovec and S. Wessendorf (eds) *The multiculturalism backlash: European discourses, policies and practices*, London: Routledge, pp 190-206.

Ley, D. and Dobson, C. (2008) 'Are there limits to gentrification?', *Urban Studies*, vol 45, no 12, pp 2471-98.

Lipman, P. (2003) 'Chicago school policy: regulating Black and Latino youth in the global city race', *Ethnicity and Education*, vol 6, no 4, pp 331-55.

Lipman, P. (2008) 'Mixed-income schools and housing: advancing the neoliberal urban agenda', *Journal of Education Policy*, vol 23, no 2, pp 119-34.

Lipman, P. (2011) *The new political economy of urban education: Neoliberalism, race and the right to the city*, New York: Routledge.

Lipman, P., Person, A. and Kenwood Oakland Community Organization (2007) *Students as collateral damage? A preliminary study of Renaissance 2010 school closings in the Midsouth*, Chicago, IL: Kenwood Oakland Community Organization.

Lofland, L. (1998) *The public realm: Exploring the city's quintessential social territory*, New York: de Gruyter.

Logan, W. (1985) *The gentrification of inner Melbourne: A political geography of inner city housing*, St Lucia, Australia: University of Queensland Press.

Lonely Planet (2009) *The Lonely Planet best in travel 2009*, Australia: Lonely Planet Publications.

Loopmans, M. and Kesteloot, C. (2009) 'Social inequalities, Brussels Studies, Citizens' Forum of Brussels', *Synopsis*, no 15, pp 1-12 [French, Dutch and English version available online at www.brusselsstudies.be.

Loopmans, M., de Decker, P. and Kesteloot, C. (2010) 'Social mix and passive revolution: a neo-Gramscian analysis of the social mix rhetoric in Flanders, Belgium', *Housing Studies*, vol 25, no 2, pp 181-200.

Lord, J.D. (1977) *Spatial perspectives on school desegregation and bussing*, Research Paper No 77-3, Washington, DC: Association of American Geographers, Commission on College Geography.

Ludwig, J., Duncan, G.J. and Hirschfield, P. (2001) 'Urban poverty and juvenile crime: evidence from a randomized housing-mobility experiment', *Quarterly Journal of Economics*, vol 116, pp 655-80.

Lupton, R. (2006) 'Neighbourhood renewal and education policy in England: what discourses of transformation and choice really mean for working class neighbourhoods and their schools', Paper presented at the Urban Affairs Association Conference, Montreal, 19-22 April.

Lupton, R. and Fuller, C. (2009) 'Mixed communities: a new approach to spatially concentrated poverty in England', *International Journal of Urban and Regional Research*, vol 33, no 4, pp 1014-28.

Lupton, R. and Power, A. (2002) 'Social exclusion and neighbourhoods', in J. Hills, J. Le Grand and D. Piachaud (eds) *Understanding social exclusion*, Oxford: Oxford University Press, pp 118-40.

Lupton, R. and Tunstall, R. (2008) 'Neighbourhood regeneration through mixed communities: a "social justice dilemma"?', *Journal of Education Policy*, vol 23, no 2, pp 105-11.

Lupton, R., Heath, N., Fenton, A., Clarke, A., Whitehead, C., Monk, S., Geddes, M., Fuller, C., Tunstall, R., Hayden, C. and Robinson, J. (2009) *Evaluation of the Mixed Communities Initiative Demonstration Projects: Initial baseline and process issues report*, June, London: Communities and Local Government.

Lupton, R., Heath, N., Fenton, A., Clarke, A., Whitehead, C., Monk, S., Geddes, M., Fuller, C., Tunstall, R., Hayden, C. and Robinson, J. (2010) *Evaluation of the Mixed Communities Initiative Demonstration Projects*, London: Communities and Local Government.

MacArthur Foundation (2005) 'Revitalizing Bronzeville: mixed-income housing is key to community strength', *Newsletter*, Spring (www.macfound.org).

MacArthur Foundation and Metropolitan Planning Council (2005) 'Building successful mixed income communities: education and quality schools', Invitational forum co-sponsored by the MacArthur Foundation and Metropolitan Planning Council in coordination with the Chicago Housing Authority, 17 November.

McCallister, L. and Fischer, C.S. (1978) 'A procedure for surveying personal networks', *Sociological Methods & Research*, vol 7, no 2, pp 131-48.

McCann, E. (2010) 'Urban policy mobilities and global circuits of knowledge: towards a research agenda', *Annals of the Association of American Geographers*, vol 101, no 1, pp 107-30.

McDonald, J. (2004) 'The deconcentration of poverty in Chicago, 1990-2000', *Urban Studies*, vol 41, no 11, pp 2119-37.

McKee, K. (2008) 'Community ownership of social housing in Glasgow: building more sustainable, cohesive communities?', *People, Place and Policy Online*, vol 2, no 2, pp 101-11.

McPherson, M., Smith-Lovin, L. and Cook, J.M. (2001) 'Birds of a feather: homophily in social networks', *Annual Review of Sociology*, no 27, pp 415-44.

Machielse, E. (1989) 'Stedelijke elite; terug van weg geweest? Een analyse van de aantrekkingskracht van de stad voor de hoge inkomensgroepen', in F. Bovenkerk and L. de Brunt (eds) *Andere stad, achter de facade van de nieuwe stedelijke vitaliteit*, Den Haag: Werkstukken Stedelijke Netwerken, pp 147-58.

Magri, S. (1995) 'Les laboratoires de l'habitation populaire en France', *Recherche*, Paris: Ministère de l'équipment, du logement, des transports et du tourisme, Plan, construction et architechture.

Malpass, P. and Murie, A. (1994) *Housing policy and practice* (4th edn), London and Hong Kong: Macmillan Press.

Mandel, C. (2005) 'Pression immobilière et rénovation urbaine: la gentrification du quartier populaire parisien de la Goutte d'Or', Mémoire de DESS, IFU.

Manley, D., Flowerdew, R. and Steel, D. (2006) 'Scales, levels and processes: studying spatial patterns of British census variables', *Computers, Environment and Urban Systems*, vol 30, pp 143-60.

Manski, C. (1993) 'Identification of endogenous social effects: the reflection problem', *Review of Economic Studies*, vol 60, pp 531-42.

Manski, C. (2000) 'Economic analysis of social interactions', *Journal of Economic Perspectives*, vol 14, no 1, pp 115-36.

Manzo, L.C. (2008) 'The experience of displacement on sense of place and well-being', in J. Eyles and A. Williams (eds) *Sense of place, health and quality of life*, Burlington, VT: Ashgate Publishing, pp 87-104.

Marcuse, P. (1985) 'Gentrification, abandonment and displacement: connections, causes and policy responses in New York City', *Journal of Urban and Contemporary Law*, vol 28, pp 195-240.

Marcuse, P. (2010 [1986]) 'Abandonment, gentrification, and displacement: the linkages in New York City', in L. Lees, T. Slater and E. Wyly (eds) *The gentrification reader*, London and New York: Routledge, pp 333-47.

Marcuse, P., Connolly, J., Novy, J., Olivo, I., Potter, C. and Steil, J. (eds) (2009) *Searching for the just city: Debates in urban theory and practice*, New York: Routledge.

Martin, L. (2007) 'Fighting for control: political displacement in Atlanta's gentrifying neighbourhoods', *Urban Affairs Review*, vol 42, no 5, pp 603-28.

Massey, D. and Denton, N. (1993) *American apartheid: Segregation and the making of the underclass*, Cambridge, MA: Harvard University Press.

Maurin, E. (2004) *Le Ghetto Français: Enquête sur le séparatisme social?*, [*The French ghetto: Enquire about the social separation?*], Paris: Le Seuil.

May, J. (1996) 'Globalisation and the politics of place: place and identity in an inner London neighbourhood', *Transactions of the Institute of British Geographers*, New Series 21, pp 194-215.

Menzl, M. (2010) *Reurbanisierung? Zuzugsmotive und lokale Bindungen der neuen Innenstadtbewohner – Das Beispiel der HafenCity Hamburg and Das Verhältnis von Öffentlichkeit und Privatheit in der HafenCity: Ein komplexer Balanceakt*, Hamburg: HafenCity Hamburg Diskussionpapier Nr 2, Hamburg: HafenCity Hamburg GmbH.

Menzl, M., Gonzalez, T., Breckner, I. and Merbitz, S. (2011) *Wohnen in der HafenCity Zuzug, Alltag, Nachbarschaft*, Hamburg: Junius Verlag

Merlot, E. (2006) 'Peuplement du parc social à la Goutte d'Or et relations sociales', ['Populating the social park in Goutte d'Or and social relations'], Master Villes, territoires, gouvernance, Evry.

Metropolitan Planning Council (2004) *CHA plan for transformation: Progress report* (www.metroplanning.org/ourwork/).

Meulenbelt, K. (1994) 'Upgrading and downgrading within the metropolitan region of Rotterdam, 1970-90', *Urban Studies*, vol 31, no 7, pp 1167-90.

Mills, C. (1988) '"Life on the upslope": the postmodern landscape of gentrification', *Environment and Planning D: Society and Space*, vol 6, no 2, pp 169-89.

Moffit, R. (2001) 'Policy interventions, low-level equilibria, and social interactions', in S. Durlauf and H.Young (eds) *Social dynamics*, London: The MIT Press, pp 45-82.

Mooney, G. and Danson, M. (1997) 'Beyond "culture city": Glasgow as a "dual city"', in N. Jewson and S. MacGregor (eds) *Transforming cities*, London: Routledge, pp 73-86.

Moran, D. (2005) *Edmund Husserl: Founder of phenomenology*, Cambridge: Polity Press.

Mulder, C.H. and Hooimeijer, P. (1999) 'Residential relocations in the life course', in L.J.G. van Wissen and P.A. Dykstra (eds) *Population issues: An interdisciplinary focus*, Den Haag: NIDI, pp 159-86.

Murdie, R. and Ghosh, S. (2010) 'Does spatial concentration always mean a lack of integration? Exploring ethnic concentration and integration in Toronto', *Journal of Ethnic and Migration Studies*, vol 36, no 2, pp 293-311.

Murphy, L. (2008) 'Third-wave gentrification in New Zealand: the case of Auckland', *Urban Studies*, vol 45, no 12, pp 2521-40.

Musterd, S. (2002) 'Response: Mixed housing policy: a European (Dutch) perspective', *Housing Studies*, vol 17, no 1, pp 139-43.

Musterd, S. (2006) 'Segregation, urban space and the resurgent city', *Urban Studies*, vol 43, no 8, pp 1325-40.

Musterd, S. and Andersson, R. (2005) 'Housing mix, social mix and social opportunities', *Urban Affairs Review*, vol 40, pp 761-90.

Musterd, S. and Ostendorf, W. (2008) 'Integrated urban renewal in the Netherlands: a critical appraisal', *Urban Research and Practice*, vol 1, no 1, pp 78-92.

Musterd, S., Ostendorf, W. and de Vos, S. (2003) 'Neighbourhood effects and social mobility: a longitudinal analysis', *Housing Studies*, vol 18, no 6, pp 877-92.

Neckel, S. (1994) 'Gefährliche Fremdheit', *Ästhetik und Kommunikation*, ['Dangerous differentness', *Aesthetics and Communication*], vol 85/6, pp 45-9.

Nevin, B. (2010) 'Housing market renewal in Liverpool: locating the gentrification debate in history, context and evidence', *Housing Studies*, vol 25, no 5, pp 715-33.

Newman, K. (2000) *No shame in my game: The working poor in the inner city*, New York: Russell Sage Foundation and Knopf.

Newman, K. and Wyly, E. (2006) 'The right to stay put, revisited: gentrification and resistance to displacement in New York City', *Urban Studies*, vol 43, no 1, pp 23-57.

Norris, M. (2005) *Mixed-tenure housing estates: Development, design, management and outcomes*, Dublin: The Housing Unit.

Oakes, J., Wells, A.S., Jones, M. and Datnow, A. (1997) 'Detracking: the social construction of ability, cultural politics, and resistance to reform', *Teachers College Record*, vol 98, no 3, pp 482-510.

Observatoire de la Santé et du Social (2008) *Baromètre social rapport: Bruxellois sur l'état de la pauvreté 2008*, Brussels: Brussels Capital Region.

ODPM (Office of the Deputy Prime Minister) (2003) *Sustainable communities: Building for the future*, London: ODPM.

OECD (Organisation for Economic Co-operation and Development) (2008) *Growing unequal? Income distribution and poverty in OECD countries*, Paris: OECD Publications.

Office of Housing (2008) *Project goals* (www.dhs.vic.gov.au/).

Office of Housing (2010) 'Current building projects' (www.housing. vic.gov.au/buildings-projects/current/).

Olszewski, L. and Sadovi, C. (2003) 'Rebirth of schools set for South Side', *Chicago Tribune*, Section 1, p 1, 19 December.

Ontario Municipal Board (2005) 'Memorandum of oral decision delivered by RA Beccarea on 13 July with subsequent written reasons and order of the board', Decision No 2673.

Oreopoulos, P. (2003) 'The long-run consequences of living in a poor neighborhood', *Quarterly Journal of Economics*, vol 118, no 4, pp 1533-75.

Orfield, G. (2001) 'Response', *Poverty & Race*, November/December (http://www.prrac.org/news.php).

Orr, L., Feins, F., Jacob, R., Beecroft, E., Sanbonmatso, L., Katz, L., Liebman, J. and Kling, J. (2003) *Moving to Opportunity Fair Housing Demonstration Program: Interim impacts evaluation*, Washington, DC: US Department of Housing and Urban Development.

Overman, H.G. (2002) 'Neighbourhood effects in large and small neighbourhoods', *Urban Studies*, vol 39, pp 117-30.

Paton, K. (2009) 'Probing the symptomatic silences of middle-class settlement: a case study of gentrification processes in Glasgow', *City*, vol 13, no 4, pp 432-50.

Peach, C. (1996) 'Good segregation, bad segregation', *Planning Perspectives*, vol 11, no 1, pp 1-20.

Peck, J. (2005) 'Struggling with the creative class', *International Journal of Urban and Regional Research*, vol 29, no 4, pp 740-70.

Peck, J. (2010) *Constructions of neoliberal reason*, New York: Oxford University Press.

Peck, J. and Tickell, A. (2002a) 'Neoliberalizing space', in N. Brenner and N. Theodore (eds) *Spaces of neoliberalism: Urban restructuring in North America and Western Europe*, Oxford: Blackwell, pp 33-57.

Peck, J. and Tickell, A. (2002b) 'Neoliberalizing space', *Antipode*, vol 34, no 3, pp 380-404.

Pedersen, W. and Swanson, J. (2010) *Community vision for change in Vancouver's Downtown Eastside*, Vancouver: Carnegie Community Action Project, June.

Pendakur, R. (1987) 'Policy analysis: Canadian housing policy and the issue of social mix', Master's Thesis, Toronto: Faculty of Environmental Science, York University.

Permentier, M., van Ham, M. and Bolt, G. (2007) 'Behavioural responses to neighbourhood reputations', *Journal of Housing and the Built Environment*, vol 22, no 2, pp 199-213.

Pfadenhauer, M. (2008) 'Markengemeinschaften: Das Brand als ,Totem' einer posttraditionalen Gemeinschaft', ['Brand communities: The brand as "totem" of a post-traditional community'], in R. Hitzler, A. Honer and M. Pfadenhauer (eds) *Posttraditionale Gemeinschaften*, [*Post-traditional Communities*], Wiesbaden: VS Verlag für Sozialwissenschaften, pp 214-27.

Phillips, M. (1993) 'Rural gentrification and the processes of class colonisation', *Journal of Rural Studies*, vol 9, no 2, pp 123-40.

Phillips, M. (2002) 'The production, symbolisation and socialisation of gentrification: impressions from two Berkshire villages', *Transactions of the Institute of British Geographers*, vol 27, no 3, pp 282-308.

Pincon, M. (1982) *Cohabiter; groupes sociaux et modes de vie dans une cité H.L.M*, Paris: Editions du Plan Construction.

Pinçon, M. and Pinçon-Charlot, M. (1989) *Dans les beaux quartiers*, [In the beautiful quarters], Paris: Seuil.

Pinçon, M. and Pinçon-Charlot, M. (2007) *Les ghettos du Gotha: Comment la bourgeoisie défend ses espaces*, [*The ghettos of Gotha: How the bourgeoisie defends their spaces*], Paris: Seuil.

Pinçon-Charlot, M. and Pinçon, M. (2004) *Sociologie de Paris*, [*The sociology of Paris*], Paris: La Découverte.

Pinto, R. (1993) *The Estate Action initiative: Council housing renewal, management and effectiveness*, Aldershot: Avebury.

Popkin, S.J. (2006) 'The HOPE VI program: what has happened to the residents?', in L. Bennett, J.L. Smith and P.A. Wright (eds) *Where are poor people to live? Transforming public housing communities*, Armonk, NY: M.E. Sharpe, pp 68-92.

Popkin, S.J., Buron, L., Levy, D. and Cunningham, M. (2000) 'The Gautreaux legacy: what might mixed-income and dispersal strategies mean for the poorest public housing tenants?', *Housing Policy Debate*, vol 11, no 4, pp 911-42.

Popkin, S.J., Katz, B., Cunningham, M., Brown, K., Gustafson, J. and Turner, M. (2004) *A decade of HOPE VI: Research findings and policy challenges*, Washington, DC: Urban Institute and Brookings Institution.

Powell, M. (2000) 'New Labour and the third way in the British welfare state: a new and distinctive approach', *Critical Social Policy*, vol 20, no 1, pp 39-60.

Power, A. (2008) 'Does demolition or refurbishment of old and inefficient homes help to increase our environmental, social and economic viability?', *Energy Policy*, vol 36, pp 4487-501.

Préteceille, E. (2006) 'La ségrégation sociale a-t-elle augmenté? La métropole parisienne entre polarisation et mixité', *Sociétés Contemporaines*, no 62, pp 69-93.

Préteceille, E. (2007) 'Is gentrification a useful paradigm to analyse social changes in the Paris metropolis?', *Environment and Planning A*, vol 39, no 1, pp 10-31.

Préteceille, E. (2009) 'La ségrégation ethno-raciale a-t-elle augmenté dans la métropole parisienne?', *Revue Française de Sociologie*, vol 50, no 3, pp 489-519.

PricewaterhouseCoopers (2007) *Plan de Développement International de Bruxelles – Schéma de base*, Rapport final au Ministre-Président de la Région de Bruxelles.

Pryor, L. (2007) 'Take off the multi-coloured glasses and the bohemian bastions are gleaming white', Sydney Morning Herald, 30 June (www.smh.com.au/news/opinion/bohemian-bastions-are-gleaming-white/2007/06/29/1182624168795.html?page=fullpage).

Purdy, S. (2004) 'By the people, for the people: tenant organizing in Toronto's Regent Park housing project in the 1960s and 1970s', *Journal of Urban History*, vol 30, no 4, p 519-48.

Putnam, R. (2000) *Bowling alone: The collapse and revival of American community*, New York: Simon & Schuster.

Raco, M. (2007) *Building sustainable communities*, Bristol: The Policy Press.

Raco, M. (2009) 'From expectations to aspirations: state modernisation, urban policy, and the existential politics of welfare in the UK', *Political Geography*, vol 38, no 7, pp 436-44.

Raffel, J.A., Denson, L.R., Varady, D.P. and Sweeney, S. (2003) *Linking housing and public schools in the HOPE VI public housing revitalization program: A case study analysis of four developments in four cities* (www.udel.edu/ccrs/pdf/LinkingHousingpdf) University of Delaware, School of Urban Affairs.

Rancière, J. (1999) *Disagreement: Politics and philosophy* (translated by Julie Rose), Minneapolis, MN: University of Minnesota Press.

Rancière, J. (2001) 'Ten theses on politics', *Theory and Event*, vol 5, no 3, pp 1-10.

Rancière, J. (2005) *The philosopher and his poor* (translated by J. Drury, C. Oster and A. Parker), Durham, NC: Duke University Press.

Randolph, B. and Wood, M. (2004) *The benefits of tenure diversification, Final report*, Sydney: Australian Housing and Urban Research Institute.

Réa, A. (2007) 'Les ambivalences de l'Etat social-securitaire', *Lien Social et Politique*, ['The ambivalence of the social security budget', *Social and Political Bond*], vol 57, pp 15-34.

Redmond, D. and Russell, P. (2008) 'Social housing regeneration and the creation of sustainable communities in Dublin', *Local Economy*, vol 23, no 3, pp 168-79.

Regent Park Collaborative Team (2002) *Regent Park revitalization study Toronto*, Toronto: Regent Park Collaborative Team.

Reijndorp, A. (2004) *Stadswijk Stedenbouw en dagelijks leven*, Rotterdam: NAi Uitgevers.

Robbins, D. (2005) 'The origins, early development and status of Bourdieu's concept of "cultural capital"', *The British Journal of Sociology*, vol 56, no 1, pp 13-30.

Robbins, D. (2006) *Bourdieu, education and society*, Oxford: Bardwell Press.

Robinson, W.S. (1950) 'Ecological correlations and behavior of individuals', *American Sociological Review*, vol 15, pp 351-7.

Robson, B. (1988) *Those inner cities*, Oxford: Clarendon Press.

Robson, B. (1994) *Assessing the impact of urban policy*, London: Department of the Environment.

Rodger, R. (1976) *Creating a livable inner city community*, Vancouver: Ministry of State for Urban Affairs and City Planning Department.

Rofe, M. (2003) '"I want to be global": theorising the gentrifying class as an emergent elite global community', *Urban Studies*, vol 40, pp 2511-26.

Rosa, H. and Strecker, D. (2010) *Theorien der Gemeinschaft zur Einführung*, [*Introduction to theories of community*], Hamburg: Junius Verlag.

Rose, D. (2004) 'Discourses and experiences of social mix in gentrifying neighbourhoods: a Montreal case study', *Canadian Journal of Urban Research*, vol 13, no 2, pp 278-316.

Rosenbaum, J. (1995) 'Changing the geography of opportunity by expanding residential choice: lessons from the Gautreaux program', *Housing Policy Debate*, vol 6, pp 231-69.

Rousseau, M. (2008) '"Bringing politics back in": la gentrification comme politique de développement urbain?', *Espaces et Sociétés*, ['"Bringing poltics back in": Gentrification as a policy of urban development?', *Space and Society*], vol 132/133, pp 75-90.

Rubinowitz, L.S. and Rosenbaum, J.E. (2002) *Crossing the class and color line: From public housing to white suburbia*, Chicago, IL: University of Chicago Press.

Sanbonmatsu, L., Kling, J.R., Duncan, G.J. and Brooks-Gunn, J. (2006) 'Neighbourhoods and academic achievement: results from the moving to opportunity experiment', *Journal of Human Resources*, vol 41, no 4, pp 649-91.

Sarkissian, W. (1976) 'The idea of social mix in town planning: an historical review', *Urban Studies*, vol 13, no 3, pp 231-46.

Savage, M. (1995) 'Class analysis and social research', in T. Butler and M. Savage (eds) *Social change and the middle classes*, London: UCL Press, pp 16-25.

Savage, M. (2008) 'Histories, belongings, communities', *International Journal of Social Research Methodology*, vol 11, no 2, pp 151-62.

Savage, M., Bagnall, G. and Longhurst, B. (2005) *Globalization and belonging*, London: Sage Publications.

Schelling, T.C. (1978) *Micromotives and macrobehaviour*, New York: W.W. Norton & Company, Inc.

Scott, J. (1999) *Seeing like a state*, New Haven, CT: Yale University Press.

Scottish Government (2007) *Firm foundations: The future of housing in Scotland, A discussion document*, Edinburgh: Scottish Government.

Scottish Government (2010) *Housing: Fresh thinking, new ideas*, Edinburgh: Scottish Government.

Scottish Neighbourhood Statistics (2009) (www.sns.gov.uk).

SEU (Social Exclusion Unit) (2001) *A new comitment to neighbourhood renewal: A national strategy action plan*, Crown Copyright.

Select Committee on Environment, Transport and Regional Affairs (2001) *Minutes of Evidence* (http://www.parliament.the-stationery-office.co.uk/pa/cm200001/cmselect/cmenvtra/166/1012403.htm).

Sennett, R. (1970) *The uses of disorder: Personal identity and city life*, New York: Alfred A. Knopf.

Sewell, J. (1994) *Houses and homes: Housing for Canadians*, Toronto: James Lorimer.

Shaton, G. (2005) 'La mixité urbaine à Bruxelles: interprétation locale à travers les discours', ['Urban mixing in Brussels: Local interpretation through the discourses'], Unpublished PhD dissertation, Brussels: Université Libre de Bruxelles.

Shaw, K. (2005) 'Local limits to gentrification: implications for a new urban policy', in R. Atkinson and G. Bridge (eds) *Gentrification in a global context: The new urban colonialism*, London: Routledge, pp 168-84.

Shaw, W.S. (2000) 'Ways of whiteness: Harlemising Aboriginal Redfern', *Geographical Research*, vol 38, no 3, pp 291-305.

Shaw, W.S. (2005) 'Heritage and gentrification: remembering "the good old days" in postcolonial Sydney', in R. Atkinson and G. Bridge (eds) *Gentrification in a global context: The new urban colonialism*, London: Routledge, pp 57-71.

Shaw, W. (2007) *Cities of whiteness*, Blackwell Publishers: USA.

Shelter (2009) *Building pressure: Access to housing in Scotland in 2009*, London: Shelter.

Shin, H.B. (2009) 'Property-based redevelopment and gentrification: the case of Seoul, South Korea', *Geoforum*, vol 40, no 5, pp 906-17.

Silverman, E., Lupton, R. and Fenton, A. (2005) *A good place for children? Attracting and retaining families in inner urban mixed income communities*, York/Coventry: Joseph Rowntree Foundation/Chartered Institute of Housing.

Simmel, G. (1903) 'Die Großstädte und das Geistesleben', ['Big cities and spiritual life'], in G. Simmel (1995) *Aufsätze und Abhandlungen 1901-1908, Band 1, [Essays and treatises 1901-1908, Volume 1]*, Frankfurt am Main: Suhrkamp Verlag, pp 116-31.

Simmel, G. (2006 [1908]) *Die Großstädte und das Geistesleben, [Big cities and spiritual life]*, Frankfurt/Main: Suhrkamp Verlag.

Simon, P. (1997) 'Les usages sociaux de la rue dans un quartier cosmopolite', ['The social practices in a street of a cosmopolitan quarter'], *Espaces et Société, [Space and Society]*, vol 90/91, pp 43-68.

Singapore Government Housing and Development Board (2010) (www.hdb.gov.sg/fi10/fi10322p.nsf/w/SellFlatEthnicIntegrationPolicy_EIP?OpenDocument" www.hdb.gov.sg/fi10/fi10322p.nsf/w/SellFlatEthnicIntegrationPolicy_EIP?OpenDocument).

Sirin, S.C. (2005) 'Socioeconomic status and academic achievement: a meta-analytic review of research', *Review of Educational Research*, vol 75, no 3, pp 417-53.

Skeggs, B. (2005) 'The re-branding of class: propertising culture', in F. Devine, M. Savage, J. Scott and R. Crompton (eds) *Rethinking class: Cultures, identities and lifestyles*, London: Palgrave, pp 46-67.

Slater, T. (2004) 'Municipally managed gentrification in South Parkdale, Toronto', *Canadian Geographer*, vol 48, no 3, pp 303-25.

Slater, T. (2006) 'The eviction of critical perspectives from gentrification research', *International Journal of Urban Research*, vol 30, no 4, pp 737-57.

Slater, T., Curran, W. and Lees, L. (2004) 'Gentrification research: new directions and critical scholarship', *Environment and Planning A*, vol 36, no 7, pp 1141-50.

Smith, A. (2002) *Mixed-income housing developments: Promise and reality*, Cambridge, MA: Joint Center for Housing Studies of Harvard University and the Neighborhood Reinvestment Corporation.

Smith, H. and Ley, D. (2008) 'Even in Canada? Concentrated immigrant poverty in gateway cities', *Annals, Association of American Geographers*, vol 98, no 3, pp 686-713.

Smith, J. (2001) 'Mixing it up: public housing redevelopment in Chicago', Paper presented to 'Area-based Initiatives in Contemporary Urban Policy' Conference, Copenhagen, 17-19 May.

Smith, J.L. (2006) 'Mixed-income communities: designing out poverty or pushing out the poor?', in L. Bennett, J.L. Smith and P.A. Wright (eds) *Where are poor people to live? Transforming public housing communities*, Armonk, NY: M.E. Sharpe, pp 282-300.

Smith, M. (2004) 'Selling salvation', *EYE Weekly*, vol 23, no 38.

Smith, N. (1979) 'Toward a theory of gentrification: a back to the city movement by capital, not people', *Journal of the American Planning Association*, vol 45, no 4, pp 538-48.

Smith, N. (1996) *The new urban frontier: Gentrification and the revanchist city*, London and New York: Routledge.

Smith, N. (2002) 'New globalism, new urbanism: gentrification as global urban strategy', *Antipode*, vol 34, no 3, pp 427-50.

Soenen, R. (2006) *Het kleine ontmoeten: Over het sociale karakter van de stad*, Antwerpen: Garant.

Soja, E.W. (2010) *Seeking spatial justice*, Minneapolis, MN: University of Minnesota Press.

Sullivan, A. and Lietz, C. (2008) 'Benefits and risks for public housing adolescents experiencing HOPEVI revitalization: a qualitative study', *Journal of Poverty*, vol 12, no 2, pp 133-54.

Swyngedouw, E. (2008) 'Where is the political? James Blaut Memorial Lecture', AAG Annual Conference, Boston, 16-21 April.

Tach, L. (2009) 'More than bricks and mortar: neighborhood frames, social processes, and the mixed-income redevelopment of a public housing project', *City & Community*, vol 8, pp 269-99.

Taub, R., Taylor, D. and Dunham, J. (1984) *Paths of neighborhood change*, Chicago, IL: University of Chicago Press.

TCHC (Toronto Community Housing Corporation) (2007a) *Social development plan, Part 1: Context*, Toronto: TCHC.

TCHC (2007c) *Social development plan, Part 3: Strategies for social inclusion*, Toronto: TCHC.

Tevanian, P. and Tissot, S. (2010) 'La mixité contre le droit a propos des ambiguïtés des politiques de lutte contre les ghettos', in P. Tevanian and S. Tissot (eds) *Les mots sont importants*, [*The words are important*], Paris: Libertalia, pp 194-203.

Thibert, J. (2007) *Inclusion and social housing practice in Canadian cities: Following the path from good intentions to sustainable projects*, Ottawa: Canadian Policy Research Networks.

Thomson, T. (2010) 'The death and life of BC's first public housing community: the Little Mountain Housing Project, Vancouver', Unpublished MA thesis, Department of Geography, University of British Columbia.

Tilly, C. (1998) *Durable inequality*, Berkeley, CA: University of California Press.

Tönnies, F. (2005 reprint) *Gemeinschaft und Gesellschaft*, Darmstadt: Wissenschaftliche Buchgesellschaft.

Toubon, J.C. and Messamah, K. (1990) *Centralité immigrée: Le quartier de la Goutte d'Or*, Paris: L'Harmattan.

Tovey, J. (2010) 'Bars open, property up: arise the "new Paddington"', Sydney Morning Herald, 13 March (www.smh.com.au/nsw/bars-open-property-up-arise-the-new-paddington-20100312-q45v.html" www.smh.com.au/nsw/bars-open-property-up-arise-the-new-paddington-20100312-q45v.html)

Tunstall, R (2002) 'Mixed tenure: In search of the evidence base', Paper delivered to the Housing Studies Association conference, York, 3rd-4th April - (www.york.ac.uk/inst/chp/hsa/papers/spring02/tunstall.pdf).

Tunstall, R. (2003) 'Mixed tenure policy in the UK: privatisation, pluralism or euphemism?', *Housing, Theory and Society*, vol 20, no 3, pp 153-9.

Tunstall, R. and Coulter, A. (2006) *Turning the tide? 25 years on 20 unpopular council estates in England*, Bristol: The Policy Press.

Tunstall, R. with Fenton, A. (2009) *Communities in recession: The impact on deprived neighbourhoods*, York: Joseph Rowntree Foundation.

Turbov, M. and Piper, V. (2005) *HOPE VI and mixed-finance redevelopments: A catalyst for neighborhood renewal*, Washington, DC: The Brookings Institution Metropolitan Policy Program.

Uitermark, J. (2003) '"Social mixing" and the management of disadvantaged neighbourhoods: the Dutch policy of urban restructuring revisited', *Urban Studies*, vol 40, no 3, pp 531-49.

Uitermark, J., Duyvendak, J.W. and Kleinhans, R. (2007) 'Gentrification as a governmental strategy: social control and social cohesion in Hoogvliet, Rotterdam', *Environment and Planning A*, vol 39, no 1, pp 125-41.

UN (United Nations) Department of Economic and Social Affairs, Population Division, Population Estimates and Projections Section (2010) *World urbanization prospects: The 2009 revision, Highlights* (http://esa.un.org/unpd/wup/).

Urban Communities (2010) www.urbancommunities.com.au/

US HUD (Department of Housing and Urban Development) (2000) *HOPE VI: Community building makes a difference*, February, Washington, DC: US HUD (www.huduser.org/publications/pdf/hope_vi.pdf).

US Office of Management and Budget HOPE VI Program Assessment, GAO 03-91, summarized at: www.whitehouse.gov/omb/expectmore/detail/10001162.2003.html.

Vale, L. (2006) 'Comment on Mark Joseph's "Is mixed-income development an antidote to urban poverty?"', *Housing Policy Debate*, vol 17, no 2, pp 259-69.

Van Criekingen, M. (2002) 'Les impacts sociaux de la rénovation urbaine à Bruxelles: analyse des migrations intra-urbaines', ['The social impacts of the urban renovation in Brussels: An analysis of intra-urban migrations'], *Belgeo*, vol 4, pp 355-76.

Van Criekingen, M. (2008) 'Towards a geography of displacement: moving out of Brussels' gentrifying neighbourhoods', *Journal of Housing and the Built Environment*, vol 23, no 3, pp 199-213.

Van Criekingen, M. (2009) 'Moving in/out of Brussels' historic core in the Early 2000s: migration and the effects of gentrification', *Urban Studies*, vol 46, no 4, pp 825-48.

Van Criekingen, M. (2010) 'Gentrifying the reurbanisation debate, not vice versa: the uneven sociospatial implications of changing transitions to adulthood in Brussels', *Population, Space and Place*, vol 16, pp 381-94.

Van Criekingen, M. and Decroly, J.-M. (2003) 'Revisiting the diversity of gentrification: neighbourhood renewal processes in Brussels and Montreal', *Urban Studies*, vol 40, no 12, pp 2451-68.

Van Criekingen, M. and Decroly, J.-M. (2009) 'Le Plan de Développement International de Bruxelles (PDI): promesses de developpements immobiliers et d'inégalites croissantes?', ['The Brussels International Development Plan (IDP): real estate development promises and growing inequlities?'], *Brussels Studies*, vol 25 [French, Dutch and English version available online at www.brusselsstudies.be].

Van Criekingen, M. and Fleury, A. (2006) 'La ville branchée: gentrification et dynamiques commerciales à Bruxelles et à Paris', ['Branching cities: Gentrification and commercial dynamics in Brussels and Paris'], *Belgeo*, vol 1, pp 113-34.

Van de Ven, L. (2008) 'Eastern promises', *National Post*, 4 April.

Van der Klaauw, B. and Ours, J. (2003) 'From welfare to work: does the neighborhood matter?', *Journal of Public Economics*, vol 87, pp 957-85.

Van der Wouden, R., Hamers, B. and Verwest, F. (2006) *Toekomstverkenning grotestedenbeleid: Een beschouwing* [*Exploration of the future big cities: Policy*], Den Haag: Ruimtelijk Planbureau.

Van Dyk, N. (1995) 'Financing social housing in Canada', *Housing Policy Debate*, vol 6, no 4, pp 815-48.

Van Eijk, G. (2010a) 'Unequal networks: spatial segregation, relationships and inequality in the city', PhD thesis, Amsterdam: IOS Press.

Van Eijk, G. (2010b) 'Exclusionary policies are not just about the "neoliberal city": a critique on theories of urban reVanchism and the case of Rotterdam', *International Journal of Urban and Regional Research*, vol 34, no 4, pp 820-34

Van Ham, M. and Manley, D. (2010) 'The effect of neighbourhood housing tenure mix on labour market outcomes: a longitudinal investigation of neighbourhood effects', *Journal of Economic Geography*, vol 10, no 2, pp 257-82.

Van Ham, M. and Manley, D. (2011: in press) 'Neighbourhood effects', in S.J. Smith, M. Elsinga, Fox O'Mahony, S.E. Ong and S. Wachter (eds) *The international encyclopedia of housing and home*, Oxford: Elsevier.

Van Ham, M., Manley, D., Bailey, N., Simpson, L. and Maclennan, D. (eds) (2011: in press) *Neighbourhood effects research: New perspectives*, Dordrecht: Springer.

Van Kempen, R. (2010) 'Restructuring large-scale highrise neighbourhoods: recent European experience', Paper presented to the Cities Centre, University of Toronto, June.

Van Kempen, R. and Priemus, H. (2002) 'Revolution in social housing in the Netherlands: possible effects of new housing policies', *Urban Studies*, vol 39, no 2, pp 237-53.

Vanden Eede, M. and Martens, A. (1994) *Quartier Nord: Le relogement des expulsés*, Bruxelles: EPO.

Vandermotten, C. (1994) 'Le plan régional de développement de la région de Bruxelles-Capitale', ['The local plan of developing the region of the capital of Brussels'], in C. Vandermotten (ed) *Planification et stratégies de développement dans les capitales européennes*, [*Planning and strategies of development in European capitals*], Brussels: Edition de l'Université de Bruxelles, pp 195-206.

Varady, D.P. (2005) 'Preface', in D.P. Varady (ed) *Desegreagating the city*, Albany, NY: SUNY Press, pp vii-xix.

Varady, D.P. and Walker, C. (2003) 'Housing vouchers and residential mobility', *Journal of Planning Literature*, vol 18, pp 17-30.

Varady, D.P., Raffel, J.A., Sweeney, S. and Denson, L. (2005) 'Attracting middle-income families in the HOPEVI public housing revitalization program', *Journal of Urban Affairs*, vol 27, no 2, pp 149-64.

Vertovec, S. (2006) *The emergence of super-diversity in Britain*, Working Paper No 06-25, Oxford: COMPASS.

Vischer Skaburskis, Planners (1980) *False Creek Area 6 Phase 1: Post-occupancy evaluation*, Vancouver: Canada Mortgage and Housing Corporation.

Völker, B. (1995) *Should auld acquaintance be forgot...? Institutions of communism, the transition to capitalism and personal networks: The case of East Germany*, Amsterdam: Thesis Publishers.

Völker, B. (1999) '15 miljoen buren – De rol van buren in persoonlijke netwerken in Nederland', in B. Völker (ed) *Buren en buurten*, Amsterdam: SISWO, pp 43-68.

Wacquant, L.J.D. (1993) 'Urban outcasts: stigma and division in the black American ghetto and the French periphery', *International Journal of Urban and Regional Research*, vol 17, pp 366-83.

Wacquant, L.J.D. (2008) *Urban outcasts: A comparative sociology of advanced marginality*, Cambridge and Malden, MA: Polity Press.

Walks, R.A. (2004) 'Suburbanization, the vote, and changes in federal and provincial political representation and influence between inner cities and suburbs in large Canadian urban regions, 1945 to 1999', *Urban Affairs Review*, vol 39, no 4, pp 411-40.

Walks, R.A. and August, M. (2008) 'The factors inhibiting gentrification in areas with little non-market housing: policy lessons from the Toronto experience', *Urban Studies*, vol 45, no 12, pp 2594-625.

Walks, R.A. and Maaranen, R. (2008) 'Gentrification, social mix, and social polarization: testing the linkages in large Canadian cities', *Urban Geography*, vol 29, no 4, pp 293-326.

Walter, F. (2008) *Baustelle Deutschland*, [Construction site Germany], Frankfurt am Main: Suhrkamp Verlag.

Ward, D. (1976) 'The urban slum: an enduring myth?', *Annals, Association of American Geographers*, vol 66, no 2, pp 323-36.

Watt, P. (2006) 'Respectability, roughness and "race": neighbourhood place images and the making of working-class social distinctions in London', *International Journal of Urban & Regional Research*, vol 30, no 4, pp 776-97.

Watt, P. (2008) 'The only class in town? Gentrification and the middle-class colonization of the city and the urban imagination', *International Journal of Urban and Regional Research*, vol 32, no 1, pp 206-11.

Weber, R. (2002) 'Extracting value from the city: neoliberalism and urban redevelopment', *Antipode*, vol 34, no 3, pp 519-40.

Weinhardt, F. (2010) *Moving into the projects: Social housing neighbourhoods and school performance in England*, Spatial Economics Research Centre Report No 22, London: London School of Economics and Political Science.

Werbner, P. (1999) 'Global pathways: working class cosmopolitans and the creation of transnational ethnic worlds', *Social Anthropology*, vol 7, no 1, pp 17–35.

Western, J. (1997) *Outcast Cape Town* (2nd edn), Berkeley, CA: University of California Press.

Wexler, H.J. (2001) 'HOPE VI: market means/public ends – the goals, strategies, and midterm lessons of HUD's Urban Revitalization Demonstration Program', *Journal of Affordable Housing and Community Development*, vol 10, pp 196–8.

Wilen, W. and Nayak, R. (2006) 'Relocated public housing residents have little hope of returning', in L. Bennett, J.L. Smith and P.A. Wright (eds) *Where are poor people to live? Transforming public housing communities*, Armonk, NY: M.E. Sharpe, pp 239–58.

Wilson, D. (2004) 'Toward a contingent neoliberalism', *Urban Geography*, vol 25, no 8, pp 771–83.

Wilson, D., Wouters, J. and Grammenos, D. (2004) 'Successful protect-community discourse: spatiality and politics in Chicago's Pilsen neighborhood', *Environment and Planning, A*, vol 36, pp 1173–90.

Wilson, W.J. (1987) *The truly disadvantaged: The inner city, the 'underclass', and public policy*, Chicago, IL: University of Chicago Press.

Wilson, W.J. (1991) 'Another look at the truly disadvantaged', *Political Science Quarterly*, vol 106, pp 639–56.

Wong, T.-C. (2006) 'Revitalising Singapore's central city through gentrification: the role of waterfront housing', *Urban Policy and Research*, vol 24, no 2, pp 181–99.

Wright, P. (2006) 'Community resistance to CHA transformation', in L. Bennett, J.L. Smith and P.A. Wright (eds) *Where are poor people to live? Transforming public housing communities*, Armonk, NY: M.E. Sharpe, pp 125–67.

Wu, F. (2009) 'Neo-urbanism in the making under China's transition', *City*, vol 13, no 4, pp 414–27.

Wu, F. (2010) 'Retreat from totalitarian society: China's urbanism in the making', in G. Bridge and S. Watson (eds) *A new companion to the city*, Oxford: Wiley Blackwell, pp 701–12.

Wyly, E.K. and Hammel, D. (2001) 'Gentrification, housing policy, the new context of urban redevelopment', in K. Fox Gotham (ed) *Research in urban sociology, Vol 6: Critical perspectives on urban redevelopment*, London: Elsevier, pp 211–76.

Wyly, E.K. and Hammel, D.J. (2005) 'Mapping neoliberal American urbanism', in R. Atkinson and G. Bridge (eds) *Gentrification in a global context: The new urban colonialism*, London and New York: Routledge, pp 18–38.

Young, I.M. (1990) *Justice and the politics of difference*, Princeton, NJ: Princeton University Press.

Young, I.M. (2000) *Inclusion and democracy*, New York: Oxford University Press.

Young, I.M. (2002) *Inclusion and democracy*, Oxford: Oxford University Press.

Young, J. (2007) *The vertigo of late modernity*, London: Sage Publications.

Zhang, Y. and Weisman, G. (2006) 'Public housings' Cinderella: policy dynamics of HOPE VI in the mid-1990s', in L. Bennett, J.L. Smith and P.A. Wright (eds) *Where are poor people to live? Transforming public housing communities*, Armonk, NY: M.E. Sharpe, pp 41–67.

Zielenbach, S. (2003) 'Assessing economic change in HOPE VI neighborhoods', *Housing Policy Debate*, vol 14, no 4, pp 621-55.

Zielenbach, S. and Voith, R. (2010) 'HOPE VI and neighborhood economic development: the importance of local market dynamics', *Cityscape: A Journal of Policy Research and Development*, vol 12, no 1, pp 99-131.

Zimmer, P. (2007) 'La politique du logement de la Région de Bruxelles-Capitale', *Bruxelles Informations Sociale*, vol 158, pp 15-29. Additional References

Zizek, S. (2000a) *The ticklish subject*, New York: Verso.

Zizek, S. (2000b) 'Class struggle or postmodernism? Yes please!', in J. Butler, E. Laclau and S. Zizek (eds) *Contingency, hegemony, universality: Contemporary dialogues on the left*, New York: Verso, pp 90-135.

Zizek, S. (2003) *The puppet and the dwarf: The perverse core of Christianity*, Cambridge, MA: The MIT Press.

Zizek, S. (2006) *The parallax view*, New York: Verso.

Zukin, S. (1987) 'Gentrification: culture and capital in the urban core', *Annual Review of Sociology*, vol 13, no 1, pp 129-47.

Index